THE UNITED STATES
AND THE ORIGINS OF THE
COLD WAR, 1941-1947

Contemporary American History Series
WILLIAM E. LEUCHTENBURG, GENERAL EDITOR

The United States
and the Origins of the
COLD WAR
1941-1947

John Lewis Gaddis

COLUMBIA UNIVERSITY PRESS

NEW YORK AND LONDON

John Lewis Gaddis is Associate Professor
of History at Ohio University

Copyright © 1972 Columbia University Press
Clothbound edition ISBN: 0-231-03289-7
Paperbound edition ISBN: 0-231-08302-5
Library of Congress Catalog Card Number: 75-186388
Printed in the United States of America

10 9 8 7

FOR BARBARA

PREFACE

Historians of the Cold War face a peculiar problem: an overwhelming, though still not complete, body of documents on United States foreign policy during and after World War II is now open for research, yet we have little reliable information about what went on inside the Kremlin during the same period. This disparity of sources makes it impractical, at present, to attempt a definitive study of the origins of the Cold War. Nor is it now feasible to make final judgments about responsibility for that conflict, although I do venture a few highly tentative suggestions in the conclusion.

My goal has been more modest. I have sought to analyze the evolution of United States policy toward the Soviet Union from the formation of the Grand Alliance in 1941 to the proclamation of the Truman Doctrine in 1947. I have proceeded on the assumption that foreign policy is the product of external and internal influences, as perceived by officials responsible for its formulation. In seeking to understand their behavior, I have tried to view problems of the time as these men saw them, not solely as they appear in retrospect. I have not hesitated to express judgments critical of American policy-makers, but in doing so have tried to keep in mind the constraints, both external and internal, which limited their options. If there is a single theme which runs through this book, it is the narrow range of alternatives open to American leaders during this period as they sought to deal with problems of war and peace.

In contrast to much recent work on the subject, this book will not treat the "Open Door" as the basis of United States foreign policy. Revisionist historians have performed a needed service by stressing the influence of economic considerations on American diplomacy, but their focus has been too narrow: many other forces—domestic politics, bureaucratic inertia, quirks of personality, perceptions, accurate or inaccurate, of Soviet intentions—also affected the actions of Washington officials. I have tried to convey the full diversity and relative significance of these determinants of policy.

Far too many people have helped in the writing of this book for me to thank them all individually, but the contributions of several deserve special mention. Robert A. Divine supervised the manuscript in its original form as a dissertation at the University of Texas, and has offered wise counsel on subsequent drafts. H. Wayne Morgan taught me most of what I know about writing style. Oliver H. Radkey first stimulated my interest in Soviet-American relations through his courses in Russian history. Robert H. Ferrell, Gaddis Smith, George C. Herring, Jr., Thomas R. Maddux, and Alfred E. Eckes, Jr., have all read the manuscript at various stages and have offered valuable suggestions. My colleague and office-mate, Lon Hamby, has generously taken time from his own book, soon to appear in this series, to wade through at least three separate drafts and to offer unfailingly helpful advice on each. I owe an especially large debt of gratitude to my editor, William E. Leuchtenburg, who, with an exemplary combination of firmness and tact, persuaded me to reconsider, reorganize, and rewrite large portions of this book. The results of his patient and constructive guidance are evident on every page. Needless to say, final responsibility for the contents remains my own.

Historians could not function without archivists and librarians. I wish to express my appreciation to the staffs of the National Archives, the Library of Congress, the Franklin D. Roosevelt, Harry S. Truman, and Dwight D. Eisenhower Libraries, and the manuscript collections at Princeton, Yale, Harvard, Rice, and the Universities of Michigan, Oklahoma, and Virginia. I owe special thanks to the long-suffering librarians at the University of Texas, Indiana University Southeast, and Ohio University, all of whom cheerfully put up with incessant requests for books, interlibrary loans, microfilm, and Xerox copies while I was writing this book. Every historian of recent United States foreign policy is indebted to the Historical Office of the Department of State, which, despite years of understaffing, has nonetheless managed to make the record of this country's diplomacy available to scholars with a degree of speed and accuracy unmatched by any other nation.

My wife, Barbara, has contributed to this project in so many ways that my gratitude to her can only be expressed on the dedication page. My son, John Michael, offered encouraging gurgles from his crib.

JOHN LEWIS GADDIS

Athens, Ohio
May, 1971

CONTENTS

ABBREVIATIONS USED IN THE FOOTNOTES

DAFR	*Documents on American Foreign Relations.* Vols. II–IX (1939–47). Boston and Princeton, 1940–49.
Eisenhower Papers	Albert D. Chandler *et al.,* eds. *The Papers of Dwight David Eisenhower: The War Years.* 5 vols. Baltimore, 1970.
FDR: Personal Letters	Elliott Roosevelt, ed. *F.D.R., His Personal Letters: 1928–1945.* 2 vols. New York, 1950.
FDR: Public Papers	Samuel I. Rosenman, ed. *The Public Papers and Addresses of Franklin D. Roosevelt.* 13 vols. New York, 1938–50.
FR	U.S. Department of State. *Foreign Relations of the United States.* Annual volumes, 1941–46. Washington, D.C., 1958–70.
FR: Casablanca	U.S. Department of State. *Foreign Relations of the United States: The Conferences at Washington, 1941–1942, and Casablanca, 1943.* Washington, D.C., 1968.
FR: Potsdam	U.S. Department of State. *Foreign Relations of the United States: The Conference of Berlin (The Potsdam Conference), 1945.* 2 vols. Washington, D.C., 1960.
FR: Tehran	U.S. Department of State. *Foreign Relations of the United States: The Conferences at Cairo and Tehran, 1943.* Washington, D.C., 1961.
FR: Washington and Quebec	U.S. Department of State. *Foreign Relations of the United States: The Conferences at Washington and Quebec, 1943.* Washington, D.C., 1970.
FR: Yalta	U.S. Department of State. *Foreign Relations of the United States: The Conferences at Malta and Yalta, 1945.* Washington, D.C., 1955.
Truman Public Papers	*Public Papers of the Presidents: Harry S. Truman, 1945–1947.* Washington, D.C., 1961–63.

THE UNITED STATES
AND THE ORIGINS OF THE
COLD WAR, 1941-1947

1

The Past as Prologue:
The American Vision of the
Postwar World

"In these past few years—and, most violently, in the past three days
—we have learned a terrible lesson." Thus did Franklin D. Roosevelt
assess the significance of Pearl Harbor in a fireside chat to the American
people on December 9, 1941. Isolationism, the President asserted, had
been a mistake: there could be no security from attack in a world ruled
by gangsters. "We don't like it—we didn't want to get in it—but
we are in it and we're going to fight it with everything we've got." The
horrors of war would also bring opportunities, however. Americans
would fight, Roosevelt proclaimed, not just for victory, but to prevent
wars from breaking out in the future. "The sources of international bru-
tality, wherever they exist, must be absolutely and finally broken down."
F.D.R. concluded forcefully: "We are going to win the war, and we are
going to win the peace that follows." [1]

Nothing shaped American plans to prevent future wars more than a
determination to avoid mistakes of the past. Washington officials
brooded deeply over the lessons of recent history. All had witnessed, and
most had participated in, the events of World War I and the interwar

[1] *FDR: Public Papers*, X, 528–30.

period. Errors of those years, they felt, had led directly to the present struggle. Vice-President Henry A. Wallace put it well: "We failed in our job after World War I. . . . But by our very errors we learned much, and after this war we shall be in position to utilize our knowledge in building a world which is economically, politically, and, I hope, spiritually sound." Roosevelt himself promised: "We have profited by our past mistakes. This time we shall know how to make full use of victory." [2]

Lessons of the past significantly conditioned Washington's plans for peace. The first essential would be to defeat completely, disarm, and occupy those nations which had started the war. Lenient treatment of Germany after World War I had only encouraged further aggression; harsher methods would be necessary after this war. But victory would mean little if political and economic conditions which had spawned the totalitarians of the 1930s remained in existence. Hence, a second requirement for peace would be to promote self-determination and to prevent future depressions. American failure to join the League of Nations had also contributed to the collapse of international order; therefore, a third prerequisite for peace would be membership in a new collective security organization. Finally, Roosevelt and his advisers clearly realized that their vision of the future would never materialize unless the members of the Grand Alliance, united now only by their common enemies, built friendly relationships which would survive victory.

Which of America's allies would more strongly resist Washington's plans for peace was not completely clear. Both Great Britain and the Soviet Union agreed on the desirability of defeating their enemies. Both accepted, though with varying degrees of commitment, the concept of international organization. Neither, however, fully supported

[2] Wallace speech to the Free World Association, May 8, 1942, *DAFR*, IV (1941–42), 66; Roosevelt speech to the International Student Assembly, September 3, 1942, *FDR: Public Papers*, XI, 353. See also Sumner Welles's speech to the *New York Herald Tribune* forum, November 17, 1942, *DAFR*, V (1942–43), 31–32; and Cordell Hull, *Memoirs*, II, 1637. For the importance of the World War I experience in shaping the policies of Roosevelt and his advisers, see Frank Freidel, *Roosevelt: The Apprenticeship*, p. 301; Robert E. Sherwood, *Roosevelt and Hopkins*, p. 227; Richard N. Gardner, *Sterling-Dollar Diplomacy*, pp. 4–5; Eric F. Goldman, *Rendezvous with Destiny*, pp. 308–9; William L. Neumann, *After Victory*, pp. 32–33; and William E. Leuchtenburg, "The New Deal and the Analogue of War," in John Braeman, Robert H. Bremner, and Everett Walters, eds., *Change and Continuity in Twentieth Century America*, pp. 82–143.

self-determination or the multilateral trading policies which Washington felt would be necessary to improve world economic conditions. Although London and Moscow approved the Atlantic Charter, which incorporated these objectives, they did so conditionally. Winston Churchill carefully exempted the entire British Empire from the document's provisions. The Russians expressed an even more sweeping reservation: "practical application of these principles will necessarily adapt itself to the circumstances, needs, and historic peculiarities of particular countries." [3]

Great Britain, however, did not have the power to insist on its postwar plans. The Soviet Union did. Like Americans, Russians could not forget the past in preparing for the future. Three devastating invasions in one hundred and thirty years had convinced Moscow of the need to seek security through territorial acquisitions and spheres of influence. Traditional Russian xenophobia, compounded by communist ideology, caused Kremlin officials to suspect Western motives and led them toward unilateral solutions of their diplomatic problems.[4] Both Washington and Moscow wanted peace, but strong internal influences caused each to conceive of it in contradictory ways. These clashing perceptions of a common goal wrecked the Grand Alliance at the moment of victory, creating an ironic situation in which simultaneous searches for peace led to the Cold War.

I

Hitler's attack on Russia in June, 1941, came at a low point in that country's relations with the United States. Recognition of the Soviet

---

[3] For the Atlantic Charter and British and Russian reservations regarding it, see *DAFR*, IV (1941–42), 209–10, 214, 216; and Theodore A. Wilson, *The First Summit*, pp. 261–62. Gaddis Smith, *American Diplomacy During the Second World War*, and Gabriel Kolko, *The Politics of War*, both stress the fact, often lost sight of in the aftermath of the Cold War, that American officials expected almost as much resistance to their postwar program from Great Britain as from the Soviet Union. A contemporary, if overdrawn, account making the same point is Elliott Roosevelt, *As He Saw It*.

[4] The definitive treatment of the motivation behind Soviet policy, in so far as this is possible given the limited sources available, is Adam B. Ulam, *Expansion and Coexistence*. Other useful interpretations include Isaac Deutscher, *Ironies of History*, pp. 147–66; Arthur M. Schlesinger, Jr., "Origins of the Cold War," *Foreign Affairs*, XLVI (October, 1967), 22–52; and Joseph R. Starobin, "Origins of the Cold War: The Communist Dimension," *ibid.*, XLVII (July, 1969), 681–96.

Union in 1933 had not dispelled the legacy of suspicion which had poisoned Russian-American relations since the Bolshevik Revolution. The
purges of the late 1930s dissipated most of the respect which the Soviet
Union had won through its economic achievements, its support of collective security, and its new "democratic" constitution of 1936. Moscow's
role in the shattering events surrounding the outbreak of World War
II—the cynical Nazi-Soviet Pact, the partition of Poland, the bungled
invasion of Finland, which made Stalin look both brutal and ridiculous
—greatly intensified American hostility. Stalin's decision to sign a non-
aggression pact with Japan in April, 1941, simply confirmed the prevailing view: that the Soviet Union was a cruel and rapacious dictatorship,
only slightly less repulsive than Nazi Germany.[5]

Despite all this, American officials quickly saw opportunity in the
Russo-German conflict. Since 1940, the Roosevelt Administration had
committed itself to aiding Great Britain against Germany by all means
short of war. If Russia could tie down Hitler's armies for any length of
time, Britain might be spared. The State Department's first official statement on the German invasion hinted cautiously at this: "In the opinion
of this Government, . . . any defense against Hitlerism, any rallying of
the forces opposing Hitlerism, from whatever source these forces may
spring, will hasten the eventual downfall of the present German leaders,
and will therefore redound to the benefit of our own defense and security." Privately Administration leaders spoke more frankly. One of them
wrote on the day after the German attack: "So long as Russia is preoc-
cupying Hitler . . . we should and will do everything in our power to
aid Britain. . . . Between them Britain and Russia may frustrate Hitler's
aims to rule the world." President Roosevelt observed late in June that if
Hitler's invasion proved to be more than simply a diversion, "it will
mean the liberation of Europe from Nazi domination." [6]

[5] The most perceptive examination of Soviet-American relations during the period
from recognition to the German invasion is Thomas R. Maddux, "American Relations
with the Soviet Union, 1933–1941" (Ph.D. dissertation, University of Michigan,
1969). William L. Langer and S. Everett Gleason, *The Challenge to Isolation* and *The
Undeclared War*, contain a detailed discussion of Russian-American relations during
the 1939–41 period. Other useful accounts include Foster Rhea Dulles, *The Road to
Teheran;* Robert P. Browder, *Origins of Soviet-American Diplomacy;* Donald G.
Bishop, *The Roosevelt-Litvinov Agreements;* and Edward M. Bennett, *Recognition of
Russia.*

[6] Statement by Undersecretary of State Sumner Welles, June 23, 1941, *DAFR,* III
(1940–41), 365; Oscar Cox to Harry Hopkins, June 23, 1941, copy in Cox Diary,

If Russian resistance to Hitler could help Britain, it followed logically that the United States should do what it could to keep the Red Army fighting. Diplomatic and military advisers gave the Russians little chance to withstand the German onslaught, but Roosevelt, impressed by Harry Hopkins' optimistic reports of his talks with Stalin late in July, chose to disregard these warnings. On August 2, while Hopkins was still in Moscow, the President admonished his special assistant for defense matters to speed up aid to Russia: "Please, with my full authority, use a heavy hand—act as a burr under the saddle and get things moving!" Three months later Roosevelt proclaimed the survival of the Soviet Union vital to the defense of the United States, and ordered that lend-lease aid be made immediately available to the Russians.[7]

Hitler's declaration of war four days after Pearl Harbor made the United States and the Soviet Union formal allies. From now on victory over Germany would depend upon cooperation with Russia, whatever past differences had been. Roosevelt appraised the value of this coalition realistically: "Put it in terms of dead Germans and smashed tanks," he told a press conference early in 1942. To General Douglas MacArthur he wrote in May that "the Russian armies are killing more Axis personnel and destroying more Axis material than all other twenty-five United Nations put together." Even after the collapse of Mussolini in July, 1943, the President could still tell the American people that "the heaviest and most decisive fighting today is going on in Russia," and that Britain and the United States had been fortunate to have been able to contribute "somewhat" to the Russian war effort.[8]

Cox MSS; Roosevelt to William D. Leahy, June 26, 1941, *FDR: Personal Letters*, II, 1177.

[7] Roosevelt to Wayne Coy, August 2, 1941, *FDR: Personal Letters*, II, 383; Roosevelt to Edward R. Stettinius, Jr., November 7, 1941, *FR: 1941*, I, 857. Examples of the pessimistic appraisals of Russian fighting ability current in the summer of 1941 can be found in Sherwood, *Roosevelt and Hopkins*, pp. 303–4; Anthony Eden, *The Reckoning*, p. 312; and Fred L. Israel, ed., *The War Diary of Breckinridge Long*, p. 207. Raymond H. Dawson, *The Decision to Aid Russia*, is the definitive treatment of the subject, but see also Robert A. Divine, *Roosevelt and World War II*, pp. 80–81; and James MacGregor Burns, *Roosevelt: The Soldier of Freedom*, pp. 110–15.

[8] Press conference, February 17, 1942, *FDR: Public Papers*, XI, 103; Roosevelt to MacArthur, May 6, 1942, quoted in Herbert Feis, *Churchill, Roosevelt, Stalin*, p. 42; fireside chat, July 28, 1943, *FDR: Public Papers*, XII, 331. See also Roosevelt to Churchill, April 3, 1942, quoted in Winston S. Churchill, *The Hinge of Fate*, p. 274; and Roosevelt to Queen Wilhelmina, April 6, 1942, *FDR: Personal Letters*, II, 1304–5.

But Roosevelt's "grand design" encompassed far more than simple military collaboration with the Soviet Union to defeat Germany— cooperation with Russia would also be vital to ensure postwar peace. Keenly aware of the realities of power, Roosevelt knew that the United States and the Soviet Union would emerge from the war as the world's two strongest nations. If they could stay together, no third power could prevail against them. If they could not, the world would be divided into two armed camps, a prospect too horrible to contemplate. "We either work with the other great Nations," F.D.R. told the Foreign Policy Association in 1944, "or we might some day have to fight them. And I am against that." [9]

The President knew that vast differences in culture, language, and ideology separated the Soviet Union from the United States. He had no illusions about the nature of Stalin's regime, which he regarded as no less rigid a dictatorship than Hitler's. But he believed the Russian form of totalitarianism to be less dangerous than that of Germany because the Kremlin had not sought world conquest through military aggression. Moscow had tried to use the Comintern to overthrow foreign governments, Roosevelt admitted, but these sporadic efforts seemed far less of a threat than Hitler's more direct methods. Much of Russia's hostility toward the West, he believed, stemmed simply from lack of knowledge: "I think the Russians are perfectly friendly; they aren't trying to gobble up all the rest of Europe or the world. They didn't know us, that's the really fundamental difference. . . . They haven't got any crazy ideas of conquest . . . , and now that they have got to know us, they are much more

[9] Speech of October 21, 1944, *FDR: Public Papers,* XIII, 352. Roosevelt clearly outlined his "grand design" in two interviews with Forrest Davis, one in December, 1942, the other in March, 1944. (See Robert A. Divine, *Second Chance,* pp. 114–15, 199.) Davis published the substance of these, without quoting the President directly, as "Roosevelt's World Blueprint," *Saturday Evening Post,* CCXV (April 10, 1943), 20 ff., and "What Really Happened at Teheran," *ibid.,* CCXVI (May 13 and 20, 1944), 12 ff., 22 ff. Other helpful summaries of Roosevelt's views on Russia include a memorandum by Archbishop Francis Spellman of a conversation with Roosevelt on September 3, 1943, published in Robert I. Gannon, *The Cardinal Spellman Story,* pp. 222–24; Edgar Snow, "Fragments from F.D.R.," *Monthly Review,* VIII (March, 1957), 399–404; W. Averell Harriman, "Our Wartime Relations with the Soviet Union," *Department of State Bulletin,* XXV (September 3, 1951), 378; Sumner Welles, *Where Are We Heading?* pp. 27–28, 36–37; William H. McNeill, *America, Britain, and Russia,* pp. 326–27, 366–67; and Burns, *Roosevelt: The Soldier of Freedom,* pp. 102–3.

willing to accept us." Proud of his decision to recognize the USSR in 1933, Roosevelt sought to bring Russia into the postwar community of peace-loving states. The post-World War I policy of treating the Soviet Union as an international pariah had been silly—after World War II it would be suicidal.[10]

The President believed that he could obtain Stalin's postwar cooperation by meeting legitimate Russian security needs, provided the Soviet Union had given up its attempts to force communism on the rest of the world. Convinced that World War I diplomats had erred in not agreeing on war aims before the fighting had stopped, Roosevelt attached great importance to reaching an early settlement with Stalin. Personal diplomacy, he felt, would demonstrate America's good intentions, thereby creating the basis for peaceful coexistence after the war. "I 'got along fine' with Marshal Stalin," F.D.R. told a nationwide radio audience after the Teheran Conference; "I believe that we are going to get along very well with him and the Russian people—very well indeed." [11]

But the President's "grand design" for cooperation with Russia was only part of a larger American scheme for preventing future wars. This vision of the future, based primarily upon the lessons of the past and shared, to a remarkable extent, by most Washington officials and by a large portion of the informed public, imposed limits on how far Roosevelt could go in accepting Stalin's postwar objectives. The President could never move too far from the American peace program without calling into question the reasons for fighting the war. The extent to which Russian postwar aims conflicted with those of the United States would thus determine, in large measure, the possibilities for keeping the alliance intact after victory.

[10] Speech to the American Youth Congress, February 10, 1940, *FDR: Public Papers,* IX, 93; Roosevelt to Myron C. Taylor, September 1, 1941, Roosevelt MSS, PSF: "Italy"; Roosevelt to Pope Pius XII, September 3, 1941, *FDR: Personal Letters,* II, 1204–5; remarks to the Advertising War Council Conference, March 8, 1944, *FDR: Public Papers,* XIII, 99; speech to the Foreign Policy Association, October 21, 1944, *ibid.,* p. 344.

[11] State of the Union address, January 11, 1944, *FDR: Public Papers,* XIII, 32; press conference, May 26, 1944, *ibid.,* pp. 135–36; fireside chat, December 24, 1943, *ibid.,* XII, 558. See also Davis, "Roosevelt's World Blueprint," pp. 109–10; and "What Really Happened at Teheran," p. 37.

II

The most obvious requirement in the American plan to prevent future wars was to render harmless those nations responsible for World War II. Early in January, 1943, Roosevelt told Congress that "if we do not pull the fangs of the predatory animals of this world, they will multiply and grow in strength—and they will be at our throats again once more in a short generation." Two weeks later at Casablanca, with Winston Churchill at his side, the President announced the doctrine of unconditional surrender: Peace could come to the world, he told the assembled press representatives, "only by the total elimination of German and Japanese war power." [12]

There was nothing accidental about this statement, despite Roosevelt's subsequent efforts to make it seem a spur-of-the-moment decision. The President had discussed unconditional surrender with the Joint Chiefs of Staff before leaving Washington, and again with the Combined Chiefs of Staff and Churchill at Casablanca. Moreover, the Advisory Committee on Postwar Foreign Policy, a group of State Department officials and private citizens set up in 1942 to advise on postwar planning, had already recommended demanding the unconditional surrender of defeated enemies. Roosevelt was fully aware of this group's conclusions before he went to Casablanca.[13]

The call for unconditional surrender grew directly out of the lessons of World War I. American officials attributed the rise of Hitler in part to German bitterness over the gap between the promises of the Fourteen Points and the realities of the Versailles treaty, in part to the myth, propagated by the Nazis, that the German army had not suffered defeat on the battlefield, but had been stabbed in the back by civilians in Berlin. This time there should be no promises of lenient treatment, and no

[12] State of the Union address, January 7, 1943, *FDR: Public Papers*, XII, 32–33; press conference, January 24, 1943, *FR: Casablanca*, p. 727. See also Roosevelt to Taylor, September 1, 1941, Roosevelt MSS, PSF: "Italy"; and Roosevelt to Jan Christiaan Smuts, November 24, 1942, *ibid.*, PSF: "Union of South Africa."

[13] Sherwood, *Roosevelt and Hopkins*, pp. 695–97; *FR: Casablanca*, pp. 506, 635; Israel, ed., *Long Diary*, pp. 264–65; Harley Notter, *Postwar Foreign Policy Preparation*, p. 127. Secretary of State Hull's retrospective assertion that unconditional surrender did not figure in the State Department's planning prior to Casablanca is obviously in error. (Hull, *Memoirs*, II, 1570.)

doubt about the fact of defeat. "We gave up unconditional surrender the last time . . . and now we have sacrificed thousands of lives because we did not do a thorough job," Mrs. Franklin D. Roosevelt wrote in June, 1944. "I think the mothers of this country . . . will not be so foolish as to ask for a negotiated peace which is what we had before." One month later, F.D.R. himself told a press conference: "Practically all Germans deny the fact they surrendered in the last war, but this time they are going to know it. And so are the Japs." [14]

The need to disavow a negotiated peace seemed particularly acute following the Anglo-American invasion of North Africa in November, 1942. Through a series of miscalculations, plans to forestall resistance to the landings had failed, forcing General Dwight D. Eisenhower and Robert Murphy, his political adviser, to negotiate a cease-fire with Admiral Jean François Darlan, the vice-premier of Vichy France. Despite its justification on military grounds, this arrangement with a notorious collaborator provoked violent criticism in the United States and Great Britain, emphasizing to Roosevelt the desirability of precluding future deals with Germany, Italy, or Japan. [15]

Unconditional surrender also fit in well with Roosevelt's strategy of military cooperation with the Soviet Union. In a moment of rashness the President in May, 1942, had promised the Russians a second front in Europe before the end of the year. Almost immediately it had become clear that this was militarily unfeasible. Churchill traveled to Moscow in August to give Stalin the bad news, and to propose the North African landings as a substitute. Stalin's obvious disappointment, together with his subsequent refusal to attend the Casablanca Conference, convinced Roosevelt that the Russian dictator had "a feeling of loneliness." The promise of unconditional surrender, F.D.R. felt, might boost Stalin's morale, a consideration of some importance since the military decisions made at Casablanca had also lessened the chances for a cross-channel attack in 1943. [16]

Stalin welcomed the proclamation of unconditional surrender but ob-

[14] Eleanor Roosevelt to Mrs. Emily C. P. Longstreth, June 12, 1944, Roosevelt MSS, OF 394; Roosevelt press conference, July 29, 1944, *FDR: Public Papers*, XIII, 210. See also Anne Armstrong, *Unconditional Surrender*, p. 40.

[15] Feis, *Churchill, Roosevelt, Stalin*, p. 110; Sherwood, *Roosevelt and Hopkins*, p. 697.

[16] Roosevelt-Molotov conversation, May 30, 1942, *FR: 1942*, III, 575–77; Feis, *Churchill, Roosevelt, Stalin*, pp. 74–80, 99–101, 115; Joint Chiefs of Staff minutes,

jected to publicizing it, complaining that it would only make the Germans fight harder. Roosevelt recognized this possibility, and stressed frequently that his policy would not mean annihilation of the German people. The President persisted in advocating unconditional surrender, however, despite repeated efforts by diplomatic and military advisers to get him to modify his stand.[17] Only by publicly pressing the point could Roosevelt assure the American people that he would not repeat the World War I mistake of negotiating with the enemy.

The policy of unconditional surrender, the first element in the American program for preventing future wars, very likely strengthened more than it weakened the anti-Axis coalition. As a "lowest common denominator," it served to unite dissimilar allies behind the goal of total victory.[18] Given Stalin's almost paranoid suspicion that his American and British partners might leave him alone to fight Hitler,[19] the policy was probably an essential first step in building a friendly relationship between the members of the Grand Alliance which would survive the end of the war.

III

Defeating those nations responsible for World War II would accomplish little, however, if conditions still existed which could produce future

meeting with Roosevelt, January 7, 1943, *FR: Casablanca*, p. 506. See also William L. Langer, "Political Problems of a Coalition," *Foreign Affairs*, XXVI (October, 1947), 84–85; John L. Chase, "Unconditional Surrender Reconsidered," *Political Science Quarterly*, LXX (June, 1955), 268–72; and Kent Roberts Greenfield, *American Strategy in World War II*, pp. 9–10.

[17] Stalin remarks, November 28, 1943, *FR: Tehran*, p. 513. Roosevelt later denied having heard Stalin criticize unconditional surrender at Teheran, but it is likely that Stalin made his comments after Roosevelt had retired on the evening of the 28th. (Hull, *Memoirs*, II, 1572; *FR: Tehran*, p. 511.) For Roosevelt's effort to soften the impact of unconditional surrender on the German people, see *FR: Casablanca*, p. 727; *FDR: Public Papers*, XII, 80, 557–58. Efforts to get Roosevelt to change the unconditional surrender policy can be traced in John P. Glennon, " 'This Time Germany Is a Defeated Nation': The Doctrine of Unconditional Surrender and Some Unsuccessful Attempts to Alter It, 1943–1944," in Gerald N. Grob, ed., *Statesmen and Statecraft of the Modern West*, pp. 109–51.

[18] Armstrong, *Unconditional Surrender*, p. 39; Chase, "Unconditional Surrender Reconsidered," pp. 271–72; Maurice Matloff, *Strategic Planning, 1943–44*, p. 40.

[19] See, for example, Stalin to Roosevelt, April 3, 1945, *FR: 1945*, III, 742.

wars. Hitler, Mussolini, and the Japanese militarists had not appeared out of nowhere; without favorable environments their movements could never have succeeded. Hoping to avoid new conflicts, American leaders looked to recent history for insight into the causes of the present struggle. In this light, the most important requirements for a peaceful postwar world seemed to lie in the political and economic spheres: politically, to afford maximum opportunity for the peoples of the world to determine their own future; economically, to prevent a recurrence of the worldwide depression of the 1930s.

President Roosevelt articulated these goals almost a year before Pearl Harbor in his "Four Freedoms" address, delivered to Congress in January, 1941. F.D.R. called for freedom of speech, freedom of religion, freedom from fear—all variants of the Wilsonian concept of self-determination—and freedom from want, which he explained as "economic understandings which will secure to every nation a healthy peacetime life for its inhabitants." Two months later, the President told the White House Correspondents' Association:

The world has no use for any Nation which, because of size or because of military might, asserts the right to goosestep to world power over the bodies of other Nations or other races. We believe that any nationality, no matter how small, has the inherent right to its own nationhood.

We believe that the men and women of such Nations, no matter what size, can, through the processes of peace, serve themselves and serve the world by protecting the common man's security; improve the standards of healthful living, provide markets for manufacture and for agriculture. Through that kind of peaceful service every Nation can increase its happiness, banish the terrors of war, and abandon man's inhumanity to man.

By following these principles, Roosevelt believed, mistakes of the past could be avoided: "We will not accept a world, like the postwar world of the 1920's, in which the seeds of Hitlerism can again be planted and allowed to grow." [20]

Self-determination was one World War I policy which, in the eyes of Roosevelt and his advisers, had not failed. Tensions of the interwar period had arisen, they believed, not from application of this principle but from violations of it. Roosevelt regarded the plebiscite method of deter-

[20] Speeches of January 6, March 15, and May 27, 1941, *FDR: Public Papers,* IX, 672, X, 69, 192.

mining boundaries and forms of government as "the most substantial contribution made by the Versailles Treaty." There was no reason why Croats should be forced, against their will, into governments with Serbs, Hungarians, Italians, or even into independence without an expression of their own views. Through plebiscites, conducted on a continuing basis, such "century-old feuds" could be settled. "The whole point of this is that peaceful determination . . . eliminates determination by war." [21]

At their meeting off the coast of Newfoundland in August, 1941, Roosevelt and Churchill easily agreed that their countries would seek no territorial gains for themselves, that they would oppose territorial changes which did not accord with the wishes of the people involved, that they would respect the right of all people to choose their own forms of government, and that they would restore "sovereign rights and self-government . . . to those who have been forcibly deprived of them." Roosevelt took these promises more seriously than did Churchill. The British Prime Minister regarded the Atlantic Charter as only "an interim and partial statement of war aims designed to assure all countries of our righteous purpose." But F.D.R. possessed a streak of idealism which led him to believe that these lofty objectives might actually be attained.[22]

Roosevelt's resolve to postpone political settlements until after the war grew out of his commitment to self-determination. People fighting for their lives or suffering occupation could hardly take time out to

[21] Roosevelt to Taylor, September 1, 1941, Roosevelt MSS, PSF: "Italy." See also Roosevelt to Smuts, November 24, 1942, *ibid.,* PSF: "Union of South Africa." Sumner Welles later described Roosevelt's faith in plebiscites as one example of the President's tendency to rely "upon a few favorite panaceas for problems that were actually too basic and far-reaching in their origins and nature to admit of any easy solutions." (*Seven Decisions That Shaped History,* p. 136.)

[22] *DAFR,* IV (1941–42), 209–10; Churchill, *The Grand Alliance,* p. 373. On Roosevelt's idealism, see Willard Range, *Roosevelt's World Order,* p. 52; and Burns, *Roosevelt: The Soldier of Freedom,* pp. 298, 549, 608. Harry Hopkins told Robert Sherwood in 1941: "You and I are for Roosevelt because he's a great spiritual figure, because he's an idealist, like Wilson, and he's got the guts to drive through against any opposition to realize those ideals. Oh—he sometimes tries to appear tough and cynical and flippant, but that's an act he likes to put on, especially at press conferences. . . . You can see the real Roosevelt when he comes out with something like the Four Freedoms. And don't get the idea that those are any catch phrases. *He believes them!* He believes they can be practically attained." (Sherwood, *Roosevelt and Hopkins,* p. 266.)

choose their future form of government. Nor should the Allies attempt to do this for them. F.D.R. regarded the secret commitments which the Allies had made to each other during World War I as one of the most serious mistakes of that conflict. These understandings had distracted the Allies from fighting the common enemy, disillusioned the public when they became known, and, because they violated the principle of self-determination, sowed the seeds of World War II. Roosevelt intended to handle things differently. He told Breckinridge Long in 1940 that he planned "to operate in the open so that there would be no secret about it. . . . There would be no 'Colonel House' business." Harry Hopkins and John G. Winant, the United States ambassador in London, warned Anthony Eden in the summer of 1941 that the American people, upon entering the war, "did not want to find after the event that we had all kinds of engagements of which they had never been told." A major American concern at the Atlantic Conference later that summer was to make sure that the British were free from secret commitments.[23]

The President's attitude reflected the tendency of Americans to distinguish sharply between political and military matters. Victory was the principal objective. Maneuvering among the Allies for postwar advantage could only help the enemy. F.D.R. wrote in the summer of 1941 that while the Allies "could all agree on objectives, we could all fight about the machinery to attain them." Two years later he told a national radio audience: "We must not relax our pressure on the enemy by taking time out to define every boundary and settle every political controversy in every part of the world. The all-important thing now is to get on with the war—and to win it." Consistently more interested in goals than means, Roosevelt betrayed considerable impatience with those who demanded to know "what are you going to do about such and such a five-square kilometer area in the world?"[24]

[23] Long Diary, February 9, 1940, Israel, ed., *Long Diary,* pp. 57–58; Eden Diary, July 21, 1941, Eden, *The Reckoning,* p. 316; Wilson, *The First Summit,* pp. 183–85. See also Welles, *Where Are We Heading?* p. 6; Notter, *Postwar Foreign Policy Preparation,* pp. 49–50; Hull, *Memoirs,* II, 1170; Neumann, *After Victory,* pp. 32–33; and Lloyd C. Gardner, *Architects of Illusion,* pp. 5–6.

[24] Roosevelt to Adolf A. Berle, June 26, 1941, *FDR: Personal Letters,* II, 1175; fireside chat, July 28, 1943, *FDR: Public Papers,* XII, 333; press conference, October 29, 1943, *ibid.,* p. 459. On Roosevelt's preoccupation with goals rather than means, see Range, *Roosevelt's World Order,* p. 28.

The strategy of postponement also took into account domestic political realities. Bipartisan agreement on foreign policy during the early stages of the war went no further than the need to defeat Germany and Japan. Not until late 1943 would leading Republicans and Democrats endorse American membership in a postwar collective security organization, and then only in guarded terms. Roosevelt feared that any detailed discussion of political settlements would provoke intense controversy within the United States, distracting attention from the war effort and possibly threatening the nation's willingness to assume future world responsibilities.[25]

The President's resolve to adjourn international politics in wartime affected American diplomacy in several areas. It was the basis of his bitter quarrel with Charles de Gaulle over formation of a provisional government in France. It caused recrimination between London and Washington over the establishment of governments in occupied Italy and liberated Greece.[26] But Roosevelt's policy met its most serious challenge when it came up against the Soviet Union's determination to protect itself from future attack by creating spheres of influence along its western border.

The weakness of both Russia and Germany after World War I had made possible the emergence of a group of small independent states in Eastern Europe. Several of these states—Poland, Finland, and the Baltic States of Latvia, Lithuania, and Estonia—had been part of the prewar Russian Empire, as had the Rumanian province of Bessarabia. The resurgence of Russian and German power in the 1930s made the independence of these countries increasingly precarious. Few people were surprised when Stalin took advantage of his 1939 pact with Hitler to incorporate into the Soviet Union eastern Poland, the Baltic States, Bessarabia, and portions of Finland. What did surprise many observers was Stalin's insistence on retaining these territories two years later, even after Hitler's attack had made Russia an ally of the United States and Great Britain.[27]

25 H. Bradford Westerfield, *Foreign Policy and Party Politics*, p. 139; McNeill, *America, Britain, and Russia*, pp. 403–5; Donald R. McCoy, "Republican Opposition During Wartime, 1941–1945," *Mid-America*, XLIX (July, 1967), 174–89.

26 Milton Viorst, *Hostile Allies*, p. 75; Smith, *American Diplomacy During the Second World War*, pp. 68–69, 151.

27 John L. Snell, *Illusion and Necessity*, p. 3. A convenient survey of the history of

Stalin at no point kept his territorial ambitions secret. As early as July, 1941, the Russians announced that they intended to retain the parts of Poland they had taken two years earlier. In December of that year, Stalin asked the British government to support his bid for all of the Baltic States and territorial concessions from Finland and Rumania. "All we ask for," he told Anthony Eden, "is to restore our country to its former frontiers." When Eden observed that Russian requirements might violate the Atlantic Charter, Stalin asked grimly whether the charter was directed against Germany or the Soviet Union.[28] Audacious as Stalin's demands seemed at a time when the German army stood just outside Moscow, they became a persistent and unvarying goal of Soviet diplomacy throughout the rest of the war.

Churchill's government, painfully aware of how London's reluctance to grant Moscow a free hand in Eastern Europe had contributed to the Nazi-Soviet Pact, was reluctantly prepared to meet Stalin's wishes. Roosevelt, however, urged the British to resist. With characteristic optimism, he hoped that in time Soviet territorial ambitions in Eastern Europe would simply go away. These claims stemmed, he believed, solely from Russian fears of a resurgent Germany. With Hitler's defeat, Moscow's appetite for additional territory should disappear.[29]

But Roosevelt's main reason for opposing Soviet territorial claims was his concern that they would violate the principles of the Atlantic Charter. Secretary of State Cordell Hull pointedly reminded F.D.R. of how the Allies' secret agreements in World War I had conflicted with the idealistic aims of President Wilson. With Roosevelt's approval, Hull warned Eden even before the British Foreign Secretary went to Moscow in December, 1941, that "above all there must be no secret accords." On learning of the extensive demands Stalin had made to Eden, Hull had his advisers in the State Department draw up a lengthy memorandum

---

this region is in Vera Micheles Dean, "The U.S.S.R. and Post-War Europe," *Foreign Policy Reports,* XIX (August 15, 1943), 125–31.

[28] *FR: 1942,* III, 495–96, 501–2. See also Eden, *The Reckoning,* p. 335; and Feis, *Churchill, Roosevelt, Stalin,* pp. 31–32.

[29] Welles memorandum of conversation with Lord Halifax, February 20, 1942, *FR: 1942,* III, 521. For the British position, see *ibid.,* pp. 532, 552; and Eden, *The Reckoning,* p. 370. Roosevelt's views on the relationship of the German question to Russian demands in Eastern Europe can be found in Jan Ciechanowski, *Defeat in Victory,* p. 100; Hull, *Memoirs,* II, 1170; and in the Welles-Halifax conversation cited above.

for the President arguing that acceptance of the Soviet Union's claims "would destroy the meaning of one of the most important clauses of the Atlantic Charter and would tend to undermine the force of the whole document." [30]

In the face of strong British pressure to accept the Russian demands, Roosevelt did consider supporting a compromise whereby inhabitants of territories to be absorbed into the Soviet Union would be allowed to leave if they wanted to. But this concession encountered strong opposition in the State Department. Assistant Secretary of State Adolf Berle labeled it a "Baltic Munich" that would put the United States into "a dangerous position, both morally and realistically, and, I may add, in terms of American politics." By early May, 1942, Hull had persuaded the President to stand firm, warning the British that if they endorsed Stalin's territorial claims the United States might be forced to dissociate itself publicly from the agreement.[31]

But the Western allies could not flatly turn Stalin down without gravely endangering the alliance. Soviet Foreign Minister V. M. Molotov arrived in London in May with instructions to insist on recognition of Russian claims. Determined to head Molotov off, Roosevelt invited him to Washington as well to discuss, as he wrote to Stalin, a "very important military proposal involving the utilization of our armed forces in a manner to relieve your critical western front." The tacit arrangement soon became clear: Stalin would postpone seeking recognition of his postwar territorial objectives in return for a British and American promise to open a second front in Europe in 1942. In London, Molotov signed an Anglo-Soviet treaty of friendship which made no mention of Russian territorial gains. In Washington shortly thereafter, Roosevelt

[30] Welles, *Seven Decisions That Shaped History,* p. 135; Hull, *Memoirs,* II, 1170; Hull to Winant, December 5, 1941, *FR: 1941,* I, 194–95; Department of State memorandum, February 4, 1942, *FR: 1942,* III, 505–12. See also William C. Bullitt to Roosevelt, December 5, 1941: "Don't let Churchill get you into any more specific engagements than those in the Atlantic Charter. Try to keep him from engaging himself vis-a-vis Russia. The treaties—if made—will be as difficult for you to handle as the secret treaties were for Wilson." (Roosevelt MSS, PSF: "Bullitt.")

[31] Eden to Halifax, transmitted to Welles on March 12, 1942, *FR: 1942,* III, 532; Welles memorandum of conversation with Halifax, April 1, 1942, *ibid.,* p. 538; Berle to Welles, April 3, 1942, *ibid.,* pp. 539–41; Hull, *Memoirs,* II, 1172. See also Nancy Harvison Hooker, ed., *The Moffat Papers,* p. 380.

formally promised the Russian foreign minister a second front in 1942.[32]

Relieved at having postponed the problem of Eastern Europe for the time being, F.D.R. told Molotov that while "there might be a proper time for raising this question, . . . the present was not the moment." Roosevelt congratulated Ambassador Winant for working out the Anglo-Soviet treaty "in thoroughly acceptable form." If the Russians had pressed for their original demands, "it would have caused almost irreparable damage to the ideals of the war." [33]

But realities of power soon overwhelmed ideals. The second front did not materialize, and by early 1943 Roosevelt had reluctantly concluded that he could not keep Stalin from taking what he wanted in Eastern Europe.[34] Unfortunately, the President, still seeking to avoid divisive controversies within the United States, failed to make this situation clear to the American people. Conditioned by wartime rhetoric to expect a peace settlement which would allow all nations to determine their own future, Americans recoiled in shock and anger as they gradually became aware of Moscow's intention to dominate the postwar governments of Eastern Europe. The resulting tension between the American principle of self-determination and Russian security needs became the single most important cause of the disintegration of the Grand Alliance.

Roosevelt did point out somewhat ruefully in his last state of the union address that while power politics should not control international relations, "we cannot deny that power is a factor in world politics, any more than we can deny its existence as a factor in national politics."

---

[32] Roosevelt to Stalin, April 11, 1942, *FR: 1942,* III, 542–43; Roosevelt-Molotov conversations, May 30 and June 1, 1942, *ibid.,* pp. 576–77, 582–83; White House press release, June 11, 1942, *ibid.,* pp. 593–94. For the relationship of the second front to Soviet territorial claims, see Harry Hopkins' memorandum of a conversation with Eden, April 9, 1942, printed in Sherwood, *Roosevelt and Hopkins,* p. 526. Robert A. Divine points out that Roosevelt probably gave his second-front pledge out of a desire to encourage the Soviet military effort on the eastern front, not as a reward for abandoning territorial demands. (*Roosevelt and World War II,* pp. 85, 89.) It seems clear, however, that the Russians believed that a bargain had been made. (See Standley to Hull, July 22, 1942, *FR: 1942,* III, 613–14.) For Roosevelt's concern about the eastern front, see chapter 3.

[33] Roosevelt-Molotov conversation, May 29, 1942, *FR: 1942,* III, 569; Roosevelt to Winant, June 17, 1942, *FDR: Personal Letters,* II, 1329.

[34] See chapter 5.

One could only hope, Roosevelt continued, that power would be "linked with responsibility, and obliged to defend and justify itself within the framework of the general good." [35] But by January, 1945, hopes that Soviet and American concepts of the "general good" would coincide seemed frail indeed.

IV

American leaders regarded reconstruction of the world's economy as important a goal as self-determination if the conditions which caused wars were to be eliminated. To them, the coincidence of world depression with the rise of dictators seemed more than accidental—almost unanimously they accepted the argument that economic distress led to war. In their planning to prevent future conflicts, Washington officials spent much time thinking about what economic measures they could take to keep such a depression from recurring. As Secretary of State Hull put it in 1944: "A world in economic chaos would be forever a breeding ground for trouble and war." [36]

The Roosevelt Administration quickly advanced clearer and more detailed suggestions in the field of postwar foreign economic policy than in other areas. This was not because top officials thought of international relations primarily in economic terms, but simply because events of the previous decade had already forced these men to devote considerable attention to the relationship between foreign policy and economics. The fact that economic diplomacy seemed less likely to provoke domestic political controversies than did other aspects of postwar planning also encouraged Administration leaders to proceed rapidly in this field.[37]

Cordell Hull provided much of the impetus behind American foreign economic policy. The aged Secretary of State had long ago convinced himself that economic nationalism caused wars. The solution, Hull believed, was to lower barriers to trade throughout the world:

[35] State of the Union address, January 6, 1945, *FDR: Public Papers,* XIII, 498.

[36] Hull, *Memoirs,* II, 1681. See also Kolko, *Politics of War,* pp. 242, 245–46.

[37] Notter, *Postwar Foreign Policy Preparation,* pp. 23–24; R. Gardner, *Sterling-Dollar Diplomacy,* p. 8. Lloyd C. Gardner, *Economic Aspects of New Deal Diplomacy,* is the most complete survey of New Deal foreign economic policy.

To me, unhampered trade dovetailed with peace; high tariffs, trade barriers, and unfair economic competition, with war. Though realizing that many other factors were involved, I reasoned that, if we could get a freer flow of trade—freer in the sense of fewer discriminations and obstructions—so that one country would not be deadly jealous of another and the living standards of all countries might rise, thereby eliminating the economic dissatisfaction that breeds war, we might have a reasonable chance for lasting peace.

There was nothing original about this concept, which went back at least to the days of David Ricardo and John Stuart Mill. Classical liberals had always viewed commerce as the main bond between nations, and most State Department economists adhered to this position.[38] But the combination of Hull's political influence with his personal tenacity gave the classical view a thrust which it might otherwise not have had in the ideologically eclectic atmosphere of the Roosevelt Administration.

Hull owed his appointment as secretary of state more to his popularity with Southern Democrats than to his expertise in foreign affairs. His high standing with Congress gave the Tennessean something of an aura of a public monument, making it impossible for Roosevelt to get rid of him or to ignore his views. Moreover, Hull was tenacious. A close associate noted that when "he gets an idea in the back of his head, it is pretty hard to shake him loose from it." Hull "had his ideas of what's right and what's wrong," Robert H. Jackson observed, "and by jingo he'll use his gun on the man that's wrong." Nothing demonstrated Hull's influence more clearly than the ease with which he forced the resignation of Roosevelt's personal friend and close adviser, Undersecretary of State Sumner Welles, in August, 1943. Hull's hatreds were implacable, Dean Acheson recalled, "not hot hatreds, but long cold ones. In no hurry to 'get' his enemy, 'get' him he usually did." [39]

[38] Hull, *Memoirs,* I, 81. See also *ibid.,* II, 1735; Hull's radio address of July 23, 1942, *DAFR,* V (1942–43), 10–11; R. Gardner, *Sterling-Dollar Diplomacy,* pp. 12–15; and Arthur W. Schatz, "The Anglo-American Trade Agreement and Cordell Hull's Search for Peace, 1936–1938," *Journal of American History,* LVII (June, 1970), 85–103. On the classical orientation of State Department economists, see Alfred E. Eckes, "Bretton Woods: America's New Deal for an Open World" (Ph.D. dissertation, University of Texas, 1969), pp. 2–3, 29–71.

[39] Donald F. Drummond, "Cordell Hull", in Norman A. Graebner, ed., *An Uncertain Tradition,* p. 186; Long Diary, November 27, 1939, Israel, ed., *Long Diary,* p. 37; Louis Fischer interview with Jackson, January 27, 1945, Fischer MSS; Julius W.

By 1940 almost all Administration leaders accepted the premise that economic distress brought war. Secretary of Agriculture Henry A. Wallace described the relationship in March of that year:

When . . . the [American] loans stopped and the Smoot-Hawley Tariff was enacted, the countries of Europe had to stop buying our goods because they had no way to pay for them. They raised their own tariffs, slapped on quotas, adopted new-fangled methods of stopping trade through import licensing and exchange control. International trade broke down. Depression became worldwide. Business collapse led to dictatorship in some countries, and dictatorship has finally plunged Europe once more into a costly war.

In his 1940 annual message to Congress, Roosevelt argued that the "destructive minefield" of trade restrictions built up during the interwar period had been "one of the contributing causes of existing wars." The United States would have to use its influence after the war, the President asserted, to see to it "that no one nation need feel compelled . . . to seek by force of arms what it can well gain by peaceful conference." [40]

The State and Treasury Departments shared the task of formulating specific plans to deal with the postwar economic situation. State assumed major responsibility for removing barriers to trade by working for renewal of the Reciprocal Trade Agreements Act and by seeking to commit other nations to liberal tariff policies. The Treasury concentrated on reforming the international monetary system by creating mechanisms to stabilize international currencies and to facilitate the flow of capital for reconstruction and development. Although relations between the two departments were not cordial—Hull with some justification suspected Treasury Secretary Henry Morgenthau, Jr., of trying to usurp State Department responsibilities—their plans for the postwar world complemented each other neatly, both looking toward restoring the free flow of world trade within a capitalist framework.[41]

Pratt, *Cordell Hull*, II, 615–19, 802–3; Dean Acheson, *Present at the Creation*, p. 9. See also Arthur M. Schlesinger, Jr., *The Coming of the New Deal*, pp. 190–91; Langer and Gleason, *The Challenge to Isolation*, pp. 7–8; and Eden, *The Reckoning*, p. 440.

[40] Wallace speech of March 12, 1940, copy in Roosevelt MSS, PPF 1820, Box 24; Roosevelt annual message, January 3, 1940, *FDR: Public Papers*, IX, 5–6. See also Roosevelt to Myron C. Taylor, September 1, 1941, Roosevelt MSS, PSF: "Italy"; Roosevelt speech of March 15, 1941, *FDR: Public Papers*, X, 69; Adolf A. Berle speech of October 15, 1942, *DAFR*, V (1942–43), 27–29; and Notter, *Postwar Foreign Policy Preparation*, p. 128.

[41] Kolko, *Politics of War*, pp. 251–52. On Treasury Department planning, see John

Fears of a postwar depression inside the United States intensified Administration concern about foreign economic policy. Fully aware that the New Deal had not solved the problem of unemployment in peacetime, Roosevelt and his associates hoped that foreign markets would help absorb the vast quantity of goods which would have to be produced if employment levels were to be maintained after the fighting had stopped. As presidential adviser Oscar Cox put it: "Jobs after the war will depend not only on our markets at home but on our markets abroad." The President committed himself in January, 1943, to government insurance against economic hazards "from the cradle to the grave." But F.D.R. was warned in the fall of 1944 that curtailment of military spending would throw at least four and a half million people out of work: "Unless steps are taken to cushion the effects of this sharp cut in total spending, the decline in business activity—in production, incomes, and employment—may snowball to alarming proportions." Finding markets for surplus products might help ease this problem of domestic reconversion. "While we shall not take advantage of any country," Roosevelt wrote to Hull in October, 1944, "we will see that American industry has its fair share in the world markets." [42]

But Washington's emphasis on reviving postwar trade stemmed from more than narrow considerations of economic self-interest. American leaders sincerely believed that opening channels of international trade would raise living standards throughout the world and lessen the danger of future war, an objective clearly in the interest of all nations. Roosevelt neatly summarized the motives behind American foreign economic policy in answering a reporter's question as to whether the United States would help rehabilitate other nations after the war: "Sure, we are going to rehabilitate them. Why? . . . Not only from the humanitarian point of view—you needn't stress that unless you want to—there's something in it—but from the point of view of our own pocketbooks, and our safety from future war." Somewhat more formally, a State Depart-

Morton Blum, *Morgenthau Diaries: Years of War,* chapter 5; and Eckes, "Bretton Woods," pp. 29–71.

[42] Oscar Cox draft of a speech for Roosevelt, dated October 2, 1944, copy in Cox Diary, Cox MSS; Roosevelt State of the Union address, January 7, 1943, *FDR: Public Papers,* XII, 31; Lauchlin Currie to Roosevelt, September 8 and 9, 1944, Roosevelt MSS, OF 396, OF 264; Roosevelt to Hull, October 17, 1944, *ibid.,* PPF 8101. See also L. Gardner, *Economic Aspects of New Deal Diplomacy,* pp. 282–83; and Kolko, *Politics of War,* pp. 252–53.

ment committee proclaimed late in 1943 that restoration of world trade would be essential "to the attainment of full and effective employment in the United States and elsewhere, to the preservation of private enterprise, and to the success of an international security system to prevent future wars." [43]

The fate of American postwar foreign economic policy clearly depended upon the attitude of other members of the Grand Alliance. Remembering Britain's vital role in the prewar world economy, Washington officials quickly began negotiations with their English counterparts to secure London's commitment to multilateral trading policies and reform of the international monetary system. The British were hesitant —an unconditional commitment to multilateralism would threaten London's sheltered export market, thus exacerbating English economic weakness—but blunt pressure from American negotiators eventually forced London to accept most of Washington's plans. Dependent on American aid for both its war effort and postwar reconstruction, Great Britain was in no position to resist.[44]

Obtaining Moscow's agreement proved to be more difficult. Despite ideological differences, American planners clearly hoped for Russian cooperation. Harry Dexter White, the Treasury Department's leading currency expert, wrote in May, 1942, that it would be an "egregious error" to exclude Russia from the International Monetary Fund and the World Bank simply because it had a socialist economy. At the Moscow Conference in October, 1943, Secretary of State Hull stressed the importance of getting the Russians to accept American economic plans. Treasury Secretary Morgenthau worked energetically throughout the Bretton Woods Conference in the summer of 1944 to secure Russian adherence to the International Monetary Fund and the World Bank. As in the case of

[43] Roosevelt press conference, November 24, 1942, *FDR: Public Papers,* XI, 492; "Summary of the Interim Report of the Special Committee on the Relaxation of Trade Barriers," December 8, 1943, printed in Notter, *Postwar Foreign Policy Preparation,* p. 622. See also Roosevelt speeches of January 7, 1943, and January 11, 1944, *FDR: Public Papers,* XII, 32, XIII, 34, 41; Berle speech of October 15, 1942, *DAFR,* V (1942–43), 23; and Harry Dexter White preliminary draft, "United Nations Stabilization Fund and a Bank for Reconstruction of the United and Associated Nations," copy in Morgenthau Diary, May 8, 1942, p. 231, Morgenthau MSS.

[44] R. Gardner, *Sterling-Dollar Diplomacy,* is the definitive treatment of these negotiations, but see also E. F. Penrose, *Economic Planning for Peace;* and L. Gardner, *Economic Aspects of New Deal Diplomacy,* pp. 275–91.

Great Britain, American officials did not hesitate to employ economic incentives to win Soviet cooperation—in this case, the prospect of a massive postwar reconstruction loan.[45] But unlike Britain, the Soviet Union, not solely dependent on the United States, eventually elected to remain aloof.

Moscow's refusal to participate in the Bretton Woods monetary system or to relax trade barriers in the areas under its control was an effect rather than a cause of the Cold War. Once the Grand Alliance had collapsed in mutual recrimination over the fate of Eastern Europe, economic cooperation became impossible. Washington chose to withhold the one instrument which might have influenced Soviet economic behavior—a postwar reconstruction loan—in hopes of extracting political concessions. Moscow responded by taking what it needed for reconstruction from the Soviet zone of Germany. The American belief that Stalin might agree to integrate the Soviet economy with those of the world's leading capitalist nations reflected a fundamental lack of sophistication which pervaded much of Washington's wartime economic planning. To attempt to construct a new world economic order without first resolving the deep political differences which divided the United States and the Soviet Union was naïve in the extreme, for, in the long run, politics turned out to be more important than economics for the leaders of both nations. The unrealistic nature of United States foreign economic planning demonstrated clearly the extent to which excessive concentration on past mistakes could impair efforts to deal with future realities.

V

But none of these measures—unconditional surrender, self-determination, the lowering of barriers to trade—seemed likely to prevent new wars if the United States reverted to isolationism. Most informed observers, both inside and outside the government, now believed that Americans had made a tragic mistake in 1919 when they refused to join the

[45] White, "United Nations Stabilization Fund," Morgenthau Diary, May 8, 1942, pp. 256–57, Morgenthau MSS; minutes, October 29, 1943 session, Moscow Foreign Ministers' Conference, *FR: 1943*, I, 665–66; Blum, *Morgenthau Diaries: Years of War*, pp. 245–50, 259–65, 275–76.

League of Nations. "Would we not . . . have been better advised," Undersecretary of State Welles asked in 1942, "if we had been willing 20 years ago to join with other free peoples of the earth in promoting an international order which . . . could have prevented . . . the total war of today?" Until the United States agreed to cooperate with other nations to police the world against threats of future aggression, there could be no guarantee of lasting peace.[46]

There was, however, considerable disagreement as to what form this cooperation should take. Many old Wilsonians favored a revival of the League of Nations, with its provisions for collective action against aggressors. A few world federalists wanted to move beyond the League to establish a true global government. Others argued that formal structures meant little; peace would come most quickly through restoration of a world balance of power. Still others saw preservation of big-power unity as the chief essential for avoiding new wars. Franklin D. Roosevelt's ideas fell into this last category.[47]

Though originally a supporter of the League of Nations, Roosevelt by the outbreak of World War II had departed substantially from the position of his former chief, Woodrow Wilson. The League's failure to keep peace in the 1930s disillusioned F.D.R., convincing him that only the prompt and effective use of force, not interminable debate, could prevent aggression. The President wrote in September, 1941:

In the present complete world confusion, it is not thought advisable at this time to reconstitute a League of Nations which, because of its size, makes for disagreement and inaction. . . . There seems no reason why the principle of the trusteeship in private affairs should not be extended to the international field. Trusteeship is based on the principle of unselfish service. For a time at least there are many minor children among the peoples of the world who need trustees in their relations with other nations and peoples, just as there are many adult nations or peoples which must be led back into a spirit of good conduct.

After Pearl Harbor Roosevelt toughened his position, arguing that in the immediate postwar period the United States, the Soviet Union, Great Britain, and China would have to act not as "trustees" but as "sheriffs"

[46] Divine, *Second Chance*, pp. 34, 68–69; Welles radio address of December 6, 1942, *DAFR*, V (1942–43), 36.

[47] Divine, *Second Chance*, p. 62.

or "policemen" for the rest of the world. The Big Four would remove from the hands of other nations, friendly as well as hostile, all weapons more dangerous than rifles. Periodic inspection would ensure against clandestine rearmament. "If any nation menaced the peace," the President explained to Soviet Foreign Minister Molotov, "it could be blockaded and then if still recalcitrant, bombed." Roosevelt acknowledged that this might be "peace by dictation," but hoped that defeated enemies would see this as being more in their interests than periodically recurring wars.[48]

F.D.R.'s concept of the Four Policemen did not preclude eventual formation of a world wide organization of nations "for the purpose of full discussion" as long as "management" was left up to the Big Four. But the President wanted to delay establishing such a body until several years after the war. The victorious allies of World War I, he believed, had set up the League of Nations too soon after the fighting had stopped. This time there would be no peace conference until the world had recovered from "shell shock," a process Roosevelt thought might take from two to four years. During the interim, the Big Four would keep order.[49]

Roosevelt doubted that the American people were yet ready for membership in a new world body. Painfully aware of Wilson's experience with the Senate, chronically prone to exaggerate domestic opposition to his foreign policy, Roosevelt hesitated to declare himself publicly in favor of a new collective security agency. During his meeting with Churchill in August, 1941, he refused to allow a commitment to post-

[48] Roosevelt to Myron C. Taylor, September 1, 1941, Roosevelt MSS, PSF: "Italy"; Roosevelt-Molotov conversation, May 29, 1942, *FR: 1942,* III, 568–69. See also an unsigned memorandum of Roosevelt's conversation with Clark Eichelberger, November 13, 1942, *FDR: Personal Letters,* II, 1366–67; Eden's account of a conversation with Roosevelt on March 15, 1943, Eden, *The Reckoning,* p. 431; Roosevelt to George Norris, September 21, 1943, *FDR: Personal Letters,* II, 1446–47; and Charles E. Bohlen's minutes of Roosevelt's conversation with Stalin, November 29, 1943, *FR: Tehran,* pp. 530–32. Two convenient summaries of Roosevelt's Four Policemen concept are Divine, *Roosevelt and World War II,* pp. 57–58; and Range, *Roosevelt's World Order,* pp. 172–76. In his May 29, 1942, conversation with Molotov, Roosevelt conditioned China's participation as one of the Four Policemen upon its ability to achieve a unified central government.

[49] Roosevelt to Taylor, September 1, 1941, Roosevelt MSS, PSF: "Italy"; press conference, September 7, 1943, *FDR: Public Papers,* XII, 375–76; Roosevelt to Norris, September 21, 1943, *FDR: Personal Letters,* II, 1446–47.

war international organization to be written into the Atlantic Charter. Throughout 1942, Roosevelt permitted subordinates to launch occasional trial balloons, but avoided personal comment on the matter.[50]

Pressure quickly mounted, however, for establishment of a collective security organization before the end of the fighting. Internationalists argued that smaller nations would resent their exclusion from the peace-keeping process. A world body representing all nations would, as Sumner Welles put it, act as a kind of "safety valve." Moreover, the United States would have more influence over its allies during the war than it would after victory. Welles believed that if Wilson had tried to commit his allies to the League of Nations before the Armistice, "the Treaty of Versailles might well have produced different results." Secretary of State Hull worried that the Four Policemen might assume responsibility for specific parts of the world, and that this might lead to spheres of influence. The "self-restraint" which the United States had shown in Latin America "might not be exercised by a great power in another region." Finally, internationalist groups throughout the country had launched a massive campaign to drum up support for a new attempt at world organization. These efforts quickly paid off, with public opinion polls by the summer of 1942 showing that three out of four Americans now favored United States membership in some form of postwar collective security organization.[51]

Roosevelt, flexible as usual, allowed the State Department to proceed with the planning for such an organization. In a carefully worded speech cleared with the President in advance, Hull called in July, 1942, for cre-

[50] Sherwood, *Roosevelt and Hopkins,* p. 360; Divine, *Second Chance,* pp. 40, 44, 49, 83–84; Wilson, *The First Summit,* p. 198; Welles, *Where Are We Heading?* p. 15. For Roosevelt's tendency to exaggerate domestic opposition, see Langer and Gleason, *The Challenge to Isolation,* pp. 5–6; and Smith, *American Diplomacy During the Second World War,* p. 9.

[51] Welles account of conversation with Roosevelt, August 11, 1941, *Where Are We Heading?* pp. 5, 19–20; Hull, *Memoirs,* II, 1644; Divine, *Second Chance,* pp. 53–69. Oscar Cox cited yet another reason for moving ahead on planning for international organization: "The persons who are good at this political field [presumably State Department officials] will have been so excluded from the conduct of the war that they will have the time and energies to devote to it." (Cox to Harry Hopkins, June 24, 1942, copy in Cox Diary, Cox MSS.) State Department planners apparently assumed from the beginning that a new world organization would be set up before the end of the war. (Notter, *Postwar Foreign Policy Preparation,* p. 102.)

ation of "some international agency . . . which can, by force, if necessary—keep the peace among nations in the future." By April, 1944, the State Department had developed a compromise plan designed to satisfy both Roosevelt and the internationalists. The United Nations would resemble the League of Nations in its universal membership— all countries fighting against Germany and Japan would be invited to join. But the United States, Great Britain, the Soviet Union, or China could, as permanent members of the Security Council, employ the veto to prevent the world organization from acting against their will. Roosevelt approved this arrangement, and authorized Hull to invite representatives of the Big Four to meet later that summer at Dumbarton Oaks, just outside Washington, to discuss the American proposal.[52]

The State Department's plan preserved the essence of Roosevelt's Four Policemen concept, but in a framework less repugnant to internationalists who feared a new Quadruple Alliance. The Security Council veto maintained the principle of big-power unity which F.D.R. knew was necessary to secure Russian cooperation. Simultaneously, the veto improved prospects for Senate endorsement of the United Nations by making it clear that the world organization could not force the United States into war against its will, thus defusing in advance a major argument used against Article X of the League of Nations. It is difficult to know whether Roosevelt himself really expected the new collective security organization to fulfill the hopes of its founders. "I dream dreams," he once wrote, "but am, at the same time, an intensely practical person." Realistically, he continued to rely on cooperation with the Soviet Union and other great powers as the best chance for keeping the peace. But at the same time his idealism led him to hope that the rule of law might eventually replace international anarchy, and that the United Nations might be the first step in that process.[53] Certain that the new organization

[52] Hull radio address, July 23, 1942, *DAFR*, V (1942–43), 9; Divine, *Second Chance*, pp. 67–68; Notter, *Postwar Foreign Policy Preparation*, pp. 93, 127–29, 533–34; Hull, *Memoirs*, II, 1652–53, 1662–63.

[53] Roosevelt to Jan Christiaan Smuts, November 24, 1942, Roosevelt MSS, PSF: "Union of South Africa"; Range, *Roosevelt's World Order*, p. 52. James MacGregor Burns has observed that Roosevelt was "a deeply divided man. . . . He was a practical man who proceeded now boldly, now cautiously, step by step toward immediate ends. He was also a dreamer and a sermonizer who spelled out lofty goals. He was both a Soldier of the Faith, battling with his warrior comrades for an ideology of peace and

could at least do no harm, Roosevelt directed his waning energies during his last year toward securing approval of the two agencies in whose hands success of the world body rested: the government of the Soviet Union and the Senate of the United States.

Soviet support proved surprisingly easy to obtain, possibly because Stalin, like Roosevelt, was not looking solely to the United Nations for postwar security. Secretary of State Hull secured Russian commitment to the principle of international organization at the Moscow Foreign Ministers' Conference in the fall of 1943, and at Dumbarton Oaks, in the summer of 1944, Big Four representatives sketched in details generally in accordance with the State Department's suggestions. At Yalta Roosevelt did have to overcome Russian reservations regarding voting procedure in the Security Council and membership in the General Assembly, but with this accomplished the Big Four were in sufficient agreement to invite their allies to San Francisco in April, 1945, to draw up and sign the United Nations Charter.[54]

Winning the Senate's approval seemed, at first, as formidable an undertaking as dealing with Moscow. Public expressions of isolationist sentiment had grown scarce after Pearl Harbor, but a distinct wariness about accepting postwar international commitments still lingered among prominent Republicans. Roosevelt and Hull worried deeply about the effect these Republicans might have in the Senate, where the opposition of any more than one-third of the membership could prevent American participation in the new world organization. Determined not to repeat Woodrow Wilson's mistakes, they resolved not to let the issue of international organization become a political football.[55]

---

freedom, and a Prince of the State, protecting the interests of his nation in a threatening world." ("FDR: The Untold Story of His Last Year," *Saturday Review*, LIII [April 11, 1970], 15.) On the United Nations as a reflection of the Four Policemen concept, see Divine, *Second Chance*, pp. 182–83.

[54] The Four-Power Declaration, signed at Moscow on November 1, 1943, announced that the United States, the Soviet Union, Great Britain, and China "recognize the necessity of establishing at the earliest practicable date a general international organization, based on the principle of the sovereign equality of all peace-loving states, and open to membership by all such states, large and small, for the maintenance of international peace and security." (*FR: 1943*, I, 756.) For subsequent negotiations with the Russians, see Divine, *Second Chance*, chapters 9–11.

[55] Hull, *Memoirs*, II, 1635–38; Roosevelt press conference, May 30, 1944, *FDR: Public Papers*, XIII, 141–43. See also Welles, *Where Are We Heading?* pp. 20–22; and Notter, *Postwar Foreign Policy Preparation*, pp. 195–96.

The President consistently stressed how the new world body would differ from the League of Nations. The United Nations, he told a press conference, would not concern itself with such questions as "whether we were to build a new dam on the Conestoga Creek," but would instead establish machinery for "talking things over with other Nations, without taking away the independence of the United States in any shape, manner, or form." When asked whether the new peace plan would resemble Wilson's Fourteen Points, F.D.R. replied hastily: "Oh, no. Oh, no. . . . Things like points, well, are principles. This is a working organization that we are talking about." Seeking to avoid the disillusionment which had greeted the League, Roosevelt repeatedly warned against expecting too much. It was unrealistic, he said late in 1944, to expect a peace-keeping organization to be set up immediately "with the telephones in, and the plumbing complete—the heating system and the electric ice boxes all functioning perfectly, all furnished with linen and silver— and with the rent prepaid." Perfectionism was as much a danger as isolationism: "Let us not forget that the retreat to isolationism a quarter of a century ago was started not by a direct attack against international cooperation but against alleged imperfections of the peace." [56]

Hull likewise was determined to avoid what he called "the crucifying consequences of . . . partisan politics." From the beginning he made certain that Republicans were represented on the State Department's Advisory Committee on Postwar Foreign Policy. Prior to the Dumbarton Oaks Conference, he submitted the State Department's plan for international organization to scrutiny by a bipartisan delegation of influential senators. After the 1944 political conventions, Hull arranged with John Foster Dulles, representing Republican nominee Thomas E. Dewey, to keep the issue out of the presidential campaign. "I have seldom worked harder on any project," Hull later wrote. "I was convinced that, if I did not reach a satisfactory agreement with him, successful American participation in an international security organization might be seriously jeopardized." Following the Yalta Conference, Roosevelt and Edward R. Stettinius, Jr., Hull's successor as secretary of state, named several prominent Republicans to the American delegation to the San Francisco

---

[56] Press conference of May 30, 1944, *FDR: Public Papers*, XIII, 141, 146; speech to the Foreign Policy Association, October 21, 1944, *ibid.*, p. 350; State of the Union address, January 6, 1945, *ibid.*, p. 498.

Conference. This strategy of bipartisanship paid off handsomely when the United Nations Charter came before the Senate on July 28, 1945—it passed by a vote of 89 to 2.[57]

But bipartisanship had its price. The necessity of reaching agreement with leading Republicans reinforced F.D.R.'s tendency to avoid public discussion of details of the postwar settlement. One reason why the Senate had rejected the League of Nations had been Wilson's tactic of embedding the charter in a peace treaty which many Americans considered unjust. If the degree to which Soviet postwar intentions conflicted with American ideals became known, bipartisan support for the United Nations might begin to erode. Republican Senator Arthur H. Vandenberg of Michigan, a staunch prewar isolationist whose vote was crucial to the Administration, made it clear that he would support American membership in the new world organization only if the peace settlement accorded with the principles of the Atlantic Charter. This situation made it even less likely that Roosevelt would attempt to prepare the American people for the demands Stalin was sure to make in Eastern Europe.[58]

International organization performed a function on the domestic front similar to that of unconditional surrender among members of the Grand Alliance. Both were "lowest common denominators": areas of agreement which all sides could endorse, while at the same time concealing differences on other, more controversial issues. Inevitably, both became panaceas, leading many to think that the attainment of unconditional surrender or the establishment of the United Nations alone would be sufficient to bring the new era of peace which everyone sought. No one illustrated the millennial quality of this thinking better than Cordell Hull in an address which he made to a joint session of Congress upon his return from the Moscow Foreign Ministers' Conference in November, 1943. Once the new international organization went into effect, the Secretary of State told the wildly applauding congressmen, "there will no longer be need for spheres of influence, for alliances, for balance of power, or any other of the special arrangements through which, in the unhappy

---

[57] Hull, *Memoirs,* II, 1635, 1656, 1693; Pratt, *Cordell Hull,* II, 718–38; Divine, *Second Chance,* pp. 270–71, 313.

[58] Vandenberg to Hull, May 3, 1944, Arthur H. Vandenberg, Jr., ed., *The Private Papers of Senator Vandenberg,* pp. 97–98; Vandenberg Diary, May 11, 1944, *ibid.,* p. 96; Westerfield, *Foreign Policy and Party Politics,* pp. 144–45. For background on Vandenberg, see C. David Tompkins, *Senator Arthur H. Vandenberg.*

past, the nations strove to safeguard their security or to promote their interest." [59] Such assertions could only lead to the very disillusionment which Roosevelt hoped to avoid.

Preoccupation with the past seriously clouded the American vision of the postwar world. Washington's commitment to unconditional surrender, self-determination, the revival of world trade, and international organization all grew out of determination to avoid mistakes which had led to World War II. None of these objectives came to grips with the realities of a postwar world which would see two great superpowers confronting each other over the corpse of Germany. Roosevelt's "grand design" for cooperation with Russia did take into account the new situation, but the President failed to build the popular consensus behind his program which would ensure its implementation. Obsessed himself by the errors of the past, Roosevelt fully supported policies designed to avoid them, never realizing the extent to which these plans would undermine his other great goal of preserving the Grand Alliance intact after victory.

[59] *Congressional Record*, November 18, 1943, pp. 9678–79. See also Armstrong, *Unconditional Surrender*, p. 39; and McNeill, *America, Britain, and Russia*, p. 501.

2

The Soviet Union and
World Revolution:
The American View, 1941-1944

Before Roosevelt's plan for postwar cooperation with the Soviet Union could go into effect, however, Americans would have to come to terms with a perplexing anomaly of the wartime situation: the fact that the United States was fighting alongside an ally officially committed to a hostile ideology. Nothing had done more to poison Soviet-American relations prior to World War II than the Kremlin's self-proclaimed ambition to work, through the Communist International, for the violent overthrow of capitalism throughout the world. As late as 1939, public opinion polls showed that most citizens of the United States, if forced to choose between communism and fascism, would have preferred the latter.[1]

[1] Warren B. Walsh, "What the American People Think of Russia," *Public Opinion Quarterly,* VIII (Winter, 1944–45), 515. One contemporary study suggested that Americans sympathized more with the basic principles of communism than with those of fascism, but that they opposed communist teachings on the single subject of property rights so intensely that, confronted with a choice, most would have chosen fascism. (Daniel Katz and Hadley Cantril, "An Analysis of Attitudes Toward Fascism and Communism," *Journal of Abnormal and Social Psychology,* XXXV [1940], 362–65.)

Yet by the end of 1941, the United States had entered the war on the side of the world's leading communist state. Through a curious kind of illogic the Russians' vigorously successful resistance to Hitler purified them ideologically in the eyes of Americans. Surely, the argument ran, any nation which was fighting so valiantly against a common enemy could not espouse so repugnant a doctrine as communism. Reassessing recent events in this light, many informed observers came to believe that Stalin had fundamentally altered the ideological orientation of his own regime; that the Soviet Union was in the process of abandoning communism in fact, if not in name.

Evidence did exist to support this argument. No Comintern congress had been held since 1935, and the activities of that organization in the years preceding the outbreak of war had been inconspicuous. Stalin had launched a campaign within the USSR to rehabilitate the heroes of pre-revolutionary Russia, and had even demonstrated a cautious tolerance of the Russian Orthodox Church. The leader of the international communist movement appeared surprisingly unsympathetic to the efforts of left-wing organizations outside the Soviet Union, and in the summer of 1943 went so far as to order abolition of the Comintern.[2] In retrospect, these seem to have been tactical maneuvers on Stalin's part to generate maximum support, both inside and outside the Soviet Union, for the struggle against Germany. But at the time many Americans interpreted them as signs that the Russians were developing a democratic system of government, in which traditional communist ideology would have no place.

Americans at no point abandoned their antipathy toward that philosophy, as bipartisan denunciations of the Communist Party of the United States during the 1944 presidential campaign showed. But the communist movement no longer appeared to be a monolithic organization directed from Moscow. By disclaiming the goal of international revolution, Stalin seemed to have removed the chief impediment to postwar cooperation with the capitalist world, thus greatly facilitating implementation of President Roosevelt's "grand design."

[2] Alexander Werth, *Russia at War*, pp. 247–49, 429–38; McNeill, *America, Britain, and Russia*, p. 316.

I

Cooperation with the United States and Great Britain in the war against
Hitler greatly improved the Soviet Union's image in the American mass
media. In the interests of Allied unity, articulate observers generally did
what they could to gloss over the less savory aspects of Stalin's regime
when reporting on the Soviet war effort. In the process, many of them
came to believe that profound changes had actually taken place inside
Russia. Stressing Stalin's apparent commitment to "socialism in one
country," they argued that Moscow was no longer interested in world
revolution and speculated that, in time, the Soviet and American systems
of government might become very much alike. Distasteful episodes in recent Russian history—the purges of the mid-1930s, the Nazi-Soviet
Pact, the seizure of the Baltic States, the partition of Poland, the Russo-
Finnish War—could be explained, if not justified, as measures to protect the Soviet Union against future German attack. Perceiving no significant conflicts of interest between Washington and Moscow, these
observers predicted that the two nations would have no difficulty in
building a peaceful relationship after the war.

The most vocal exponent of this point of view was Joseph E. Davies,
a wealthy Wisconsin lawyer who had served as American ambassador to
the Soviet Union from January, 1937, through June, 1938. Davies owed
his appointment more to friendship with Roosevelt and generous campaign contributions than to knowledge of Russia. Foreign Service officers
attached to the Moscow Embassy resented his selection as a replacement
for William C. Bullitt, whom they respected, and for a time considered
resigning in protest. The new ambassador's willingness to condone the
Moscow purge trials produced paroxysms of rage among trained Embassy experts like the young George F. Kennan, who recalled being sent
regularly "to fetch the ambassador his sandwiches, while he exchanged
sententious judgments with the gentlemen of the press concerning the
guilt of the victims." [3]

[3] "Joseph E. Davies," *Current Biography, 1942,* pp. 177–80; Richard H. Ullman,
"The Davies Mission and United States-Soviet Relations, 1937–1941," *World Politics,*
IX (January, 1957), 222–27; George F. Kennan, *Memoirs,* pp. 82–83.

Nevertheless, Davies proved to be more accurate than the professional diplomats in predicting the Nazi-Soviet Pact of 1939. In 1941, almost alone he maintained that the Soviet Union would withstand Hitler's invasion. Though Davies later admitted privately that his predictions had merely been lucky guesses, they won him considerable influence with the American public and the Roosevelt Administration as an expert on Russian affairs. Davies used his position to work for closer ties between the United States and the Soviet Union and, despite poor health, brought to this task energy, enthusiasm, and a shrewd sense of publicity. Following the German attack on Russia, he spoke frequently in support of extending lend-lease to the Soviet Union. He also obtained from the State Department an unusual grant of permission to publish records of his Russian experiences in a book, *Mission to Moscow,* which appeared late in 1941.[4]

Mission to Moscow was an astonishing mixture of the ephemeral and the significant. It contained confidential reports from Davies to the State Department and the President, excerpts from Davies' personal journal, and records of private conversations with high government officials, interspersed with tediously detailed descriptions of the Batum Botanical Gardens and the Crimean wine-making industry. Despite its unevenness, *Mission to Moscow* offered a titillating glimpse into State Department files on an issue of great current interest. It became an immediate best-seller and met with a highly favorable initial reaction. The *Cincinnati Post* called it "tingling history." The *New York Herald Tribune* said that the book placed Davies firmly in the tradition of such other American shirtsleeve diplomats as Benjamin Franklin and Will Rogers. The *Houston Post* found it "perhaps the most valuable book to be published on the subject of Russia in the past decade." On the inside front cover of his personal copy, Franklin D. Roosevelt wrote: "This book will last." [5]

[4] Elbridge Durbrow memorandum of conversation with Davies, February 3, 1943, *FR: 1943,* III, 504; Joseph E. Davies, *Mission to Moscow.* Davies' predictions were not always accurate. In June, 1942, he wrote: "A surprise Japanese attack upon Russia seems almost certain sometime this summer." ("Russia Will Hold This Summer," *Saturday Evening Post,* CCXIV [June 20, 1942], 89.) Despite this, Arthur Krock could still write in January, 1943: "Mr. Davies has proved himself a better expert on Russian military capacity than most of the professional soldiers on whose judgment the United States Government relied for at least the first year of the Soviet-German war." (*New York Times,* January 14, 1943.)

[5] Reviews quoted on book jacket, *Mission to Moscow;* Ullman, "The Davies Mis-

In this volume and in a series of articles written between 1941 and 1943, Davies gave the American people a new view of the Soviet Union. At the end of *Mission to Moscow,* he proclaimed that "the Russia of Lenin and Trotsky—the Russia of the Bolshevik Revolution—no longer exists." Communism had proved itself to be an inefficient system of production. Through a long and occasionally cruel process, the Soviet government had evolved into "a system of state socialism operating on capitalistic principles [which is] steadily and irresistibly swinging to the right." The Russians did not seek to revolutionize the world, but rather to create an egalitarian society in which all men would be governed according to ethical principles. Even if some form of communism did survive inside Russia, Davies argued, it would prove less of a threat to American institutions than fascism. Communism was based, "after all, on the same principle of the 'brotherhood of man' which Jesus preached." [6]

Stalin himself was no bloody-handed tyrant: "A child would like to sit in his lap and a dog would sidle up to him." Davies explained the unpleasant aspects of the Russian dictator's regime by asserting that since the mid-1930s the Soviet Union had been preparing for war with Germany. Stalin had used the purges not to eliminate potential rivals but to eradicate German spies. Fifth columnists did not exist in Russia, Davies pointed out, for the simple reason that the Russians had shot them all. The Nazi-Soviet Pact came only after Britain and France had demonstrated at Munich that they would not oppose German aggression. Russia had seized territory from Poland, the Baltic States, and Finland in 1939 and 1940, but solely for the purpose of gaining additional territory in which to resist the expected German invasion. Hitler's attack on the Soviet Union in 1941 had come as no surprise; the Russians had been getting ready for it for years. [7]

Victory over Germany, Davies asserted, clearly would depend upon

---

sion," p. 220. See also the summary of reviews in *Book Review Digest, 1942,* pp. 187–88.

[6] Davies, *Mission to Moscow,* pp. 34, 511, 551–52. See also Davies, "How Russia Blasted Hitler's Spy Machine," *American Magazine,* CXXXII (December, 1941), 110; "What We Didn't Know about Russia," *Reader's Digest,* XL (March, 1942), 46; "The Soviets and the Post-War," *Life,* XIV (March 29, 1943), 49; and a statement prepared for the American Library Association, January 30, 1944, Davies MSS, Box 14.

[7] Davies, *Mission to Moscow,* p. 357. See also the Davies articles previously cited.

cooperation with Moscow. The fact that the Soviet Union had a communist government was of no concern: "If I have a man fighting with me, I am not inquiring about his religion or what church he goes to, or what party he votes with, while he is helping me to save my wife and children and liberties from possible enslavement or destruction. I am going to give him the benefit of the doubt." Americans who criticized the Soviet form of government only helped Hitler: "The way in which they live and conduct their government . . . is exclusively their own business." Davies felt that there was no reason why the United States and the USSR could not coexist peacefully after the war. Russia's chief preoccupation would be security from future attack; its main goal would be internal industrial development. The "riddle" of how to deal with the Russians was no riddle at all: the United States should adopt "the simple approach of assuming that what they say, they mean; that they are honest in their beliefs, speak the truth and keep their promises." [8]

Subsequent events made Davies' views seem naïve, even foolish, but they did not appear so at the time. Many prominent Americans allowed their hopes for cooperation with the USSR to push them into similar outbursts of wishful thinking. General Douglas MacArthur, for example, cabled from his besieged headquarters on Corregidor in February, 1942, that "the hopes of civilization rest on the worthy banners of the courageous Red Army." Vice-President Henry A. Wallace told a Soviet-American friendship rally late in 1942 that overemphasis on political democracy in the United States had produced extremes of rugged individualism, states' rights, and even anarchy, while overemphasis on economic democracy in the Soviet Union had created an oppressive bureaucracy. Somewhere there had to be "a practical balance" between the two. Theologian Reinhold Niebuhr, later a vigorous critic of Wallace and the USSR, took a similar position early in 1943:

Ideally, collaboration between the Communist and the democratic world might lead to a wholesome exchange of political experience. . . . We have, on the whole, more liberty and less equality than Russia has. Russia has less liberty and more equality. Whether democracy should be defined primarily in terms of liberty or of equality is a source of unending debate.

[8] Davies speech to the Community War Fund Rally, Jacksonville, Florida, November 17, 1943, Davies MSS, Box 14; speech to the Governors' Conference, Columbus, Ohio, June 21, 1943, *Vital Speeches,* IX (August 1, 1943), 638–40; "The Soviets and the Post-War," p. 49.

The Soviet Union was a dictatorship, Niebuhr admitted, but it shared with the United States a belief in justice "which transcends the interests of any one particular race or nation." [9]

During the early years of the war, the most popular American periodicals repeatedly ran articles describing the Soviet Union in uncritical terms. *Life* outdid all its competitors with a special issue on Russia in March, 1943, which proclaimed, among other things, that Lenin was "perhaps the greatest man of modern times," that the Russians were "one hell of a people . . . [who] to a remarkable degree . . . look like Americans, dress like Americans and think like Americans," that the NKVD was "a national police similar to the FBI," and that Americans should "not get too excited" about the fact that the Russians lived "under a system of tight, state-controlled information. . . . If the Soviet leaders tell us that the control of information was necessary to get the job done, we can afford to take their word for it." The normally cautious *New York Times* proclaimed in an April, 1944, editorial: "It is not misrepresenting the situation to say that Marxian thinking in Soviet Russia is out. The capitalist system, better described as the competitive system, is back." [10]

Even presumably dispassionate scholars succumbed to the new mood. Sir Bernard Pares, a distinguished British historian of Russia, told an American radio audience in June, 1943, that "whatever else she is, Russia is not at the present time Communistic, and no one there pretends she is." Professor Ralph Barton Perry of Harvard called attention to "the steady swerving of Soviet policy away from a strict and narrow Marxian

[9] MacArthur message quoted in Sherwood, *Roosevelt and Hopkins,* p. 497; Wallace speech of November 8, 1942, printed in the *New Republic,* CVII (November 23, 1942), 667; Niebuhr, "Russia and the West," *Nation,* CLVI (January 16, 1943), 83; "Russia as an Ally in War and Peace," *University of Chicago Round Table,* February 21, 1943, p. 5. See also Edward L. and Frederick H. Schapsmeier, *Prophet in Politics: Henry A. Wallace and the War Years, 1940–1965,* p. 34. Paul Willen, "Who 'Collaborated' with Russia?" *Antioch Review,* XIV (September, 1954), 259–83; Lawrence S. Wittner, *Rebels Against War,* pp. 115–18; and Richard R. Lingeman, *Don't You Know There's a War On?* pp. 207–8, 222, 225–27, successfully recapture the euphoric mood with which many Americans viewed Russia during the early stages of the war.

[10] *Life,* XIV (March 29, 1943), *passim; New York Times,* April 4, 1944. For a brief survey of American periodical treatment of Russia during the war, see Willen, "Who 'Collaborated' with Russia?" pp. 262–67.

ideology in the direction of ideas that we can call, in very broad terms, democratic." Foster Rhea Dulles, of Ohio State University, published an elaborate history of Russian-American relations from Catherine the Great to the Teheran Conference to demonstrate the absence of conflict between the two nations. Yale historian George Vernadsky, defending Stalin's 1939-40 seizures of territory as protective measures against Germany, argued that in wartime "it is often necessary to re-examine our interpretations of the past, making whatever revisions in it seem to be required by the march of the news." [11]

Wendell Willkie, the Republican Party's unsuccessful 1940 presidential candidate, expressed as well as anyone the new view of Russia which the events of World War II had produced. Willkie visited the Soviet Union during a 1942 round-the-world tour arranged with the cooperation of President Roosevelt. Never a man to cloak his intentions, the Indiana Republican frankly told his Russian hosts that he had come to obtain information which would improve the Soviet Union's image in the United States. If he saw anything in Russia which might create an unfavorable impression among Americans, Willkie continued, he would remain silent about it.[12]

Willkie described his trip to Russia in *One World,* a brief, simply written plea for international cooperation which had sold three million copies by the time of his death in October, 1944. Acknowledging that brutal methods had been used to put the Bolsheviks in power, Willkie

[11] "Death of the Comintern," *University of Chicago Round Table,* June 6, 1943, p. 16; "Russia's Foreign Policy," *ibid.,* September 12, 1943, pp. 2–3; Dulles, *The Road to Teheran;* Vernadsky, "A Review of Russian Policy," *Yale Review,* XXXI (March, 1942), 514, 525–29. For evidence that China scholars demonstrated a similar susceptibility to wishful thinking during the war, see Tang Tsou, *America's Failure in China,* I, 227–30. Kenneth S. Davis, a journalist, carried the revisionist approach to an extreme by arguing that Stalin had signed the Nazi-Soviet Pact to buy time for war preparations and, when ready, had deliberately provoked the German attack: "It is entirely possible that when the final history of this great world crisis is written, Stalin will stand out as the man who saved the civilized world in spite of itself through one of the most profoundly brilliant pieces of strategy that has ever been employed by a national leader during an international conflict." ("Have We Been Wrong about Stalin?" *Current History,* I [September, 1941], 11.)

[12] Undated report by Ambassador William H. Standley on Willkie's visit, *FR: 1942,* III, 645–47. See also the accounts in William H. Standley and Arthur A. Ageton, *Admiral Ambassador to Russia,* pp. 274–77; and Werth, *Russia at War,* pp. 481–86.

asserted that the Soviet government had nonetheless significantly improved the life of the Russian people. He did not try to excuse the Nazi-Soviet Pact, but pointed out that the democracies had little to be proud of either, having acquiesced in the Munich agreement and the sale of scrap iron to Japan. Willkie saw little reason to fear the Soviet Union in the future: "Russia is neither going to eat us or seduce us." In an article written shortly after his return to the United States, he said: "I believe it is possible for Russia and America, perhaps the two most powerful countries in the world, to work together for the economic freedom and the peace of the world. At least . . . there is nothing I ever wanted more to believe." [13]

To its credit, the Roosevelt Administration generally avoided attempts to picture the Soviet Union as a budding democracy or to defend past actions of Stalin's regime, preferring instead to justify collaboration with Russia in terms of military necessity. The one significant exception to this pattern occurred before American entry into the war, when President Roosevelt became worried that powerful religious organizations might oppose lend-lease shipments to Russia because of that country's restrictions on freedom of worship. In August, 1941, the White House arranged on two days' notice to fly Dr. Daniel A. Poling, president of the International Christian Endeavor, to London in a bomber to defend aid to the Soviet Union before a meeting of his organization. On September 3, F.D.R. pointedly advised Pope Pius XII that "leaders of all churches in the United States . . . should not . . . by their present attitude on this question directly assist Germany in her present objectives." [14] Since the Pope presumably had little influence over American Protestant denominations, it may be assumed that Roosevelt had potential Catholic opposition chiefly in mind.

"If Moscow could get some publicity back to this country regarding the freedom of religion [in Russia]," Roosevelt told Soviet Ambassador Constantine Oumansky on September 11, "it might have a very fine edu-

---

[13] Wendell Willkie, *One World*, pp. 85–86; "We Must Work with Russia," *New York Times Magazine*, January 17, 1943, pp. 5 ff. Sales figures for *One World* are given in Ellsworth Barnard, *Wendell Willkie*, p. 412.

[14] Long Diary, August 29, 1941, Israel, ed., *Long Diary*, p. 213; Roosevelt to Pope Pius XII, September 3, 1941, *FDR: Personal Letters*, II, 1204–5. See also Roosevelt to Myron C. Taylor, September 1, 1941, Roosevelt MSS, PSF: "Italy"; Sherwood, *Roosevelt and Hopkins*, pp. 372–73; and Range, *Roosevelt's World Order*, pp. 130–31.

cational effect before the next lease-lend bill comes up in Congress." As if to jog the Russians' memory, the President some days later read to a press conference Article 124 of the largely unimplemented 1936 Soviet Constitution, which contained guarantees of religious freedom. Roosevelt regarded this question as one of "outstanding importance . . . from the standpoint of public opinion in the United States," Secretary of State Hull cabled Ambassador Laurence A. Steinhardt in Moscow. "It is desired that you make every endeavor to see that some statement of this kind is made by the Soviet authorities at the earliest possible moment." The Russians dutifully complied on October 4, 1941, publicly proclaiming that freedom of worship was allowed in the Soviet Union so long as it did not challenge the authority of the state.[15]

Like Davies and Wallace, Roosevelt saw some possibility that the Soviet and American systems of government might, through evolution, become similar. The President once explained to Sumner Welles that since 1917 the USSR had advanced "from the original form of Soviet Communism . . . toward a modified form of state socialism," while at the same time the United States had progressed "toward the ideal of true political and social justice":

He believed that American democracy and Soviet Communism could never meet. But he told me that he did believe that if one took the figure 100 as representing the difference between American democracy and Soviet Communism in 1917, with the United States at 100 and the Soviet Union at 0, American democracy might eventually reach the figure 60 and the Soviet system might reach the figure of 40.

As long as this trend toward convergence continued, Roosevelt saw no reason to regard conflict between the communist and capitalist worlds as inevitable.[16] Unlike many prominent figures during the war, however, the President refrained from publicly encouraging the belief that time would erase ideological differences between the two nations.

After Pearl Harbor, the Roosevelt Administration felt little need to polish the Soviet Union's image in the United States. For most Ameri-

[15] Roosevelt-Oumansky conversation, September 11, 1941, *FR: 1941*, I, 832; Hull to Steinhardt, October 2, 1941, *ibid.*, pp. 1000–1; Steinhardt to Hull, October 6, 1941, *ibid.*, pp. 1002–3. See also Ciechanowski, *Defeat in Victory*, pp. 54–55.

[16] Welles, *Where Are We Heading?* pp. 37–38. See also a memorandum by Archbishop Francis Spellman of a conversation with Roosevelt on September 3, 1943, printed in Gannon, *The Cardinal Spellman Story*, pp. 223–24.

cans, the simple fact that the Russians were fighting Hitler was reason enough to accept them as allies without worrying too much about ideological conflicts. As one Georgia newspaper editor put it: "I'd be willing to fight alongside the Devil himself to win this war." [17] The uncritical descriptions of Russia which became so prevalent in the mass media during World War II reflected the desire of those Americans sophisticated enough to concern themselves with contradictions in international affairs to find complete ideological consistency in the war aims of the anti-Axis coalition. This well-intentioned but misguided effort generated a false sense of euphoria which led to disillusionment and recrimination later on, when it became apparent that, aside from common interest in defeating their enemies, the Soviet Union and the United States had radically different concepts of what the postwar world should be like.

II

Not all Americans accepted the view that the fires of war had purified the Stalinist dictatorship. A small but diverse group of observers argued that the Soviet Union still had a totalitarian form of government, and doubtless would continue to have one after the war. They acknowledged Stalin's apparent abandonment of the goal of world revolution, but refused to exclude the possibility that the Kremlin might still use the world communist movement to promote its policies. These observers protested attempts to excuse events of the past decade in Russia as farsighted measures to prepare for war with Germany, and anticipated some postwar conflicts with the Soviet Union. Still, none of them opposed the alliance with Stalin against Hitler, arguing only that it should be based firmly on considerations of national interest, not on fruitless and occasionally ludicrous efforts to whitewash the Moscow regime.

William Henry Chamberlin, former Moscow correspondent for the *Christian Science Monitor* and author of several books and articles on Russia, typified this point of view. The Stalin who had proved to be such a "courageous, clear-sighted, astute, tenacious leader of his armies and his people," Chamberlin observed, was the same man who had slaugh-

[17] S. C. Heindel to Senator Elbert Thomas, June 14, 1943, Thomas MSS, Box 56, "Davies" file.

tered his own associates and signed the pact with Hitler. The Soviet regime which had inspired millions of Russians to give their lives in its defense was the same one which had "starved its recalcitrant peasants and decimated its pre-revolutionary intelligentsia." These paradoxes constituted an "enigma," to be sure, but in Chamberlin's view hiding them would gain nothing.

Chamberlin strongly deprecated efforts "to prettify Stalin, whose internal homicide record is even longer than Hitler's," or to falsify the recent history of the USSR. Aid to Russia should be based "squarely on considerations of American national interests in defeating Hitler." Such frankness would not, as many feared, impair relations with Moscow— the Russians based their alliance with the United States on their own national interests, not on the attitudes of the American public. Failure to be frank, however, would inevitably bring disillusionment after the war. Peaceful postwar association with Russia was possible, Chamberlin believed, provided the Russians really had given up their ambition to foment world revolution. American economic assistance in Soviet reconstruction efforts could serve as an especially useful device to cement good relations. But such a relationship would not get very far unless Americans gave up their peculiar habit of regarding moral excellence as a prerequisite for wartime collaboration.[18]

A small group of articulate observers, many of them like Chamberlin disillusioned former admirers of the Soviet regime, supported his call for a more realistic attitude toward Russia. Eugene Lyons, Louis Fischer, Max Eastman, and John Dewey all vigorously criticized wartime efforts to obscure distasteful facts about the Soviet Union. William C. Bullitt warned President Roosevelt in 1943 that simply because the Red Army had fought well, Americans should not leap to the conclusion that Stalin had embraced the Four Freedoms: "Since this thesis implies a conversion of Stalin as striking as the conversion of Saul on the road to Damascus,

[18] The following articles are representative of Chamberlin's point of view during the war: "Russia: An American Problem," *Atlantic Monthly*, CLXIX (February, 1942), 148–56; "The Russian Enigma: An Interpretation," *Harper's*, CLXXXV (August, 1942), 225–34; "Russia as a Partner in War and Peace," *Saturday Evening Post*, CCXV (November 14, 1942), 124; "Information, *Please*, about Russia," *Harper's*, CLXXXVIII (April, 1944), 405–12; "W. L. White and His Critics," *American Mercury*, LX (May, 1945), 625–31; "Can We Do Business with Stalin?" *ibid.*, LXI (August, 1945), 194–201.

. . . we have to suspect that this view is the product of the fatal vice in foreign affairs—the vice of wishful thinking." State Department experts on Russia, many of whom had served with Bullitt in Moscow, tried repeatedly to point out potential sources of conflict with the Soviet Union, but with little effect. American socialists and pacifists tended to maintain a critical attitude toward Russia throughout the war.[19]

A minor triumph of sorts for these critics came in the spring of 1943 when reviewers panned an elaborate Warner Brothers film version of *Mission to Moscow*, starring Walter Huston as Joseph Davies. The movie contained numerous historical inaccuracies: it showed Marshal M. N. Tukhachevsky admitting his guilt in a Moscow courtroom when in fact he had been shot without a public trial; it depicted Chinese victims of Japanese bombs being treated in Soviet hospitals; it implied strongly that all pre-Pearl Harbor isolationists had been Republicans. These revisions of history, together with the film's emphatic anti-British bias and reverential treatment of Roosevelt, attracted widespread criticism. James Agee, writing in the *Nation,* called the movie "a great, glad two-million-dollar bowl of canned borscht, eminently approvable by the Institute of Good Housekeeping." John Dewey, who had conducted an extensive investigation of the Moscow purge trials, charged angrily that the film "may serve the interests of Soviet propaganda. It does not serve the interests of 'truth about Russia.' " Columnist Dorothy Thompson delivered the sharpest barb: "It has been suggested that this film needs cutting. It does—indefinitely." [20]

Davies felt that these criticisms overlooked the film's utility as an attack on isolationism and as a means of establishing confidence in the

[19] Eugene Lyons, "The Purification of Stalin," *American Mercury,* LIV (January, 1942), 109–16; "Cooperating with Russia," *ibid.,* LVI (May, 1943), 536–45; "The Progress of Stalin-Worship," *ibid.,* LVI (June, 1943), 693–97; Max Eastman, "To Collaborate Successfully, We Must Face the Facts about Russia," *Reader's Digest,* XLIII (July, 1943), 1–14; Fischer letter to the editor, *Nation,* CLX (June 23, 1945), 706–8; Dewey letter to the editor, *New York Times,* January 11, 1942; Ruth Byrns, "John Dewey on Russia," *Commonweal,* XXXVI (September 18, 1942), 511–13; Bullitt to Roosevelt, January 29, 1943, Roosevelt MSS, PSF: "Bullitt"; Kennan, *Memoirs,* especially chapters 8–10; Wittner, *Rebels Against War,* pp. 118–19; Willen, "Who 'Collaborated' with Russia?" pp. 278–79.

[20] *Time,* XLI (May 10 and 17, 1943), 23–24, 19–20; James Agee, *Agee on Film,* p. 37. See also Chamberlin, "Information, *Please,* about Russia," pp. 406–7, and Lyons, "Progress of Stalin-Worship," pp. 696–97.

Soviet Union as an ally. He later wrote to producer Jack Warner that "within six weeks after the first showing of 'Mission to Moscow,' all of the leaders of the Republican Party . . . made public declarations against Isolation, which the picture so eloquently preached against." When Davies returned to Moscow in May of 1943 on a special mission for President Roosevelt, he arranged a personal screening of the film for Joseph Stalin and other members of the Kremlin hierarchy.[21] But the unfavorable reception which American critics gave the film, together with the bored response of the general public, indicated that efforts to reconcile United States and Russian war aims in all respects had now begun to strain the limits of credibility.

Nevertheless, most American observers carefully refrained from criticizing the Soviet Union while the war was on. The one conspicuous exception was William L. White, son of the famous Kansas editor William Allen White, who accompanied United States Chamber of Commerce President Eric Johnston on a trip to the Soviet Union in the summer of 1944. White's account of this trip, published early in 1945, combined customary praise for the Red Army's fighting abilities with a number of mildly critical remarks concerning the low Russian standard of living, the oppressiveness of the state security apparatus, and the inefficiency of Soviet industrial techniques. White's book provoked a torrent of criticism. Johnston hastily dissociated himself from its conclusions. Several American correspondents in Moscow published a statement labeling the book "a highly biased and misleading report." The *New York Times* reviewer charged that "Mr. White fires no guns for fascism, but he rolls ammunition for it." Yet one year later, a far more hostile description of life in Russia from the *Times*'s own Russian correspondent, Brooks Atkinson, attracted generally favorable acclaim culminating in an invitation from President Truman for Atkinson to visit the White House.[22]

[21] Draft of letter from Davies to Rex Stout, March 21, 1944, Davies MSS, Box 14; Davies to Warner, August 31, 1945, *ibid.,* Box 19; Werth, *Russia at War,* p. 673; C. L. Sulzberger, *A Long Row of Candles,* p. 213.

[22] William L. White, *Report on the Russians.* A serialization of White's book which appeared in the *Reader's Digest,* XLV (December, 1944), 101–22, and XLVI (January, 1945), 106–28, did much to attract attention to it. On the reception of White's book, see *Time,* XLV (March 26, 1945), 61–62; Chamberlin, "W. L. White and His Critics," pp. 625–31; and White, "Report on the Critics," *Saturday Review,* XXIX (October 6, 1946), 15–17. Atkinson's account appeared in the *New York*

It is difficult to say what effect these conflicting views of Russia had on public opinion as a whole. Wartime polls showed that roughly one out of five Americans firmly distrusted the Soviet Union during the war and saw little chance of good relations in the future. A somewhat larger group—approximately 35 percent of the population—anticipated no difficulties in arranging postwar cooperation with the USSR. The remaining 45 percent oscillated between optimism and pessimism according to the course of events, or expressed no opinion. But the over-all level of interest in foreign affairs during the 1940s remained surprisingly low. Estimates indicate that 30 percent of American voters paid no attention whatever to international developments. Forty-five percent of the electorate was aware of important events, but incapable of discussing them intelligently. Only about one out of four American adults consistently demonstrated any thorough knowledge of foreign affairs.[23]

Significantly, the minority of Americans who did keep up with international developments tended to rate possibilities of postwar cooperation with the Soviet Union higher than did poorly informed citizens. College graduates showed a greater willingness to trust Russia than did Americans with high school or grade school educations. Businessmen, professional leaders, and white-collar workers exhibited less suspicion of Soviet intentions than did low income groups.[24] The existence of a favorable attitude toward the USSR among well-educated and presumably prosperous Americans would seem to indicate that critics of Russia had little impact in counteracting the flood of sympathetic and often inaccurate information about the Soviet Union which appeared in the mass media during the war.

Times on July 7–9, 1946, and as "Russia, 1946," in *Life*, XXI (July 22, 1946), 85–94. See also the *New York Times*, July 13, 1946, for Atkinson's reception at the White House.

[23] Gabriel A. Almond, *American People and Foreign Policy*, p. 53; Martin Kriesberg, "Dark Areas of Ignorance," in Lester Markel, ed., *Public Opinion and Foreign Policy*, pp. 51–52. Generalizations on public attitudes toward the Soviet Union are based on responses to the question, asked repeatedly in wartime opinion polls: "Do you think Russia can be trusted to cooperate with us after the war?" Data on responses are given in Hadley Cantril and Mildred Strunk, eds., *Public Opinion, 1935–1946*, pp. 370–71; and are presented in graph form in Hadley Cantril, "Opinion Trends in World War II," *Public Opinion Quarterly*, XII (Spring, 1948), 38.

[24] Cantril and Strunk, eds., *Public Opinion*, p. 371; Walsh, "What the American People Think of Russia," p. 520; Willen, "Who 'Collaborated' with Russia?" p. 281; Jerome Bruner, *Mandate from the People*, p. 113.

III

One key determinant of postwar relations between Russia and the West would be the extent to which traditional communist ideology still influenced the foreign policy of the USSR. If, as appeared likely to many observers during the war, the Kremlin had abandoned its old goal of world revolution, then chances for peaceful Soviet-American coexistence after Germany's defeat would be good. If, on the other hand, the Soviets continued to nurse revolutionary ambitions, lasting peace would be difficult to achieve. President Roosevelt's entire "grand design" for postwar cooperation with the Soviet Union rested on the assumption that Moscow had stopped trying to impose communism on the rest of the world.[25]

The Soviet Union's main instrument for fomenting world revolution in the past had been the Communist International, or Comintern, which it had established in 1919. This organization had not been conspicuously successful—indeed communism failed to take root permanently anywhere outside the Soviet Union during the interwar period. But as long as the Comintern remained in existence it provided evidence of the Kremlin's symbolic, if not actual, espousal of world revolution. Loy Henderson, assistant chief of the State Department's Division of European Affairs, warned Undersecretary of State Sumner Welles in April of 1942 that although little had been heard of the Comintern lately, "we have no information which would cause us to believe that it is not continuing quietly to function with headquarters in the Soviet Union." Elbridge Durbrow, another Division of European Affairs official, told Joseph Davies early in 1943 that any postwar agreements with the Soviet Union "would have to include a very concrete and definite understanding that the activities of the Comintern would have to be liquidated." Nothing would do more to improve relations between Russia and the rest of the world, Cordell Hull observed in May, than the final and definite prohibition of further Comintern activities.[26]

Under these circumstances, news from Moscow on May 22, 1943, that

[25] On this point, see Welles, *Where Are We Heading?* pp. 37–38.

[26] Henderson to Welles, April 9, 1942, *FR: 1942,* III, 436; Durbrow memorandum of conversation with Davies, February 3, 1943, *FR: 1943,* III, 503–4; Hull memorandum of conversation with Eduard Beneš, May 18, 1943, *ibid.,* pp. 529–30.

the Comintern had been dissolved made a great impression in the United States. Admiral William H. Standley, at that time American ambassador in the Soviet Union, regarded this development as an event of major importance which symbolized Russia's confidence in its allies. Hull told the press that cessation of Comintern activities would contribute greatly to wartime and postwar cooperation. Eric Johnston found the news to be the most encouraging since the battle of Stalingrad, while Wendell Willkie termed the step "a very wise move" which would do much to dissipate misunderstandings among the Allies. Assistant Secretary of State Breckinridge Long noted in his diary that dissolution of the Comintern would destroy one of Germany's main propaganda assets, Europe's fear of communization should the Russians win the war. Representative Martin Dies, chairman of the House Committee to Investigate Un-American Activities and long one of the most avid "Red-baiters" in Congress, went so far as to speculate that abolition of the Comintern might even make it possible to do away with his own committee.[27]

Joseph E. Davies, who was in Moscow when the abolition of the Comintern was announced, reported to President Roosevelt that the Russians appeared to be sincere in abandoning interference in the internal affairs of other countries. In an article written for the United Press later that summer, Davies explained that the Russians now clearly intended "to cooperate with, and not to stir up trouble for, their neighbors, with whom they are pledged to collaborate to win the war and the peace." By abolishing the Comintern, Davies said, Stalin had dealt the death blow to Trotsky's program of violent world revolution. Trotsky's widow, living in exile in Mexico, lent credence to Davies' conclusion when she proclaimed bitterly that dissolution of the Comintern constituted the final betrayal of the Bolshevik Revolution.[28]

Davies was hardly an objective observer but, as usual, he was not alone in his views. Many people who in later years would be far less sympathetic to the Soviet Union than Davies accepted his explanation of the Comintern's abolition. Senator Tom Connally of Texas, chairman of

[27] Standley to Hull, May 25, 1943, *FR: 1943*, III, 534–35; Hull press conference of May 24, 1943, quoted *ibid.*, pp. 535–36; *New York Times*, May 23, 1943; Long Diary, May 23, 1943, Israel, ed., *Long Diary*, p. 314; Dies comment in the *New York Times*, May 23, 1943.

[28] Davies to Roosevelt, May 29, 1943, Roosevelt MSS, PSF 18: "Russia"; *New York Times*, May 24 and August 1, 1943.

the Senate Foreign Relations Committee, commented that "Russians for years have been changing their economy and approaching the abandonment of communism, and the whole Western world will be gratified at the happy climax of their efforts." Despite the fact that he had little regard for Davies, Ambassador Standley agreed that Stalin had acted sincerely. From now on, Standley thought, the Russians would try to convert the world to communism not through subversive activities but simply by setting a good example. General Patrick J. Hurley, acting as a personal representative of President Roosevelt, told Chiang Kai-shek in November, 1943, that Stalin had stopped supporting communist activities outside of the Soviet Union. The Russian dictator, Hurley maintained, now realized that communism could succeed inside Russia without being forced on the rest of the world. George Messersmith, the influential American ambassador in Mexico, believed that communism in the conventional sense no longer existed within the Soviet Union, and that "the rabid communists are all found outside Russia today." Representative John W. McCormack of Massachusetts told the House of Representatives succinctly: "Dissolution of the Communist International . . . means the renunciation of world revolution." [29]

Some observers did acknowledge the possibility that communism might take root in Europe on its own, without assistance from the Soviet Union. The economic and social devastation of war had undermined the old order, and communists were rapidly winning popularity throughout Europe by leading resistance movements against the Germans. John Scott, *Time*'s correspondent in Stockholm, warned Secretary of State Hull late in 1943 that public opinion in the occupied countries was swinging away from distant governments-in-exile toward communist and other resistance groups. Vera Micheles Dean, of the Foreign Policy Association, wrote that Europe was ripe for revolution, but that such up-

[29] *New York Times,* May 23, 1943; Harold H. Burton Diary, October 19, 1943, Burton MSS, Box 138; Hurley to Roosevelt, November 20, 1943, *FR: Tehran,* pp. 102–3; Messersmith to Hull, January 4, 1944, Hull MSS, Box 53, Folder 165; *Congressional Record,* June 6, 1943, p. A2778. For Standley's opinion of Davies see Standley and Ageton, *Admiral Ambassador to Russia,* chapter 22. Standley had changed his view of the dissolution of the Comintern by 1955: "The Comintern never was dissolved; it just went underground for the duration of the war. The dissolution was reported as a measure to help allay the prejudice and suspicion of the American people." (*Ibid.,* p. 373.)

heavals as might occur would spring primarily "from maladjustments within the countries where they take place." Walter Duranty, a former *New York Times* correspondent in Moscow, told a radio audience early in 1943: "We may have anarchy in Europe. We may have all sorts of dreadful Red and Black movements, of which I am afraid. But my impression and belief is that the Russians will not foster or push such movements. On the contrary, they would rather tend to stem them." [30]

But the prospect of indigenous communist regimes in Europe aroused surprisingly little concern in the United States during the war. Believing as they did in the concept of self-determination, Americans felt that they could not consistently demand for Europeans the right to choose democratic forms of government without at the same time allowing those who wanted it to embrace communism. John McCormack told his colleagues in the House of Representatives:

Most of us in opposing national socialism or communism, recognize the right of the people of other nations to have any kind of a government they want that does not violate the international law of decency.

It was the advocacy by Soviet Russia of world revolution, violating the laws of nations, . . . that properly aroused resentment and opposition.

"We don't care whether Russia is Communist at home," the *Washington Times-Herald* editorialized, "but we didn't like Russia's efforts to promote Communist revolutions here." [31]

[30] Scott to Hull, December 23, 1943, Hull MSS, Box 53, Folder 165; Dean, "The U.S.S.R. and Post-War Europe," pp. 132–33, 138; "Russia as an Ally in War and Peace," *University of Chicago Round Table*, February 21, 1943, p. 12. On postwar Europe's susceptibility to revolution see also Demaree Bess, "Will Europe Go Communist after the War?" *Saturday Evening Post*, CCXVI (January 22, 1944), 15; Heinz H. F. Eulau, "The New Soviet Nationalism," *Annals of the American Academy of Political and Social Science*, CCXXXII (March, 1944), 28; and William H. Chamberlin, "Russia and Europe, 1918–1944," *Russian Review*, IV (Autumn, 1944), 9.

[31] *Congressional Record*, June 3, 1943, p. A2778; *Washington Times-Herald* editorial, date not given, reprinted *ibid.*, November 15, 1943, p. A4861. See also Bruner, *Mandate from the People*, p. 106. Gabriel Kolko, *The Politics of War*, argues that officials of the United States government during World War II attributed the rise of the "Left" in Europe to the growing influence of the Soviet Union, and deliberately set out to counteract it. But Kolko cites as his main evidence to support this thesis the efforts of Anglo-American military authorities to disarm resistance groups in liberated countries, a development which can more logically be accounted for in terms of the need for secure communications behind the advancing armies and requirements for restoring civilian government. Kolko's interpretation ignores Roosevelt's hopes for post-

In contrast to the general trend of opinion in the United States, State Department experts refused to attach much significance to the abolition of the Comintern. The Division of Far Eastern Affairs noted in August, 1943, that the Soviet Union still had "as one of its paramount political objectives the creation of well disposed and ideologically sympathetic governments in nearby areas." Ambassador W. Averell Harriman wrote President Roosevelt from Moscow in November that although the Russians had recently shown little interest in exporting communism, they might still do so "if it proves to be the only way they can get the kind of relationships they demand from their western border states." Elbridge Durbrow of the Division of Eastern European Affairs argued early in 1944 that communist parties outside the Soviet Union would continue to follow Moscow's orders, even though no formal centralized agency existed to guide them. Indeed, dissolution of the Comintern might actually strengthen the world communist movement by giving individual party organizations a semblance of independence, thus enabling them to attract greater popular support in their respective countries. Harriman agreed. "Communist form of governments [*sic*] is not a present objective of the Soviets," he wrote in April, 1944, "although full opportunity for political expression of the Communist parties [does] appear [to be] a fixed objective." [32]

Communist activities in Latin America caused particular concern to State Department officials. Charles E. Bohlen noted in May of 1943 that Mexico was the center for Comintern operations in the Western hemisphere, and that the appointment of the Soviet ambassador to that country was "more than merely a routine diplomatic assignment." Harriman early in 1944 called Hull's attention to the fact that the Soviets maintained unusually large diplomatic staffs in several Latin American coun-

---

war cooperation with the Soviet Union, and focuses too narrowly on economic factors as the primary domestic influence on American diplomacy. The tendency to ascribe revolutionary developments to the machinations of Moscow did become a prominent characteristic of United States foreign policy, but not until at least 1946.

[32] Division of Far Eastern Affairs memorandum, August 19, 1943, *FR: Washington and Quebec*, pp. 627–29; Harriman to Roosevelt, November 4, 1943, *FR: Tehran*, p. 154; Durbrow memorandum, "Certain Aspects of Present Soviet Policy," February 3, 1944, *FR: 1944*, IV, 813–19; Harriman to Hull, April 20, 1944, *ibid.*, p. 863. See also an unsigned memorandum prepared in the Division of European Affairs, "Current Problems in Relations with the Soviet Union," March 24, 1944, *ibid.*, pp. 839–42.

tries, although there was no evidence that these diplomats were engaging in subversive activities. Marion Parks, of the department's Office of American Republic Affairs, observed in March of 1944 that the Russians had done everything possible to increase their influence in Latin America. Communist movements there were proceeding along much the same lines as they had prior to dissolution of the Comintern, and "connections are generally believed to exist between the [Soviet diplomatic] missions and local Communist groups." [33]

But the State Department did not regard continued communist activity as evidence that the Soviet Union still sought world revolution. George F. Kennan, counselor at the American Embassy in Moscow, wrote in the summer of 1944 that "it is a matter of indifference to Moscow whether a given area is 'communistic' or not. All things being equal, Moscow might prefer to see it communized, although even that is debatable. But the main thing is that it should be amenable to Moscow influence, and if possible to Moscow authority." Elbridge Durbrow pointed out that "the Comintern has been and still is used primarily as an instrument of Soviet foreign policy." The Russians might well try to take advantage of the revolutionary conditions which were sure to exist in Europe after the war, but if they did, it would be for reasons of national interest, not because of a determination to impose communism on the rest of the world.[34]

Outside of official circles, the hierarchy of the Catholic Church constituted the most vocal center of skepticism regarding Soviet ideological intentions. A bitter heritage of distrust had long separated the Vatican from the Kremlin. The Church's traditional hostility toward communism, the Soviet Union's persecution of religion, and the violent confrontation between Catholics and communists during the Spanish Civil War all had contributed to the mutual hostility. The outbreak of World War II had done nothing to alleviate this bitterness, and as it became more and more likely that heavily-Catholic Poland would fall within a Soviet

[33] Bohlen memorandum of May 19, 1943, *FR: 1943,* III, 530–31; Harriman to Hull, January 18, 1944, *FR: 1944,* IV, 806–7; Parks memorandum on "Activities of Soviet Diplomatic Representatives in the Other American Republics," March 28, 1944, *ibid.,* pp. 843–54.

[34] Kennan memorandum, "Russia—Seven Years Later," September, 1944, *FR: 1944,* IV, 908–9; Durbrow memorandum, "Certain Aspects of Present Soviet Policy," February 3, 1944, *ibid.,* p. 817.

sphere of influence, relations between Stalin and the Pope worsened.

As early as February, 1942, the Catholic journal *America* had warned its readers that the effort to convince Americans that they need not fear communism would neither strengthen national morale nor further war aims, "since it is based upon a lie." *Catholic World* noted in the spring of 1943 that admiration for Soviet military achievements threatened to obscure the fact that Stalin still wanted world revolution. Russia's alliance with the West was merely a marriage of convenience; when Germany was defeated Stalin would resume his attempts to communize Europe.[35]

Dissolution of the Comintern failed to alter the conviction of several prominent Catholic leaders that communism posed as great a threat as fascism. Monsignor Fulton J. Sheen persistently advocated this point of view: "Communism is the Asiatic form of fascism and fascism is the European form of communism. There is no essential difference in ideology between the Nazis, the Fascists, and the Communists; all absorb the individual into the collectivity. There is as little difference between communism and fascism as there is between burglary and larceny." Early in 1944 Sheen warned a State Department official that while Russia might be willing to help the Allies eradicate Nazi Germany, this did not mean that the Kremlin would cooperate in other areas. "Irreligious atheism," Sheen observed, "is not only the internal policy of Soviet Russia, but is also to be its external policy in a Soviet Europe." Father James Gillis, the editor of *Catholic World,* described the danger of Russian communism in similar terms for his readers in the fall of 1944:

The greatest potential menace to permanent peace is Soviet Russia. Fascism is not and never was as dangerous as Communism. Naziism, the most virulent form of Fascism, is about to be destroyed. Another evil, imperialism, British, French, Dutch, will be amended and gradually abolished. But Fascism, Naziism, Imperialism combined—if that could be—would not be so serious a threat to peace and to international cooperation as Russian Communism.

Three Catholic archbishops warned President Roosevelt in December that Stalin had been trained "in the school of revolutionaries who plotted the overthrow of all the governments of the world and the establish-

---

[35] "Not Untimely," *America,* LXVI (February 7, 1942), 490; C. P. Thomas, "Prelude to Invasion," *Catholic World,* CLVII (May, 1943), 149–54.

ment of a world domination of communism." The Russian leader instinctively distrusted noncommunist nations and was "seeking to establish the domination of the Soviet Union over other nations by promoting, subsidizing, and directing Communistic minority groups in other countries." [36]

Catholic critics of communism found a conspicuous spokesman in William C. Bullitt, the former American ambassador to the Soviet Union. Bullitt had gone to Moscow in 1933 an enthusiastic supporter of the Moscow regime, but in one of the abrupt shifts from admiration to hatred which characterized his life, he soon became bitterly anti-Soviet. In August of 1943 he had told Roosevelt: "Hitler's aim was to spread the power of the Nazis to the ends of the earth. Stalin's aim is to spread the power of the communists to the ends of the earth. Stalin, like Hitler, will not stop. He can only be stopped." [37] Bullitt's influence with the President waned as cooperation with Russia increased, however, and the summer of 1944 found him without an official position, free to express publicly his personal views.

Bullitt did so with customary vigor in a widely read article which appeared in *Life* in September. Entitled "The World from Rome," it purported to give the views of the hierarchy of the Catholic Church, although Bullitt employed only the euphemism "Romans" throughout. The "Romans," Bullitt said, viewed the American decision to aid Stalin without first securing his promise not to dominate postwar Eastern Eu-

[36] *Washington Times-Herald,* February 2, 1944, reprinted in the *Congressional Record,* February 2, 1944, p. A547; memorandum by unidentified State Department official of conversation with Sheen, February 18, 1944, Department of State Records, 861.404/2-1844 EG; James M. Gillis, "Getting Wise to Russia," *Catholic World,* CLX (October, 1944), 1–6; Archbishops Edward Mooney, A. Stritch, and Francis Spellman to Roosevelt, December 13, 1944, Department of State Records, 700.0011 PEACE/12-1344 Ai. Les K. Adler and Thomas G. Paterson, "Red Fascism: The Merger of Nazi Germany and Soviet Russia in the American Image of Totalitarianism, 1930's–1950's," *American Historical Review,* LXXV (April, 1970), 1046–64, deals with the tendency to equate communism with fascism both before and after World War II, but neglects Catholic efforts to do this during the war.

[37] Bullitt to Roosevelt, August 10, 1943, Roosevelt MSS, PSF: "Bullitt." Bullitt's persistent Russophobia had alienated the President by this time, as had the former ambassador's recent smear campaign against Sumner Welles, which had brought about the Undersecretary of State's forced resignation. On this matter, see Acheson, *Present at the Creation,* p. 46; Israel, ed., *Long Diary,* pp. 324–25; and Burns, *Roosevelt: The Soldier of Freedom,* p. 350. For insight into Bullitt's personality, see Beatrice Farnsworth, *William C. Bullitt and the Soviet Union, passim;* and Kennan, *Memoirs,* pp. 79–81.

rope as "one of the biggest mistakes of the war." Events in Poland had already made the Atlantic Charter "a dead letter, a mere expression of a pious hope that will never seriously be supported by either the United States or Great Britain." Moscow's call for "friendly democratic governments" along its borders was merely a ploy to allow communist elements "to organize themselves strongly enough to destroy all democratic liberties and install a soviet totalitarian regime." Alarmingly apocalyptic in tone, the article warned: "Rome again sees approaching from the East a wave of conquerors. . . . Will the result of this war be the subjugation of Europe by Moscow?" The "Romans" and Bullitt clearly feared such a development.[38]

"The World from Rome" stirred up a hornet's nest of criticism. The exiled Italian scholar Gaetano Salvemini accused Bullitt of using the label "Romans" to project his own and the Catholic Church's point of view. *Life*'s editors observed lamely that the Russophobic tone of Bullitt's writing should not have surprised anyone, since everyone already knew that Bullitt was a Russophobe. One of *Life*'s readers commented tartly that the Church hierarchy could more effectively halt the spread of communism by raising the standard of living of its own communicants than by talking to people like Bullitt.[39]

There were others who doubted the Kremlin's sincerity in abolishing the Comintern. Former Russian correspondent Louis Fischer told a radio audience that "Stalin has only torn up a label. He loses nothing. He must be laughing at us for being so naïve as to celebrate the death of a name." Max Eastman, another prominent critic of the Stalinist regime, asked: "Why should we expect a sudden end to the World Communist conspiracy just because the bosses of the Comintern have ostentatiously burned their letterheads?" Alexander Barmine and Victor A. Kravchenko, two former Soviet officials who had defected to the United States, warned loudly of Russian duplicity. A dwindling band of isolationists like Representative Hamilton Fish of New York continued to refer ominously to "the bloody hand of Communism." [40]

[38] *Life,* XVII (September 4, 1944), 94–109.

[39] Gaetano Salvemini, "Mr. Bullitt's Romans," *New Republic,* CXI (October 2, 1944), 423–26; letters to the editor column, *Life,* XVII (September 25, 1944), 2–10. For a survey of public reaction to Bullitt's article, see Department of State, "Fortnightly Survey of American Opinion," No. 11, September 19, 1944.

[40] "Will Russia's Abolition of the Comintern Help Win the Peace?" *Town Meeting of the Air,* May 27, 1943, pp. 8–9; Eastman, "To Collaborate Successfully, We Must

But the skepticism of the State Department, the Catholic hierarchy, and others about dissolution of the Comintern did not extend to the general public. Opinion polls demonstrated that as the war progressed, more and more Americans came to believe that the Russians really had abandoned their plans for world revolution. A poll taken in August of 1944 showed that only 20 percent of a national sample expected Russia to try to spread communism to Europe after the war. Another poll sent to President Roosevelt in November concluded that a majority of the population accepted as sincere the Soviet government's contention that its main objective was to build up a strong socialist state, not to spread communism. Most Americans at this time would have agreed with Richard Lauterbach, former head of the *Time-Life* Russian bureau, who observed that "more people talk about world revolution in New York than they do in Moscow." [41]

IV

Antipathy for communism remained strong within the United States throughout the war, but Americans directed this hostility against their own communists, not Russian ones. Harry Hopkins explained to Molotov in 1942 that the American Communist Party was made up of "disgruntled, frustrated, ineffectual, and vociferous people—including a comparatively high proportion of distinctly unsympathetic Jews." Two years later, during a trip to the Soviet Union, Eric Johnston undertook to explain to the Russians why communists were so unpopular in the United States: "Our American Communists . . . lack originality and realism. They still follow and imitate what they think is your current policy. If you take pepper they sneeze. If you have indigestion, they belch. They annoy our trade unions much more than they annoy our

Face the Facts about Russia," p. 11; Barmine, "The New Communist Conspiracy," *ibid.*, XLV (October, 1944), 27–33; *New York Times*, April 4, 1944; *Time*, XLV (January 1, 1945), 14.

[41] Almond, *American People and Foreign Policy*, pp. 93–94; Bruner, *Mandate from the People*, p. 113; Report on "Public Understanding of Russian Intentions, Policies, Performances," prepared for Roosevelt by Hadley Cantril, November 10, 1944, Roosevelt MSS, OF 857, Box 3; *New York Times*, October 21, 1944. See also Walsh, "What the American People Think of Russia," p. 514.

employers." John L. Lewis early in 1944 indignantly berated American communists for trying to "hang on to the coattails of the Red Army" by equating friendship for Russia with sympathy for communism. It was an "outrageous contention" to assert that the United States could not fight side by side with Russia while simultaneously combating communists at home. Congressman John Rankin of Mississippi went so far as to blame the Detroit race riot of 1943 on American communists, but noted that in the Soviet Union communism was so unpopular that the Russians were running it out of the country.[42]

Such slanders hurt Earl Browder, the unlikely head of the Communist Party of the United States, who was once described as looking more like a lyric poet than a revolutionary. Too many people, he complained, thought that "now that the Soviet Union is our ally . . . the Communists of the Soviet Union are okey, since they are indispensable, but that does not mean that we need tolerate them in the United States." Following the Teheran Conference, the American Communist Party made every effort to fit itself into the domestic political establishment. Browder at one point proclaimed that "if J. P. Morgan supports this coalition [of Russia and the United States] and goes down the line for it, I as a Communist am prepared to clasp his hand." When told on another occasion that he sounded like a member of the National Association of Manufacturers, Browder replied: "That's fine. I'm awfully glad to hear that." In May of 1944 the Communist Party of the United States dissolved itself, became the "nonpartisan" Communist Political Association, and proclaimed its support of Franklin D. Roosevelt for President.[43]

This latest gyration of the American Communist Party failed to appease its critics. The expansion of federal government power during the New Deal and World War II had convinced some Americans that a

[42] Hopkins-Molotov conversation, May 29, 1942, *FR: 1942*, III, 570–71; Johnston speech of June 3, 1944, *FR: 1944*, IV, 967*n; New York Times*, February 29, 1944; *Congressional Record*, July 1, 1943, p. A3371. Congressman Rankin attributed much of the racial tension in the United States to the activities of communists: "Many innocent, unprotected white girls . . . have been raped and murdered by vicious Negroes, who have been encouraged by those alien-minded Communists to commit such crimes." (*Ibid.*)

[43] "Earl Browder," *Current Biography, 1944*, pp. 69–73; Browder debate with George Sokolsky, March 21, 1943, on "Is Communism a Menace?" *New Masses*, April 6, 1943, p. 16; Irwin Ross, "It's Tough to Be a Communist," *Harper's*, CXCII (June, 1946), 532.

form of collectivism, possibly even communism, might develop indigenously in the United States. As the presidential election of 1944 approached, Republican orators found it convenient to play on these fears as a means of pillorying the Roosevelt Administration. The Communist Political Association's endorsement of Roosevelt made it easier for Republicans to link communism with the New Deal. Highly effective campaigning for the Democrats by Sidney Hillman's Political Action Committee of the Congress of Industrial Organizations worried many Republicans, causing them to try to discredit that organization by labeling it communist.[44] Thus communism became an issue during the 1944 presidential campaign but not, oddly enough, because of the activities of the Comintern.

Republicans went to great lengths to make it clear that opposition to domestic communism did not imply disrespect for the Soviet Union. Fundamental differences existed between Russian and American economic and social systems, Thomas E. Dewey said in April, 1944, but these dissimilarities in no way made friction between the two countries inevitable. Former President Herbert Hoover assured the Republican National Convention in June that Russia was no longer truly communist: "The Communist Internationalism of Russia has been driven out by the nationalist aspiration to free Mother Russia and expand the empire." [45]

During the campaign the Republican vice-presidential candidate, John W. Bricker, repeated with depressing monotony the charge that communists wanted Roosevelt to win the election. Bricker accused Roosevelt of having pardoned Earl Browder from prison, where he had been sent for falsifying his passport, in order to win communist support for a fourth term. The President depended for his reelection, Bricker asserted,

[44] Leon Friedman, "Election of 1944," in Arthur M. Schlesinger, Jr., ed., *History of American Presidential Elections, 1789–1968,* IV, 3015, 3033–35. One of the most vivid denunciations of the Political Action Committee came from a Democrat, Representative Philip J. Philbin of Massachusetts, who charged that the organization was "inspired by internal Communists, revolutionary Socialists, Syndicalists and an assorted variety of social reform crackpots, fellow travellers, brave-new-world, starry-eyed dreamers, dangerous un-American alien radicals, and other diverse subversive elements." (*Congressional Record,* June 20, 1944, p. A3179.)

[45] Dewey speech of April 28, 1944, reprinted in the *Congressional Record,* 1944 appendix, pp. A2022–A2023; Hoover speech of June 27, 1944, reprinted *ibid.,* pp. A3425–A3428.

on big city bosses and "Communist and radical elements." Merging his condemnations of the Communist Party and the Political Action Committee, Bricker charged in Dallas late in October that "the great Democratic party has become the Hillman-Browder communistic party with Franklin Roosevelt at its front." Representative Clare Boothe Luce of Connecticut made the same accusation, asserting that on orders of Moscow the American Communist Party "has gone underground, after the fashion of termites, into the Democratic party." [46]

Dewey himself used the communist issue more cautiously than Bricker and other Republicans. Speaking in Charleston, West Virginia, in October, he maintained that communists were supporting Roosevelt because the New Deal was moving toward state ownership of the nation's productive facilities. Under these circumstances, "government would tell each of us where we could work, at what, and for how much." This might be either communism or fascism, but whatever it was Dewey was against it. The Republican candidate climaxed his use of the communist issue with a speech in heavily-Catholic Boston on November 1:

Naziism and fascism are being crushed out in the world. But the totalitarian idea is very much alive and we must not slip to its other form, communism. . . . Today that pagan philosophy is sweeping through much of the world. As we look abroad we see that in country after country its advocates are making a bid for power. We would be fools not to look for that same danger here. And we haven't far to look.

After uttering this dire warning, however, Dewey took care to ensure that his remarks would not reflect on the Soviet Union. New Dealers, he charged, were trying to convince the American people that they

must love communism or offend our fighting ally, Russia. Not even the gullible believe that. In Russia, a Communist is a man who supports his government. In America, a Communist is a man who supports the fourth term so that our form of government may more easily be changed.

The question of communism in the United States, Dewey concluded, had nothing whatsoever to do with the Soviet Union. [47]

Republican use of the communist issue caused some concern within the Democratic camp. In a radio address early in October, Roosevelt ex-

[46] *New York Times,* September 21, 26, October 17, 26, 1944.
[47] *Ibid.,* October 8, November 2, 1944.

plicitly rejected the support of the American communists: "I have never sought and I do not welcome the support of any person or group committed to communism or fascism or any other foreign ideology which would undermine the American system of government or the American system of free competitive enterprise and private property." At the same time Roosevelt, like Dewey, felt called upon to stress that anticommunism did not mean anti-Sovietism. Repudiation of American communists should not "interfere with the firm and friendly relationship which this nation has in this war . . . with the people of the Soviet Union. The kind of economy that suits the Russian people . . . is their own affair." [48]

Roosevelt's speech failed to quiet Democratic anxieties. A Chicago party worker assured Harry Hopkins that the American public was deeply concerned about communism: "This current talk about Browder and Hillman, socialization of industry, business, education, etc., is something that people are talking about." Oscar Cox, one of Hopkins' chief assistants, drafted a speech for Foreign Economic Administrator Leo T. Crowley which asserted that

President Roosevelt and the Administration are not only strongly opposed to the doctrines of communism for the United States, but by their progressive leadership they have prevented communism from getting a foothold and becoming a real power in this country—a foothold and a real power which communism might well have gotten if the breadlines and apple-selling of Hooverism had continued.

Senator Robert F. Wagner of New York felt it necessary to inform a Manhattan audience that "neither Franklin Roosevelt nor I are any closer to the Communists than we are to the Hottentots." [49]

Democratic sensitivity over the communist issue became so great at one point that the Administration took the unusual step of indirectly asking Stalin not to endorse Roosevelt. On two occasions in October, Samuel Rosenman, the President's speech-writer, expressed fear to Joseph Davies that any intimation from Moscow that Stalin favored Roosevelt's reelection might hurt the Democratic Party. Davies offered to send a

[48] Sherwood, *Roosevelt and Hopkins,* pp. 328–29; Roosevelt radio address of October 5, 1944, *FDR: Public Papers,* XIII, 323–24.

[49] James K. Finn to Hopkins, October 29, 1944, Hopkins MSS, Box 120; Cox first draft, Crowley campaign speech, October 16, 1944, copy in Cox Diary, Cox MSS; *New York Times,* October 10, 1944.

personal message to the Soviet leader conveying this concern and asking him to have Russian newspapers "pipe down" in their commentary on American politics. Undersecretary of State Edward R. Stettinius, Jr., telephoned Davies from the White House on October 20 approving the idea, and on the same day Davies dispatched to Stalin through the Soviet Embassy in Washington the following personal note:

I earnestly hope that the recent public statements by Governor Dewey, the Republican candidate, will not be replied to or commented on by the Soviet press for the present. They would be republished here and seized upon by hostile forces, and charged by them to be an intrusion into the private political affairs of our country by a foreign Government. It would be directed to arouse resentment among certain of our people, who other wise would be favorable.[50]

The Democrats need not have worried. Popular antipathy for communism did not translate itself into votes against the Administration's Russian policy. Nor did Republican charges of American communist support for Roosevelt significantly cut into the President's majority. Senator Arthur H. Vandenberg concluded from the results that "there is a wide difference of opinion in the country regarding Communism—and a majority of our electorate has just indicated that it does not seem very worried about it." [51] Vandenberg's conclusion was only partially correct. Americans bitterly opposed communism inside the United States, but simply found it difficult to take Earl Browder and his pitiful band of followers seriously. Should the Soviet Union resume, or appear to resume, its efforts to spread communism outside its borders, however, the threat would seem much more ominous.

Americans both inside and outside the government demonstrated a substantial lack of sophistication in assessing the relationship between ideology and Soviet foreign policy during World War II. Influenced by a domestic tradition which attached little importance to political theory, they tended to underrate the importance of ideological considerations in other countries. Prominent "experts" on Russia showed only dim awareness of the degree of tactical flexibility which Marxist-Leninist doctrine

[50] Davies Journal, October 8, 14, and 20, 1944; Davies to Stalin, October 20, 1944, Davies MSS, Box 15.

[51] Vandenberg to James V. Oxtoby, Jr., November 15, 1944, Vandenberg MSS.

allowed, and hence frequently overemphasized the significance of Stalin's attempts to sweep ideology under the rug in the interests of the war effort. Furthermore, "informed" observers failed to take into account the ability of a totalitarian regime to rally widespread public support, especially in periods of national crisis. Confronted with evidence that the Russian people were willing to fight for their government, many Americans jumped illogically to the conclusion that the Soviet Union had suddenly become a democracy.[52] These inaccurate perceptions left the United States ill-prepared for postwar developments, including Joseph Stalin's firm assurance to all concerned that reports of his conversion to the liberal democratic tradition had been highly exaggerated.

[52] Tang Tsou reaches similar conclusions regarding American perceptions of Chinese Communism in *America's Failure in China,* I, 204–5, 219–21. See also Kenneth E. Shewmaker, *Americans and Chinese Communists, 1927–1945: A Persuading Encounter.*

3

※※

Cooperating for Victory:
Defeating Germany and Japan

In August, 1943, William C. Bullitt submitted a lengthy memorandum to his old friend Franklin Roosevelt warning of an imminent "political catastrophe" in Europe. The United States and Great Britain had rightly judged Hitler's conquest of Europe to be "an intolerable menace to . . . their free institutions," Bullitt asserted, but "domination of Europe by Stalin's Communist dictatorship would be as great a threat." Unfortunately, the British and Americans needed Russia's help in the war against Germany if they were to keep their casualties within tolerable limits. The problem, therefore, was to find some way to prevent "the domination of Europe by the Moscow dictatorship without losing the participation of the Red Army in the war against the Nazi dictatorship."

Bullitt's argument reflected a central dilemma of American military strategy during World War II: victory over the Axis depended upon co-operation with the Soviet Union, yet defeat of Germany and Japan would mean a vast increase in Russian power in Europe and the Far East, a development which might well preclude realization of such vital postwar objectives as self-determination and the revival of multilateral trade. Bullitt's solution to this problem was to devise operations against Germany which would place Allied forces in a position to counteract Russian influence in Eastern Europe—an Anglo-American invasion of the Balkans would accomplish this, he believed—while at the same time making further aid to the Soviet Union, both for wartime and for postwar purposes, contingent upon Moscow's acceptance of Washington's war aims. "War is an attempt to achieve political objectives by fighting," he reminded Roosevelt, "and political objectives must be kept in mind in planning operations." [1]

F.D.R. did not have to be warned of risks of collaborating with Moscow. "I don't dispute your facts," he told Bullitt. "They are accurate. I don't dispute the logic of your reasoning." But the President made it clear that he did not intend to follow Bullitt's advice:

I just have a hunch that Stalin is not that kind of man. Harry [Hopkins] says he's not and that he doesn't want anything but security for his country, and I think that if I give him everything I possibly can and ask nothing from him in return, *noblesse oblige,* he won't try to annex anything and will work with me for a world of democracy and peace.

Bullitt retorted that Stalin was "a Caucasian bandit whose only thought when he got something for nothing was that the other fellow was an ass," but Roosevelt cut him off: "It's my responsibility and not yours; and I'm going to play my hunch." [2]

As was often the case with Roosevelt, his "hunch" was based on sound reasoning. No one could yet exclude the possibility that Stalin, if pressed too hard, might make a separate peace with Hitler. Even if the Russian dictator did agree to support American war aims, there could be no assurance that he would keep his promise. Furthermore, Roosevelt was extremely conscious of the limits of American power. United States troops could not counteract Russian moves in Eastern Europe without imposing unacceptable demands on the nation's manpower pool and productive facilities—already stretched to the limit by simultaneous operations against Germany and Japan.[3] Such a maneuver would also

[1] Bullitt to Roosevelt, August 10, 1943, Roosevelt MSS, PSF: "Bullitt." See also Bullitt to Roosevelt, January 29 and May 12, 1943, *ibid.*

[2] Bullitt, "How We Won the War and Lost the Peace," *Life,* XXV (August 30, 1948), 94. Bullitt is vague about the precise date when this conversation took place, but there is no doubt that it substantially reflects Roosevelt's position.

[3] The United States could have considerably increased the size of its armed forces, but only at the expense of vital war production. On this point, see Matloff, *Strategic Planning, 1943–44,* pp. 115–16. Greenfield, *American Strategy in World War II,* pp. 6–7, 75–76; and Richard M. Leighton, "OVERLORD Revisited: An Interpretation of

endanger prospects for Soviet assistance in the Far East, which American military leaders badly wanted. Finally, the President felt certain that public opinion would not tolerate keeping United States forces overseas after the war, a clear necessity if Soviet influence was to be contained.[4] Roosevelt therefore rejected Bullitt's suggestion that he reorient military strategy in accordance with postwar political objectives. Instead he concentrated on achieving total victory over the Axis, trusting that a mutual desire to avoid further conflict would compel Russians and Americans to coexist peacefully after the war.

Roosevelt failed to see, however, how his strategy for winning the war might undermine his effort to build trust between Washington and Moscow. F.D.R. sought to defeat the Axis through the maximum possible use of American industrial power, but with the minimum possible expenditure of American lives.[5] Such a policy precluded launching military operations when chances for success were not high. Yet to the Russians, who did not enjoy the luxury of deciding where and how they would fight Germany, a "blood sacrifice" in the form of an early second front seemed the acid test of Anglo-American intentions. Roosevelt led the Russians to expect such a front in Europe in 1942, but then endorsed a British proposal to invade North Africa, thereby delaying the full cross-channel attack until 1944. At the time, each decision appeared to be in the best interests of the anti-Axis coalition, but the two-year gap between promise and performance convinced the Russians that their capitalist comrades had decided to let them carry the main burden of the war. The resulting atmosphere of suspicion was hardly conducive to

American Strategy in the European War, 1942–1944," *American Historical Review,* LXVIII (July, 1963), 928, 937, both emphasize the limitations which logistical considerations imposed on United States strategic planning.

[4] On this point, see William R. Emerson, "F.D.R.," in Ernest R. May, ed., *The Ultimate Decision,* pp. 168–72.

[5] Kent Roberts Greenfield argues that Roosevelt believed "that the role of America was from first to last to serve as 'the arsenal of Democracy,' and that its proper contribution to victory was to confront its enemies with a rapidly growing weight of material power that they could not hope to match; then to use it to crush them with a minimum expenditure of American lives." (*American Strategy in World War II,* p. 74.) See also Kolko, *The Politics of War,* pp. 14, 20; Burns, *Roosevelt: The Soldier of Freedom,* pp. 86, 546; and Richard M. Leighton and Robert W. Coakley, *Global Logistics and Strategy, 1940–1943,* pp. 137–40.

Roosevelt's "grand design" for placing postwar Soviet-American relations on a firm basis of mutual understanding.

I

In planning initial military operations against the Axis, Roosevelt had two basic requirements. Despite the fact that Japan's attack on Pearl Harbor had brought the United States into the war, he insisted on taking the offensive against Hitler. Almost a year earlier, British and American military chiefs had decided that should their two countries become involved in war with both Germany and Japan, their principal effort would be directed toward defeating Germany first. Roosevelt fully supported this strategy, because only through it could he ensure attainment of one of his major political objectives—the survival of Great Britain. The President's second requirement followed logically from the first: that American troops should engage the Germans as soon as possible. Acutely sensitive to public opinion, F.D.R. feared that if action against the Nazis was delayed, domestic pressure to pay the Japanese back for Pearl Harbor would become irresistible. It was "very important to morale," he told Army Chief of Staff General George C. Marshall late in 1941, "to give this country a feeling that they are in the war, [and] to give the Germans the reverse effect, to have American troops somewhere in active fighting across the Atlantic." [6]

At the ARCADIA conference in Washington at the end of 1941, Winston Churchill proposed an Anglo-American invasion of North Africa as a first step in "closing the ring" on Germany, to be followed in 1943 by landings on the European continent itself. Roosevelt expressed interest in this idea, especially when the Prime Minister suggested that Vichy authorities might be persuaded to "invite" Allied troops into areas under their control with little or no resistance. American military officials re-

[6] Marshall memorandum of conversation with Roosevelt, December 23, 1941, quoted in Maurice Matloff and Edwin L. Snell, *Strategic Planning for Coalition Warfare, 1941–42*, p. 105. See also Stimson to Hopkins, August 4, 1943, *FR: Washington and Quebec*, p. 445; and Greenfield, *American Strategy in World War II*, p. 59. For the "Germany first" decision, see Louis Morton, "Germany First: The Basic Concept of Allied Strategy in World War II," in Kent Roberts Greenfield, ed., *Command Decisions*, pp. 11–47.

sponded skeptically, however, arguing that the North African project relied too much on tenuous lines of communication and would make only
an indirect contribution to victory. Moreover, the Americans darkly suspected the British of being "motivated more largely by political than by
sound strategic purposes." General Marshall and his advisers favored
more forthright methods: "We've got to go to Europe and fight," General Dwight D. Eisenhower, deputy chief of the Army's War Plans Division, wrote early in 1942, "we've got to begin slugging with air at West
Europe; to be followed by a land attack as soon *as possible*." [7]

One of the main reasons why American strategists wanted an early invasion of Europe was their desire to help Russia. The Red Army's
staunch resistance to Hitler had strongly reinforced the logic of the
"Germany first" decision. "We would be guilty of one of the grossest
military blunders of all history," Eisenhower observed, "if Germany
should be permitted to eliminate an Allied army of 8,000,000 men." Eisenhower believed that two things would be necessary to keep the Soviet
Union in the war: direct lend-lease aid, and "the early initiation of operations that will draw off from the Russian front sizable portions of the
German Army, both air and ground." An invasion of France launched
from Great Britain seemed the most practical way to accomplish this
objective. In addition to relieving Russia, it would strike the Germans in
the most direct manner possible, permitting maximum utilization of
shipping and air power without endangering the security of the British
Isles. General Marshall endorsed Eisenhower's conclusions, and by the
end of March, 1942, had won Roosevelt's tentative approval of them.
"Your people and mine demand the establishment of a front to draw off

[7] Undated memorandum by Major General Stanley D. Embick, quoted in Matloff
and Snell, *Strategic Planning, 1941–42*, p. 104; Eisenhower desk diary note, January 22, 1942, *Eisenhower Papers*, I, 66. For the British proposal, see Churchill, *The
Grand Alliance*, pp. 545–55. The ARCADIA discussions are covered in Matloff and
Snell, chapter 5; and *FR: Casablanca*, pp. 3–415. Suspicion of British motives was
widespread among American military officials at this time. General Marshall later recalled: "On one occasion our people brought in an objection to something the British
wanted. I didn't see anything wrong with the British proposal, but our planners . . .
explained that there was an ulterior purpose in this thing. . . . Later [Sir Charles]
Portal [Chief of the Royal Air Force] said that he had drafted the proposal and that
it was taken from a memorandum of ours. And it was a fact; he showed it to me. . . .
Our own paragraph was the key of our objection." (Marshall interview with Forrest C.
Pogue, October 29, 1956, quoted in Pogue, *Marshall: Ordeal and Hope*, p. 264.)

pressure on the Russians," F.D.R. wrote Churchill early in April, "and these people are wise enough to see that Russians are today killing more Germans and destroying more equipment than you and I put together." [8]

But ROUND-UP, the American plan for invading France, had one great liability: it could not take place until the spring of 1943, the earliest date at which the necessary military build-up in Great Britain would be complete. Roosevelt felt that he could not wait this long. "I am becoming more and more interested in the establishment of a new front this summer," he informed Churchill in March, 1942. F.D.R. knew that from the strictly military point of view it made sense to delay landings in France until 1943, but as president he had to take into account political considerations as well: "The necessities of the case call for action in 1942—not 1943," he told his military advisers. "I regard it as essential that active operations be conducted in 1942." General Marshall later recalled that he learned an important lesson from this incident: "The leader in a democracy has to keep the people entertained. . . . The people demand action. We couldn't wait to be completely ready." [9]

Aside from his desire to maintain domestic support for the "Germany first" strategy, Roosevelt had an additional political reason for wanting to avoid delay. Late in May, 1942, Soviet Foreign Minister Molotov had come to Washington to discuss the question of a second front. The Russians hoped to hold out, Molotov said, but "it was only right to look at the darker side of the picture." Hitler might be able to defeat the Red Army unless the Anglo-Americans could begin offensive action soon to draw off forty German divisions. The Soviet government wanted "a straight answer": could it expect a second front by the end of the year? Over Marshall's objections, Roosevelt authorized Molotov to inform Sta-

[8] Eisenhower memorandum, July 17, 1942, *Eisenhower Papers*, I, 389; Eisenhower to Marshall, February 28, 1942, *ibid.*, p. 151; Roosevelt to Churchill, April 3, 1942, quoted in Churchill, *The Hinge of Fate*, p. 274. On the reasoning behind plans for the cross-channel attack, see Eisenhower, *Crusade in Europe*, p. 45; Matloff and Snell, *Strategic Planning, 1941–42*, pp. 177–79, 181–85; Pogue, *Marshall: Ordeal and Hope*, p. 305; and Sherwood, *Roosevelt and Hopkins*, pp. 519–20.

[9] Roosevelt to Churchill, March 9, 1942, quoted in Sherwood, *Roosevelt and Hopkins*, p. 518; Roosevelt memorandum of May 6, 1942, quoted in Gordon Harrison, *Cross-Channel Attack*, p. 24; Marshall interview with Forrest Pogue, November 13, 1956, quoted in Pogue, *Marshall: Ordeal and Hope*, p. 330. See also Harry Hopkins to Roosevelt, March 14, 1942, quoted in Sherwood, *Roosevelt and Hopkins*, p. 519.

lin that the United States and Great Britain would attack the Germans somewhere in Europe before the end of 1942.[10]

Like his military chiefs, F.D.R. was seriously concerned about the Red Army's capacity to repel another German summer offensive, and hoped to encourage the Russians by promising that help was on the way. Furthermore, Molotov had just signed the Anglo-Soviet treaty of friendship without pressing for endorsement of Russian boundary claims in Eastern Europe. In return for this concession to American sensibilities, Moscow clearly expected assurances about the second front. It is unclear how literally Stalin interpreted Roosevelt's promise. Churchill warned Molotov that, while the Western allies would do their best, they would not engage in suicidal operations simply to meet the President's timetable. Stalin himself admitted to American ambassador William H. Standley in July that wanting a second front and actually having one were two different things. But the second-front pledge was widely publicized inside the Soviet Union, leading Standley to comment that if it was not fulfilled, "these people will be so deluded in their belief in our sincerity of purpose . . . that inestimable harm will be done to the cause of the United Nations." [11]

Faced with the President's call for action before the end of the year, War Department strategists began pushing SLEDGEHAMMER, an operation involving quick landings on the French coast in the fall of 1942. Although logistical limitations made success doubtful, Eisenhower favored taking the risk because even a failure would at least convince the Russians "that we are trying to assist." But SLEDGEHAMMER soon encountered the unyielding opposition of the British. The terrible memory of World War I made Churchill and his generals even more determined than Roosevelt to keep casualties down. With this in mind, they favored striking at Germany through a series of amphibious landings around the

[10] Roosevelt-Molotov conversation, May, 1942, *FR: 1942,* III, 577, 582–83; Pogue, *Marshall: Ordeal and Hope,* pp. 326–27. The public communiqué issued after the Molotov visit announced that "in the course of the conversations full understanding was reached with regard to the urgent tasks of creating a Second Front in Europe in 1942." (White House press release, June 11, 1942, *FR: 1942,* III, 594.)

[11] Divine, *Roosevelt and World War II,* pp. 88–89; Churchill, *The Hinge of Fate,* p. 297; Standley to Hull, June 22 and July 22, 1942, *FR: 1942,* III, 598, 612. For the relationship of the second front to Soviet boundary claims, see chapter 1.

periphery of Hitler's Europe, together with a tight naval blockade and heavy aerial bombardment. The British supported an eventual invasion of the European continent, but hoped to postpone it until other measures had severely weakened German resistance. Painfully aware that the SLEDGEHAMMER landings, if they took place, would involve mostly British troops, the Prime Minister and his Chiefs of Staff decided in July, 1942, to veto the operation.[12]

American military planners reacted violently to this news. Secretary of War Henry L. Stimson warned Roosevelt that Churchill had a chronic addiction to "half-baked" diversionary schemes, and solemnly advised the President to read up on the disastrous World War I Dardanelles campaign. The Joint Chiefs of Staff recommended that if the British repudiated SLEDGEHAMMER, the United States should abandon its "Germany first" strategy and assume the offensive against Japan. But the President refused to consider this drastic proposal. Placing Anglo-American unity above all else, he ordered the Joint Chiefs to accept Churchill's alternative plan for engaging the Germans in 1942: an autumn invasion of North Africa. Eisenhower, who would command the North African operation, viewed the demise of SLEDGEHAMMER bitterly:

The whole thing seems to me to be absurdly simple. I believe in direct methods, possibly because I am too simple-minded to be an intriguer or to attempt to be clever. However, I am no longer in the places where these great questions have to be settled. My only job is to carry out my directives as well as I can.[13]

Pleased by the President's decision, Churchill volunteered to fly to Moscow in August to tell Stalin that there would be no second front in

[12] Eisenhower memorandum, July 17, 1942, *Eisenhower Papers*, I, 389. See also Greenfield, *American Strategy in World War II*, p. 58; Matloff and Snell, *Strategic Planning, 1941–42*, pp. 278–84; Harrison, *Cross-Channel Attack*, pp. 26–32. Samuel Eliot Morison, *Strategy and Compromise*, chapter 4, presents the traditional interpretation of the conflict between British and American strategic concepts, a view now modified somewhat by Leighton, "OVERLORD Revisited," pp. 921–23; and Greenfield, *American Strategy in World War II*, chapter 2. For British reservations regarding SLEDGEHAMMER, see Pogue, *Marshall: Ordeal and Hope*, pp. 315–18; Churchill, *The Hinge of Fate*, pp. 282–83; and McNeill, *America, Britain, and Russia*, p. 174.

[13] Pogue, *Marshall: Ordeal and Hope*, pp. 340–42; Matloff and Snell, *Strategic Planning, 1941–42*, pp. 268–70; Leo Meyer, "The Decision to Invade North Africa," in Greenfield, ed., *Command Decisions*, pp. 182–88; Eisenhower to Fox Conner, August 21, 1942, *Eisenhower Papers*, I, 485.

Europe in 1942. "It was like carrying a large lump of ice to the North Pole," he later wrote. Russian cinema audiences enthusiastically cheered films of the Prime Minister's visit, erroneously interpreting his two-fingered "victory" sign as a promise of a second front. Stalin took the news with bitterness, but eventually managed to work up some enthusiasm for the North African operation as the next best thing. "May God prosper this undertaking," he remarked to Churchill with un-Marxian emphasis.[14]

Whether or not Stalin really expected a European second front in 1942, he did manage to reap considerable propaganda advantages from his allies' failure to fulfill Roosevelt's pledge. Wendell Willkie remarked while visiting Moscow in September that the American people might have to "prod" their generals a bit to get the second front under way, a comment which provoked Roosevelt into making cutting remarks about unnamed "typewriter strategists." In an October newspaper interview, Stalin observed that the second front still occupied a "primary place" in Soviet military planning, and that without it, lend-lease assistance to Russia was "of little effect." The Soviet leader called pointedly for "complete and timely fulfillment by Allies of their obligations." On the eve of the North African landings, Joseph E. Davies told reporters that the Russian leaders had shown remarkable tolerance and forbearance in their requests for a second front. Roosevelt obliquely responded to these criticisms in a press conference on November 10: "If you had all the luck on your side and the other fellow made all the mistakes," F.D.R. observed, one might be able to throw a military plan together on the spur of the moment and have it work. "But after all, where hundreds of thousands of lives are involved; we do try to conduct war operations by what is known as a reasonable chance of success." [15]

Roosevelt's decision to invade North Africa demonstrated the degree to which both military and political considerations influenced American

[14] Churchill's classic account of this conference is in *The Hinge of Fate*, pp. 411–37. See also Harriman to Roosevelt, August 13, 1942, *FR: 1942*, III, 620; and Standley to Hull, August 25, 1942, *ibid.*, 634.

[15] Undated report by Ambassador Standley on Willkie's trip, *FR: 1942*, III, 647; Sherwood, *Roosevelt and Hopkins*, pp. 634–35; Stalin interview with Henry Cassidy, *Pravda*, October 5, 1942, quoted in *FR: 1942*, III, 461; *New York Times*, November 8, 1942; *FDR: Public Papers*, XI, 462–63. See also Loy Henderson to Hull, October 15, 1942, *FR: 1942*, III, 464–66.

strategy. On strictly military grounds, a cross-channel attack in the spring of 1943 seemed to offer the quickest way to victory. But, for political reasons, F.D.R. could not delay action that long: domestic support for the "Germany first" strategy might wane, while the Russians, if no help came by the end of the year, might seek a separate peace. Roosevelt could not get a second front in Europe in 1942 without alienating the British, however, so he settled for a compromise—North Africa. The President later explained to a press conference:

> We did agree to start a second front of sorts [in 1942], and when it came down to the point, it seemed best to start it at a place called Algiers. . . . That was done. Now, . . . you can write pages and pages on what you mean by a second front. . . . No . . . two people in this room will agree. . . . At least, action was taken.[16]

But Roosevelt failed to take into account the political impact which the North African decision would have on his own plan for postwar cooperation with the Soviet Union.

II

The invasion of North Africa, as American military leaders feared, precluded establishment of a second front in Europe in 1943. Temporary but unexpected resistance by the Vichy French, together with German tenacity, prevented the operation from going as quickly as had been hoped. Not until May, 1943, did the Germans give up in Tunisia. Moreover, Roosevelt and Churchill decided at Casablanca to follow the North African victory with an attack on Sicily, in an effort to knock Italy out of the war. This made landings in France impossible in 1943, although the final decision to put off the invasion was not made until later that year. In retrospect, it seems clear that postponement of the cross-channel attack saved the British and Americans from a major military disaster.[17] But the delay severely strained the alliance with the Soviet Union, leaving the Russians to feel, with considerable justification, that they had been left to do most of the fighting against Germany.

[16] Press conference of February 23, 1943, Roosevelt MSS, PPF 1-P, Vol. XXI.
[17] Harrison, *Cross-Channel Attack*, pp. 38–45, 89; Matloff, *Strategic Planning, 1943–44*, p. 131; Eisenhower, *Crusade in Europe*, p. 71; Morison, *Strategy and Compromise*, pp. 46–47.

The absence of a second front brought Soviet-American relations to a low point in the summer of 1943, leading some observers to consider the possibility that Stalin might yet conclude a separate peace with Germany. Joseph E. Davies reported from Moscow in May that many Soviet leaders believed their Anglo-American allies wanted "a weakened Russia at the peace table and a Red Army that is bled white." He warned: "If Great Britain and the United States fail to 'deliver' on the western front in Europe this summer, it will have far reaching effects upon the Soviets that will be effective both on their attitude in the prosecution of this war and in their participation in the reconstruction of the peace." Davies mentioned the existence of "an appeasement group" in the Soviet Union, and thought it possible that the Russians might content themselves with simply liberating their own territory, without trying to bring about the total defeat of Germany. State Department Russian expert Charles E. Bohlen noted in June that while there was no evidence that the Russians would try to deal with Hitler, the possibility could not be ruled out for the simple reason that "a dictatorship responsive . . . to the views of one man is of necessity unpredictable." [18]

In July, 1943, the Soviet government announced formation of a "Free Germany" Committee, composed of German exiles in Russia, a move which Ambassador Standley interpreted as evidence that Moscow intended to follow "an independent policy" in Central and Eastern Europe. State Department officials saw even more ominous implications in the Russian action: Stalin, they feared, was clearing the way for negotiations with a pro-Soviet government in Germany should Hitler be overthrown. Assistant Secretary of State Breckinridge Long noted in his diary that "if Russia should pull out of the war it would leave us in a terrible situation in Europe and would make it infinitely more difficult for us to conquer Japan." As late as October, 1943, Roosevelt was still sufficiently concerned about Stalin's intentions to ask Standley: "What do you think, Bill, will he make a separate peace with Hitler?" [19]

[18] Davies to Roosevelt, May 29, 1943, Roosevelt MSS, PSF 18: "Russia"; Bohlen memorandum of June 24, 1943, *FR: 1943*, III, 668n. See also Sherwood, *Roosevelt and Hopkins*, p. 734; and Feis, *Churchill, Roosevelt, Stalin*, pp. 134–35.

[19] Standley to Hull, July 22 and 23, 1943, *FR: 1943*, III, 552–54; Hull to Standley, July 30, 1943, *ibid.*, pp. 557–58; James C. Dunn to Major General George V. Strong, August 11, 1943, cited in Matloff, *Strategic Planning, 1943–44*, p. 286n; Long Diary, August 9, 1943, Israel, ed., *Long Diary*, p. 320; Standley and Ageton, *Admiral Ambassador to Russia*, p. 498. For other expressions of concern about a separate peace

But the prospect of a new Nazi-Soviet Pact, though worrisome, grew increasingly remote as the military situation on the eastern front improved. Gradually it became clear that the Red Army's victory at Stalingrad in the winter of 1942–43 had marked a decisive turning point. After smashing German resistance in massive battles around Kursk, Orel, and Kharkov in the summer of 1943, the Russians began an advance on a broad front which within two years would carry them to Berlin. Anglo-American efforts in the Mediterranean seemed paltry by comparison—Stalin had complained publicly in February, 1943, that "the Red Army alone is bearing the whole weight of the war." [20] The chief danger now seemed to be not that the Russians would stop fighting but that they would regard their victories as having earned them the right to demand a dominant role in shaping the peace settlement.

General Marshall warned Roosevelt in March that if the Russians got to Germany before the Western allies, "a most unfortunate diplomatic situation" would follow. By August he was speculating whether "in the event of an overwhelming Russian success, . . . the Germans [would] be likely to facilitate our entry into the country to repel the Russians." Secretary of War Stimson observed that further delay in launching the cross-channel attack would have dangerous implications, for "Stalin won't have much of an opinion of people who have done that and we will not be able to share much of the postwar world with him." Ambassador Standley, writing from Moscow on August 10, noted that the absence of a second front gave the Russians a definite political advantage:

It . . . prepares the ground for a strong stand in the field of foreign policy. To the extent that people believe that the Soviet Union carried the major burden of winning the war and that the United States and Great Britain withheld assistance which they could have given, they will be more inclined

see William C. Bullitt to Roosevelt, August 10, 1943, Roosevelt MSS, PSF: "Bullitt"; William D. Leahy, *I Was There*, p. 185; Sherwood, *Roosevelt and Hopkins*, p. 734; and *FR: 1943*, III, 246, 621–23, 667–68, 674, 682, 684–87, 690, 695–99, and 708–9. For retrospective assessments of the validity of these fears, see Snell, *Illusion and Necessity*, pp. 125–26; Feis, *Churchill, Roosevelt, Stalin*, p. 143; and McNeill, *America, Britain, and Russia*, p. 324.

[20] Stalin "order of the day," issued on the 25th anniversary of the establishment of the Red Army, February 23, 1943, *FR: 1943*, III, 506–8. Churchill summarizes developments on the eastern front in 1943 with his customary succinctness in *Closing the Ring*, pp. 221–23.

to support a claim that the Soviet Union should have the greatest voice in determining the peace.

Moreover, unless the British and Americans extended significant military assistance to the Russians in the struggle against Germany, they could hardly expect much help from Stalin in the war against Japan. A strategic estimate prepared late in the summer of 1943 concluded that "the most important factor the United States has to consider in relation to Russia is the prosecution of the war in the Pacific." If the Far Eastern conflict had to be carried on without Russia's help, "the difficulties will be immeasurably increased and operations might become abortive." [21]

The Joint Chiefs of Staff summarized the relationship between strategy and politics in a memorandum prepared in September, 1943. The end of the war, they recognized, would place the Soviet Union in a dominant position throughout Eastern and Central Europe, giving it the power to impose whatever territorial settlements it wanted. But the United States still depended on Russian assistance to win the war against Germany—a separate Russo-German peace would make large-scale Anglo-American military operations on the European continent impossible. Furthermore, Russian help would be needed against Japan.[22] Although the Joint Chiefs drew no conclusions from their analysis, its implications were clear: the price of military aid from the Soviet Union against Germany and Japan would be a significant expansion of Russian influence after the war.

But President Roosevelt showed little inclination to let such postwar considerations affect his plans for operations against Germany. F.D.R. did mention to the Joint Chiefs on two occasions in 1943 the need to beat the Russians to Berlin, but after his cordial meeting with Stalin at Teheran in December said nothing more about this. When General Ei-

[21] Marshall memorandum of conversation with Roosevelt, March 30, 1943, quoted in Matloff, *Strategic Planning, 1943–44,* pp. 68–69; Combined Chiefs of Staff minutes, meeting of August 20, 1943, Quebec, *FR: Washington and Quebec,* p. 911; Stimson Diary, May 17, 1943, quoted in Henry L. Stimson and McGeorge Bundy, *On Active Service in Peace and War,* p. 527; Standley to Hull, August 10, 1943, *FR: 1943,* III, 562; General James H. Burns to Harry Hopkins, August 10, 1943, *FR: Washington and Quebec,* pp. 624–27. See also Sherwood, *Roosevelt and Hopkins,* pp. 748–49.

[22] JCS 506, "Instructions Concerning Duty as Military Observer at American-British-Soviet Conference," September 18, 1943, cited in Matloff, *Strategic Planning, 1943–44,* pp. 292–93.

senhower concluded in March, 1945, that the German capital was "no longer a particularly important objective," Roosevelt registered no complaints. The President made no effort to accelerate plans for the 1944 cross-channel attack, now code-named OVERLORD, in hopes of establishing a counterweight to growing Soviet influence in Europe. Instead he carefully delayed the invasion until Anglo-American forces had accumulated sufficient resources to ensure its success without seriously hampering operations under way in other theaters, particularly the Pacific.[23]

If any postwar consideration shaped Washington's strategy, it was the desire to minimize overseas political responsibilities after Germany's surrender. Throughout the summer and fall of 1943 Churchill, though never explicitly repudiating plans for OVERLORD, continually pushed for additional operations in the Mediterranean and the Balkans. War Department planners regarded the Prime Minister's motives as blatantly political: he hoped, they believed, to let Russia defeat Germany while Britain used American resources to prop up the remains of its empire. The Joint Chiefs defended OVERLORD as a purely military operation which would bring all anti-Axis forces together in the most efficient manner possible for the sole purpose of defeating Germany, without involving the United States in complicated postwar political entanglements. Roosevelt agreed, commenting that it was "unwise to plan military strategy based on a gamble as to political results." [24]

[23] Combined Chiefs of Staff minutes, meeting with Roosevelt and Churchill, Quebec, August 23, 1943, quoted in Matloff, *Strategic Planning, 1943–44*, p. 226; Joint Chiefs of Staff minutes, meeting with Roosevelt, en route to Teheran, November 19, 1943, *FR: Tehran*, p. 255; Eisenhower to Marshall, March 30, 1945, *Eisenhower Papers*, IV, 2561. Gabriel Kolko argues that American strategists did seek to counteract growing Soviet influence in Europe by establishing a military presence there as soon as possible. But his view does not explain the decision to invade North Africa, which delayed the entry of United States troops into Western and Central Europe by at least a year. Moreover, much of his argument rests upon the existence of RANKIN (C), a contingency plan for a quick descent on the continent in the event of a German collapse. Kolko maintains that this plan was "entirely politically conceived," but offers no firm evidence for this conclusion. A summary of RANKIN prepared for the Combined Chiefs of Staff in August, 1943, noted specifically that the plan was to be carried out *in cooperation with* the Russians. (Kolko, *The Politics of War*, chapter 1, especially pp. 28–30; memorandum by Sir Frederick Morgan, "Digest of Operation 'Rankin,' " August 14, 1943, *FR: Washington and Quebec*, p. 1018. See also Matloff, *Strategic Planning, 1943–44*, pp. 225–27; William M. Franklin, "Zonal Boundaries and Access to Berlin," *World Politics*, XVI [October, 1963], 5–7; and Sir Frederick Morgan, *Overture to Overlord*, pp. 57, 104–22.)

[24] Joint Chiefs of Staff minutes, meeting with Roosevelt, August 10, 1943, quoted

Still, in view of the North African experience, Stimson and his associates could not help worrying that F.D.R.'s "impulsive nature" might cause him to yield again to Churchill's blandishments. Shortly before the Teheran Conference, Roosevelt assured his concerned Secretary of War that he "wouldn't touch the Balkans." Stimson replied: "Well, you can't even talk about them . . . without frightening people. . . . Remember, no more Balkans." These fears proved groundless. American military chiefs, still deeply suspicious of British political designs, had exaggerated Churchill's opposition to OVERLORD. Moreover, at Teheran Stalin came out firmly in favor of the cross-channel attack, insisting that a commander be appointed quickly, "otherwise nothing would come out of the operation." Impressed, Roosevelt resolved any doubts he may have had, endorsed unequivocally the 1944 landings in France, and named General Eisenhower supreme commander of the Allied Expeditionary Forces. "I thank the Lord Stalin was there," Stimson wrote in his diary; "he saved the day." [25]

The successful invasion of Normandy in June, 1944, justified to American strategists their emphasis on military considerations and, at least for the time being, relieved Stalin's doubts regarding the willingness of his allies to fight the Germans on a large scale. Congratulating Roosevelt and Churchill, the Russian dictator proclaimed that "the history of warfare knows no other like undertaking from the point of view of its scale, its vast conception, and its masterly execution." For the moment, as Churchill noted, "harmony was complete." [26]

Delivery of the second front in Europe placed the Western allies in a favorable position to press for Russian creation of a second front in the Far East, where for three years the United States and Great Britain had been fighting Japan without the help of the Soviet Union. The Pacific

in Matloff, *Strategic Planning, 1943–44*, p. 215. See also *ibid.*, pp. 173–75, 178–79; Stimson to Roosevelt, August 10, 1943, Stimson Diary, Stimson MSS; and Emerson, "F.D.R.," pp. 168–72. American military planners almost certainly misjudged British motives in advocating further operations in the Mediterranean and the Balkans. On this point, see John Ehrman, *Grand Strategy*, V, 111–18; Leighton, "OVERLORD Revisited," p. 922; and Greenfield, *American Strategy in World War II*, pp. 41–45.

[25] Stimson Diary, October 29, November 4, December 5, 1943, Stimson MSS; minutes, 2d plenary meeting, November 29, 1943, *FR: Tehran*, p. 535; Eisenhower, *Crusade in Europe*, pp. 206–8. See also Harrison, *Cross-Channel Attack*, pp. 118–26; and Matloff, *Strategic Planning, 1943–44*, pp. 356–69.

[26] Stalin to Churchill, June 11, 1944, quoted in Churchill, *Triumph and Tragedy*, p. 8.

war seemed likely to drag on for some time after the fighting ended in
Europe, and threatened to take a heavy toll in American casualties. Supply difficulties, together with Chiang Kai-shek's reluctance to fight, had
dashed hopes of employing Chinese manpower in the struggle against
Japan. A Soviet attack through Manchuria would provide a valuable
substitute, containing Japanese armies on the mainland of Asia while
American forces invaded the home islands. The atomic bomb remained a
purely hypothetical weapon at this time, known to only a few top military leaders, with no assurance that it would work. Hence, United States
officials received with great pleasure Stalin's promise, given at the Moscow Foreign Ministers' Conference in October, 1943, to enter the war
against Japan after Germany's surrender.[27]

At the Teheran Conference in December, however, Stalin made it
clear that he would expect political compensation for furnishing military
assistance in the Far East. The Soviet leader did not specify his exact requirements, but acknowledged that Roosevelt's suggestion of a Pacific
warm-water port under international control "would not be bad." One
year later, in December, 1944, Stalin became more precise. Pulling out a
map of the Far East, he indicated to Ambassador Harriman that the Soviet Union would want the Kurile Islands and lower Sakhalin, leases at
Port Arthur and Dairen, control of the Chinese Eastern and South Manchurian railroads, and recognition of the independence from China of
Outer Mongolia. At the Yalta Conference in February, 1945, Roosevelt
agreed substantially to these demands and undertook to secure Chiang
Kai-shek's approval of them. In return, Stalin promised to go to war
against Japan within "two or three months" after Germany's defeat, and
to conclude a pact of "friendship and alliance" with Chiang's Nationalist
government in China.[28]

[27] Louis Morton, "Soviet Intervention in the War with Japan," *Foreign Affairs,* XL
(July, 1962), 653–57; Ernest R. May, "The United States, the Soviet Union, and the
Far Eastern War, 1941–1945," *Pacific Historical Review,* XXIV (May, 1955),
153–63; Matloff, *Strategic Planning, 1943–44,* pp. 292–93, 433–37, 500–1, 536;
and Hull, *Memoirs,* II, 1309–11.

[28] Roosevelt-Churchill-Stalin meeting, November 30, 1943, *FR: Tehran,* pp.
567–68; Harriman to Roosevelt, December 15, 1944, *FR: Yalta,* pp. 378–79;
"Agreement Regarding Entry of the Soviet Union into the War Against Japan," February 11, 1945, *ibid.,* p. 984. The Yalta Far Eastern agreement differed from Stalin's
original demands by providing for internationalization of the port of Dairen and
joint Sino-Soviet operation of the Manchurian railroads. (George A. Lensen, "Yalta
and the Far East," in John L. Snell, ed., *The Meaning of Yalta,* p. 152.)

The Yalta Far Eastern agreement was a classic example of Roosevelt's failure to coordinate military strategy with his postwar political objectives. The Joint Chiefs of Staff, speaking strictly in military terms, advised that Soviet entry into the Japanese war would reduce American casualties and hasten Tokyo's surrender. But Roosevelt failed to consult with his civilian advisers regarding the political consequences of this strategy. The State Department knew nothing of Stalin's demands because Ambassador Harriman had communicated them directly to Roosevelt through Navy Department channels. Working independently, State Department experts had prepared two papers advising against the outright transfer of lower Sakhalin and the Kuriles to the Soviet Union, but these were unaccountably left out of the briefing book prepared for the President's use at Yalta. Ironically, the Joint Chiefs had some time earlier concluded that if Stalin entered the Japanese war, he would do so only when convinced that Japan could be defeated at small cost to himself. Nothing which the United States could promise would affect his timing one way or another.[29] But the Joint Chiefs did not regard it as part of their job to furnish advice on nonmilitary matters, and apparently never passed this prescient conclusion on to the President.

Roosevelt's second-front diplomacy, in both Europe and the Far East, reflected his over-all strategy of seeking victory over the Axis as quickly as possible with the minimum possible loss of American lives. Despite the Soviet Union's minor role in the war against Japan, this strategy paid off handsomely in Europe. For three years, from June of 1941 to June of 1944, the Soviet Union carried the main burden of the fight against Hitler. On the day Anglo-American forces established the long-awaited second front in Normandy, the Red Army was still confronting more than 250 German and satellite divisions along the thousand-mile eastern front. British and American troops, in France and Italy, faced less than 90 enemy divisions. Partly because of Russian military successes, the United States Army got through the war with less than half

---

[29] Edward R. Stettinius, Jr., *Roosevelt and the Russians: The Yalta Conference*, pp. 95–96; *FR: Yalta*, pp. 378n, 379–83, 385–88; Matloff, *Strategic Planning, 1943–44*, p. 206; JCS memorandum, "U.S.S.R. Capabilities and Intentions in the Far East," November 18, 1943, *FR: Tehran*, p. 242. See also Morton, "Soviet Intervention in the War with Japan," p. 662. Harriman later argued that Roosevelt agreed to Stalin's territorial demands in order "to limit Soviet expansion in the East and to gain Soviet support for the Nationalist Government of China." ("Our Wartime Relations with the Soviet Union," *Department of State Bulletin*, XXV [September 3, 1951], 373.)

the number of divisions prewar plans had indicated would be necessary for victory. Casualty figures reflect with particular vividness the disproportionate amount of fighting which went on in the east. A conservative estimate places Soviet war deaths—civilian and military—at approximately 16 million. Total Anglo-American losses in all theaters came to less than a million.[30]

But Roosevelt's reluctance to incur heavy American casualties could not help but undermine his plans for postwar cooperation with the USSR. The long delay in establishing the second front confirmed Soviet fears that their capitalist allies had deliberately let communist Russia bear the brunt of the fighting. As a result, the suspicion with which Stalin had always viewed his Anglo-American associates intensified considerably. Convinced that they had won the war, the Russians showed little inclination to compromise on major postwar objectives which the West found unacceptable. Roosevelt probably felt that he had no other choice—the American people would not have supported sacrificial operations to meet the Russian timetable for a second front. Given ideological differences, it seems likely that the Russians would still have distrusted their allies, even if the Anglo-Americans had hurled their forces against Hitler's Europe in 1942. But by promising such a maneuver in 1942, and then delaying it until 1944, Roosevelt needlessly aggravated Soviet hostility toward the West, thereby imperiling his own hopes for the postwar world.[31]

III

Second-front strategy was not the only limitation on the effectiveness of Roosevelt's plans to build a cordial relationship with the Soviet Union.

[30] On June 6, 1944, Hitler had available on the eastern front, in Finland, and the Balkans 199 German divisions and 63 Finnish, Rumanian, Hungarian, and Bulgarian divisions. On the same day there were 61 German divisions available in France and the Low Countries, plus 25 German and 4 Italian divisions in Italy. (Harrison, *Cross-Channel Attack*, Appendix G.) Estimates of casualties are from Gordon Wright, *The Ordeal of Total War, 1939–1945*, pp. 263–65. For the American manpower situation, see Maurice Matloff, "The 90-Division Gamble," in Greenfield, ed., *Command Decisions*, pp. 365–81.

[31] On this point, see Burns, *Roosevelt: The Soldier of Freedom*, p. 374.

The success of a policy depends not simply upon its proclamation at the top but also on the manner in which it is executed at lower levels. Virtually without exception, subordinate officials responsible for dealing with the Russians from day to day became convinced that the President's openhanded policy was unwise. Moscow felt no obligation to reciprocate American generosity, they argued; the only way to ensure cooperation was to handle negotiations on a strict *quid pro quo* basis. As a result, these officials carried out Roosevelt's program grudgingly, making every effort behind the scenes to get it revised.

There can be no doubt that the Russians were difficult to deal with. Language problems alone meant that negotiations took at least twice as long as with the British. Americans serving in Russia found the officially sanctioned suspicion of foreigners oppressive, and puzzled over the rapidity with which Stalin and his top associates could shift from cordiality to bitter vindictiveness, and back again. Soviet administrative practices made negotiations even more frustrating—no Russian official could agree to anything, it seemed, without consulting Stalin himself. The Russians kept far fewer records than the British or the Americans, but pride kept them from admitting this. Instead they would turn aside Anglo-American requests for information with elaborate but hardly believable excuses—in one case General John R. Deane, head of the American military mission in Moscow, was asked to delay a visit to the front for a few days because "Marshal Vasielievsky would have kidney trouble until July 20." Requests for action would inevitably be countered with blunt references to the nonexistence of the second front. The sluggishness of the state bureaucracy infuriated the impatient Americans, who attached great importance to administrative efficiency. "I was in a high dudgeon much of the time," Deane later recalled.[32]

Soviet attitudes toward lend-lease were particularly galling. Representatives from Moscow would arrive in the United States with long lists of demands, made without regard to American priorities or supply capabili-

[32] John R. Deane, *The Strange Alliance*, pp. 20–21, 34–35, 49–50, 91–92, 98–99, 111, 203. For other accounts of the difficulties of dealing with the Russians, see Kennan, *Memoirs*, pp. 560–65; Standley and Ageton, *Admiral Ambassador to Russia, passim;* and Philip E. Mosely, "Some Soviet Techniques of Negotiation," in Raymond Dennett and Joseph E. Johnson, eds., *Negotiating with the Russians*, pp. 271–303. The other essays in this volume also provide valuable insights into the difficulties of dealing with the Russians, based on firsthand experience.

ties. Secretary of Agriculture Claude R. Wickard's experience with a
group of Russian food commissioners was typical: "They simply walked
in, all of them sober-faced, never cracked a smile, smart as they could
be. . . . They said, 'Here is what we want.' And they'd just sit there.
There wasn't much negotiation to it. It was simply a demand. . . .
Sometimes we got the idea that they were just darn, downright stubborn." At the direction of President Roosevelt, lend-lease authorities
made no effort to evaluate Soviet needs, or to determine the uses to
which the Russians put the equipment they received. Despite this generous attitude, accorded to no other ally, lend-lease aid did not seem to
make the Russians any easier to deal with. Stalin continued to berate his
allies over the absence of a second front, while ignoring Western requests for an exchange of military information. Furthermore, the Soviet
government showed few signs of appreciation for the aid it had received,
a tendency which provoked Ambassador Standley into complaining publicly about Russian ingratitude at a Moscow press conference in March,
1943.[33]

Despite adverse reaction in Washington to Standley's criticism of an
ally in wartime, American military officials had come to feel by this
time that the United States could safely attach conditions to future
lend-lease shipments without impairing the over-all war effort. The War
Department's Operations Division had asserted in January, 1943, that
lend-lease should be continued only if Moscow adopted a more cooperative attitude: "The time is appropriate for us to start some straight-
from-the-shoulder talk with Mr. Joseph Stalin." When the Third Lend-
Lease Protocol came up for negotiation in the spring of 1943, the
Pentagon supported insertion of a provision giving American military
attachés in Russia the same travel rights and access to information as Soviet representatives had in the United States. Early in 1944, Ambassador
Harriman and General Deane reported from Moscow that the Russians

---

[33] Wickard interview with Dean Albertson, in Albertson, *Roosevelt's Farmer:
Claude R. Wickard in the New Deal*, p. 267; Standley press conference statement,
March 8, 1943, *FR: 1943*, III, 631–32. See also Matloff, *Strategic Planning, 1943–44*,
p. 281; Deane, *The Strange Alliance*, pp. 89–91, 98–99, 102; Leighton and Coakley,
Global Logistics, 1940–43, pp. 551–52; Standley and Ageton, *Admiral Ambassador to
Russia*, pp. 331–49; and George C. Herring, Jr., "Lend-Lease to Russia and the Ori-
gins of the Cold War, 1944–1945," *Journal of American History*, LVI (June, 1969),
94–96.

were misusing American equipment, and that closer scrutiny should be exercised over USSR aid requests. General Marshall suggested to President Roosevelt in March, 1944, the possibility of using lend-lease as a "trump card" to ensure Soviet military cooperation with Allied plans for the invasion of France. But the White House consistently blocked all of these attempts to employ lend-lease as a bargaining device. When the Joint Chiefs of Staff raised the question of how lend-lease termination should be handled after the war, Roosevelt curtly told them that he would make the necessary arrangements himself.[34]

Aside from lend-lease, military cooperation between the United States and the USSR had not been close during the early years of the war. But during the last half of 1943, as serious planning for the second front in Europe got under way, the need arose for some coordination of strategy with Moscow. Moreover, the Russians had not yet formally committed themselves to enter the war against Japan. With these problems in mind, President Roosevelt decided to reorganize the American diplomatic staff in Moscow—Harriman replaced Standley as ambassador, while the Joint Chiefs of Staff sent Deane to the Soviet capital as their representative. The main goal of the Harriman-Deane mission was to improve diplomatic and military contacts with the Russians.[35] As such, it would provide a good test of what kind of relations could be expected with the Soviet Union after the war.

The Harriman-Deane operation began auspiciously enough, with Stalin's promise late in October, 1943, to enter the Far Eastern war upon the defeat of Germany. The Russians also quickly approved "in principle" proposals for a more effective exchange of weather information, better air transport facilities, and creation of a base in the Ukraine for the

---

[34] War Department Operations Division Policy Committee, "Weekly Strategic Resume," January 23, 1943, quoted in Matloff, *Strategic Planning, 1943–44,* p. 282; Marshall to Roosevelt, March 31, 1944, *ibid.,* p. 497. For the Washington reaction to Standley's statement, see Sherwood, *Roosevelt and Hopkins,* pp. 705–6; Israel, ed., *Long Diary,* p. 300; and Cox Daily Calendar, March 9, 1943, Cox MSS. Negotiations on the Third Lend-Lease Protocol are covered in Matloff, *Strategic Planning, 1943–44,* pp. 282–83; and *FR: 1943,* III, 737–81. See also Deane, *The Strange Alliance,* pp. 89–91; Richard M. Leighton and Robert W. Coakley, *Global Logistics and Strategy, 1943–1945,* pp. 671, 685–86; Matloff, *Strategic Planning, 1943–44,* p. 498; *FR: 1944,* IV, 1035–36, 1055–58; Herring, "Lend-Lease to Russia," pp. 95–97.

[35] Matloff, *Strategic Planning, 1943–44,* pp. 289–91; Deane, *The Strange Alliance,* pp. 47–48.

refueling, rearming, and repair of American bombers operating over Nazi-occupied Europe. But Deane soon discovered that agreement "in principle" meant little—negotiations on putting these proposals into effect did not begin until February, 1944, and then only after continuous pressure from the Americans. Military collaboration never worked well. The Russians showed great reluctance to let United States pilots fly over Soviet territory. German bombers quickly located the joint Russian-American air base and seriously damaged it. Although Moscow did arrange for the "escape" of a group of American airmen interned in the Soviet Union after bombing Japan, efforts to secure proper treatment for United States prisoners-of-war liberated by the advancing Red Army proved unavailing. Attempts to establish air bases in Siberia for use against Japan also failed.[36]

By the end of 1944, Deane had developed serious reservations regarding the possibility of cooperation with Moscow. In a long letter to General Marshall, he complained:

I have sat at innumerable Russian banquets and become gradually nauseated by Russian food, vodka, and protestations of friendship. Each person high in public life proposes a toast a little sweeter than the preceding on Soviet-British-American friendship. It is amazing how these toasts go down past the tongues in the cheeks. After the banquets we send the Soviets another thousand airplanes, and they approve a visa that has been hanging fire for months. We then scratch our heads to see what other gifts we can send, and they scratch theirs to see what else they can ask for.

Unconditional aid to the Russians made sense when they were fighting for survival, Deane argued, but "they are no longer back on their heels; . . . if there's one thing they have plenty of, it's self-confidence. The situation has changed, but our policy has not." The Russians

simply cannot understand giving without taking, and as a result even our giving is viewed with suspicion. Gratitude cannot be banked in the Soviet

[36] Deane, *The Strange Alliance,* pp. 20–21, 47–48, 55, 59–63, 107–25, 182–201. See also, on shuttle-bombing, Matloff, *Strategic Planning, 1943–44,* pp. 498–500; and on prisoners-of-war, Stimson Diary, March 2 and 16, 1945, Stimson MSS. The Russians did make some effort to exchange "intelligence" information with the Americans. Deane tells of being informed in great secrecy by an NKVD agent that an American engineer working in the Baku oil fields had been overheard to describe Roosevelt as a "son of a bitch who should be taken out and shot." Deane "thanked them profusely and said I certainly would see that corrective action was taken." (*The Strange Alliance,* p. 59.)

Union. Each transaction is complete in itself without regard to past favors. The party of the second part is either a shrewd trader to be admired or a sucker to be despised. . . . In short, we are in the position of being at the same time the givers and the supplicants. This is neither dignified nor healthy for U.S. prestige.

Deane recommended allowing the Soviet Union only such aid as could be shown to be vital to the war effort. Everything else should be furnished on a *quid pro quo* basis. If American requests for cooperation were left unanswered after a reasonable length of time, the United States should act on its own, simply informing the Russians of what it was going to do. Deane's letter impressed Marshall and Secretary of War Stimson sufficiently for them to send it to President Roosevelt, with the information that Harriman also had endorsed its contents.[37]

Other officials experienced in dealing with the Russians had already expressed similar judgments. Standley, Harriman's predecessor in Moscow, had warned Roosevelt in March, 1943, that the policy "of continuing to accede freely to their requests . . . seems to arouse suspicion of our motives in the Oriental Russian mind rather than to build confidence." William C. Bullitt, another former ambassador, urged Roosevelt early in 1943 to use "the old technique of the donkey, the carrot, and the club . . . to make Stalin move in the direction in which we want him to move." Bullitt's "carrot" was the prospect of American aid for Russian reconstruction; his "club" was the possibility of denying that aid and restricting lend-lease shipments. Bullitt had lost much of his influence by this time, but subordinate Foreign Service officers who had served with him in Moscow in the 1930s still occupied important positions in the State Department, from which they pressed for a tougher negotiating posture with the Russians. George F. Kennan had never considered the USSR a proper ally for the United States, and argued that aid should be sent to Russia only to the extent that it promoted American self-interest. Loy W. Henderson warned in the summer of 1943 that "if we show the slightest weakness and equivocation . . . the Soviet Government will at once bring tremendous pressure on us and in the end our relations will be more unfavorably affected than they would be if we display firmness at the outset." [38]

[37] Stimson to Roosevelt, January 3, 1945, enclosing Deane to Marshall, December 2, 1944, *FR: Yalta*, pp. 447–49.
[38] Standley to Roosevelt, Hull, and Welles, March 10, 1943, *FR: 1943*, III, 510;

Harriman himself had gone to Moscow late in 1943 with a feeling of optimism regarding the possibilities of postwar Soviet-American cooperation. By the summer of 1944, however, the difficulties of dealing with the Russians on a day-to-day basis had convinced him that Roosevelt's policy of unconditional aid would have to be changed. Soviet authorities had "misinterpreted our generous attitude toward them as a sign of weakness," Harriman warned Harry Hopkins; "the time has come when we must make clear what we expect of them as the price of our good will." From now on, the Ambassador advised the State Department, the United States should cooperate with and support the Russians wherever possible, but if disagreements arose Washington should make it clear that it would not back down.[39]

These criticisms of his Russian policy appear to have had an effect on the President. By early 1945 he seems to have accepted Harriman's view that economic aid for postwar Russian reconstruction should be withheld until Moscow adopted a more cooperative attitude in the political sphere.[40] Even more significantly, Roosevelt had decided by this time not to tell the Russians of the highly secret Anglo-American project to develop the atomic bomb.

During the summer of 1944, Dr. Vannevar Bush, director of the Office of Scientific Research and Development, and Dr. James B. Conant, president of Harvard University and chairman of the National Research Council, had become concerned that the Soviet Union's continued exclusion from the bomb project might damage postwar relations with that country. Bush warned Secretary of War Stimson that any American attempt to monopolize the bomb after the war would only stimulate a crash development program in the Soviet Union. Because the scientific principles applies in building the bomb were no secret, the Russians would almost surely succeed in this effort, touching off a dangerous armaments race. In September, Supreme Court Justice Felix Frankfurter

---

Bullitt to Roosevelt, January 29, 1943, Roosevelt MSS, PSF: "Bullitt"; Kennan, *Memoirs*, pp. 57, 133–34; Henderson to Ray Atherton, June 11, 1943, *FR: 1943*, III, 544. For background on the training of Russian experts in the Foreign Service, see Kennan, *Memoirs*, pp. 61–62, 68–70, 84; and Maddux, "American Relations with the Soviet Union, 1933–1941," pp. 134–40.

[39] Harriman to Hopkins, September 10, 1944, *FR: 1944*, IV, 989; and Hull, September 20, 1944, *ibid.*, p. 997. For Harriman's earlier feeling of optimism, see his messages to Roosevelt of July 5 and November 4, 1943, *FR: Tehran*, pp. 15, 152–55.

[40] On this point, see chapter 6.

sent Roosevelt a memorandum from the Danish physicist Niels Bohr which strongly advocated bringing the Russians in on the secret while they were still allies. Roosevelt seemed impressed enough with Bohr's argument to send the scientist to see Churchill, who gruffly dismissed the idea. Upon Bohr's return, however, the President intimated that, despite the Prime Minister's attitude, he would be willing to consider approaching Stalin on the subject.[41]

But when Churchill joined the President at Hyde Park following the Quebec Conference later that month, the two men signed a secret agreement explicitly rejecting the idea that "the world" should be told about the bomb before its use. The memorandum further stated: "Enquiries should be made regarding the activities of Professor Bohr and steps taken to ensure that he is responsible for no leakage of information particularly to the Russians." Stimson told Roosevelt on the last day of 1944 that, although troubled by the possible repercussions, he did not favor telling the Russians about the bomb "until we were sure to get a real *quid pro quo* from our frankness." Roosevelt apparently agreed, for this policy remained in force up to the time of his death.[42]

It seems likely that the difficulties of dealing with Moscow on small matters, which Standley, Harriman, Deane, and other American officials in the Soviet Union complained so vigorously about, contributed at least in part to Roosevelt's decision to be less than candid with his Russian ally on the very big matter of the atomic bomb. The almost unanimous support for a *quid pro quo* policy from such experts "in the field" must have caused the President to wonder whether his plan to win Stalin's trust through a program of unconditional aid had not failed. And what-

[41] Richard G. Hewlett and Oscar E. Anderson, Jr., *A History of the United States Atomic Energy Commission: The New World, 1939–1946*, pp. 325–28; Frankfurter to Roosevelt, September 8, 1944, in Max Freedman, ed., *Roosevelt and Frankfurter: Their Correspondence, 1928–1945*, pp. 728–36; Burns, *Roosevelt: The Soldier of Freedom*, pp. 455–58.

[42] Roosevelt-Churchill agreement of September 19, 1944, quoted in Margaret Gowing, *Britain and Atomic Energy, 1939–1945*, p. 447; Stimson Diary, December 31, 1944, Stimson MSS. Bush broached the subject to the Secretary of War again after the Yalta Conference early in 1945, but Stimson remained dubious: "I am inclined to tread softly and to hold off conferences on the subject until we have some much more tangible 'fruits of repentance' from the Russians." (*Ibid.*, February 13, 1945.) There is evidence that, during the last month of his life, F.D.R. was reconsidering his decision not to tell the Russians about the bomb. See J. W. Pickersgill and D. W. Forster, *The Mackenzie King Record, 1944–1945*, pp. 326–27.

ever their effect on Roosevelt himself, it is clear that Harriman and his
Moscow colleagues exerted a strong influence on the late President's successor when Harry S. Truman turned to them for advice on how to handle the Russians.[43]

IV

Stalin's lack of trust in his Western allies manifested itself with particular vividness in connection with the surrender of Germany and its
satellites. Despite the approach of victory, the Soviet leader seemed unable to free himself from the fear that his capitalist associates might yet
make common cause with Germany in a joint crusade against Bolshevism. Even if London and Washington refused such a deal, Hitler might
achieve a similar effect by letting Anglo-American troops advance into
Germany while he devoted all his efforts to holding the Russians back.
The reluctance of Roosevelt and Churchill to absorb heavy casualties
probably made the second possibility seem especially real from Moscow's
point of view. Accordingly, Stalin watched with a wary eye as Allied
military successes brought attempts, first by Hitler's satellites, then by
Germany itself, to end the war.

Stalin's fears surfaced initially in the summer of 1943, when Italy became the first member of the Axis to seek peace. Shortly after the fall of
Mussolini in July, the famous Soviet author, Ilya Ehrenburg, cornered
Associated Press correspondent Henry Cassidy in Moscow and, presumably acting on instructions, vigorously criticized the Americans and British for failing to consult the Russians on the Italian situation. The Soviets had understood the necessity of dealing with Admiral Darlan,
Ehrenburg said, but negotiating with Badoglio was too much. Did this
mean that London and Washington would deal with Goering when the
time came? When Cassidy responded by bringing up Moscow's recent
creation of the Free Germany Committee, Ehrenburg observed cynically
that two could play at the game of negotiating with the enemy.[44]

Western officials recognized clearly enough the importance of keeping
Moscow informed. On the day after Mussolini fell, British Foreign Secre-

---

[43] See chapter 7.
[44] Standley to Roosevelt and Hull, July 30, 1943, *FR: 1943*, III, 555–56.

tary Anthony Eden reminded Ambassador John G. Winant that Russia would have to be consulted in dealing with the Italians. Winant needed no prompting. "When the tide turns and the Russian armies are able to advance," he pointed out to the State Department, "we might well want to influence their terms of capitulation and occupancy in Allied and enemy territory." Ambassador Standley, concerned by Ehrenburg's bitter remarks, also strongly recommended establishing some mechanism for advising the Russians of Italian developments. State Department officials agreed, and early in August asked Standley to tell the Russians that they would be kept fully abreast of events in Italy and that suggestions or inquiries from them would be welcome.[45]

It soon became clear, however, that the Russians wanted more than just information—they wanted a role in running the occupation of Italy. Using a garbled British telegram on Italian surrender terms as an excuse, Stalin late in August complained that the information he had received on negotiations with Badoglio had been "absolutely inadequate." The Americans and British had been treating the Russians "as a passive third observer"; it was "impossible to tolerate such [a] situation any longer." The time had come, Stalin asserted, to establish a "military-political commission," composed of representatives from all three major allies, for the purpose of "considering the questions concerning the negotiations with the different Governments dissociating themselves from Germany." [46]

Roosevelt and Churchill worried that creation of such a commission would introduce unnecessary complications into an already tangled military situation. Could the Russians not simply send a representative to Eisenhower's headquarters, the President asked early in September. Stalin replied brusquely that this would "by no means" substitute for the military-political commission, "which is necessary for directing on the spot

[45] Winant to Hull, July 26, 1943, *FR: 1943,* II, 335; Standley to Roosevelt and Hull, July 30, 1943, *FR: 1943,* III, 555–56; Hull to Winant, August 1, 1943, *FR: 1943,* II, 340; Hull to Standley, August 3, 1943, *ibid.,* pp. 344–45. See also the comments of the British ambassador to the Soviet Union, Sir Archibald Clark Kerr, on the importance of inter-Allied consultation, reported in Maxwell M. Hamilton to Hull, August 8, 1943, *ibid.,* pp. 347–48.

[46] Stalin to Roosevelt and Churchill, August 22 and 24, *FR: 1943,* II, 353–54, I, 783. For the matter of the garbled telegram, see Standley to Hull, August 25, 1943, *FR: 1943,* II, 354.

the negotiations with Italy. . . . Much time has passed, but nothing is done." Faced with this virtual ultimatum, the Anglo-American leaders reluctantly agreed to establish the commission, with headquarters to be located in Algiers.[47]

The Western allies quickly demonstrated, however, that they envisaged a far narrower role for the commission than did the Russians. The group would receive full information on negotiations with defeated enemies, Roosevelt told Stalin, but it would not have plenary powers. In his instructions to General Eisenhower, the President emphasized that the commission would operate "under the Allied Commander in Chief." The Russians protested this interpretation, but Roosevelt held firm. Churchill concurred, arguing that "we cannot be put in a position where our two armies are doing all the fighting but Russians have a veto and must be consulted on any minor violation of the armistice terms." Stalin apparently attached considerable importance to the military-political commission, naming as his delegate Assistant Commissar of Foreign Affairs Andrei Vishinsky. Roosevelt indicated the significance with which he regarded the new agency by designating as United States representative Edwin C. Wilson, former ambassador to Panama.[48]

American officials realized that the decision to minimize Moscow's role in the occupation of Italy might give the Russians a convenient excuse later on to restrict Anglo-American activities in Rumania, Bulgaria, and Hungary. But Roosevelt did not expect the Russians to allow their allies much influence in this area whatever happened in Italy. Eastern Europe would simply have to get used to Russian domination, he told Archbishop Francis Spellman in September, 1943. Early in October, he reminded Churchill that the occupation of Italy would "set the precedent for all such future activities in the war." When the Red Army entered Rumania early in 1944, the Joint Chiefs of Staff noted that it was

[47] Roosevelt to Stalin, September 6, 1943, *FR: 1943,* I, 784; Stalin to Roosevelt, September 8, 1943, *ibid.,* p. 785; Roosevelt to Stalin, September 10, 1943, *ibid.*

[48] Roosevelt to Stalin, September 10, 1943, *FR: 1943,* I, 785; Stalin to Roosevelt, September 12, 1943, *ibid.,* p. 786; Roosevelt to Eisenhower, September 22, 1943, *FR: 1943,* II, 374; Molotov to Hamilton, September 26, 1943, *ibid.,* pp. 377–78; Adolf A. Berle to Winant, September 28, 1943, *FR: 1943,* I, 790. Churchill's comment is quoted in an *aide-mémoire* from the British Embassy to the State Department, October 11, 1943, *FR: 1943,* II, 385–86. See also Leo Pasvolsky's minutes of a conference between Roosevelt, Hull, and other State Department officials, October 5, 1943, *FR: 1943,* I, 541.

"only natural and to be expected" that the Russians would handle the surrender negotiations, since only their forces were on the scene:

The present Rumanian situation is analogous to the Italian situation at the time of her surrender to the British and ourselves. Since Russian participation in Italian operations was impracticable, the western Allies handled the matter of Italian surrender . . . and Russian participation in the Italian situation has been limited to representation on the Allied Control Commission.

Secretary of State Hull noted on March 30 that, in view of the Italian precedent, it seemed logical to accord the Russians prime responsibility for working out armistice terms for Rumania, Hungary, and Bulgaria.[49]

Subsequent State Department opposition to Churchill's suggestion that Moscow be given a dominant role in these three countries in return for recognition of British interests in Greece, Yugoslavia, and Hungary related not to armistice negotiations or military occupation but to the fear that specifically assigned areas of responsibility might harden into permanent spheres of influence. The distinction between wartime and postwar arrangements was a fine one, since provisional governments set up under military occupation would almost certainly influence political developments in the Balkans after Germany's surrender. Roosevelt hoped that these two matters could be kept separate, however, and acquiesced in Churchill's deal with the Russians on the condition that it not prejudice the final peace settlement.[50]

[49] Spellman memorandum of conversation with Roosevelt, September 3, 1943, printed in Gannon, *The Cardinal Spellman Story,* pp. 223–24; Roosevelt to Churchill, October 4, 1943, *FR: 1943,* II, 383; Leahy to Hull, March 28, 1944, *FR: 1944,* IV, 161; Hull to Lincoln MacVeagh, March 30, 1944, *ibid.,* p. 164. Several historians have viewed the Italian precedent as an explanation for subsequent Soviet behavior in Eastern Europe. See, for example, McNeill, *America, Britain, and Russia,* p. 310; Kolko, *The Politics of War,* pp. 39, 50–52, 128, 130–31; and John Bagguley, "The World War and the Cold War," in David Horowitz, ed., *Containment and Revolution,* pp. 97–104. Given the long-standing Soviet determination to control Eastern Europe, however, it seems highly unlikely that the Russians would have given their Western allies any significant role in the occupation of former German satellites there, even if London and Washington had met Moscow's wishes with regard to Italy. For Soviet ambitions in Eastern Europe, see chapters 1 and 5.

[50] Churchill, *Triumph and Tragedy,* pp. 61–65, 196–97; Hull, *Memoirs,* II, 1452–53; Roosevelt to Harriman, enclosing a message to Stalin, October 4, 1944, *FR: Yalta,* pp. 6–7; Roosevelt to Churchill, October 4, 1944, *ibid.,* p. 7; Yalta Briefing Book Paper, "American Policy Toward Spheres of Influence," undated, *ibid.,* pp.

The one enemy whose surrender all three allies expected to receive together was, of course, Germany. As representatives from the collapsing Reich began making peace overtures early in 1945, Stalin's almost frantic reaction showed that, despite creation of the second front and all of Roosevelt's efforts at personal diplomacy, Russian-American relations still had not been placed on a basis of mutual trust. Even at this late date, the Soviet leader apparently still worried that his capitalist allies might make a deal with Hitler.

Early in March, 1945, Office of Strategic Services agents in Switzerland informed Washington that General Karl Wolff, a high-ranking S.S. officer, had arrived in Berne to discuss the possible surrender of German forces in northern Italy. American officials notified Moscow of this within two days. The Russians responded by requesting that Soviet officers be sent to observe the negotiations, but after due consideration the Joint Chiefs of Staff advised against accepting this proposal. This was purely a military surrender in the field, the Joint Chiefs argued, and the Russians would never have allowed American representatives to observe comparable discussions on the eastern front. To bring the Russians in would introduce "into what is almost entirely a military matter an unavoidable political element." President Roosevelt agreed, fearing that the presence of Soviet officers might affect the willingness of the Germans to surrender. On March 15, Ambassador Harriman informed the Russians that their representatives could sit in on the formal surrender negotiations at Allied Headquarters in Italy, but not on the preliminary talks at Berne.[51]

Moscow reacted immediately and violently. The Russians found the American attitude "utterly unexpected and incomprehensible," Molotov told Harriman, and demanded that negotiations with the Germans at Berne be broken off. Roosevelt responded that these talks were solely for the purpose of establishing contact—no surrender would be arranged without Soviet participation. Molotov retorted ominously that "it is not

---

103–6. Herbert Feis argues that by October, 1944, Roosevelt had privately come to agree with Churchill regarding the need for a division of spheres of influence in Eastern Europe. (*Churchill, Roosevelt, Stalin,* p. 451.)

[51] *FR: 1945,* III, 722–31. For background on the OSS operation in Switzerland and northern Italy, see Allen Dulles, *The Secret Surrender.*

a question of incorrect understanding of the objectives of this contact or misunderstanding—it is something worse." The Americans and the British had been negotiating with the German High Command "behind the back of the Soviet Government which has been carrying on the main burden of the war against Germany." Roosevelt replied directly to Stalin on March 24, assuring him that "in such a surrender of enemy forces in the field, there can be no political implications whatever and no violations of our agreed principle of unconditional surrender." Stalin's reply, on the 29th, charged that the Germans had already used the discussions with the Anglo-Americans to shift three additional divisions from northern Italy to the Russian front. Five days later he made the startling accusation that

the negotiations . . . have ended in an agreement with the Germans, on the basis of which the German commander on the Western front—Marshal Kesselring, has agreed to open the front and permit the Anglo-American troops to advance to the East, and the Anglo-Americans have promised in return to ease for the Germans the peace terms.

The Russians, Stalin concluded, would never have done such a thing. Roosevelt responded sharply on April 4: "Frankly I cannot avoid a feeling of bitter resentment toward your informers, whoever they are, for such vile misrepresentations of my actions or those of my trusted subordinates." [52]

Negotiations with the Germans in Italy failed to bear fruit immediately, however, and quickly receded into the background as the other events of early April—the invasion of Germany, the Polish crisis, and Roosevelt's death—crowded in on policy-makers. But Soviet behavior had left American officials gravely worried. Admiral William D. Leahy, Chief of Staff to the Commander in Chief, saw in the Berne incident "a clear demonstration of the dangerous undesirability of having unnecessary allies in war." To Ambassador Harriman, the affair suggested that the Russians intended "to dominate all matters relating to Germany in ways not yet fully disclosed." Secretary of War Stimson noted that Moscow's "quarrelsome" reaction "indicated a spirit in Russia which bodes evil in the coming difficulties of the postwar scene." Soviet accusations of

[52] *FR: 1945*, III, 731–46. General Marshall and Admiral Leahy drafted Roosevelt's April 4 reply. (Leahy, *I Was There*, pp. 391–92.)

Anglo-American collaboration with Germany revealed to Stimson "an astonishing situation in Stalin's mind and the minds of his staff." [53]

The Berne episode also worried Roosevelt, but he was determined not to let it wreck the Soviet-American partnership. On the day he died, he drafted a telegram to Stalin noting that "the Berne incident . . . now appears to have faded into the past without having accomplished any useful purpose," and that "mutual distrust and minor misunderstandings" of this type should not be allowed to happen in the future. Before presenting this message to Stalin, Harriman wired from Moscow asking the President if he did not want to eliminate the word "minor" in describing the quarrel, which to Harriman hardly seemed "minor" at all. Roosevelt replied that the message should be delivered as written, "as it is my desire to consider the Berne misunderstanding a minor incident." [54]

But, in a sense, Harriman was right. The balefully suspicious manner in which Stalin reacted to news of the Berne discussions revealed as nothing else had the failure of Roosevelt's wartime policy toward the Soviet Union. The President had sought to make Stalin trust him, feeling that only in this way could postwar Soviet-American cooperation be assured. To this end, he had furnished the Russians with lend-lease supplies on an unconditional basis, had twice traveled halfway around the world to meet with the Soviet leader, and had incurred considerable political risk at home in order to satisfy Moscow's postwar territorial demands.[55] Yet Roosevelt refused to pay the one price which might, but only might, have convinced Stalin of his sincerity—the massive American casualties which would have been necessary to establish an early second front. There were limits to how far even Roosevelt could go in trying to overcome Soviet suspicion. While the bankruptcy of his policy of openhandedness was not fully apparent at the time of his death, events such as Berne make it seem unlikely that Roosevelt, had he lived, would have continued it much longer.

[53] Leahy, *I Was There*, p. 336; Harriman to Stettinius, March 17, 1945, *FR: 1945*, III, 734; Stimson Diary, March 17 and April 4, 1945, Stimson MSS. See also Deane, *The Strange Alliance*, pp. 165–66.

[54] *FR: 1945*, III, 756–57.   [55] On this point, see chapter 5.

4

※※※※※※※※※※※※※※※※※※※※※※※※※※※※※※※※※※※※※※※

Repression versus Rehabilitation: The Problem of Germany

Moscow's nervousness over the problem of surrender made it clear that agreement on how to treat defeated enemies would be a major prerequisite for postwar inter-Allied cooperation. Since the United States had done most of the fighting against Japan, it could expect a decisive role in shaping occupation policies for that country. Hitler's European satellites presented no serious threat to future peace; moreover, by the end of 1944 the Big Three had tacitly agreed that Italy would fall within an Anglo-American sphere of influence, while the Soviet Union would assume responsibility for Finland, Rumania, Bulgaria, and Hungary. Germany, however, posed a far more difficult problem: it was the only enemy against which all three allies had fought in roughly equal proportion,[1] and in which each was determined to exert its influence to prevent still another outburst of aggression which might lead to a third world war.

The Big Three shared an obvious interest in keeping Germany under control, but unless they could agree before the end of the fighting on how to do this, disputes among the victors would almost certainly arise.

[1] The fact that the Soviet Union's casualties far exceeded those of Great Britain and the United States should not be allowed to obscure the fact that Britain fought Germany alone from June, 1940, to June, 1941, or that American industry, through lend-lease, provided much of the matériel used to bring about Germany's defeat.

Neither the Russians nor the Anglo-Americans had ever completely overcome their fears of a separate peace; both would tend to regard any conflicts over occupation policy as evidence that former allies were conspiring with a former foe. Even if such suspicions did not develop on their own, the absence of a common program would place the Germans in an excellent position to play one occupying power off against the other. Efforts to work our tripartite policies for Germany failed, however, largely because of conflict and confusion within the United States government.

The conflict revolved around whether policies of repression or rehabilitation would best keep Germany pacified. Advocates of repression, including the Treasury Department and, somewhat less firmly, President Roosevelt, saw aggressive characteristics in all Germans and argued that Hitler had accurately reflected these tendencies. The Versailles treaty had not kept the peace because it had been too lenient—after World War II the victors would have to treat Germany more severely so that successors to Hitler could not arise. Proponents of rehabilitation, centered chiefly in the State Department, likewise attributed the rise of Hitler to the Versailles settlement but blamed the pact's harshness, not its generosity. The treaty's punitive economic provisions and war guilt clause, they insisted, had led to the social and economic situation which bred Nazism. Security from future Hitlers could come only by reforming conditions within Germany so that totalitarianism would have no appeal. For this, a moderate peace would be necessary.[2]

Confusion, arising out of failure to coordinate wartime strategy with postwar political objectives, kept the Roosevelt Administration from choosing between these two approaches until it was too late. The President and his military advisers, concerned almost exclusively with winning the war, saw no need to consider plans for the occupation of defeated enemies until the end of the fighting was near. State Department officials, desperately seeking policy guidance in this field, found the military obstructive, the President preoccupied, and often gave up in frustra-

---

[2] For summaries of these two points of view, together with descriptions of their British and Russian counterparts, see John L. Snell, *Wartime Origins of the East-West Dilemma over Germany*, chapter 1. See also Walter L. Dorn, "The Debate over American Occupation Policy in Germany in 1944–1945," *Political Science Quarterly*, LXXII (December, 1957), 484–85.

tion. When the approach of victory made it impossible to ignore occupation policy much longer, the government moved in two directions at once. The War Department, thinking solely of the short-range problem of military government, came out in favor of repression as a matter of administrative convenience. The State Department, worried about long-range political and economic problems in Europe, continued to insist upon rehabilitation. Roosevelt lent comfort to both sides at different times, leaving the controversy unresolved at his death. The absence of a clear-cut American position precluded meaningful discussions with Great Britain and the Soviet Union prior to the end of the war, thus making divergent occupation policies in Germany virtually inevitable.

I

The debate over Germany within the Roosevelt Administration began in the spring of 1943 when British Foreign Secretary Anthony Eden came to Washington to discuss postwar issues. During the ensuing talks, Harry Hopkins expressed concern that the Allies had not yet reached an understanding "as to which armies would be where and what kind of administration should be developed." Hopkins worried that unless such agreements were made, "one of two things would happen—either Germany will go Communist or [an] out and out anarchic state would set in." The State Department, he thought, should formulate a plan in collaboration with the British, and then seek the approval of the Russians. Roosevelt agreed, instructing Hull to begin consultations with the War Department, London, and eventually Moscow on "the question of what our plan is to be in Germany and Italy during the first few months after Germany's collapse." [3]

The State Department's Advisory Committee on Postwar Foreign Policy had already initiated studies on this question, and by the end of the summer was ready with its first recommendations. The best way to guard against future aggression, the department argued, would be to en-

[3] Hopkins memorandum, conversation with Roosevelt and Hull, March 17, 1943, *FR: 1943*, III, 26; Roosevelt to Hull, March 23, 1943, *ibid.*, p. 36. For the March, 1943, discussions with Eden see *ibid.*, pp. 1–48, and Eden, *The Reckoning*, pp. 430–41.

courage the emergence of democratic institutions inside Germany. For such a policy to succeed, the peace settlement would have to be designed to provoke "a minimum of bitterness" from the German people. Occupation controls should be kept "to the minimum in number and in severity which will be compatible with security." The German economy would have to be allowed to revive to the point that it could provide "a tolerable standard of living" for the German people. Finally, the other occupying powers would have to agree on similar policies for their zones. If friction developed among the Russians, British, and Americans, Germany would be in a position to shift the balance of power from one side to another—a situation which could have disastrous consequences for future peace. Hence, the department concluded, Washington should work for a generous peace which would foster the growth of democracy inside the defeated Reich.[4]

From this it followed logically that the dismemberment of Germany would be self-defeating. Forcible partition, State Department planners believed, would contribute nothing to security: economic and military disarmament would do that. It would cause resentment among the German people, however, and would necessitate the imposition of elaborate controls to prevent surreptitious attempts at reunification. Moreover, dismemberment might lead to the formation of spheres of influence, possibly provoking conflicts among the victors. Imposed partition, one department adviser told Hull, "would be little short of a disaster both for Germany and for us." [5]

The State Department's plans for a moderate peace also precluded the use of reparations for punitive purposes. Department officials expected some of the victors, especially the Soviet Union, to demand extensive goods and services from Germany for use in reconstructing their war-damaged economies. Yet Hull's advisers feared that the indiscriminate

[4] Recommendation by the State Department Interdivisional Country Committee on Germany, September 23, 1943, printed in Notter, *Postwar Foreign Policy Preparation*, p. 559.

[5] *Ibid.*, p. 558; draft by Harley Notter of a Hull memorandum to Roosevelt, September, 1943, Hull MSS, Box 52, Folder 159. One State Department official who did support dismemberment was Undersecretary of State Sumner Welles, but his influence ceased abruptly with his resignation from the department in August, 1943. For Welles's views, see his memorandum of a conversation with Anthony Eden and Lord Halifax on March 16, 1943, *FR: 1943*, III, 19–22; and his *The Time for Decision*, pp. 336–61.

extraction of reparations would wreck what remained of the German economy, thereby ruining efforts to promote democratic institutions and possibly burdening the United States with a massive relief operation. Furthermore, economic collapse in Germany might threaten the recovery of Europe as a whole, and thus endanger the department's goal of reviving a multilateral system of world trade. "It is to the long-range interest of the United States that Germany be prosperous," the department concluded, "but that, at the same time, [the] German economy should not again be directed to war-like purposes." [6]

Ambiguities existed in the State Department's proposal. Its success would depend upon agreement by other occupying powers to implement similar policies, for democratic institutions in one zone would do little good if totalitarianism took root again in the others. Yet the Russians had thus far shown little willingness to tolerate democracy in areas under their control, and seemed unlikely to endorse any occupation plan which did not allow them a substantial volume of reparations.[7] The State Department still had to decide how much of Germany's industrial plant could be dismantled to prevent rearmament and provide reparations without causing economic chaos. But by the end of 1943 the department had accomplished more toward planning the occupation of Germany than had any other agency of government. As was so often the case in the Roosevelt Administration, however, the Chief Executive's grant of authority in this area did not give Hull and his advisers a free hand. Both the President and the War Department possessed certain prejudices regarding Germany which from the first undercut State's efforts to move toward a moderate peace.

Roosevelt's attitudes toward Germany stemmed largely from personal experiences in that country. F.D.R. had attended school there as a boy, acquiring simultaneously knowledge of the language and a strong distaste for German arrogance and militarism: "The talk among us children became stronger each year toward an objective—the inevitable war with France and the building up of the Reich into the greatest world power. Even then we were taught to have no respect for English-

[6] "U.S. Proposal with Regard to Questions of Reparations," Moscow Conference Document No. 39, October, 1943, *FR: 1943*, I, 740–41; Postwar Programs Committee memorandum, "The Treatment of Germany," August 5, 1944, *FR: 1944*, I, 312.

[7] On this point, see Harriman to Roosevelt, November 4, 1943, *FR: Tehran*, p. 154.

men and we were taught that Americans were mere barbarians, most of whom were millionaires." In 1919, as assistant secretary of the navy, Roosevelt returned to the Rhineland, now occupied by United States troops. To his disgust, he found occupation authorities reluctant to fly the American flag, lest they unduly humiliate the Germans. F.D.R. angrily complained to General Pershing, arguing that the Germans had to be made to understand in no uncertain terms that they had lost the war.[8] This determination to bring the fact of defeat home to the German people became a key element in the policy Roosevelt followed a quarter of a century later as President.

"After the first World War we tried to achieve a formula for permanent peace, based on magnificent idealism," Roosevelt told Congress in 1943. "We failed. But, by our failure, we have learned that we cannot maintain peace at this stage of human development by good intentions alone." This time, the victors would have to occupy all of Germany, plus additional strategic bases throughout the world. To guard against future aggression, Roosevelt strongly supported the division of Germany into from three to five states. Prussian militarism had led to the rise of Hitler; partition would make totalitarianism in postwar Germany impossible. "When Hitler and the Nazis go out, the Prussian military clique must go with them," Roosevelt argued; "the war-breeding gangs of militarists must be rooted out of Germany—and out of Japan—if we are to have any real assurance of future peace."[9]

The President's hopes for peacetime collaboration with the Soviet Union did much to shape his policy toward Germany. Harsh occupation policies, like unconditional surrender, appealed to him in part because he

---

[8] Snell, *Dilemma over Germany*, pp. 30–31; Lucius D. Clay, *Decision in Germany*, p. 5; Roosevelt to Colonel Arthur Murray, March 4, 1940, Roosevelt MSS, PSF: "Great Britain: A. Murray"; Frank Freidel, *Franklin D. Roosevelt: The Ordeal*, p. 13. "When I was eleven in 1893, I think it was, my class was started on the study of 'Heimatkunde'—geography lessons about the village, then about how to get to neighboring towns and what one would see, and, finally, on how to get all over the Province of Hesse-Darmstadt. The following year we were taught all about roads and what we would see on the way to the French border. I did not take it the third year but I understand the class was 'conducted' to France—all the roads leading to Paris." (Roosevelt to Murray, cited above.)

[9] Roosevelt messages to Congress, January 7 and September 17, 1943, *FDR: Public Papers*, XII, 33, 391. For Roosevelt's ideas on partition, see the record of his conversations with Anthony Eden, March 15 and 22, 1943, *FR: 1943*, III, 16–17, 36.

felt they would improve Russian-American relations. F.D.R. believed that Stalin wanted additional territory in Eastern Europe as protection against a resurgent Germany. Several times the President expressed the view that if German disarmament could be guaranteed, Soviet interest in Eastern Europe would wane. Roosevelt told Robert Murphy in 1944 that the occupation of Germany had to be arranged in such a way as to convince the Soviet Union of America's good intentions. Cooperation with Russia was the most important postwar objective of the United States, the President emphasized, and Germany would be the proving ground for that cooperation.[10]

Roosevelt discussed dismemberment with top State Department officials in October, 1943, shortly before Secretary Hull's departure for the Moscow Foreign Ministers' Conference. Insisting that he knew Germany better than did the department's experts, F.D.R. at first accused Hull and his advisers of exaggerating the undesirable effects of partition, but later he acknowledged sheepishly that he had not visited Germany for many years and that dismemberment might not work after all. The President's position, though ambivalent, caused Hull to skirt the issue of partition when he presented the State Department's plans to his British and Russian colleagues in Moscow later that month. There had been a tendency to favor partition "in high quarters in the United States," Hull said, "but as the discussions progressed and conflicting and often very convincing arguments were advanced for and against, there was an increasing disposition to keep an open mind on this point." Molotov and Eden agreed that the question needed further study.[11]

When the Big Three met at Teheran one month later, however, the full measure of Stalin's determination to deal harshly with Germany became apparent. The Soviet leader repeatedly emphasized the need to occupy strong positions within Germany to prevent rearmament, and at one point proposed a toast to the "liquidation" of between 50,000 and

[10] Memorandum by Sumner Welles of a conversation with Lord Halifax, February 20, 1942, *FR: 1942,* III, 521; memorandum by Jan Ciechanowski of Roosevelt's conversation with General Wladyslaw Sikorski, March 24, 1942, in Ciechanowski, *Defeat in Victory,* p. 100; Robert Murphy, *Diplomat among Warriors,* p. 227.

[11] Hull, *Memoirs,* II, 1265–66, 1287; Leo Pasvolsky minutes, Roosevelt meeting with State Department officials, October 5, 1943, *FR: 1943,* I, 541–43; minutes of the seventh meeting of the foreign ministers, Moscow, October 25, 1943, *ibid.,* pp. 631–32.

100,000 members of the German officers corps. Roosevelt offered to settle for 49,000, a "joke" which caused Churchill to stalk angrily from the
room. When the President revived his plan for the dismemberment of
Germany, Stalin endorsed it enthusiastically. Churchill expressed reservations, proposing instead the detachment of Prussia from the rest of
Germany, but Stalin refused to go along. Prussians were no different
from other Germans, he argued, they all fought like devils. The Big
Three reached no final agreements, referring the German question to the
newly formed European Advisory Commission, but their discussion did
indicate tentative endorsement of the principle of partition. Characteristically, Roosevelt neglected to inform the State Department of this significant development.[12]

Beyond dismemberment, the President's ideas on Germany remained
vague. In line with his desire to postpone political decisions until after
the war, Roosevelt felt in 1943 that it was simply too early to begin
planning detailed occupation policies. He was open to suggestions, but
would commit himself firmly to nothing. Discussing what to do with
Germany after victory was really a waste of time, the President had told
a press conference in July: "I think it takes people's thoughts off winning the war to talk about things like that now." [13]

Military officials carefully avoided involvement in planning the occupation of Germany. "The formulation of long-view political, social and
economic policies is properly the function of civilian agencies of the government," an officer in the Army's Military Government Division wrote
in 1942; "their 'implementation,' during any period of military necessity,
is the function of the military command." Army planners expected their
responsibility for military government in Germany to last only until
order had been restored, possibly no more than a few weeks, after which
the task of occupation would be turned over to civilian authorities appointed by the United States government. "You are not politicians . . .
but soldiers," General Eisenhower told a group of Civil Affairs officers

[12] Minutes, Roosevelt-Churchill-Stalin meetings of November 28 and December 1,
1943, *FR: Tehran,* pp. 509–12, 532–33, 553–54, and 600–4. See also Charles Bohlen's memoranda of November 28 and December 15, 1943, *ibid.,* pp. 513, 846–47;
Lord Moran, *Churchill: The Struggle for Survival, 1940–1965,* p. 152; and Blum,
Morgenthau Diaries: Years of War, pp. 340–41.

[13] Paul Y. Hammond, "Directives for the Occupation of Germany: The Washington
Controversy," in Harold Stein, ed., *American Civil-Military Decisions,* p. 324; Roosevelt press conference, July 13, 1943, Roosevelt MSS, PPF 1-P, Vol. XXII.

under his command shortly before D-Day; "[your task is] to help us win the war." [14]

But at the same time, the Army was determined not to allow civilians to interfere in the operation of military government during the brief period when it would be necessary. Civilian meddling in three similar situations—in Southern states occupied by the Union Army during the Civil War, in the Philippines following the Spanish-American War, and in the Rhineland after World War I—had been, in the words of an Army expert on the subject, "demoralizing, costly, and ludicrous." Civilians would play a role in military government—political and economic matters could not be completely ignored in dealing with defeated enemies—but the Army hoped "to forestall their seizing its direction or control." [15]

The experience of invading and occupying North Africa seemed to confirm the wisdom of this policy. As early as July, 1942, General Eisenhower was complaining about interference from civilian officials, each of whom "feels that he has a distinct and separate mission in life and never stops to think that . . . winning the war normally involves also the Army, Navy, and Air Force." Late in November, three weeks after the landings, he wrote to General Marshall: "The sooner I can get rid of all these questions that are outside the military in scope, the happier I will be! Sometimes I think I live ten years each week, of which at least nine are absorbed in political and economic matters." Shortly thereafter Eisenhower described the civilian representatives hovering around his headquarters as "locusts," and advocated imposing "a single staff authority over the whole gang." [16]

[14] Colonel Jesse I. Miller to Colonel Edward S. Greenbaum, December 21, 1942, in Harry L. Coles and Albert K. Weinberg, *Civil Affairs: Soldiers Become Governors,* p. 56; Dorn, "Debate over American Occupation Policy," p. 487; Forrest C. Pogue, *The Supreme Command,* pp. 83–84. See also Coles and Weinberg, *Civil Affairs,* pp. 19–20, 26. The Army established a School of Military Government at Charlottesville, Virginia, in the spring of 1942 to train officers for the tasks of military government. Charges that the school was turning out American *gauleiters* caused the Army to become especially sensitive to the need to keep this training free from political overtones. On this point, see Stimson and Bundy, *On Active Service,* pp. 553–54; and Hajo Holborn, *American Military Government: Its Organization and Policies,* pp. 3–4.

[15] Miller to Greenbaum, July 23 and 30, 1942, in Coles and Weinberg, *Civil Affairs,* pp. 16, 17–18.

[16] Eisenhower to General Brehon Somervell, July 27, 1942, *Eisenhower Papers,* I,

Hoping to avoid the mistakes of North Africa before reaching enemy territory, the Army in March of 1943 established a Civil Affairs Division within the War Department to coordinate political and economic planning as it affected military government. The division was supposed to refrain from policy-making, which the Army still regarded as a civilian responsibility, but to ensure that the execution of policy during periods of military government came under Army control. War Department planners quickly realized, however, that the best way to control the execution of policy was to impede the formulation of it. The Joint Chiefs of Staff decided in April that "requirements of secrecy and security" precluded consulting civilian agencies about occupation policy prior to launching military operations. By May, General John Hilldring, director of the Civil Affairs Division, had informed State Department officials "that they would have to take second place to the War Department in questions of military government," and was working to commit other government agencies to this principle.[17] Resolved on the one hand to avoid making policy itself, but determined on the other not to let civilians interfere, the Army fell back on the simple practice of evaluating occupation measures in terms of whether or not they accorded with the nebulous doctrine of "military necessity."

But even this non-policy had political and economic implications. No one knew for certain how long military government would last. Occupation measures implemented solely on the basis of "military necessity" could well undermine long-range plans for the treatment of Germany being considered in the civilian branches of the government. Despite its studied position of policy neutrality, therefore, the War Department's attitudes would significantly affect the manner in which Americans administered their occupation zone.

The contradictions implicit in the views of the State Department, the War Department, and the White House pointed up the need for closer

---

423; Eisenhower to Marshall, November 30, 1942, *ibid.*, II, 781; Eisenhower to Major General George V. Strong, December 4, 1942, *ibid.*, II, 794. See also Coles and Weinberg, *Civil Affairs*, pp. 30–31; and Holborn, *American Military Government*, p. 7.

[17] Hammond, "Directives for the Occupation of Germany," pp. 320–21; Joint Chiefs of Staff to Secretaries Stimson and Knox, April 10, 1943, in Coles and Weinberg, *Civil Affairs*, p. 70; minutes, War Department General Council meeting, May 31, 1943, *ibid.*, p. 97; Merle Fainsod, "The Development of American Military Government Policy During World War II," in Carl J. Friedrich and associates, *American Experiences in Military Government in World War II*, p. 31.

coordination between these agencies of government before any definitive United States recommendations on the treatment of Germany were submitted to the British and the Russians. No such coordination had taken place, however, by the end of 1943. The State Department had formulated a comprehensive long-range plan for the occupation of Germany, but had not yet reconciled it with the attitudes of the President and the War Department. Roosevelt had informally discussed the German question with Churchill and Stalin at Teheran, but had not informed the State Department of the purport of these conversations. The War Department, preoccupied with "military necessity," had resolved to consult civilians on the question of Germany as little as possible. Meanwhile, plans were under way to establish an Anglo-American-Soviet commission to work out common policies for the surrender and occupation of defeated enemies, a development which found the United States government seriously unprepared.

II

The Grand Alliance, like other coalitions in world history, was held together primarily by hatred for a common enemy. Hitler's defeat would remove the alliance's chief reason for existence, raising the question of whether the British, Russians, and Americans could overcome inevitable differences in national interests to continue cooperation in the postwar period. Fear on the part of any one ally that his associates were conspiring with his enemies would make such collaboration impossible, hence the need for agreement on common policies for the occupation of Germany before the fighting stopped. Neither the Big Three nor their foreign ministers had sufficient time or energy to resolve such a complex issue themselves, as their inconclusive talks at Moscow and Teheran had shown. Washington's inadequate integration of wartime and postwar planning wrecked a promising effort to work out occupation policies at the tertiary level—through the European Advisory Commission.

The EAC evolved from the military-political commission which Stalin had pressured his Anglo-American allies into establishing in September, 1943, following the surrender of Italy.[18] Despite their reluctance to give

[18] On this matter, see chapter 3.

the Russians a major role in the occupation of that country, the British saw little reason to postpone consideration of general political issues. Accordingly, at the Moscow Foreign Ministers' Conference in October, Anthony Eden suggested transforming the military-political commission into an advisory council for Italy and creating a new tripartite European Advisory Commission, located in London, to handle not only negotiations with defeated enemies but all political matters which the Big Three chose to refer to it. Eden's proposal quickly won Soviet approval. The Americans were less enthusiastic, but Hull warily accepted Eden's plan after stipulating that it would not preclude use of regular diplomatic channels if these were considered desirable. As finally agreed in the Moscow Conference protocol, the EAC was assigned the broad task of "making recommendations to the three Governments upon European questions connected with the termination of hostilities." In addition, it was specified that one of the commission's first jobs would be to furnish detailed suggestions on "the terms of surrender to be imposed upon each of the European states with which any of the three Powers are at war, and upon the mechanism required to ensure the fulfillment of those terms." [19]

But the United States quickly moved to restrict the EAC's role as much as possible. Secretary of State Hull instructed Ambassador John G. Winant, American representative on the commission, to avoid discussing general political questions, limiting his activities instead to drawing up surrender terms and organizing joint occupation machinery for defeated enemies. Winant protested this narrow grant of authority, pointing out that the British wanted the EAC to deal with establishment of control in all countries, friendly and unfriendly, occupied by the Allies. "If we present the Russians only with *faits accomplis* on these subjects, as we were obliged to do in the case of Italy, we can only expect to learn of their actions and policies in Eastern Europe in a similar manner." Winant's complaints evoked no sympathy among Washington officials, most of whom were motivated, as George F. Kennan later observed, "by a

---

[19] *FR: 1943*, I, 554, 571–72, 605–8, 706, 710–11, 756–57. For British motives in proposing establishment of the EAC, see Eden, *The Reckoning*, pp. 476, 492–93; Sir Llewellyn Woodward, *British Foreign Policy in the Second World War*, p. 246n; and Philip E. Mosely, "The Occupation of Germany: New Light on How the Zones Were Drawn," *Foreign Affairs*, XXVIII (July, 1950), 581.

lively concern lest the new body should at some point and by some mischance actually do something." [20]

Winant's instructions reflected the Roosevelt Administration's reluctance to make postwar political commitments before the end of the war. Late in 1943, the President had emphasized to the Joint Chiefs of Staff the need to keep the EAC a purely advisory body—to ensure that the Big Three made all major decisions. Others within the Administration, remembering 1919, feared that any secret political arrangements made during the war might provoke a resurgence of isolationism inside the United States. "If we get the war being run from London," Secretary of War Stimson proclaimed, "we will have the United States isolationist when the end of the war comes." Assistant Secretary of War John J. McCloy echoed this sentiment:

On every cracker barrel in every country store in the U.S. there is someone sitting who is convinced that we get hornswoggled every time we attend a European conference. European deliberations must be made in the light of the concepts of the new continent because that continent has now, for better or for worse, become a determining factor in the struggles of the old one. What may be lost through not moving to London in the way of better and more accessible records or a greater familiarity with local conditions, will be made up in a readier assumption of responsibility on the part of the U.S. and perhaps in a greater obectivity of decision.

Still others, including Secretary of State Hull, worried that if the EAC took up political questions it would impair the authority of the future collective security organization. "I believe that you will appreciate the possible long-term repercussions on American public opinion," Hull told Winant, "should the impression be gained that this Commission . . . is secretly building the new world." [21]

Even with its authority restricted to the surrender and occupation of defeated enemies, the EAC could have served as a valuable forum for tripartite discussions on Germany had Washington cooperated. But inade-

---

[20] Hull to Winant, December 23, 1943, *FR: 1943,* I, 812; Winant to Hull, January 4 and 6, 1944, *FR: 1944,* I, 1–3, 10; Kennan, *Memoirs,* p. 166.

[21] Joint Chiefs of Staff minutes, meeting with Roosevelt, November 15, 1943, *FR: Tehran,* pp. 197–98; Stimson Diary, October 28, 1943, Stimson MSS; McCloy to Harry Hopkins, November 25, 1943, *FR: Tehran,* p. 418; Hull to Winant, January 9, 1944, *FR: 1944,* I, 12. See also Dorn, "Debate over American Occupation Policy," p. 488.

quate coordination of wartime and postwar planning created a bureaucratic snarl within the Roosevelt Administration which made it virtually
impossible for the American representative on the EAC to take any
action at all. Representatives from the State, War, and Navy departments had established in December, 1943, a joint body known as the
Working Security Committee to draw up instructions for Winant. Before
these could be sent, however, each representative had to clear them with
his own department, thus giving each agency a veto over what proposals
Winant could make in the EAC. Securing State and Navy Department
clearance created no serious problems. But War Department representatives, made up of officers from the Civil Affairs Division, at first refused
to take any part whatever in drafting instructions for Winant, arguing
that the occupation of defeated enemies was purely a military matter.
When, upon receipt of orders from above, CAD officers did agree to participate in the Working Security Committee, they seemed reluctant to
approve any policy at all, at one point even vetoing a reply to a telegram from Winant asking when he could expect instructions. Negotiating with CAD officials, State Department representatives came to feel,
required every bit as much patience as dealing with the Russians themselves.[22]

There were several reasons for this difficulty. Since its formation in
the spring of 1943, the Civil Affairs Division had carefully avoided involving itself in the formulation of occupation policy, hoping to allow
maximum discretion to Army commanders during periods of military
government. Consequently, Division officers required weeks of study before they could pass judgment on State Department proposals. But this
was not the whole problem. The Joint Chiefs of Staff also had to clear
instructions to Winant before War Department representatives on the
Working Security Committee could endorse them. But the Joint Chiefs,
presumably seeking to stay out of policy-making in "political" fields, refused to consider papers which had not received final State Department
approval. The State Department, not wanting to trespass on "military"
matters and hoping to allow Winant negotiating room, submitted only
tentative suggestions which would not become official policy until approved by the Working Security Committee, and then by the EAC. The

[22] Hammond, "Directives for the Occupation of Germany," pp. 329–30; Mosely,
"Occupation of Germany," pp. 583–86.

resulting stalemate might have been circumvented had some mechanism existed for coordinating policy between the civilian and military agencies of government. But efforts to establish such a mechanism had failed because the Joint Chiefs, for reasons of security, refused to allow civilian officials access to their deliberations. Since both Roosevelt and the War Department distrusted the EAC anyway, neither made any serious effort to resolve the problem. All of this left Winant, in the words of one of his assistants, "stranded without instructions on the policy that he should follow, without freedom to propose a policy of his own, and without a mandate to comment on the policies proposed by other member countries." [23]

The chaotic manner in which the United States government finally arrived at a policy on German occupation zones illustrated vividly the consequences of this failure of coordination. Late in 1943 the State Department submitted to the Working Security Committee a plan to draw the zones in such a way that all three occupying powers would have access to Berlin. CAD representatives on the committee refused to consider this proposal, arguing that zonal boundaries were military matters, and would probably be determined by the location of each nation's armies at the end of hostilities. Early in 1944, the British placed before the EAC a plan to divide Germany into three zones, with the Russians in the east, the Americans in the southwest, and the British in the northwest. Berlin was to be an area under tripartite responsibility lying deep within the Soviet zone. The Russians quickly indicated their approval. Winant was without instructions, however, and could only report these developments to Washington with the comment that he "would appreciate being informed as to our present position on this question." [24]

[23] Hammond, "Directives for the Occupation of Germany," pp. 330–33; Penrose, *Economic Planning for Peace*, p. 233. Walter L. Dorn, who advised the War Department on civil affairs in Germany during this period, later observed: "Nothing is more apparent than the anxious solicitude on the part of the War Department to keep the American Army of Occupation out of politics, while the Department of State and the American Delegation in E.A.C. seemed determined to saddle this army with a whole shoal of essentially political tasks which threatened to outrun the limited administrative capabilities of an army of occupation." ("Debate over American Occupation Policy in Germany," p. 487.)

[24] Mosely, "Occupation of Germany," pp. 586–89; William M. Franklin, "Zonal Boundaries and Access to Berlin," *World Politics*, XVI (October, 1963), 8–9, 13–15; Winant to Hull, February 16, 1944, *FR: 1944*, I, 173. For the British and Russian proposals on zonal boundaries see *ibid.*, pp. 150–53, 177–78.

These developments caught the Civil Affairs Division off guard, causing it to revise its previous position that the EAC should not deal with
occupation zones. Late in February, 1944, it sent to the State Department for referral to Winant a Joint Chiefs of Staff memorandum, prepared three months earlier, proposing very different zonal boundaries
from those under consideration in the EAC. This plan gave the United
States a huge northwest zone bordering on Berlin, with noticeably
smaller zones for the Russians in the east and the British in the southwest. It pushed back the boundary of the Soviet zone, which the British
and the Russians had already agreed on, from 50 to 150 miles to the
east. It cut across existing German administrative boundaries, and made
no provision for tripartite occupation of Berlin. It neglected to draw
zonal boundaries all the way to the Czech-German frontier, thus leaving
undefined the border between the British and Soviet zones. Efforts to
elicit some clarification of this extraordinary plan from War Department
representatives on the Working Security Committee proved unavailing,
so the State Department simply forwarded this strange document to
Winant with the comforting assurance that it would be "self-
explanatory." [25]

It was hardly that. Winant refused to submit the plan to the EAC
and dispatched his counselor, George F. Kennan, back to Washington to
protest. Kennan quickly cleared up the matter by going directly to the
President. The War Department's proposal, Kennan found, stemmed
from a rough sketch of German occupation zones which Roosevelt had
casually drawn on a National Geographic Society map for the Joint
Chiefs of Staff in November, 1943. Subsequent discussions in the EAC
had made presentation of this proposal unfeasible, as Roosevelt readily
acknowledged. But officials in the Civil Affairs Division, confronted un-
expectedly with the need to instruct Winant on zonal boundaries, had
resurrected the plan and insisted on its submission to the EAC, regardless of the unfortunate effect this would have had on negotiations there.
State Department reservations about this procedure had been turned
aside by the assertion that the plan represented the wishes of the Com-

[25] Stettinius to Winant, March 8, 1944, enclosing C.C.S. 320/4 (Revised), prepared
by the Joint Chiefs of Staff and dated December 4, 1943, *FR: 1944*, I, 195–96; memorandum by George F. Kennan, April 4, 1944, *ibid.,* pp. 208–9; Franklin, "Zonal
Boundaries," pp. 17–18; Mosely, "Occupation of Germany," pp. 591–92. See also a
State Department map, illustrating the differences between the JCS proposal and that
accepted by the British and the Russians, in *FR: 1944,* I, facing p. 196.

mander in Chief, and hence was not subject to negotiation. Highly amused by this set of events, F.D.R. quickly shelved the War Department document and authorized Winant to accept the zonal boundaries proposed by the British and the Russians.[26]

Roosevelt's action failed to break the stalemate over occupation zones, however, for though willing to accept the boundaries suggested by the British, he objected strongly to their assignment of southwestern Germany as the American area of responsibility. The President had been led by Admiral William D. Leahy, former ambassador to Vichy, to expect a postwar revolution in France, a development which would threaten the Army's lines of communication if United States troops were occupying southwestern Germany. " 'Do please don't!' ask me to keep any American forces in France," F.D.R. had written Churchill in February. "I just cannot do it! I would have to bring them all back home. . . . I denounce and protest the paternity of Belgium, France and Italy. You really ought to bring up and discipline your own children. In view of the fact that they may be your bulwark in future days, you should at least pay for their schooling now!"

Roosevelt failed to sway the Prime Minister, however, and at length the President's military advisers persuaded him to accept the southwestern zone, largely on grounds that existing troop deployments would make it easier for Americans to occupy that part of Germany. But F.D.R. insisted that the British give the United States two enclaves in their northwestern zone at the ports of Bremen and Bremerhaven. American military authorities went to great lengths to negotiate with the British a precise agreement allowing access to these ports from the United States zone. Ironically, in view of later events, the War Department continued to resist efforts to make similar arrangements with the Russians for access to Berlin, arguing that this was purely a "military" matter which commanders on the scene could work out during the actual invasion of Germany.[27]

[26] Kennan, *Memoirs,* p. 171; Hull to Winant, May 1, 1944, *FR: 1944,* I, 211. See also Franklin, "Zonal Boundaries," pp. 18–19. The map on which Roosevelt sketched his plan for occupation zones is reproduced in Matloff, *Strategic Planning, 1943–44,* facing p. 341. Joint Chiefs of Staff minutes of their meeting with Roosevelt, which took place on November 19, 1943, are in *FR: Tehran,* pp. 253–56, 261.

[27] Roosevelt to Churchill, February 29, 1944, *FR: 1944,* I, 189. See also Franklin, "Zonal Boundaries," pp. 19–21; and Mosely, "Occupation of Germany," pp. 593, 596–97, 604. Harold Macmillan later observed that "Admiral Leahy was one of those

The EAC was not a totally useless organization. In addition to its tortured but eventually fruitful work on occupation zones, the commission managed after tedious negotiations to hammer out tripartite agreements on surrender terms and control machinery for Germany.[28] But these represented merely the framework, not the substance, of a common policy. More significant than the agreements reached in the EAC were the matters which could not be submitted to it at all because of imperfect political-military coordination in Washington. The most important of these concerned the question of reparations.

Realizing the urgency of settling the reparations issue with the Russians, the State Department early in 1944 submitted to the Working Security Committee for referral to the EAC a set of general recommendations on the economic treatment of Germany, together with specific suggestions on reparations policy. The Joint Chiefs of Staff held these documents for two months, then refused to approve them because plans for military operations against Germany had not progressed far enough to determine how they would be affected by these economic proposals. State Department officials carefully rewrote their suggestions, pointedly emphasizing their nonmilitary character, but these also failed to clear the Joint Chiefs. Hoping that successful landings in France might have changed the military's attitude, the State Department tried once again late in July, this time submitting a lengthy general statement of policy on the postwar treatment of Germany. Again the Joint Chiefs waited for two months, then informed the department that while the papers in question contained "important considerations of military interest," these were "so involved with important political considerations as not to be separable into sections." The Joint Chiefs blandly suggested resubmitting the document to the Working Security Committee, on which, they somewhat superfluously pointed out, "there is military representation." [29]

---

men who, although unable to converse with any Frenchman in intelligible French, believed himself the supreme exponent of the French mentality." (*The Blast of War,* p. 160.)

[28] These agreements are printed in *FR: Yalta,* pp. 110–27.

[29] Hammond, "Directives for the Occupation of Germany," pp. 336–38; James C. Dunn to Admiral William D. Leahy, July 22, 1944, *FR: 1944,* I, 251–52; Leahy to Hull, September 29, 1944, *ibid.,* p. 343. Undersecretary of State Stettinius had informed Winant on June 10, 1944, that both the War Department and the Joint Chiefs were pressing for action in the EAC now that the invasion of France was in progress. (*Ibid.,* p. 233.)

Not surprisingly, State Department officials soon began to consider the possibility of bypassing the Working Security Committee, and hence the EAC, to get reparations talks with the Russians under way. Tripartite agreement on German economic policy was urgent, Hull advised Winant in August, 1944, and "in view of the need for instituting discussions in the near future it may be impracticable to proceed through EAC." Winant agreed. Reparations policy could not be established without agreement on an over-all economic program for Germany, he advised the department, and this in turn would require study of the European economy as a whole, a subject far beyond the commission's limited mandate.

Winant suggested holding reparations talks in Moscow so that Russian negotiators could refer quickly back to their government for instructions, thus eliminating one frequent source of delay in the EAC. The ambassador discreetly avoided reference to the other great impediment to EAC operations—clearance problems in Washington—but Philip E. Mosely, his political adviser, noted shortly thereafter:

One of these days we shall have to agree on a lot of policies with regard to Germany, and unless we can have some papers approved by the JCS [Joint Chiefs of Staff] we shall be in a position of merely commenting on the carefully prepared British papers or charging with a feather duster at . . . Russian statements of policy. . . . [There is] danger of a breakdown of tripartite understanding with respect to Germany if our EAC delegation here cannot be provided in advance with statements of US Government policy. After all tripartite policy with regard to Germany is the real touchstone of Allied post-war cooperation. . . . It was for this reason that I suggested to the Ambassador that it might be valuable to propose having reparation discussions in Moscow.

Negotiations failed to get under way in the fall of 1944, however, because of the sudden outbreak of controversy within the Roosevelt Administration over the Morgenthau Plan. "Speed on these matters is not an essential at the present moment," Roosevelt advised Hull on October 20. "I dislike making detailed plans for a country which we do not yet occupy." [30] As a result, American officials made no effort to discuss repa-

---

[30] Hull to Winant, August 16 and 22, 1944, *FR: 1944,* I, 271–72, 276; Winant to Hull, August 14 and 19, 1944, *ibid.,* pp. 274–76; Mosely to James W. Riddleberger, September 5, 1944, *ibid.,* pp. 331–32; Roosevelt to Hull, October 20, 1944, *FR: Yalta,* p. 158. For the effect of the Morgenthau controversy in postponing negotiations

rations with the Russians until early 1945, when Roosevelt and Churchill met Stalin at Yalta.

"I do not think that any conference or commission created by governments for a serious purpose has had less support from the governments creating it than the European Advisory Commission," Winant complained in the fall of 1944; "at least I do not know of any like example in recorded history." The EAC had established the machinery for the occupation of Germany, but attempts to move beyond this to the content of policy had failed, chiefly because American military authorities would not clear instructions to Winant on nonmilitary matters. The War Department and the Joint Chiefs of Staff refused to allow civilian agencies to formulate long-range policy for Germany lest this impair in some way the freedom of action of the Army's military governors. Determined to stay out of policy-making itself, the military nevertheless shaped the course of future events by preventing anyone else from making policy. But Army authorities could never have maintained this paradoxical position had they not had at least tacit support from the White House. Seeking to preserve *his* freedom of action in the political sphere, Roosevelt had always regarded the EAC warily: "We must emphasize the fact that the European Advisory Commission is 'Advisory' and that you and I are not bound by this advice," he reminded Hull late in 1944; "if we do not remember that word 'advisory' they may go ahead and execute some of the advice, which, when the time comes, we may not like at all." [31]

III

Anglo-American forces landed in Normandy in June of 1944, and by the end of July had broken out of their beachheads to begin driving the Germans out of France. "The enemy in the West has had it," an intelligence summary from General Eisenhower's headquarters concluded late in August; "two and a half months of bitter fighting have brought the end of the war in Europe within sight, almost within reach." Even the

with the Russians on Germany, see Moseley, "Occupation of Germany," p. 596; and McNeill, *America, Britain, and Russia,* p. 491.

[31] Winant to Hull, October 7, 1944, *FR: 1944,* I, 351; Roosevelt to Hull, October 20, 1944, *FR: Yalta,* p. 158.

normally cautious General Marshall succumbed to this mood of optimism, advising his senior commanders on September 13 that the war against Germany would probably end before November. The rapidly changing military situation made all the more urgent the need for Washington officials to decide how they would treat the Germans after V-E Day, and to secure their allies' approval of these plans. As Secretary of War Stimson later observed, "The armies had outrun the policy makers." [32]

Under these circumstances, the consistent reluctance of the Joint Chiefs of Staff to approve proposals for the postwar treatment of Germany failed to stop such planning; it simply caused government officials who needed guidance in this field to seek it through channels other than the Working Security Committee. In the spring of 1944, President Roosevelt had formed an interdepartmental Executive Committee on Economic Foreign Policy, made up of representatives from the State, Treasury, Agriculture, Commerce, and Labor departments, the Foreign Economic Administration, and the United States Tariff Commission. The War Department was not represented. Encouraged by this omission, the State Department in June decided to submit to the ECEFP the general statement on economic policy for Germany which it had been unable to clear through the Working Security Committee. Department officials realized that some form of interdepartmental consultation would have to take place in Washington before this document could serve as a basis for eventual reparations talks with the Russians. The ECEFP considered the State Department's plan for two months, and after making some revisions approved it on August 4, 1944.[33]

The resulting document reflected the State Department's continued support for a moderate peace as the best guarantee against future aggression. While it called for measures which would guarantee payment of

[32] SHAEF Weekly Intelligence Summary, August 26, 1944, quoted in Pogue, *Supreme Command*, pp. 244–45; Marshall to senior commanders, September 13, 1944, *Eisenhower Papers*, IV, 2117; Stimson and Bundy, *On Active Service*, p. 566. See also Hammond, "Directives for the Occupation of Germany," pp. 340–41.

[33] Hammond, "Directives for the Occupation of Germany," p. 342. State Department officials had not yet decided to hold reparations talks outside the EAC at the time that they submitted their economic proposals to the ECEFP. Their original intent had been not to bypass the Joint Chiefs of Staff but to improve their bargaining position with that body by securing prior ECEFP endorsement of their plan. (*Ibid.*, p. 343.)

restitution and reparations to Germany's victims, prevent reconversion of the German economy to war purposes, and eliminate "German economic domination in Europe," the plan also proposed integrating the defeated Reich into "the type of world economy envisaged by the Atlantic Charter." This would require maintaining a tolerable standard of living and would preclude indiscriminate destruction of Germany's industrial capacity. Punitive policies would not work: "An indefinitely continued coercion of more than sixty million technically advanced people . . . would be at best an expensive undertaking and would afford the world little sense of real security." [34]

Meanwhile, similar proposals for the occupation of Germany were under discussion at Supreme Headquarters, Allied Expeditionary Forces, in Great Britain. In preparing for the invasion of Western Europe, General Eisenhower had set up "country units" within the SHAEF organization to plan civil affairs operations in liberated and enemy territories. Since Anglo-American forces were likely to move into Germany within a few months, the German "country unit," in the absence of firm directives from Washington, quickly found it necessary to begin drawing up specific guidelines for the use of military government authorities. By August, 1944, it had produced a *Basic Handbook for Military Government of Germany.*[35]

SHAEF's "country unit" planners were chiefly civilian experts who had been recruited into the Army, however, and their guidelines for Germany differed from the War Department's doctrine of "military necessity" in several important ways. The SHAEF handbook emphasized the need for centralized tripartite administration of occupied Germany

---

[34] "Germany: General Objectives of United States Economic Policy with Respect to Germany," memorandum by the Executive Committee on Economic Foreign Policy, approved August 4, 1944, *FR: 1944*, I, 278–87. See also "The Treatment of Germany," a memorandum by the State Department Committee on Postwar Problems, dated August 5, 1944, *ibid.*, pp. 306–25; Hammond, "Directives for the Occupation of Germany," pp. 342–46; Blum, *Morgenthau Diaries: Years of War*, pp. 331–32; and John L. Chase, "The Development of the Morgenthau Plan Through the Quebec Conference," *Journal of Politics*, XVI (May, 1954), 327–28.

[35] Dale Clark, "Conflicts over Planning at Staff Headquarters," in Friedrich and associates, *American Experiences in Military Government*, pp. 211–17. See also Pogue, *Supreme Command*, p. 353; and Harold Zink, "American Civil-Military Relations in the Occupation of Germany," in Harry Coles, ed., *Total War and Cold War: Problems in Civilian Control of the Military*, pp. 212–15.

rather than the Army's policy of seeking maximum freedom of action for military government authorities in the American zone. SHAEF's planners seemed to place the economic welfare of the German people above the interests of the occupying army, a view which the Army's recently revised field manual on military government had explicitly repudiated. But most important, the SHAEF handbook assumed that the end of the war would find the German governmental and economic structure intact, prepared to serve the purpose of the occupying authorities. General Eisenhower had warned the Combined Chiefs of Staff on August 23, 1944, that there probably would be no functioning German government to surrender to the Allies, and that under the circumstances he as supreme commander felt unable to assume responsibility for control and support of the German economy.[36] Hence, the Army was on the verge of repudiating the SHAEF handbook at the moment of its appearance.

This proved not to be necessary, however, for the handbook, together with the State Department's proposals for the economic treatment of Germany, recently approved by the ECEFP, provoked a violent outburst from an agency of government not hitherto involved in planning occupation policy—the Treasury. The resulting furor drastically altered the direction of postwar planning for Germany within the United States government and prevented any serious consultation with the other occupying powers until the summer of 1945, several months after the surrender of Germany.

Assistant Secretary of the Treasury Harry Dexter White had sat in on discussions of the State Department's plan in the ECEFP during the summer of 1944. At the same time Colonel Bernard Bernstein, a former Treasury official, had been keeping his old department advised on SHAEF planning from his vantage point in the Finance Division of the German "country unit." Their observations produced fruit early in August, 1944, when Treasury Secretary Henry Morgenthau, Jr., made a trip to Europe. During the flight, White showed Morgenthau the ECEFP document, while in England Bernstein summarized the substance of SHAEF's handbook. Both struck the Treasury Secretary as too soft on

[36] Clark, "Conflicts over Planning at Staff Headquarters," pp. 218–19; Penrose, *Economic Planning for Peace,* p. 242; Eisenhower to the Combined Chiefs of Staff, August 23, 1944, FWD 13128(SCAF 68), Eisenhower MSS. For a summary of the Army field manual on military government, see Fainsod, "Development of American Military Government Policy," pp. 31–34.

Germany, and he immediately began a campaign to replace them with a harsher program which came to be known as the Morgenthau Plan.[37]

Morgenthau and White first enunciated this plan at a meeting with Ambassador Winant and several of his advisers outside London on August 12. Too many Englishmen and Americans, Morgenthau argued, were leaning toward a "soft" peace, the same mistake made after World War I. The only sure way to prevent future wars would be to eliminate not only Germany's war-making capacity but its industrial plant as well, converting that nation into a "pastoral" country. Specifically, Morgenthau objected to indications that occupying forces planned to assume responsibility for the German economy. Economic chaos would be a good thing, the Treasury Secretary thought—it would bring the fact of defeat home to the German people. There should be no attempts to set up a "WPA" program in the ruins of the Third Reich.[38]

Morgenthau's plan evoked a mixed reaction. Winant remained noncommittal, but two of his assistants, Philip E. Mosely and E. F. Penrose, argued strongly against the idea. Mosely warned that any attempt to wreck Germany's industry would make that country dependent on Russia, thus opening all of Europe to Soviet domination. Penrose pointed out that an agricultural economy could not support the population of Germany, whereupon Morgenthau suggested dumping surplus Germans in North Africa. British Foreign Secretary Anthony Eden endorsed the general idea of toughness toward Germany, but maintained a discreet silence regarding the merits of Morgenthau's specific proposal. General Eisenhower admitted to Morgenthau that he had not thought much about postwar treatment of Germany, but he enthusiastically supported elimination of German war plants. Back in Washington, Secretary of State Hull seemed sympathetic, reminding Morgenthau of his proposal, vigorously applauded by the Russians at Moscow the year before, to shoot all German and Japanese leaders upon capture. Only Secretary of War Stimson expressed outright opposition to the plan on grounds that it would cause starvation inside Germany.[39]

[37] Blum, *Morgenthau Diaries: Years of War,* pp. 333–34; Chase, "Development of the Morgenthau Plan," pp. 326–31; Zink, "American Civil-Military Relations in the Occupation of Germany," pp. 213–14.

[38] Penrose, *Economic Planning for Peace,* pp. 245–46; Blum, *Morgenthau Diaries: Years of War,* p. 338.

[39] Blum, *Morgenthau Diaries: Years of War,* pp. 338–42; Penrose, *Economic Planning for Peace,* pp. 247–50; Eisenhower, *Crusade in Europe,* p. 287. Morgenthau's ac-

In the final analysis, however, the fate of the Morgenthau Plan rested with President Roosevelt. Inclined since the beginning of the war to favor harsh treatment of Germany, F.D.R. by August of 1944 had, if anything, stiffened his views. "We have got to be tough with Germany and I mean the German people not just the Nazis," he told Morgenthau on August 19; "we either have to castrate the German people or you have got to treat them in such a manner so they can't just go on reproducing people who want to continue the way they have in the past." Two days later, Roosevelt wrote to Senator Kenneth McKellar: "It is amazing how many people are beginning to get soft in the future terms [for] the Germans and the Japs." On the 25th, Morgenthau sent Roosevelt a memorandum summarizing the SHAEF handbook for Germany. Roosevelt read it overnight, and the next day sent a stinging rebuke to Stimson, demanding that the document be withdrawn:

This so-called "Handbook" is pretty bad. . . . It gives me the impression that Germany is to be restored just as much as the Netherlands or Belgium, and the people of Germany brought back as quickly as possible to their pre-war estate.

It is of the utmost importance that every person in Germany should realize that this time Germany is a defeated nation. I do not want them to starve to death, but, as an example, if they need food to keep body and soul together beyond what they have, they should be fed three times a day with soup from Army soup kitchens. That will keep them perfectly healthy and they will remember that experience all their lives. . . .

There exists a school of thought both in London and here which would, in effect, do for Germany what this Government did for its own citizens in 1933 when they were flat on their backs. I see no reason for starting a WPA, PWA, or a CCC for Germany when we go in with our Army of Occupation.

Too many people here and in England hold to the view that the German people as a whole are not responsible for what has taken place—that only a few Nazi leaders are responsible. That unfortunately is not based on fact. The German people as a whole must have it driven home to them that the whole nation has been engaged in a lawless conspiracy against the decencies of modern civilization.[40]

---

count of his interview with Eisenhower described the General as charging advocates of a soft peace with seeking to build up Germany as a bulwark against Russia. Eisenhower's account mentions nothing of this, however.

[40] Morgenthau account of conversation with Roosevelt, August 19, 1944, quoted in Blum, *Morgenthau Diaries: Years of War*, p. 342; Roosevelt to McKellar, August 21, 1944, Roosevelt MSS, PPF 3715; Roosevelt to Stimson, with copies to Morgenthau and Hull, August 26, 1944, printed in Blum, pp. 348–49.

Heartened by Roosevelt's reaction, Morgenthau encouraged his staff to toughen the Treasury's plan. "The President is hungry for this stuff," he told them late in August. "I wouldn't be afraid to make the suggestion just as ruthless as is necessary." Even then, Morgenthau felt his advisers had not gone far enough. Over the objections of White and other Treasury officials, he insisted on including in the plan a proposal to dismantle the industry of the Ruhr and Saar, and flood all the coal mines. "Just strip it," he told White, "I don't care what happens to the population. . . . I would take every mine, every mill and factory and wreck it. . . . Steel, coal, everything. Just close it down." [41]

Morgenthau reached the height of his influence at the Quebec Conference in mid-September. Attending at Roosevelt's special invitation, the Treasury Secretary managed to get the President and Winston Churchill to initial a document calling for conversion of Germany "into a country primarily agricultural and pastoral in character." But in so doing, Morgenthau overplayed his hand. He also proposed, and Roosevelt approved, an unconditional grant of $6.5 billion in lend-lease aid to Britain for the period between the defeat of Germany and that of Japan. This infuriated Hull, who had sought to tie continuation of lend-lease to concessions on trade policy. From this time on the Secretary of State joined subordinates in his department and Secretary of War Stimson in firmly opposing Morgenthau's scheme. Moreover, a series of leaks to the press late in September resulted in publication of the plan. The public response was overwhelmingly critical, and Republicans began making plans to use Morgenthau as a campaign issue in the election later that fall. [42]

Roosevelt immediately backtracked. "No one wants to make Germany a wholly agricultural nation again," he assured an indignant Hull on September 29. Several days later, he admitted to Stimson that Morgenthau had "pulled a boner." When Stimson showed the President the

[41] Blum, *Morgenthau Diaries: Years of War,* pp. 350–54. For the final version of the Morgenthau Plan, see *ibid.,* pp. 356–59; and Henry Morgenthau, Jr., *Germany Is Our Problem.*

[42] Blum, *Morgenthau Diaries: Years of War,* pp. 377–78; Hull, *Memoirs,* II, 1613–14. For public reaction to the Morgenthau Plan, see the Department of State, "Fortnightly Survey of American Opinion on International Affairs," No. 12, October 5, 1944. Hull's implication that he had opposed the Morgenthau Plan from the beginning (*Memoirs,* II, 1605–6) is, at best, misleading. On this point, see Hammond, "Directives for the Occupation of Germany," pp. 370–71; and Penrose, *Economic Planning for Peace,* p. 253.

memorandum he and Churchill had initialed at Quebec, F.D.R. was startled, admitting that he had approved the document without much thought. The whole furor had resulted from inaccurate newspaper reporting, Roosevelt misleadingly asserted on October 9; "there is obviously no 'idea of turning [the] German economy upside down and expecting it to work.' " The President's major campaign speech on foreign policy, delivered in New York on October 21, took a noticeably moderate position on the postwar treatment of Germany. Early in November, F.D.R. allowed State Department officials to draft a letter for him arguing that "German productive skill and experience should be utilized for the general economic welfare of Europe and the world" as long as this did not threaten peace.[43]

Morgenthau's plan for the "pastoralization" of Germany is understandable as a reflection of irrational wartime hatred for a cruel and stubborn enemy. Nor is it surprising that many government officials, not wanting to appear "soft" on Germany, at first supported the plan.[44] Upon reflection, however, the impractical and inhumane aspects of the proposal quickly became clear, causing support for it within the Roosevelt Administration to crumble even before unwanted publicity brought about the President's disavowal. What is surprising is that the spirit of the Morgenthau Plan survived its official repudiation and went on to influence profoundly the occupation policies which the United States initially implemented inside Germany.

The Treasury Secretary's proposal appealed to lower-echelon War Department officials as a means of simplifying the task of military government. Morgenthau's plan appeared just as Army authorities had begun to worry about being stuck with responsibility for reviving the German economy, which seemed likely to collapse completely before V-E Day. By asserting that economic chaos in Germany was not inconsistent with American objectives, Morgenthau gave the Army a convenient excuse for avoiding this burden, which threatened to ensnarl military government officials in a tangle of distasteful nonmilitary complications.

[43] Roosevelt to Hull, September 29, 1944, *FR: Yalta,* p. 155; Stimson Diary, October 3, 1944, quoted in Stimson and Bundy, *On Active Service,* p. 581; Roosevelt to Pierre Jay, October 9, 1944, Roosevelt MSS, OF 198-A; speech to the Foreign Policy Association, October 21, 1944, *FDR: Public Papers,* XIII, 352–53; Roosevelt to Nicholas Murray Butler, November 11, 1944, Roosevelt MSS, PPF 445.

[44] On these points, see Clark, "Conflicts over Planning at Staff Headquarters," pp. 212–13; and Snell, *Dilemma over Germany,* p. 13.

Roosevelt's blast at the SHAEF handbook, provoked by Morgenthau, had come just as the Army itself was moving toward repudiating the ideas contained in that document. The ex-civilians in SHAEF's German "country unit" had failed to reflect the concern of professional officers within SHAEF and the War Department to insulate military government from political and economic complications. Accordingly, Civil Affairs Division representatives attached to SHAEF, upon hearing of Roosevelt's complaint, had gladly ordered fundamental modifications to bring the handbook into line with Morgenthau's position: Occupation authorities would make no effort to rehabilitate the German economy beyond what was necessary for military purposes. They would import and distribute no relief supplies except where absolutely necessary to prevent disease and disorder. They would carry out a rigorous program to purge former Nazis from German governmental positions. Finally, they would treat Germany as a defeated, not a liberated, country.[45]

Simultaneously, the impending collapse of Germany had convinced Washington officials that General Eisenhower needed a new directive on the administration of military government after V-E Day. An existing directive, issued by the Combined Chiefs of Staff in April, 1944, applied only to German territory occupied before the official surrender. Hopes were not high that the EAC could agree on tripartite postwar occupation policy in the near future. Hence, representatives from the State, War, and Treasury departments decided early in September to begin drafting an interim directive on Germany which Eisenhower could use from the end of the fighting until the Allies finished working out long-range occupation policies.[46]

Morgenthau's influence significantly affected the preparation of this document, which was completed on September 23, after the Treasury Secretary's trip to Quebec but before news of his plan had leaked to the press. The interim directive began by instructing Eisenhower to take actions only "of short term and military character, in order not to prejudice whatever ultimate policies may be later determined upon." This nod

[45] SHAEF Civil Affairs Division order of September 15, 1944, cited in Pogue, *Supreme Command,* p. 356. See also Hammond, "Directives for the Occupation of Germany," p. 356. For the conflict between ex-civilians and military professionals inside SHAEF, see Clark, "Conflicts over Planning at Staff Headquarters," pp. 214–20.

[46] Hammond, "Directives for the Occupation of Germany," pp. 328–29, 371.

to War Department sensibilities out of the way, the directive then went on to make policy with a vengeance, largely in accord with Treasury Department wishes. Like the revised handbook, it emphasized treating Germany as a defeated, not a liberated, nation. American military authorities would do nothing to rehabilitate the German economy except to avoid disease or disorder that might threaten occupation forces. German officials would retain primary responsibility for the economy's functioning. But the directive also called for an elaborate "denazification" program, including the arrest of all Nazis and Nazi sympathizers, down to and including local party and government authorities. Since most German officials were Nazis, this meant, as State Department representatives pointed out, a policy of "planned chaos." The War Department accepted the Treasury's suggestions, however, and State, demoralized by the Morgenthau affair, went along. The Joint Chiefs of Staff cleared the interim directive in record time—one day—assigning it in the process the file number by which it became known: JCS 1067.[47]

In the light of Stimson's determined opposition to the Morgenthau Plan, the War Department's decision to approve the document seems puzzling. But in this case, Stimson's views failed to reflect the position of his own department. Assistant Secretary of War McCloy, who represented the Army during the drafting of JCS 1067, placed primary emphasis on obtaining some kind of directive for Eisenhower, regardless of its content. A German collapse in 1944 still seemed possible, and Eisenhower urgently needed instructions. Furthermore, Civil Affairs Division officers both in Washington and at SHAEF saw in Morgenthau's doctrine of "planned chaos" a means of avoiding the involvement with civil affairs which military government planners had long dreaded. Finally, as a unilateral order from the Joint Chiefs to the commander of the United States zone in Germany, JCS 1067 had the additional advantage of bypassing the tripartite Control Council due to be set up in Berlin, thus increasing the authority of American military government officials. Eisenhower was duly grateful. "I want you to know how much I appreciate your efforts," he wrote McCloy early in November, "to protect us

[47] "Directive to SCAEF Regarding the Military Government of Germany in the Period Immediately Following the Cessation of Organized Resistance (Post-Defeat)," September 22, 1944, *FR: Yalta*, pp. 143–54. See also Hammond, "Directives for the Occupation of Germany," pp. 371–77, 390–91.

from a complex system of advisers which would only add to the difficulties of a straight forward problem of military government." [48]

"Military necessity" thus finally forced the War Department to define its position on the occupation of Germany. This gave the State Department little comfort, however, for JCS 1067, if put into effect for even a brief period of time, seemed likely to undermine the department's longrange objectives in that country. The interim directive to Eisenhower reflected too much of the spirit of the Morgenthau Plan. By forbidding military government officials from rehabilitating the economy beyond the point necessary to safeguard American troops, JCS 1067 would preclude attainment of a "tolerable" standard of living for the German people, one of the major prerequisites, in the State Department's view, for the emergence of democratic institutions inside Germany. By emphasizing the autonomy of the zonal commander, the directive also threatened to detract from the authority of the Allied Control Council in Berlin, thus making tripartite agreement on occupation policies more difficult to achieve. At the same time, however, the interim directive had been cleared by the Joint Chiefs of Staff, an advantage long-suffering State Department officials were not inclined to take lightly. Hence, early in November, they hit on the strategy of proposing JCS 1067 to the EAC as a tripartite policy for Germany, but only after revising it thoroughly to eliminate as many traces as possible of the Morgenthau Plan. [49]

Acting Secretary of State Stettinius warned President Roosevelt on November 11 that the British and the Russians would never accept Morgenthau's tactic of "planned chaos." Stressing the importance of tripartite cooperation in Germany, Stettinius recommended changing JCS

[48] Penrose, *Economic Planning for Peace,* p. 271; Hammond, "Directives for the Occupation of Germany," pp. 401–2; Dorn, "Debate over American Occupation Policy," pp. 492, 494–95; Coles and Weinberg, *Civil Affairs,* pp. 139–41; Clark, "Conflicts over Planning at Staff Headquarters," pp. 230–31; Eisenhower to McCloy, November 1, 1944, *Eisenhower Papers,* IV, 2269. McCloy later asserted that the War Department approved JCS 1067 with the expectation that the American zonal commander would modify its unrealistic provisions in the process of applying it. (Dorn, "Debate over American Occupation Policy," p. 501.) JCS 1067 had originally been planned as an Anglo-American directive, but the British Chiefs of Staff never approved it. (Hammond, "Directives for the Occupation of Germany," pp. 376–77.)

[49] *FR: 1944,* 407–8, 410–11; Hammond, "Directives for the Occupation of Germany," pp. 393, 397–400. See also Fainsod, "Development of American Military Government Policy," p. 34; and Clark, "Conflicts over Planning at Staff Headquarters," pp. 230–31.

1067 to allow occupation authorities to take "all possible steps in the initial phases of occupation to prevent development of a chaotically unmanageable economic situation." Roosevelt at first indicated sympathy for this point of view, but after consulting Morgenthau asked the State Department to redraft its suggestion. Further efforts by department officials to elicit a firm statement of policy from the White House proved fruitless.[50]

Attempts by State Department representatives to win War and Treasury support for the changes they wanted in JCS 1067 turned out to be equally frustrating. James W. Riddleberger, chief of the Division of Central European Affairs, complained in December that War Department negotiators "were obviously under categorical instructions to adhere as closely as possible to the original" for fear of offending the Treasury. As a result, little could be done to the political section of the document except to "improve the arrangement, the phrasing and the German." Emile Despres, one of the department's German experts, later noted how War and Treasury officials had come to share a common interest in a "limited liability" concept of military government which would preclude assuming responsibility for operation of the German economy:

The War Department favors this limited definition of the Army's tasks because (1) they favor a simple, clear-cut military occupation, (2) they wish, by limiting the task, to minimize the need for consultation and negotiation among the commanders of the several zones of occupation, and (3) they wish to keep the job within the capabilities of the occupation forces. The Treasury supports the doctrine of limited liability because (1) they consider that extreme disruption in Germany is not in conflict with Allied interests, and (2) acceptance of any responsibility for the minimum functioning of the German economy would cause us to make compromises with respect to elimination of Nazis.[51]

The State Department therefore failed in its first attempt to reconcile the Army's short-range plans for military government with its own long-range objective of transforming Germany into a democracy.

[50] Stettinius to Roosevelt, November 11, 1944, *FR: 1944,* I, 398–403; Leo Pasvolsky memorandum, Stettinius-Roosevelt conversation, November 15, 1944, *ibid.,* pp. 409–10; Blum, *Morgenthau Diaries: Years of War,* pp. 390–93.

[51] Riddleberger to James C. Dunn and H. Freeman Matthews, December 14, 1944, *FR: 1944,* I, 420; Despres to William L. Clayton and Edward S. Mason, February 15, 1945, *FR: 1945,* III, 412–13. See also Dorn, "Debate over American Occupation Policy in Germany," pp. 487, 498–500.

IV

The State Department did regain some influence over German policy as a whole, however, as President Roosevelt began preparations for the second Big Three meeting early in 1945. F.D.R.'s embarrassment over publication of the Morgenthau Plan had weakened the Treasury Secretary's position, despite the fact that Roosevelt, as he told State Department officials in November, was still "determined to be tough with Germany." Formation in December of the State-War-Navy Coordinating Committee, composed of assistant secretaries from each department, did much to improve civil-military consultation on major policy questions. Communication between the President and the State Department increased substantially after Stettinius became secretary of state upon Hull's retirement late in November, and, at the request of Harry Hopkins, appointed Charles E. Bohlen as special liaison officer to the White House. Significantly Roosevelt invited Stettinius, but not Morgenthau, to accompany him to Yalta to meet Churchill and Stalin.[52]

The State Department's briefing book papers on Germany, prepared for the President's use at Yalta, stressed the importance of preventing each occupying power from following unilateral policies, even if this meant "curtailing to some degree the freedom of action of the commander of the United States Zone." Tripartite agreement on centralized administration would ensure that the industrialized parts of Germany under Anglo-American control would receive badly needed food shipments from the predominantly agricultural Soviet Zone. Furthermore, the department added cautiously, "establishment of a comprehensive military government would prevent the equally undesirable development of the importation into Germany of a substantially ready-made provisional government perhaps recognized by and functioning under special

[52] Blum, *Morgenthau Diaries: Years of War*, pp. 382–83; Pasvolsky memorandum, Roosevelt-Stettinius conversation, November 15, 1944, *FR: Yalta*, p. 172; Snell, *Dilemma over Germany*, pp. 116–17; Stettinius, *Roosevelt and the Russians*, pp. 29–31. On the development of the State-War-Navy Coordinating Committee, see *FR: 1944*, I, 1466–70; Ray S. Cline, *Washington Command Post*, pp. 322–27; and Ernest R. May, "The Development of Political-Military Consultation in the United States," *Political Science Quarterly*, LXX (June, 1955), 161–80.

foreign auspices." In the economic field, the department called for reducing, but not destroying, the German industrial plant in order to prevent rearmament and provide reparations. Efforts should be directed toward the eventual "assimilation—on a basis of equality—of a reformed, peaceful and economically non-aggressive Germany into a liberal system of world trade." Finally, in economics as in other areas, the Big Three should endeavor to reach agreements before the termination of hostilities, so as to "minimize the danger of new European rivalries." [53]

On the sensitive issue of reparations a firm resolve not to repeat past mistakes shaped the State Department's position. "We were most anxious," Stettinius later recalled, "to avoid the disastrous experience of reparations after World War I." To prevent a recurrence of the currency transfer problems which had plagued the Allies in the interwar period, the department advocated having Germany make payments in kind—goods and services—rather than in money. A fixed time limit—preferably five but not more than ten years—should govern how long Germany would have to pay. The department advised against stating Germany's reparations obligation in terms of a specific sum of money, because no one knew what the German capacity to pay would be at the end of the war. Such an approach would also "avoid difficulties with public opinion in the Allied countries, which is likely to regard any given amount of reparation as inadequate." Finally, it should be made clear to all concerned that, unlike its policy in the 1920s, "the U.S. will not finance the transfer of reparation either directly by extending loans or credits to Germany, or indirectly by assuming a burden of supplying at its own expense essential goods or equipment to Germany." President Roosevelt strongly supported these recommendations, explaining to Admiral Leahy on the way to Yalta that he was determined to "avoid the pitfalls that had made the World War I reparations actually a burden on America." [54]

[53] Yalta briefing book papers, "The Treatment of Germany" and "Economic Policies Toward Germany," *FR: Yalta,* pp. 178–93. On Roosevelt's use of these documents, see the conflicting accounts in Stettinius, *Roosevelt and the Russians,* p. 30; James F. Byrnes, *Speaking Frankly,* p. 23; and Leahy, *I Was There,* p. 343.

[54] Stettinius, *Roosevelt and the Russians,* p. 299; Yalta briefing book paper, "Reparation and Restitution Policy Toward Germany," January 16, 1945, *FR: Yalta,* pp. 194–97; Leahy, *I Was There,* p. 343. For the influence of the post-World War I experience on planning reparations policy, see Penrose, *Economic Planning for Peace,*

At Yalta, the Russians agreed to a ten-year time limit and reparations in kind, to be taken partly by the physical removal of heavy industrial equipment, partly by seizing production from surviving facilities. The Soviet proposal diverged from the Anglo-American position, however, in two important respects: The Russians called for tripartite agreement on a fixed monetary sum to be taken out of Germany, suggesting the figure of $20 billion, of which half would go to the USSR. They also assigned first priority to the extraction of reparations, making no firm provisions for preventing starvation or maintaining the German standard of living. The Russians never advocated going as far as Morgenthau's plan for the indiscriminate destruction of German industry—indeed the Soviets several times expressed opposition to the Treasury's scheme, which would have precluded reparations from current production—but their proposals nonetheless raised fears among the British and Americans of mass starvation in the industrialized but food-poor Western zones. The United States had lent Germany "over ten billion dollars" after World War I, Roosevelt pointed out. This time it would not repeat the mistake. Germany should pay reparations, but not to the point of causing economic chaos, for he "did not wish to contemplate the necessity of helping the Germans to keep from starving." If one wanted a horse to pull a wagon, Churchill remonstrated, one had at least to give it fodder. True enough, Stalin replied, "but care should be taken to see that the horse did not turn around and kick you." [55]

The conflict over reparations proved too deep to resolve at Yalta, so

pp. 218–19; Jacob Viner, "German Reparations Once More," *Foreign Affairs,* XXI (July, 1943), 659–73; "What Should Germany Pay?" *Fortune,* XXIX (February, 1944), 134–38, 231; and William Diebold, Jr., "What Shall Germany Pay? The New Reparations Problem," in the Council on Foreign Relations series, "American Interests in the War and the Peace," April, 1944. For an illuminating discussion of the whole reparations issue, written from a revisionist point of view, see Bruce Kuklick, "The Division of Germany and American Policy on Reparations," *Western Political Quarterly,* XXIII (June, 1970), 276–93.

[55] Bohlen minutes, Second Plenary Meeting, February 5, 1944, *FR: Yalta,* pp. 620–21. See also the Soviet proposal, "Basic Principles of Exaction of Reparations from Germany," submitted to the foreign ministers on February 7, 1945, *ibid.,* p. 707. A. A. Sobolev, vice-chairman of the Russian delegation to the Dumbarton Oaks Conference, had told Leo Pasvolsky in September, 1944, that he was "certain that Mr. Morgenthau's type of thinking was not acceptable to the Soviet Government." (Pasvolsky memorandum of conversation with Sobolev, September 28, 1944, Hull MSS, Box 61, Folder 250.) See also Blum, *Morgenthau Diaries: Years of War,* pp. 386, 398–99; Penrose, *Economic Planning for Peace,* pp. 281–82; and Kolko, *The Politics of War,* pp. 324, 326–27.

the Big Three simply referred it to a new tripartite commission, which would hold meetings in Moscow. The Americans reluctantly agreed to accept the Soviet figure of $20 billion as a "basis for negotiations," but the British refused even to go this far. The other Yalta decisions on Germany were equally vague: the three heads of government postponed until later final settlement of the issues of dismemberment, war criminals, and the Polish-German border. The only definite agreement on Germany which Roosevelt, Churchill, and Stalin reached was their decision to give France an occupation zone and a seat on the Allied Control Council.[56]

State Department officials were pleased, however, with the extent to which Roosevelt had followed their advice at Yalta. The President's firm stand on reparations seemed to indicate that he had abandoned, once and for all, Morgenthau's policy of "planned chaos" in Germany. Upon his return to Washington, Roosevelt instructed Secretary of State Stettinius to assume responsibility for implementing the conference decisions.[57] Stettinius was attending an inter-American meeting in Mexico City at the time, but his subordinates in the department, pleasantly surprised by this unaccustomed grant of authority, quickly seized the opportunity to launch a second effort to purge all traces of the Morgenthau Plan from JCS 1067.

Acting Secretary of State Joseph C. Grew instructed Ambassador Winant not to present the revised version of that document to the European Advisory Commission. Meanwhile department officials, working under the direction of Assistant Secretary of State James C. Dunn, rapidly prepared a completely new draft directive, incorporating provisions which the State Department had sought all along. This document explicitly deemphasized the autonomy of zonal commanders, endorsed a moderate denazification policy, and called for a "substantial degree of centralized financial and economic control" from the now quadripartite Control Council. Stettinius approved the new directive upon his return to Washington on March 10, and sent it to the White House. To the delight of the State Department, Roosevelt returned it several days later with the marginal notation: "OK, FDR." [58]

[56] Yalta Conference protocol, February 11, 1945, *FR: Yalta,* pp. 978–80.

[57] Roosevelt to Stettinius, February 28, 1945, *FR: 1945,* III, 433.

[58] Grew to Winant, February 28, 1945, cited in Hammond, "Directives for the Occupation of Germany," p. 415; Stettinius to Roosevelt, March 10, 1945, enclosing "Draft Directive for the Treatment of Germany," *FR: 1945,* III, 433–38. Apparently a

The State Department's initiative caused consternation in both the Pentagon and the Treasury, although for different reasons. Stimson and McCloy disliked the new directive's emphasis on central administration from the Control Council in Berlin. The Secretary of War complained on March 15 that "we were not going to get a four-headed body comprising three great nations [presumably France did not qualify in this respect] to achieve uniformity in the application of details of policy." Morgenthau charged heatedly that the new policy appeared to mean "that the power of the German Empire would be continued and reconstructed." Later the Treasury Secretary cornered Stettinius and extracted from the Secretary of State the admission that subordinates had handed him the new draft directive upon his return from Mexico, that he had been tired, and that he "really didn't know what was in it." State Department officials had gone off "on a frolic of their own," McCloy complained to Morgenthau on the 17th; "we've got a right to sulk." Morgenthau agreed: "It's damnable, an outrage." On March 20, the Treasury Secretary took Roosevelt a memorandum arguing that the State Department document "goes absolutely contrary to your views," and citing specific departures from JCS 1067. Roosevelt, obviously in poor health, admitted to Morgenthau that he did not remember signing the State Department's directive, and wanted to rescind it.[59]

Now consternation reigned in the State Department. Undersecretary of State Grew found the President's absent-mindedness "amazing." Stettinius, from his farm in Virginia, told his associates that if he were in Washington he was sure he could jog the President's memory. But on March 22, Roosevelt complained that he had been "sold a bill of goods" and informed the State Department that the March 10 document would

report by an official of the Foreign Economic Administration, James A. Perkins, calling for complete revision of JCS 1067, also influenced the State Department initiative. The conclusion of Perkins' report, dated March 3, 1945, is quoted in Hammond, "Directives for the Occupation of Germany," pp. 414–15.

[59] Minutes, Stettinius-Stimson-Morgenthau meeting, March 15, 1945, *FR: 1945,* III, 454–55; Blum, *Morgenthau Diaries: Years of War,* pp. 403–8. See also Hammond, "Directives for the Occupation of Germany," pp. 418–20. A memorandum prepared on March 16, 1945, by an unidentified State Department official pointed out: "The Treasury and War Departments advocate the same policy for different reasons: Treasury wants chaos; War wants decentralization and complete authority for its zone commander." (*FR: 1945,* III, 457.)

have to be rewritten. The following day representatives from the State, War, and Treasury departments met and agreed on a new policy statement, making minor concessions to the State Department position but for the most part reasserting the philosophy of JCS 1067. Roosevelt approved the document on the same day, marking it: "OK, FDR., superseding memo of March 10, 1945." [60]

JCS 1067 still needed further revision before it could be put into effect, a process which took until May, 1945. Harry S. Truman, who had become President upon Roosevelt's death in April, approved the final version on May 11, 1945, three days after Germany's surrender. Still very much a Treasury document, it called for broad denazification policies but left responsibility for the German economy for the most part up to the Germans. The War Department, seeking to minimize the political and economic responsibilities of the American zonal commander, had firmly resisted State Department attempts to modify these provisions. "This is a big day for the Treasury," Morgenthau noted in his diary after Truman had signed the directive. "[I] hope somebody doesn't recognize it as the Morgenthau Plan." [61]

Hence, by the time of Germany's surrender, the United States still had not decided between repression and rehabilitation as the best way to prevent future aggression. The American plan on reparations, endorsed by Roosevelt at Yalta, followed the State Department's desire to maintain a tolerable standard of living inside Germany, both as a means of encouraging the emergence of democratic institutions there, and in hopes of promoting the economic revival of Europe. American occupation policy, however, still reflected the Treasury's call for a peace of vengeance, not because of the intrinsic merit of this idea, which Roosevelt had repudiated, but because the Army simply considered it more convenient than the State Department's program. Neither side had made any serious attempt to develop its plans for Germany in the light of possible difficulties with the Soviet Union. Events of the spring of 1945

[60] Blum, *Morgenthau Diaries: Years of War,* pp. 407, 410–12; Grew memorandum of telephone conversation with Stettinius, March 22, 1945, *FR: 1945,* III, 469–70; "Memorandum Regarding American Policy for the Treatment of Germany," March 23, 1945, *ibid.,* pp. 471–73.

[61] Blum, *Morgenthau Diaries: Years of War,* p. 460. For the final revisions of JCS 1067, see Hammond, "Directives for the Occupation of Germany," pp. 422–27.

made it impossible to ignore the problem of Russia any longer, however, and would by the time of the next Big Three meeting in July force a badly needed rationalization of American policy on the postwar treatment of Germany.

5

※⟨⟨⟨※

Security versus Self-Determination: The Problem of Eastern Europe

In contrast to their confusion over Germany, Washington officials knew what they wanted in Eastern Europe: maximum possible self-determination for the people of that region without impairing the unity of the Grand Alliance. Unfortunately these two goals—both fundamental elements in the American program for preventing future wars—conflicted with each other. Stalin had made it clear since the summer of 1941 that he would not tolerate hostile states along his western border, yet in most of Eastern Europe free elections, if held, would produce governments unfriendly to Moscow.[1] The existence of two clear objectives thus did not simplify the task of Roosevelt and his advisers, because both could not be attained. A choice would have to be made, in the light of American interests, between self-determination for Eastern Europe and cooperation with the Soviet Union.

With characteristic optimism, Roosevelt hoped he could avoid making this decision. Throughout the war he worked to convince the East Europeans that they had nothing to fear from Russia and that they could afford to choose governments acceptable to Moscow. Simultaneously he sought to persuade Stalin that the defeat and disarmament of Germany, together with maintenance of big-power unity into the postwar period,

[1] McNeill, *America, Britain, and Russia*, p. 535.

would do more to guarantee Soviet security than would territorial gains and spheres of influence in Eastern Europe. If a choice became inevitable, however, Roosevelt knew in which direction he would move. Self-determination he had always regarded as an ideal to be striven for, but not practically attainable in all situations.[2] Cooperation with the Soviet Union, though, was essential both to win the war and to keep the peace after victory. By the end of 1943, the President had cautiously indicated to the Russians that they could count on a free hand in Eastern Europe.

At the same time, however, the President hoped that Stalin would be discreet, for any appearance of abandoning self-determination would cause F.D.R. serious political problems inside the United States. Several million Polish-Americans might defect from the Democratic Party in 1944, endangering Roosevelt's chances for reelection. Even more important, any flagrant violations of the Atlantic Charter might give critics of international organization sufficient ammunition to kill American participation in the United Nations, just as Wilson's departures from the Fourteen Points a quarter-century earlier had contributed to the Senate's rejection of the League of Nations. For these reasons, Roosevelt felt that he could not publicly back away from his promises of a peace settlement which would allow the people of Europe to determine their own future, even though he knew that the likelihood of this happening in countries bordering Russia was small.

But by failing to prepare the American people for Stalin's demands in Eastern Europe, Roosevelt inadvertently undermined the domestic consensus necessary for his postwar policy of cooperation with the Soviet Union. Having been led by the President's own rhetoric to expect self-determination everywhere, Americans reacted angrily when the Soviet Union proceeded to extract territorial concessions from its neighbors, and to impose spheres of influence on them. Interpreting these actions as first steps in a renewed bid for world revolution, Americans, lessons of the past firmly in mind, gradually came to regard Stalin as an aggressor with unlimited ambitions who, like Hitler, would have to be resisted and contained.

[2] Range, *Roosevelt's World Order*, pp. 33–34; Feis, *Churchill, Roosevelt, Stalin*, p. 22.

I

When the second front did not materialize as promised in 1942, Stalin felt free to reassert his territorial claims, not only to the Baltic States and portions of Finland and Rumania, but to eastern Poland as well. Even more ominously, the Russians broke diplomatic relations with the Polish government-in-exile in London in April, 1943, after the Poles had asked the International Red Cross to investigate German charges that the Russians had massacred several thousand Polish officers at Katyn Woods in 1940.[3] The Red Army's massive victory at Stalingrad early in 1943 had drastically shifted the military balance on the eastern front in favor of the Russians, making it apparent that Stalin soon would be in a position to impose his will on Eastern Europe. Roosevelt gradually came to realize, as the British had before him, that he would have to work out some kind of accommodation with the Russians on this matter while the war was still on.

When Anthony Eden came to Washington in March of 1943, he found the President far more willing to accept Soviet territorial demands than he had been a year earlier. Roosevelt still thought that Russian absorption of the Baltic States would "meet with a good deal of resistance" in the United States, and hoped the Kremlin might make its action more palatable by holding plebiscites. But, "realistically, the Russian armies would be in the Baltic States at the time of the downfall of Germany and none of us can force them to get out." The President took a similar position on Poland:

The big powers would have to decide what Poland should have and . . . he, the President, did not intend to go to the Peace Conference and bargain with Poland or the other small states; as far as Poland is concerned, the important thing is to set it up in a way that will help maintain the peace of the world.

Both Eden and Roosevelt agreed, in addition, that Stalin would want, and should get, boundary concessions from Finland and Rumania.[4]

[3] On this matter, see *FR: 1943*, III, 323–27, 374–93.

[4] Harry Hopkins memorandum of Roosevelt-Eden conversation, March 15, 1943, *FR: 1943*, III, 13–18. See also *ibid.*, pp. 34–36; and Eden, *The Reckoning*, pp.

The President's position on Eastern Europe changed little in the months between Eden's visit and Roosevelt's first meeting with Stalin at Teheran. In a magazine interview published in April, F.D.R. expressed the hope that Stalin's territorial claims could be satisfied "through a combination of plebiscite and trusteeship techniques" without violating the Atlantic Charter. Three months later, he frankly warned Polish ambassador Jan Ciechanowski that the United States would not fight Stalin to prevent him from taking eastern Poland and the Baltic States. In September, the President told Archbishop Francis Spellman that there would be no point in opposing Stalin's territorial demands because the Russian leader had the power to take these areas, regardless of what Britain and the United States did. It would be better to yield to Stalin's requests gracefully. At about the same time, Roosevelt repeated this conclusion to W. Averell Harriman, his new ambassador in Moscow, but added that he would try to keep Stalin from going too far by stressing the unfavorable world reaction this would provoke, by agreeing to dismember Germany in hopes of making the Russians feel more secure, and by offering American economic assistance in repairing Soviet war damage. Shortly after this, the President informed Secretary of State Hull that he intended to appeal to Stalin "on the grounds of high morality." Neither England nor the United States would fight to save the Baltic States, he would tell Stalin, but Russia would improve its standing in the eyes of the world if it would hold plebiscites in the territories it planned to take over.[5]

Roosevelt's advisers generally agreed that the United States could do little to prevent Stalin from taking the territory he wanted. Joseph E. Davies reported after a trip to Moscow in the summer of 1943 that the Russians "are going to take back what they consider was wrongfully taken from them." John D. Hickerson, assistant chief of the State Department's Division of European Affairs, warned that any attempt to reestablish the boundaries of September 1, 1939, in Eastern Europe would be "sheer military fantasy." Professor Isaiah Bowman of Johns

431–32. Eden says that Roosevelt mentioned favorably the Curzon line as the eastern boundary of Poland, but there is no indication of this in the American records.

[5] Forrest Davis, "Roosevelt's World Blueprint," pp. 20 ff.; Ciechanowski, *Defeat in Victory*, p. 186; Gannon, *The Cardinal Spellman Story*, p. 223; Feis, *Churchill, Roosevelt, Stalin*, pp. 174–75; Hull, *Memoirs*, II, 1266. On the authenticity of the Davis article as an expression of Roosevelt's views, see Divine, *Second Chance*, pp. 114–15.

Hopkins University, once a member of Woodrow Wilson's "Inquiry" and now on the State Department's Advisory Committee on Postwar Foreign Policy, favored making the Poles return some of the land they had taken when they "had Russia down" after World War I. Soviet incorporation of the Baltic States would shock American opinion, Bowman felt, but there was little the United States could do about it short of going to war with Russia. Admiral William D. Leahy, as Chief of Staff to the Commander in Chief Roosevelt's most influential military adviser, thought it "inconceivable" that Stalin would allow Poland and the Baltic States to regain their independent status after the war. By employing its superior military power and by threatening to make a separate peace with Germany, Russia could, Leahy thought, keep the United States and Britain from interfering.[6]

Early in November, Ambassador Harriman sent Roosevelt an informed estimate of Soviet intentions in Eastern Europe, based on information he had picked up during the Moscow Conference of Foreign Ministers in October. The Russians would insist strongly on their 1941 frontiers, Harriman wrote. They believed that the British had already agreed to these boundaries, and that American failure to discuss the issue up to this point indicated that Washington had no serious objections. "The problem of Poland is even tougher than we believed." The Russians would not content themselves simply with territorial gains at the expense of Poland, but would insist on having a "friendly" government installed in Warsaw. They regarded the Polish government-in-exile in London as "hostile, and therefore completely unacceptable to them." Above all, the Soviets were determined to have nothing resembling the old "cordon sanitaire" in Eastern Europe.[7]

There was no real ambiguity about Stalin's objectives in Eastern Europe, therefore, when Roosevelt embarked for Teheran late in November, 1943. Nor was there much doubt as to what the American response would be. The President had worried over this matter for almost two years, and had for some time realized that the United States and Great

[6] Davies to Roosevelt, May 29, 1943, Roosevelt MSS, PSF 18: "Russia"; Hickerson to Hull, August 10, 1943, Department of State records, 840.50/2521; Bowman to Hull, September 27, 1943, Hull MSS, Box 52, Folder 159; Leahy, *I Was There*, p. 185.

[7] Harriman to Roosevelt, November 4, 1943, *FR: Tehran*, p. 154.

Britain lacked the power to deny Stalin what he wanted. Roosevelt would use his influence to persuade Stalin to be magnanimous, while at the same time working to convince the East Europeans that their own best interests lay in cooperation with the Soviet Union. But under no circumstances would the United States fight for self-determination in Eastern Europe. The one question still unsettled was how to present this policy in the United States as anything other than a violation of the Atlantic Charter. Charles E. Bohlen saw the dilemma clearly. The basic underlying difficulty in Soviet-American relations, he wrote in the fall of 1943, would be convincing the American people to abandon their traditional aversion to power politics in order to secure cooperation with the Soviet Union in the postwar world.[8]

With similar considerations in mind F.D.R., after the Teheran Conference had been under way for several days, invited Stalin to his quarters for a private discussion relating to American politics. An election was coming up in 1944, Roosevelt said, and while he did not want to run again, he might have to if the war was still on. The President reminded Stalin that there were six or seven million Polish-Americans in the United States, and that "as a practical man he did not wish to lose their vote." He, personally, agreed with Stalin that the Russo-Polish border should be moved to the west and that the Poles should obtain territorial compensation at the expense of Germany. He hoped, however, Stalin would understand that he could not, for political reasons, "publicly take part in any such arrangement at the present time." Stalin replied, reassuringly, that "now [that] the President [had] explained, he had understood."

Roosevelt went on to say that there were also a number of Lithuanians, Latvians, and Estonians in the United States. While he himself realized that these states had once been part of Russia, and while the American government certainly did not intend to go to war to prevent the Russians from reoccupying them, "the big issue in the United States, insofar as public opinion went, would be the question of referendum and the right of self-determination." Roosevelt expressed his personal confidence that inhabitants of the Baltic States would, in any future plebiscite, cheerfully ratify their own incorporation into the Soviet Union. Stalin pointed out that the Baltic States had enjoyed little autonomy

[8] Bohlen to James C. Dunn, September 7, 1943, Hull MSS, Box 52, Folder 159.

under Nicholas II, "who had been an ally of Great Britain and the United States," and that no one had brought up public opinion at that time. The Soviet leader could not quite understand why the question was being raised now. Roosevelt replied that "the truth of the matter was that the public neither knew nor understood." To which Stalin responded: "They should be informed and some propaganda work should be done." Roosevelt now became more direct, telling Stalin that "it would be helpful for him [Roosevelt] personally if some public declaration in regard to the future elections . . . could be made." Stalin answered that there would be "plenty of opportunities for such an expression of the will of the people." [9]

It is impossible to know precisely what Stalin made of this peculiar conversation, which represented Roosevelt's only significant statement on the problem of Eastern Europe at Teheran. The President did make it clear that the United States would not oppose the territorial changes Stalin wanted, but that the Russian leader must not expect public acknowledgment of this until after the 1944 campaign. Any promise of elections or plebiscites which Stalin might give to make these changes more acceptable to the American people would be appreciated. Roosevelt said nothing about guaranteeing self-determination in the rest of Eastern Europe, but it seems likely that Stalin emerged from this talk convinced that the President's main concern would be to present Russian policy to the American public in the most favorable light, not to secure literal compliance with the principles of the Atlantic Charter.

II

Polish-American concern over the fate of Eastern Europe was real enough. Congressmen with Polish-American constituencies had begun to worry over this issue long before the Teheran Conference. Representative John Dingell of Michigan had warned Roosevelt in August, 1943, that "we Americans are not sacrificing, fighting, and dying to make permanent and more powerful the Communistic Government of Russia and to make Joseph Stalin a dictator over the liberated countries of Europe."

[9] Bohlen notes, Roosevelt-Stalin conversation, December 1, 1943, *FR: Tehran*, pp. 594–95.

When Secretary of State Hull returned from the Moscow Foreign Ministers' Conference in November with no territorial guarantees for Eastern Europe, expressions of alarm intensified. Senator John A. Danaher of Connecticut reminded his colleagues that "there are literally thousands upon thousands of boys of Polish extraction who . . . are fighting all over the world in the firm belief that they are going to help restore the pre-war borders of the homeland of their parents." Senator Arthur H. Vandenberg of Michigan wrote the editor of a Detroit Polish-language newspaper that

> if the Atlantic Charter means *anything,* it *must* mean a new Poland when it says that there are to be "no territorial changes that do not accord with the freely expressed wishes of the peoples concerned"; and when it promises to "respect the right of all peoples to choose the form of Government under which they will live"; and when it asserts that "sovereign rights and self-Government are to be restored to those who have been forcibly deprived of them."

On November 16, ten members of the House of Representatives asked Hull to reassure Polish-Americans that the United States would continue to assist Poland and all other "freedom-loving nations." [10]

Polish diplomats in Washington viewed the Moscow declaration's silence on territorial questions with foreboding. Ambassador Jan Ciechanowski noted a strong atmosphere of private pessimism beneath the official optimism in government circles: "I actually met with expressions of sympathy and condolence on the part of numerous political friends." Another Polish official compared the Moscow declaration to a doughnut, with the hole representing the question of territory: "What can you do with the central question unsolved? It should have been a cookie." Such expressions of anxiety took on more ominous overtones when the Office of Strategic Services warned on November 10 that the Polish government-in-exile planned "to mobilize political feeling in the United States to back Polish claims against Soviet Russia." The report said that the Poles hoped to work among Polish-Americans, Catholics, and Middle Westerners, that they anticipated making use of anti-British sentiment

[10] Dingell to Roosevelt, August 19, 1943, Department of State records, 760C.61/2093; *Congressional Record,* November 1, 1943, p. 8929; Vandenberg to Frank Januszewski, November 6, 1943, Vandenberg MSS; congressmen to Hull, November 16, 1943, Department of State records, 740.0011 MOSCOW/278. See also Representative B. J. Monkiewicz to Roosevelt, August 18, 1943, *ibid.,* 760C.61/2096.

in the United States, and that they would not hesitate to seek help from "friendly" congressmen. The apparent objective of this campaign was to make it impossible for Roosevelt to "move in any serious way against the Polish interest." [11]

These developments alarmed Hull, who had always resented efforts by minority groups to influence foreign policy.[12] He warned Ciechanowski that Polish criticism of American diplomacy was assuming a "thoroughly unfriendly nature" and cabled Roosevelt, then on his way to Teheran, that the Poles were desperate and might engage in "unfortunate public outbursts." The Secretary of State assured the President that "we are making every effort here . . . to convince the Poles, official and unofficial, that they must take a calmer outlook and not prejudice their case by undue public agitation regarding our policies." [13]

Early in January, 1944, the Red Army crossed Russia's prewar border into what had been Poland. Several days later, the Soviet government issued a public statement calling for a "strong and friendly Poland," but insisting that "Ukrainian and White Russian" lands which had been part of Poland now become part of the Soviet Union. The Poles would receive compensation through the return "of the ancient Polish lands taken from Poland by the Germans." The proclamation further warned that the Polish government-in-exile in London had demonstrated an unwillingness to carry on friendly relations with the USSR, and implied that Moscow might sponsor a new and more sympathetic government in Warsaw.[14]

The State Department noted shortly thereafter that its mail on the

[11] Ciechanowski, *Defeat in Victory*, p. 228; *Newsweek*, XXII (November 15, 1943), 17; DeWitt C. Poole, Foreign Nationalities Branch, Office of Strategic Services, to Adolf A. Berle, November 10, 1943, Department of State records, 760C.61/2119.

[12] Hull, *Memoirs*, II, 1315. Hull complained bitterly against "interfering minorities" who, "aided by the improvement of methods for diffusing information and propaganda, have raised a voice and exerted a pressure in foreign affairs far out of proportion to their numbers. . . . On many occasions, when the international relations of our Government require the most delicate and careful handling . . . , some of these groups scatter poison or otherwise play havoc with them." (*Ibid.*, II, 1738.)

[13] Hull memorandum of conversation with Ciechanowski, November 19, 1943, *FR: 1943*, III, 484–85; Hull to Roosevelt, November 23, 1943, *FR: Tehran*, p. 384. Ciechanowski, in his account of the November 19 meeting, does not mention the Secretary of State's warnings against domestic Polish agitation. (*Defeat in Victory*, pp. 234–43.)

[14] Harriman to Hull, January 11, 1944, *FR: 1944*, III, 1218–20.

Polish question had increased sharply, as had petitions on the subject addressed to Congress. Most of this material came from individuals of Polish descent or from Polish-American organizations. On January 6, the chairman of the National Council of Americans of Polish Descent wrote to Roosevelt that American acquiescence in Russia's decision "to keep her share of the loot grabbed with Hitler" could only be interpreted as "a sign of approval and coresponsibility." Representative Joseph Mruk of New York warned Roosevelt one week later that if Russia absorbed eastern Poland the war would be "lost idealistically and morally—even before we have been able finally to win it militarily." Congressman John Lesinski of Michigan told a meeting of Polish-Americans in Detroit that if Stalin was allowed "to gobble up Poland" he would take all of Europe as well.[15]

In March, 1944, a group of Polish-American leaders decided to form a nationwide movement embracing every major Polish organization in the United States. Coordinating committees were established in Detroit, Chicago, New York, and other centers of Polish-American strength for the purpose of electing 4,000 delegates to a Polish-American congress, to be held in Buffalo at the end of May. Each delegate was to contribute $25.00 to support the congress' work. White House assistant David K. Niles, who wrote a lengthy report on the affair for Roosevelt, noted with professional admiration that the congress would "go down in history as the most colossal piece of organizational work. There is really something to learn from the Poles in the manner this congress was created."

The principal aim of the ostensibly nonpartisan congress was to marshal Polish-American opinion in opposition to any new partition of Poland. But Niles noted that the main organizers of the congress, Charles Rozmarek of Chicago, Frank Januszewski, publisher of the Detroit *Polish Daily News,* and Michael F. Wegrzynek, chairman of the National Council of Americans of Polish Descent, were all Republicans. Leaders of the congress received advice and support, though apparently not financial assistance, from the Polish government-in-exile, the American Cath-

15 "Public Attitudes on Foreign Policy," report no. 13, February 29, 1944, Department of State records, 711.00 PUBLIC ATTITUDES/7A; M. F. Wegrzynek to Roosevelt, January 6, 1944, printed in *Congressional Record,* 1944 appendix, p. A158; Mruk to Roosevelt, January 14, 1944, Roosevelt MSS, OF 463-A, Box 4; Lesinski speech of January 30, 1944, copy, *ibid.*

olic hierarchy, and several isolationist members of the United States Congress. At the congress' first meeting in Buffalo moderate groups prevented the passage of resolutions directly critical of the Roosevelt Administration. But Niles warned that there was "terrific resentment against the Administration" among leading Polish-Americans "which will eventually crystalize in some unfriendly form." [16]

The possible impact of Polish-American disaffection on the forthcoming election clearly worried Administration officials. As early as February, Oscar Cox had advised Harry Hopkins that Polish-Americans might desert the Democratic Party, and in the process "start enough of a rumpus to swing over other groups before November of 1944." During the spring the White House received thousands of printed postcards, all of them urging Roosevelt to oppose "the fourth partition of Poland." On May 3, Polish Constitution Day, some 140 congressmen inserted into the *Congressional Record* material on Poland, much of it furnished by Polish-American groups, calling for application of the Atlantic Charter to the Russo-Polish controversy. Assistant Secretary of State Breckinridge Long noted later that month that it would be difficult to solve the boundary dispute between Russia and Poland in such a way as to satisfy the Polish-Americans, who might well hold the balance of political power in states like Illinois, Ohio, New York, and Pennsylvania.[17]

Because of the sensitive political situation, propaganda activities of the Polish government-in-exile caused special anxiety in Washington. Joseph E. Davies complained that the London Poles were constantly distributing expensive propaganda booklets in the United States and that they "would readily pay thousands of dollars to throw a monkey-wrench into American public opinion against Russia." Isador Lubin, an aide to Harry Hopkins, noted with concern the appearance of several articles in the Detroit Polish-language press calling on Polish-Americans not to

[16] Memorandum by Niles, May 26, 1944, Roosevelt MSS, PSF: "Poland." See also Department of State, "Fortnightly Survey of American Opinion," No. 5, June 21, 1944; and Joseph A. Wytrwal, *America's Polish Heritage: A Social History of the Poles in America,* pp. 262–63. Niles later wrote to Grace Tully: "I think we sort of handled the Buffalo conference so that we pulled some of the fangs out of it." (Niles to Tully, June 6, 1944, Roosevelt MSS, PSF: "Poland.")

[17] Cox to Hopkins, February 7, 1944, Hopkins MSS, Box 324; postcards in Roosevelt MSS, OF 463, Box 1; Department of State, "Fortnightly Survey of American Opinion," No. 3, May 19, 1944; Long Diary, June 13, 1944, Israel, ed., *Long Diary,* p. 354.

contribute their "sweat" to lend-lease production for Russia. At Roosevelt's request Lubin submitted to him several pamphlets critical of American and British policy put out by the Polish Information Center which had, Lubin observed indignantly, received financial assistance from the American government. Concern over this matter was great enough to cause both Roosevelt and the State Department to warn Polish Prime Minister Stanislaw Mikolajczyk against holding public meetings with Polish-American groups when he visited the United States in June of 1944.[18]

During his conversations with Mikolajczyk, President Roosevelt repeatedly stressed the need for the London Poles to work out a reconciliation with the Soviet Union. There were five times as many Russians as Poles, the President said, "and let me tell you now, the British and the Americans have no intention of fighting Russia." Roosevelt observed that if he were in the position of the Poles, he would agree to territorial concessions and changes in the make-up of the Polish government. Stalin, he assured Mikolajczyk, had no intention of extinguishing Polish liberty, if for no other reason than that this would alienate American public opinion. The President urged the Polish prime minister to meet with Stalin personally, because "in this political year I cannot approach Stalin with a new initiative about Poland." [19]

The President's assurances to Mikolajczyk represented no change from his previous position. The Poles would have to accept territorial changes, but Roosevelt hoped the pressure of world opinion would moderate Soviet demands. Shortly before Mikolajczyk arrived in Washington, Roosevelt instructed Harriman to tell Stalin that the Polish problem "will be kept out of 'politics' " and to express the hope "that the Soviets would give the Poles 'a break.' " When Harriman conveyed this information to Molotov, the Russian foreign minister interrupted to ask whether Roose-

[18] Davies Journal, April 25, 1944, Davies MSS, Box 14; Lubin to Dean Acheson, April 3, 1944, Department of State records, 760C.61/2287; Lubin to Roosevelt, June 5, 1944, Roosevelt MSS, PSF: "Poland"; James C. Dunn to Edward R. Stettinius, Jr., May 24, 1944, *FR: 1944*, IV, 874; Bohlen memorandum of conversation with Ciechanowski, May 24, 1944, *ibid.*, III, 1272.

[19] The fullest account of the Roosevelt-Mikolajczyk conversations is in Ciechanowski, *Defeat in Victory*, but see also Mikolajczyk's record of the talks, in Edward J. Rozek, *Allied Wartime Diplomacy: The Pattern in Poland*, pp. 220–21; Stanislaw Mikolajczyk, *The Rape of Poland*, pp. 59–60; and Stettinius calendar notes, June 7, 1944, Stettinius MSS, Box 240.

velt's attitude was still the same as that expressed at Teheran. Harriman replied, "of course," and Molotov said that Stalin would be gratified to hear this news.[20]

The Russian leader made his own abortive effort to improve relations with Polish-Americans in the spring of 1944 when he personally invited the Reverend Stanislaus Orlemanski, an obscure parish priest from Springfield, Massachusetts, to visit the Soviet Union. Orlemanski's efforts in helping to organize the pro-Soviet Kosciusko Polish Patriotic League in the United States had apparently led Stalin to believe, with wild inaccuracy, that Orlemanski represented Polish-American opinion. The Massachusetts priest received a cordial welcome in Moscow, and enjoyed a two-hour talk with Stalin and Molotov. The Russian dictator promised Orlemanski that he would not interfere in Polish internal affairs after the war, that he would allow freedom of religion in the Soviet Union, and that it might even be possible for the Kremlin to cooperate with the Vatican. Both the American chargé d'affaires in Moscow and an Office of Strategic Services representative who interviewed Orlemanski upon his return felt that Stalin's comments represented a sincere bid to improve relations with Poland, Polish-Americans, and the Catholic Church.[21]

Whatever Stalin's intentions were with regard to the Orlemanski visit, they backfired. The priest's trip provoked violent objections from the Polish government-in-exile, the Polish-American community, and American Catholics. Ambassador Ciechanowski informed the State Department that his government viewed the affair with "the greatest concern and disappointment." Michael J. Ready, general secretary of the National Catholic Welfare Conference, charged that Orlemanski's trip was "like other missions to Moscow, . . . a political burlesque, staged and directed by capable Soviet agents." Congressman Dingell told the

[20] Stettinius memorandum of conversation with Harriman, May 23, 1944, *FR: 1944,* IV, 873–74; Harriman to Roosevelt, June 7, 1944, *ibid.,* III, 1276–77.

[21] On Orlemanski's visit to Moscow, see *FR: 1944,* III, 1398–99, 1402–11, IV, 868–69; Hull, *Memoirs,* II, 1442–44; and Werth, *Russia at War,* pp. 844–47. The estimates of Stalin's intentions are in Maxwell M. Hamilton to Hull, May 9, 1944, *FR: 1944,* IV, 869; and a memorandum by DeWitt C. Poole of conversations with Orlemanski on May 15–16, 1944, Department of State records, 760C.61/2334. Stalin also invited Professor Oscar Lange of the University of Chicago, a native of Poland, to come to Moscow at this time. Lange later became the postwar Polish government's first ambassador to the United States.

House of Representatives that Orlemanski had "soiled his sacerdotal robes of priesthood to kowtow to Stalin and to others who betrayed the Polish people and the Roman Catholic Church into the hands of their enemies." The crowning blow came when Orlemanski's bishop reprimanded him for making the trip without permission.[22] President Roosevelt found Orlemanski's account of his talk with Stalin "extremely interesting" and expressed a desire to talk with the priest "off the record," but Secretary of State Hull, still smarting under a barrage of criticism, cast cold water on the idea. So ended one of the more curious episodes in wartime Soviet-American relations.[23]

Meanwhile, Republicans were preparing to capitalize on the discontent of ethnic minorities with the Administration's foreign policy. Senator Vandenberg saw the potentialities of the issue clearly. He proposed to Thomas E. Dewey late in March, 1944, that the Republican platform's foreign policy plank incorporate the language of the Atlantic Charter "because *this is the point* at which the Roosevelt Administration is deserting the hopes and prayers of all our American nationals from Poland, Finland, Latvia, Lithuania, Estonia, etc." Vandenberg opposed making definite promises to the Poles "because our current defaults to Mr. Stalin are rapidly putting him in 'the driver's seat.' " It would be difficult to make any specific pledge on Poland "which would actually be worth the paper it is written on." But the senator added: "There is no doubt in my mind . . . that Polish voters will be more responsive to us this Fall than in many years." [24]

[22] James C. Dunn memorandum of conversation with Ciechanowski, May 2, 1944, *FR: 1944,* III, 1407; *New York Times,* May 1, 1944; *Congressional Record,* May 3, 1944, p. 3931; Poole memorandum of conversation with Orlemanski, May 27, 1944, Roosevelt MSS, PSF: "Poland." Orlemanski told Poole that he had not talked with his bishop since his return from Moscow, but "the parish had just bought a fine new bell. Maybe the bishop would come and bless it and then everything would be fine again." (*Ibid.*)

[23] Roosevelt to Hull, May 31, 1944, Department of State records, 760C.61/2334; Hull to Roosevelt, June 2, 1944, *ibid.* When Mikolajczyk was in Washington Roosevelt mentioned Orlemanski's report to him, suggesting the rather breathtaking possibility that, since Stalin obviously had no desire to assume the tsars' old position as head of the Russian Orthodox Church, he might favor a reunion of the Russian Orthodox and Roman Catholic Churches under the leadership of the Pope. (Ciechanowski, *Defeat in Victory,* pp. 308–9.)

[24] Vandenberg to Dewey, March 30, 1944, and Milton Carmichael, April 29, 1944, Vandenberg MSS. See also *Newsweek,* XXIII (May 1, 1944), 29–30.

Dewey himself avoided dealing with the Polish issue explicitly during the campaign, confining his remarks instead to the need to be "fair and upright in our dealings with the smaller nations." He did criticize the "dim secrecy" surrounding Roosevelt's negotiations on Poland, but admitted that "Poland has had differences with Russia that go deep into history and for which there's no simple solution." In a series of discreet conversations with Republican leaders in October, however, Ambassador Ciechanowski did obtain private expressions of sympathy for the Polish position. Herbert Hoover told Ciechanowski that Roosevelt had double-crossed the Poles at Teheran, and that their only hope was to appeal to American public opinion. John Foster Dulles promised the Polish ambassador that he would try to win Dewey's support for the Polish cause, and Dewey himself informed Ciechanowski that he disliked Roosevelt's acquiescent Polish policy and would, if elected, take a firmer position against Soviet demands.[25]

Democratic political leaders, already concerned about the outcome of the election, found Republican activity among Polish-Americans increasingly alarming. Representative George C. Sadowski of Michigan observed that "the Republicans are wringing their hands and shedding crocodile tears for poor Poland." Senator Joseph C. O'Mahoney of Wyoming sent word to Samuel Rosenman that many Polish-Americans in Illinois and Ohio were "emotionally disturbed." The secretary of the Polish-American Businessmen's Association of Chicago wrote plaintively to Roosevelt that

it is really hard to talk to some of our people. And elections are coming soon. Will you kindly talk to your friends, Messrs. Winston Churchill and Joseph Stalin, and really do something substantial, and soon, for those poor suffering Polish souls in Poland? We have here at least 300,000 Polish votes. There are millions of Polish votes all over [the] USA, and it is hard to talk to them. . . . Will you kindly take this trouble under your consideration?

[25] *New York Times,* September 9, October 9 and 18, 1944; Ciechanowski reports to Mikolajczyk of conversations with Hoover on October 6 and 20, Dulles on October 20, and Dewey on October 8, 1944, cited in Rozek, *Allied Wartime Diplomacy,* pp. 300–1. Ciechanowski later wrote: "I was frequently asked by various campaign managers, and especially by election agents of the New Deal, what I thought would be the most appropriate way to obtain the support of what they called 'the Polish vote' for the Democratic machine. Of course I steadily refused to discuss these matters." (*Defeat in Victory,* p. 347.)

Convinced that Roosevelt would have to do something to neutralize Polish-American criticism, Attorney General Frances Biddle suggested that the President meet briefly with a delegation from the Polish-American Congress and "say something that would hearten the Poles." Other Democratic leaders enthusiastically seconded the proposal. Senator Joseph Guffey asked Roosevelt to receive the delegation because "it will help us greatly in Pennsylvania." Mayor Edward J. Kelly of Chicago told Democratic National Committee chairman Robert Hannegan that while the general situation in Illinois was good, he was worried about the Poles and considered it "absolutely imperative that the President arrange immediately to see the group of Polish leaders." [26]

Roosevelt yielded to the importunings of his advisers and received the Poles at the White House on Pulaski Day, October 11, 1944. Charles Rozmarek, president of the Polish-American Congress, asked the President for assurance that he would prevent imposition of a puppet regime on Poland and would oppose forced transfers of populations there. Roosevelt replied blandly that "you and I are agreed that Poland must be reconstituted as a great nation" and assured the Polish-Americans that "world opinion" would back up that objective. While this interview produced little information that could encourage the Polish-Americans, it did at least relieve the anxieties of Democratic politicians. Roosevelt saw Rozmarek again in Chicago on October 28. Following this interview Rozmarek endorsed the President for reelection, because "he assured me that . . . he will see to it that Poland is treated justly at the peace conference." [27]

Election results showed Democratic anxieties about the Polish vote to have been highly exaggerated. One report, prepared for the Democratic National Committee, estimated that 90 percent of Polish-American voters remained within the Roosevelt coalition. Rozmarek's last-minute endorsement of Roosevelt appeared in retrospect as an effort to save face

[26] Sherwood, *Roosevelt and Hopkins,* pp. 819–20; *Congressional Record,* May 3, 1944, p. 3940; record of telephone conversation with O'Mahoney, October, 1944, Rosenman MSS, Ms. 62–4, Box 2, Roosevelt Library; Frank Nurczyk to Roosevelt, September 13, 1944, Roosevelt MSS, OF 463-A, Box 4; Biddle to Roosevelt, September 28 and October 7, 1944, *ibid.,* OF 463-A, Box 1; Guffey to Roosevelt, October 7, 1944, *ibid.;* Hannegan to Edwin M. Watson, October 7, 1944, *ibid.*

[27] White House press release, October 11, 1944, Roosevelt MSS, OF 463-A, Box 1; *New York Times,* October 29, 1944.

once leaders of the Polish-American Congress realized they could not swing the Polish vote to Dewey. In a post-mortem on the election Frank Januszewski, vice-president of the congress, complained to Senator Vandenberg that the Republican Party had directed its attack against the New Deal, which had been good to Polish-Americans, not against the diplomacy of the Roosevelt Administration. Vandenberg himself perceived an even greater difficulty. The tragedy of the situation, he wrote to Januszewski, was "that we cannot prove that they [the Poles] have been 'sold down the river' (if they have) and we cannot conscientiously promise them that they can rely upon us for a better deal when we collide with Stalin at the Peace Table." [28]

Attempts to employ ethnic voting to influence the 1944 election probably harmed more than they helped Poland's interests. Promises to withhold or deliver the Polish-American vote distracted the Roosevelt Administration's attention from the question of Poland itself to the problem of appeasing Polish-American leaders.[29] They also contributed to the obsessive cautiousness which paralyzed Roosevelt's East European policy in 1944, preventing badly needed efforts to tell the American people what kind of peace settlement they could expect in that part of the world.

III

But Roosevelt's concern over political retaliation from Polish-Americans was not the only reason why he felt unable to prepare the American people for postwar developments in Eastern Europe. Key senators, many of them former isolationists, had made it clear that they would support American membership in the new world organization only if the peace settlement reflected the principles of the Atlantic Charter. Any indications that the big powers were preparing to divide Europe up into spheres of influence might be as damaging to the United Nations as the

[28] Report by Press Research, Inc., on the Polish lobby, June 4, 1945, copy in Democratic National Committee records, Box 155, Truman Library; Januszewski to Vandenberg, November 22, 1944, Vandenberg MSS; Vandenberg to Januszewski, October 31, 1944, *ibid.*

[29] Louis L. Gerson, *The Hyphenate in Recent American Politics and Diplomacy,* p. 140.

Allies' World War I secret agreements had been to the League of Nations. Full disclosure of Soviet intentions in Eastern Europe could well wreck the domestic consensus which Roosevelt regarded as necessary for successful prosecution of the war, and provoke a return to isolationism once peace had come.

The Senate had already passed a resolution early in November, 1943, calling for "the United States, acting through its constitutional processes, [to] join with free and sovereign nations in the establishment and maintenance of international authority with power to prevent aggression and to preserve the peace of the world." Approval of this innocuous statement, proposed by Chairman Tom Connally of the Foreign Relations Committee after prodding from internationalists, was never in doubt. In the course of the debate, however, several former isolationists expressed concern over Soviet intentions in Eastern Europe. Senators Robert R. Reynolds and Edwin C. Johnson proposed amending the Connally resolution to guarantee the postwar independence and territorial integrity of that area. "If the Atlantic Charter means what it says," Johnson intoned, "and if our ideals of justice and freedom . . . are not pure flimflam, then my resolution is in order and timely." [30]

The views of Reynolds and Johnson hardly represented a majority position in the Senate, as the 85-to-5 vote in favor of the unamended Connally resolution showed.[31] But their action reflected a growing tendency on the part of old isolationists to make incorporation of the Atlantic Charter into the peace settlement their price for supporting American membership in the new international organization. Since the opposition of only 33 senators could keep the United States out of the United Nations, Roosevelt Administration officials could not afford to ignore this development.

Secretary of State Hull, whose department had assumed chief responsibility for planning the United Nations, understood the danger clearly enough. Early in 1944 he cabled Ambassador Harriman that he was "much disturbed" by the Soviet government's approach to the Polish problem. The Russians should understand that American support for an international organization would depend upon Moscow's willingness "to

---

[30] *Congressional Record,* November 1 and 2, 1943, pp. 8939–40, 9006.

[31] For the debate over the Connally resolution, see Divine, *Second Chance,* pp. 147–54.

abandon unilateralism and to seek its ends by free and frank discussion with a Polish Government that is not hand-picked." If the Soviet Union insisted on imposing a puppet government in Poland, Americans would interpret this as a regression to power politics. Such action would seriously affect the Senate's attitude toward the new collective security organization. If "some authorized person or official in Russia [could] reiterate fairly often Russia's interest in . . . the movement of international cooperation," Hull later told Soviet Ambassador Andrei Gromyko, this would "help to clear the air." Time and time again during the first half of 1944 Hull urged upon the patient but noncommittal Gromyko the need for the Soviet Union to seek its objectives through cooperation and consultation with its allies, not through unilateral action.[32]

Hull's admonitions had little apparent effect on the Russians, but his concern over public opinion did appear to be well founded. At the time of the Moscow Conference in November, 1943, surveys indicated that 54 percent of Americans thought that Russia could be trusted to cooperate with the United States after the war. But by the end of January, 1944, this figure had declined to 42 percent. Even allowing for the usual margin of error, this poll demonstrated, as a State Department analyst noted, "a significant decline in public confidence in Russian cooperation after the war." Even more ominously, a National Opinion Research Center poll, released in December, 1943, showed that while "a majority of the American public believes that following the war Russia will not be content with her pre-war boundaries, . . . a majority also believes that Russia should *not* extend them." Considerable doubt existed as to how the United States should respond to this situation—39 percent of the sample thought Washington should try to stop the Soviet Union from taking territory which belonged to Poland before the war, while 38 percent opposed this—but the evidence was clear that Americans would not look favorably upon Soviet violations of self-determination in Eastern Europe.[33]

---

[32] Hull to Harriman, January 25, 1944, *FR: 1944*, III, 1234–35; Hull memoranda of conversations with Gromyko on March 11, 19, 29, April 13, 20, May 7, and June 1, 1944, Hull MSS, Box 61, Folder 250, *FR: 1944*, IV, 854, Department of State records, 760C.61/2298. See also Hull to Harriman, December 23, 1943, *FR: 1943*, III, 611–12; *idem*, January 15 and February 9, 1944, *FR: 1944*, III, 1228–29, IV, 824–26.

[33] "Public Attitudes on Foreign Policy," reports No. 6, December 21, 1943, and

Criticism of Russian "unilateralism" in the Senate reflected the grow-ing public concern. Styles Bridges of New Hampshire questioned whether the United States was trying to restrain those of its allies "who might have territorial or power ambitions." "I have seemed to sense," Bridges warned, "a gradual drifting away from the principles of the At-lantic Charter." Harlan Bushfield of South Dakota observed that for a thousand years Russian rulers had dreamed of acquiring a warm-water outlet to the sea. "Today is Russia's opportunity. Does anyone doubt that she will make the most of it?" Burton K. Wheeler of Montana told his colleagues that, despite the fact that sympathy for the Soviet Union had "grown tremendously" in recent years, if Russia overran Poland, Fin-land, the Baltic and Balkan States, public sentiment would change very rapidly.[34]

Secretary of State Hull was, at this time, quietly trying to get Senate leaders to approve the State Department's plans for an international or-ganization. Fears that the Big Three had already settled the main fea-tures of the peace in secret led Senator Arthur H. Vandenberg, a key Re-publican member of the Foreign Relations Committee, to inform Hull that the Senate could not endorse the department's program without knowing what the terms of the peace settlement would be. Otherwise, senators would be signing "the most colossal 'blank check' in history." Vandenberg wrote in his diary:

Over all these negotiations . . . hung the shadow of a doubt as to whether we (or even Hull himself) was in possession of *full* information as to what peace terms may have *already* been agreed upon between Roosevelt, Stalin and Churchill. . . . We all believe in Hull. But none of us is *sure* that Hull *knows* the whole story.

Allen Drury, a congressional correspondent for the United Press, ob-served that "the fatal cleavage in government" which had ruined Wood-row Wilson's plans for the League of Nations was developing again.

No. 12, February 21, 1944, Department of State records, 711.00 PUBLIC ATTITUDES/6, 7A. See also Cantril and Strunk, eds., *Public Opinion*, p. 1169; and Bruner, *Mandate from the People*, pp. 121–22. Samuel Rosenman submitted the re-sults of the January, 1944, poll to Roosevelt on February 17, 1944. (Roosevelt MSS, OF 857, Box 3.)

[34] *Congressional Record*, January 14, March 7, April 21, May 3, 1944, pp. 186, 2302, 3623–24, 3888.

"Congress just doesn't like to be hoodwinked, bypassed, patronized, lied to, or affronted in the field of foreign policy." [35]

Publication in May of a two-part *Saturday Evening Post* article by Forrest Davis giving Roosevelt's account of the Teheran Conference further increased tension in the Senate. The article abounded in careless phrases sure to arouse senatorial ire. Davis pictured Roosevelt as "gambling" that the Soviet Union would be willing to collaborate with the West, a policy "bordering at times on what has been termed appeasement." The account stressed F.D.R.'s repeated and patient attempts to make friends with Stalin, and revealed for the first time publicly the concept of the Four Policemen. All of this served to confirm the suspicions of senators who believed that the Big Three had already drawn the major outlines of the peace settlement. Robert A. Taft of Ohio accused the President of basing his policy "on the delightful theory that Mr. Stalin in the end will turn out to have an angelic nature." Vandenberg wrote that "if the Post articles are right, . . . all the ideology of the 'Atlantic Charter' is already 'out the window.' " [36]

Hull eventually secured cautious oral approval of the State Department's plans for international organization from Senate leaders, but he failed to get the written commitment he had hoped to use to dispel doubts about congressional willingness to join the new organization. Senatorial suspicion of Roosevelt's secret diplomacy at Teheran, particularly with regard to Eastern Europe, was primarily responsible for the tentative nature of this commitment. Representatives of the United States, the Soviet Union, Great Britain, and China, meeting at Dumbarton Oaks from August through October, 1944, also endorsed the key features of the department's plans, leaving unresolved only the questions of voting procedure in the Security Council and the Soviet Union's demand

[35] Vandenberg to Hull, May 3, 1944, Vandenberg, ed., *Private Papers*, pp. 97–98; Vandenberg Diary, May 23, 1944, *ibid.*, pp. 101–2; Drury Diary, May 8, 1944, Allen Drury, *A Senate Journal: 1943–1945*, p. 162.

[36] Forrest Davis, "What Really Happened at Teheran," *Saturday Evening Post*, CCXVI (May 13 and 20, 1944), 13 ff., 22 ff.; Taft radio address of June 8, 1944, *Congressional Record*, 1944 appendix, p. A2901; Vandenberg Diary, May 26, 1944, Vandenberg, ed., *Private Papers*, pp. 103–4. See also Israel, ed., *Long Diary*, pp. 348, 356. Edgar Snow asked Roosevelt on May 26, 1944, whether Davis' articles had accurately reflected his views. Roosevelt replied: "Yes, Forrest did a good job." (Snow, "Fragments from F.D.R.," p. 400.)

for multiple votes in the General Assembly. But agreement on the organizational structure of the future United Nations did not necessarily ensure Senate approval. Vandenberg wrote early in the fall of 1944: "The *nature* of the peace—whether it is calculated to be just and equitable —has an important bearing upon the nature and extent of our commitment to forever underwrite its terms." [37]

Cordell Hull finally retired as secretary of state at the end of November, 1944, after heading the Department of State for twice as long as any other man. Sick, tired, and bitter over long years of being bypassed by the President, the Secretary could take comfort in the flood of praise he received from colleagues in government, the press, and the public. One editorial in *Life,* however, struck a discordant note. It recalled Hull's "big moment" when he had stood before Congress in 1943 promising that "there will no longer be need for spheres of influence, for alliances, for balance of power, or any other of the special arrangements . . . of the unhappy past." "But who believes that?" *Life* asked: "Not the heads of the governments of Russia, Britain, France, or even the U.S. Things aren't working out that way. The old chasm between words and events, which characterized so much of the Hull era, still yawns." [38] *Life*'s bluntness reflected a growing awareness in the United States toward the end of 1944 that the gap between the realities of the peace settlement and the principles of the Atlantic Charter was indeed going to be large.

Unilateral British and Russian actions in Eastern Europe intensified this sense of uneasiness. Churchill's hostility to the emergence of left-wing governments in liberated countries became painfully obvious with his forcible suppression of the Greek uprising in December, 1944. At the same time, the Russians were moving toward establishment of a puppet government in Poland, a process completed with Soviet recognition of the Lublin regime early in 1945. Ironically British actions in Greece aroused the greater amount of concern in the United States. The confrontation there was sharper than in Poland, and, according to opinion

[37] Divine, *Second Chance,* pp. 200–3, 220–28; Vandenberg to Mrs. John K. Ormond, September 30, 1944, Vandenberg MSS.

[38] "Mr. Hull," *Life,* XVII (December 11, 1944), 26. See also Pratt, *Cordell Hull,* II, 765–66; and Israel, ed., *Long Diary,* p. 388.

polls, Americans distrusted Britain more than they did Russia.[39] But both cases demonstrated a disturbing Anglo-Russian tendency to divide postwar Europe into spheres of influence—a tendency which the United States was doing nothing to stop.

President Roosevelt accidentally aggravated the situation by casually revealing at a press conference on December 19, 1944, that he and Churchill had never actually signed the Atlantic Charter. F.D.R. immediately realized his mistake and at his next press conference stressed that the ideals of the Charter were more important than whether a signed document existed. But the damage had already been done. News that the Charter had not been signed came as a shock to a nation accustomed to placing great faith in written documents. Senator Vandenberg, a good judge of such matters, proclaimed that Roosevelt's statement had "jarred America to its very hearthstones." [40]

Much of the criticism Roosevelt received now came from his own supporters. The President's new secretary of state, Edward R. Stettinius, Jr., had already angered liberals by filling high State Department positions with such establishment figures as Joseph C. Grew, William L. Clayton, James C. Dunn, and Nelson A. Rockefeller. Roosevelt's cavalier dismissal of the Atlantic Charter, together with British and Russian actions in Eastern Europe, convinced many liberals that the ideals of the war had been abandoned. Edgar Ansel Mowrer, columnist for the *New York Post,* accused Roosevelt of compromises, postponements, and evasions: "Yet still unrepentantly he wisecracks, he postures, he ducks, he does everything but come clean and tell the country what he is up to." Former Undersecretary of State Sumner Welles criticized the apparent lack of unity among the Allies, and called upon Roosevelt to assert bold leadership. Allen Drury charged Roosevelt with "four years of sloppy diplomacy, personal intrigue and tin-horn politicking on a world-wide scale." [41]

[39] Stettinius to Roosevelt, "American Opinion on Recent European Developments," December 30, 1944, Roosevelt MSS, PSF 30: "Stettinius." This survey of public opinion indicated that of the one-third of the public dissatisfied with the extent of Big Three cooperation, 54 percent blamed Britain while only 18 percent blamed Russia.

[40] *New York Times,* December 20, 22, 1944; *Congressional Record,* January 10, 1945, p. 166.

[41] *Time,* XLV (January 8, 1945), 13; Drury Diary, December 17, 1944, Drury,

In the Senate, isolationists like Burton K. Wheeler no longer found themselves alone when they warned that the United States would not join the world organization unless Russia and Britain changed their policies. Even such a dedicated internationalist as Senator Joseph Ball of Minnesota was worried: "If the present trend of unilateral decisions by the Allied nations in the liberated areas of Europe continues, it may do irreparable damage to the principles of international collaboration set forth in the Dumbarton Oaks proposals." With Senators Harold Burton, Carl Hatch, and Lister Hill, Ball proposed that the Senate set standards in advance for the kind of peace settlement it would accept. Perfectionism, Joseph E. Davies observed in his diary, was proving to be just as dangerous to international cooperation as isolationism: "The altruistic impulse among some of our ablest public men [which] insists upon a perfect structure of World Peace" failed to take into account such obvious "facts of life" as Russian insistence on friendly governments in Eastern Europe, British requirements for control of important sea-lanes, and even American demands for postwar strategic bases in the Pacific.[42]

The President had hoped to get the Senate to approve membership in the United Nations before explosive situations like Poland and Greece could come up, the *New Republic*'s knowledgeable "TRB" wrote early in 1945, but now "the fat is in the fire." For whatever reason, whether intimidation by Polish-Americans, concern over the Senate, or declining health,[43] Roosevelt had not prepared the American people for the kind of peace settlement which he knew would be necessary in Eastern Europe. George F. Kennan, then counselor at the American Embassy in Moscow, saw the problem clearly. The Soviets, he wrote to Ambassador

---

Senate Journal, p. 313. On Stettinius' State Department appointments, see Sherwood, *Roosevelt and Hopkins*, pp. 837–38; and Divine, *Second Chance*, pp. 253–55. The appointment of a poet, Archibald MacLeish, as assistant secretary of state for public and cultural relations failed to placate outraged liberals.

[42] Drury, *Senate Journal*, p. 318; *New York Times*, December 26, 1944; Davies Journal, December 9, 1944, Davies MSS, Box 15.

[43] On this matter, see Herman E. Bateman, "Observations on President Roosevelt's Health During World War II," *Mississippi Valley Historical Review*, XLIII (June, 1956), 82–102; and the important new information in Howard G. Bruenn, "Clinical Notes on the Illness and Death of President Franklin D. Roosevelt," *Annals of Internal Medicine*, LXXII (April, 1970), 579–91. See also the *New Republic*, CXII (January 8, 1945), 51. Since 1943 "TRB" has been Richard L. Strout.

Harriman, had never stopped thinking in terms of spheres of influence. The American people,

for reasons which we do not need to go into, have not been aware of this quality of Soviet thought, and have been allowed to hope that the Soviet government would be prepared to enter into an international security organization with truly universal power to prevent aggression. We are now faced with the prospect of having our people disabused of this illusion.[44]

Such were the unhappy circumstances in which the Roosevelt Administration began planning for the next meeting of the Big Three, at which there would have to take place a settlement of East European questions which both the Soviet Union and the American public could accept.

IV

The President's advisers had public opinion much on their minds as they prepared for Yalta. A summary of opinion polls sent to Roosevelt early in January, 1945, concluded that recent events "have increased public skepticism concerning the ability of the major powers to live up to the ideals of the Atlantic Charter and the United Nations." Another analysis prepared for the President by Secretary of State Stettinius called attention to "a significant *decline* in public confidence in the conduct of our foreign policy in the past six months." [45] Concern over this matter affected Administration planning on the two critical East European issues with which the Big Three would have to deal: the question of boundaries, and the problem of who was to govern the countries of this area.

F.D.R.'s tacit approval of Stalin's territorial claims at Teheran had, for all practical purposes, settled the boundary problem in advance. The President's counselors continued to support the wisdom of this decision. Bernard Baruch, never one to withhold advice, wrote Roosevelt that Stalin's demand for Polish territory was understandable because the Russians feared Germany. It would be useless "to demand of Russia what

[44] Kennan to Harriman, December 19, 1944, quoted in Kennan, *Memoirs*, p. 222. See also Brooks Emeny to John Foster Dulles, December 22, 1944, Dulles MSS; and Joseph M. Jones, *The Fifteen Weeks*, pp. 102–3.

[45] Hadley Cantril to Grace Tully, January 11, 1945, Roosevelt MSS, OF 857, Box 3; Stettinius to Roosevelt, December 30, 1944, *ibid.*, PSF 30: "Stettinius."

she thinks she needs and most of which she now possesses." Secretary of War Stimson thought Russian insistence on the Curzon Line reasonable in the light of history—"it certainly does not seem to be worth a quarrel with Russia." State Department briefing-book papers prepared for Roosevelt's use at Yalta recommended the Curzon Line as a basis for the Polish-Russian boundary but, reflecting a promise the President had made to Polish Prime Minister Mikolajczyk the previous summer, suggested trying to get Stalin to leave the province of Lvov inside Poland. Stalin's claims at the expense of Finland, Rumania, and the Baltic States were not mentioned.[46]

State Department officials did worry, however, about how disclosure of these agreements would affect public opinion. Stettinius wrote Roosevelt that while Americans would not categorically oppose Stalin's territorial demands, they would object to Russian acquisition of Polish territory without Polish consent. Americans would accept any boundary settlement which the Russians, the London Poles, and the Lublin Poles reached together, but any Russian agreement with the Lublin Poles alone would probably not be regarded by American opinion as expressing the will of the Polish people.[47]

John D. Hickerson, now deputy director of the State Department's Office of European Affairs, explained the boundary problem clearly in a memorandum to Stettinius: Everyone knew that the Soviet Union intended to reabsorb the Baltic States, Bessarabia, and parts of East Prussia and pre-1939 Poland. "I personally don't like it although I realize that the Soviet Government has arguments on its side. The point is [that] it has been done and nothing which it is in the power of the United States Government to do can undo it." Under the circumstances, Hickerson favored accepting Moscow's territorial claims, using whatever bargaining power the United States had left to persuade the Russians to cooperate in the postwar international organization. The United States would also need Soviet support to defeat Germany and Japan—"the importance

---

[46] Baruch to Roosevelt, January 4, 1945, Baruch MSS, "Memoranda—President Roosevelt, 1945"; Stimson memorandum for conversation with Stettinius, January 22, 1945, Stimson MSS, Box 418; Yalta briefing book paper, "Suggested United States Policy Regarding Poland," *FR: Yalta,* pp. 230–34. For Roosevelt's promise regarding Lvov, see Ciechanowski, *Defeat in Victory,* p. 305; and Mikolajczyk, *The Rape of Poland,* pp. 59–60.

[47] Stettinius to Roosevelt, December 30, 1944, Roosevelt MSS, PSF 30: "Stettinius."

of these two things can be reckoned in terms of American lives." Hickerson felt, however, that concessions of this kind could not be made without repercussions inside the United States. Accordingly, he recommended an immediate program involving off-the-record discussions with congressmen, newspapermen, and radio commentators to prepare the public for these developments.[48]

The complexion of governments in the newly liberated nations of Eastern Europe concerned the State Department more than did boundaries. Stettinius warned Roosevelt early in January of a widespread public belief that both Britain and Russia were actively supporting factions of their choice in liberated countries. "The public disapproves of such unilateral action." The Secretary of State felt that a positive statement clarifying the American position on liberated Europe "would tend to find support and furnish a frame of reference, which the public clearly desires." On January 18, Stettinius recommended to the President establishment of an Emergency High Commission for Liberated Europe, composed of the governments of the United States, Great Britain, the Soviet Union, and France, which would "assist in establishing popular governments and in facilitating the solution of emergency economic problems in the former occupied and satellite states of Europe." Announcement of such a commission at the Big Three meeting "would reassure public opinion in the United States and elsewhere." [49]

Archibald MacLeish, assistant secretary of state for public and cultural relations, worried that "the wave of disillusionment which has distressed us in the last several weeks" would increase if Americans got the impression that "potentially totalitarian provisional governments" were being set up in liberated countries. "It would be a blessing to the world if we could walk straight up to this question." The Big Three should agree first, that the peoples of the liberated areas are to have an opportunity, when conditions permit them to express their will, to decide for themselves what

[48] Hickerson to Stettinius, January 8, 1945, *FR: Yalta,* pp. 94–96.

[49] Stettinius to Roosevelt, January 6, 1945, Roosevelt MSS, PSF 29: "State Department"; Stettinius to Roosevelt, January 18, 1945, *FR: Yalta,* pp. 97–98. A Yalta briefing book paper on spheres of influence commented: "It would be unfortunate . . . if any temporary arrangement should . . . appear to be a departure from the principle adopted by the three Governments at Moscow [in 1943], in definite rejection of the spheres of influence idea. . . . Any arrangement suggestive of spheres of influence cannot but militate against the establishment and effective functioning of a broader system of general security in which all countries will have a part." (*Ibid.,* p. 105.)

kind of government they want; second, that they can have any kind of government they want, so long as it is not a government, the existence of which would endanger the peace of the world—and a fascist government, in our opinion, does endanger the peace of the world by its mere existence.

Leo Pasvolsky, special assistant to the secretary of state in charge of planning for the United Nations, wrote Stettinius that creation of the proposed Emergency High Commission for Liberated Europe "would be the most powerful antidote that we can devise for the rapidly crystallizing opposition in this country to the whole Dumbarton Oaks idea on the score that the future organization would merely underwrite a system of unilateral grabbing." [50]

Roosevelt, Churchill, and Stalin met for the second time during the war at Yalta on the coast of the Black Sea in February, 1945. F.D.R.'s choice of advisers to accompany him reflected his preoccupation with how the public would react to this meeting. To interpret the Yalta agreements to the Congress, he took along James F. Byrnes, director of the Office of War Mobilization and Reconversion, popularly known as the "Assistant President" in charge of the home front. Byrnes, having had no experience in foreign affairs, was genuinely surprised at being asked to go. As a conservative South Carolina Democrat whom Roosevelt had pointedly passed over for the vice-presidential nomination in 1944, however, Byrnes had little reason to follow the President blindly, and was therefore a good choice for this assignment. Less clear were Roosevelt's reasons for asking Edward J. Flynn, Democratic "boss" of the Bronx, to join the Yalta entourage. Apparently Roosevelt's extreme sensitivity to Catholic opinion made him feel the necessity of including a prominent Catholic like Flynn, who later made a special report to the Pope on religious conditions in Russia. The President also broke sharply with his previous custom by, for the first time, taking the Secretary of State to a major wartime conference with the Russians. [51]

[50] MacLeish to Joseph C. Grew, January 24, 1945, *FR: Yalta*, pp. 101–2; MacLeish to James C. Dunn, January 19, 1945, *ibid.*, pp. 427–28; Pasvolsky to Stettinius, January 23, 1945, *ibid.*, p. 101. At a preliminary meeting on the island of Malta, Stettinius told Anthony Eden that public sentiment made it extremely important for the Big Three to find a solution to the Polish problem. Otherwise the American people, especially Catholics, would be "greatly disturbed," and the prospect of American membership in the international organization might be endangered. (Minutes of Eden-Stettinius meeting, February 1, 1945, *ibid.*, pp. 499–500.)

[51] James F. Byrnes, *All in One Lifetime*, pp. 252–53; Ernest K. Lindley, "Byrnes,

Little was said at Yalta about Russia's boundaries with its East European neighbors. Roosevelt told Stalin that, as he had noted at Teheran, he was "in general" in favor of the Curzon Line as the eastern boundary of Poland. Reminding the Russian leader again of the six or seven million Poles in the United States, however, the President observed that "most Poles, like the Chinese, want to save face. . . . It would make it easier for me at home if the Soviet Government could give something to Poland." Roosevelt suggested, merely as a "gesture," that the Russians leave the predominantly Polish city of Lvov and the surrounding oil fields within the new Poland, even though they were on the Russian side of the Curzon Line. Stalin refused. The Curzon Line, he pointed out with malicious accuracy, had originally been drawn by the Allies after World War I. How could he return to Moscow and have it said of him that he was less Russian than Curzon and Clemenceau? [52] This ended discussion of the Russo-Polish boundary.

Far more difficult to resolve was the problem of who was to govern Poland—the Lublin Poles, the London Poles, or a combination of both. Roosevelt told Stalin that the American public opposed recognition of the Lublin government on the grounds that it represented a minority of the Polish people. In the same breath, however, the President also said that he wanted a government in Poland "that will be thoroughly friendly to the Soviet [Union] for years to come. That is essential." It seems unlikely that Roosevelt realized the contradiction implicit in this statement—the fact that a government in Warsaw representative of the will of the Polish people would almost inevitably have been hostile to the Soviet Union.[53]

The Russians insisted that the Lublin Poles form the nucleus of any

---

the Persuasive Reporter," *Newsweek,* XXV (March 12, 1945), 42; Edward J. Flynn, *You're the Boss,* pp. 185–206; *Time,* XLV (April 2, 1945), 22; Stettinius, *Roosevelt and the Russians,* p. 3.

[52] H. Freeman Matthews notes, 3d plenary meeting, February 6, 1945, *FR: Yalta,* pp. 677–78. The final communiqué reflected the Russian position on boundaries: "The three Heads of Government consider that the eastern frontier of Poland should follow the Curzon Line with digressions from it in some regions of five to eight kilometers in favor of Poland. They recognize that Poland must receive substantial accessions of territory in the north and west. . . . The final delimitation of the western frontier of Poland should await the Peace Conference." (*Ibid.,* pp. 973–74.)

[53] Matthews notes, 3d plenary meeting, February 6, 1945, *FR: Yalta,* pp. 677–78; McNeill, *America, Britain, and Russia,* p. 535.

new Polish provisional government. The British argued that a wholly new Polish government should be constituted, composed of representatives from both the London and Lublin regimes. On February 9, the American delegation suggested as a compromise that "the present Polish Provisional Government be reorganized into a fully representative government based on all democratic forces in Poland and including democratic leaders from Poland abroad." The American proposal became the basis for the final agreement: "The Provisional Government which is now functioning in Poland should . . . be reorganized on a broader democratic basis with the inclusion of democratic leaders from Poland itself and from Poles abroad. This new Government should then be called the Polish Provisional Government of National Unity." This accord left intact the essence of the Russian position that the Lublin regime should serve as the basis for the new Polish provisional government, a fact which did not escape Roosevelt. Two weeks before his death he reminded Churchill that "we placed, as clearly shown in the agreement, somewhat more emphasis on the Lublin Poles than on the other two groups from which the new Government is to be drawn." [54]

Roosevelt agreed to this compromise because he believed the reorganized Polish provisional government would remain in power only until it could hold elections to determine the will of the Polish people. Stalin encouraged this belief, telling the President that "unless there is a catastrophe on the front and the Germans defeat us" it might be possible to hold elections in Poland within a month. Roosevelt placed great importance on these elections:

He [Roosevelt] felt that the elections was [*sic*] the crux of the whole matter, and since it was true, as Marshal Stalin had said, that the Poles were quarrelsome people not only at home but also abroad, he would like to have

[54] Bohlen notes, 5th plenary meeting, February 8, 1945, *FR: Yalta*, pp. 776–79; American delegation draft, "Suggestions in Regard to the Polish Governmental Question," February 9, 1945, *ibid.*, pp. 815–16; Yalta Conference communiqué, February 12, 1945, *ibid.*, pp. 973–74; Roosevelt to Churchill, March 29, 1945, *FR: 1945*, V, 189. According to Joseph E. Davies, Byrnes admitted to him on June 6, 1945, that "there was no intent [at Yalta] that a new government was to be created independent of the Lublin Government. . . . There was no justification under the spirit or letter of the agreement for insistence by Harriman and the British Ambassador that an entirely new Government should be created. . . ." (Davies Journal, June 6, 1945, Davies MSS, Box 17.) For a clear discussion of the Yalta negotiations on Poland, see Martin F. Herz, *Beginnings of the Cold War*, pp. 80–85.

some assurance for the six million Poles in the United States that these elections would be freely held, and he said he was sure if such assurance were present that elections would be held by the Poles there would be no doubt as to the sincerity of the agreement reached here.

Roosevelt emphasized that the first Polish election should be "beyond question": "It should be like Caesar's wife. I did not know her but they said she was pure." Stalin replied: "They said that about her but in fact she had her sins." [55]

The final communiqué reflected Roosevelt's wishes by pledging the new provisional government "to the holding of free and unfettered elections as soon as possible on the basis of universal suffrage and secret ballot." Anglo-American efforts to have the communiqué specify Big Three supervision of the elections failed, however, because Molotov thought this would be "offensive to the Poles." After negotiations had ended, Admiral Leahy warned Roosevelt that the agreement on Poland was "so elastic that the Russians can stretch it all the way from Yalta to Washington without ever technically breaking it." The President replied wearily: "I know, Bill—I know it. But it's the best I can do for Poland at this time." [56]

Roosevelt never tried to implement Stettinius' suggestion for an Emergency High Commission on Liberated Europe. He did persuade Churchill and Stalin to sign a "Declaration on Liberated Europe" which reaffirmed the principles of the Atlantic Charter and called for the formation of provisional governments in Eastern Europe "broadly representative of all democratic elements in the population and pledged to the earliest possible establishment through free elections of governments responsive to the will of the people." The declaration lacked enforcement machinery, however, providing only that when necessary the Big Three would "consult together on the measures necessary to discharge the joint responsibilities set forth in this declaration." James F. Byrnes later admitted candidly that the President had proposed the Declaration on Liberated Europe because of concern inside the United States about the for-

---

[55] Matthews notes, 5th plenary meeting, February 8, 1945, *FR: Yalta,* p. 790; Bohlen notes, 6th plenary meeting, February 9, 1945, *ibid.,* p. 854.

[56] Yalta Conference communiqué, February 12, 1945, *FR: Yalta,* p. 973; Bohlen notes, 6th plenary meeting, February 9, 1945, *ibid.,* pp. 842–43; Leahy, *I Was There,* pp. 315–16.

mation of spheres of influence in Eastern Europe. Roosevelt's reluctance to apply the declaration less than two weeks after Yalta when the Russians imposed a puppet government on Rumania doubtless indicated to Moscow that the President did not expect literal compliance with the terms of the agreement.[57]

President Roosevelt was pleased with what he had accomplished at Yalta. The commitment from the Russians to allow free elections in Eastern Europe promised to allay American fears of a Russian sphere of influence. While the agreement on organizing a Polish provisional government was a compromise, Roosevelt regarded it as only a temporary one. Resolution of the dispute over voting in the United Nations Security Council, together with the agreement to meet in San Francisco in April to draw up a charter for the world organization, indicated that the Russians sincerely wanted the new collective security effort to succeed. Secretary of State Stettinius described Yalta as a "most successful meeting," giving every evidence that the Russians wanted to cooperate with the United States. Harry Hopkins thought that at Yalta "the Russians had proved that they could be reasonable and farseeing and there wasn't any doubt in the minds of the President or any of us that we could live with them and get along with them peacefully for as far into the future as any of us could imagine." [58]

On March 1, 1945, Roosevelt, looking tired, reported in person to a joint session of Congress on the Yalta Conference. He delivered his speech sitting down, in an unusual public acknowledgment of his infirmity. His hands shook as he read the text. Yalta, he said, provided the foundation for a lasting peace settlement which would bring order and security to the world. It would not be a perfect settlement at first. "But it can be a peace—and it will be a peace—based on the sound and just principles of the Atlantic Charter." The Declaration on Liberated Europe had halted a trend toward the development of spheres of influ-

[57] Yalta Conference communiqué, February 12, 1945, *FR: Yalta*, pp. 977–78; *New York Times*, February 14, 1945. On the Rumanian situation, see Feis, *Churchill, Roosevelt, Stalin*, pp. 564–67; and Byrnes, *Speaking Frankly*, p. 53. William H. McNeill has argued that Stalin must have viewed the Declaration on Liberated Europe as "a harmless piece of rhetoric, soothing to the Americans." (*America, Britain, and Russia*, p. 559.)

[58] James V. Forrestal Diary, March 13, 1945, Walter Millis, ed., *The Forrestal Diaries*, p. 35; Stimson Diary, March 13, 1945, Stimson MSS; Sherwood, *Roosevelt and Hopkins*, p. 870.

ence which, "if allowed to go unchecked, . . . might have had tragic results." The compromise on Poland, "under the circumstances, is the most hopeful agreement possible for a free, independent, and prosperous Polish state." But, in the final analysis, success or failure of the Yalta agreements would depend on the United States Congress. "Unless you here in the halls of the American Congress—with the support of the American people—concur in the decisions reached at Yalta, and give them your active support, the meeting will not have produced lasting results." [59]

<h1 style="text-align:center">V</h1>

President Roosevelt achieved considerable success in making palatable to the American people the Yalta decisions on Eastern Europe. Taking the Big Three's pledge to hold free elections in Poland and the rest of Eastern Europe as an assurance that these countries would not suffer the imposition of unrepresentative regimes, most Americans at the time viewed the agreements as the best possible solution to the problem. While some observers regarded the Polish arrangements as imperfect, they were seen as necessary compromises. The *New York Times* commented that although the agreements might disappoint some people, they still surpassed most expectations. *Time* said of Yalta that "no citizen of the U.S., the U.S.S.R., or Great Britain could complain that his country had been sold down the river." A public opinion poll taken shortly after the conference ended revealed that only 9 percent of those questioned saw the results of the Yalta Conference as unfavorable to the United States.[60]

But, as the President had said, the ultimate outcome of Yalta would depend upon the attitude of the United States Congress. Roosevelt, Wilson's unfortunate precedent firmly in mind, did his best to ensure that the compromises he had made would not endanger prospects for American membership in the new world organization. Even before his per-

[59] *FDR: Public Papers,* XIII, 570–86; *Time,* XLV (March 12, 1945), 17; Drury, *Senate Journal,* pp. 371–73.

[60] Department of State, "Fortnightly Survey of American Opinion," No. 21, February 20, 1945; *New York Times,* February 13, 1945; *Time,* XLV (February 19, 1945), 15–16; American Institute of Public Opinion poll, February 20, 1945, cited in Cantril and Strunk, eds., *Public Opinion,* p. 1084.

sonal appearance on Capitol Hill, the President had begun working to present the Yalta agreements to Congress in the most favorable light. For this purpose, Byrnes flew back to Washington as soon as the conference ended and immediately set to work. In private conversations with congressional leaders and in a public press conference, he emphasized as major achievements of the conference the Declaration on Liberated Europe and the Big Three's agreement to meet at San Francisco in April to organize the United Nations. Byrnes performed his job well. "The Crimean communiqué was favorably received by the public and by the Congress," he wrote Roosevelt; "with few unimportant exceptions, the . . . press was very favorable." Although reluctant to discuss specific details, congressional leaders of both parties expressed general satisfaction with the results of the conference. Senate majority leader Alben Barkley cabled Roosevelt that the Yalta communiqué had made "a profound impression" when read on the floor of the Senate. The *New Republic's* "TRB" detected some notes of caution in Washington's reaction, but pointed out that Roosevelt had already achieved more than Wilson in winning congressional approval of the peace settlement.[61]

Public criticism of the Yalta agreements was limited to Polish-American groups, chronic Roosevelt critics like David Lawrence, who saw Yalta as "a confirmation of lynch law in international affairs," and old isolationists like Senator Burton K. Wheeler, who warned that the Declaration on Liberated Europe was a rhetorical gesture which would in no way prevent Russian control of Eastern Europe. The isolated nature of these complaints became clear when the House Foreign Affairs Committee refused even to report out New York Representative William Barry's resolution condemning the agreement on Poland.[62]

But the most important potential critic of the Yalta Polish agreement, though publicly silent, rumbled ominously in private. Senator Arthur H.

[61] Byrnes to Roosevelt, February 17, 1945, Roosevelt MSS, OF 4675: "Crimea Conf."; Lindley, "Byrnes, the Persuasive Reporter," p. 42; *Time*, XLV (February 26, 1945), 15–16; *New York Times*, February 13, 1945; Barkley to Roosevelt, February 12, 1945, quoted in Sherwood, *Roosevelt and Hopkins*, p. 870; *New Republic*, CXII (February 26, 1945), 294.

[62] Athan G. Theoharis, *The Yalta Myths*, pp. 27–29; David Lawrence, "The Tragedy of Yalta," *U.S. News*, XVIII (March 2, 1945), 26–27; *New York Times*, February 14, 1945; *Congressional Record*, February 26, 1945, p. 1470. See also Department of State, "Fortnightly Survey of American Opinion," Nos. 21, 22, and 23, February 20, March 7 and 20, 1945.

Vandenberg, acutely sensitive to East European problems because of his large Polish-American constituency in Michigan, had warned Secretary of State Hull in 1944 that he would not support American membership in a postwar international organization unless a "just" peace settlement was obtained. As the Republican Party's most influential congressional spokesman on foreign affairs, Vandenberg could well generate sufficient votes in the Senate to kill the United Nations Charter. The Michigan senator considered the Big Three's handling of the Polish question to have been definitely unjust. "I think the Polish settlement was *awful*," he wrote Bernard Baruch. The Yalta compromise was not only unfair, Vandenberg complained to the State Department, but might cause an unfortunate psychological reaction among the American people. The senator took an even blunter position in an off-the-record conversation with Washington reporters: "If a Dumbarton Oaks treaty is ever killed here in the Senate, over its body will stand the shadow of Poland." [63]

The unforeseen repercussions of a dramatic speech Vandenberg had made on the floor of the Senate one month earlier, however, severely limited his freedom to criticize the Yalta Polish agreement. Vandenberg had intended in this address, delivered on January 10, 1945, to propose a method of halting Soviet expansion without endangering the wartime alliance or the final peace settlement. Much to the senator's surprise, the speech had a vastly different effect.

Vandenberg had begun with a characteristically florid jab at President Roosevelt's "jocular, and even cynical, dismissal of the Atlantic Charter as a mere collection of fragmentary notes":

These basic pledges cannot now be dismissed as a mere nautical nimbus. They march with our armies. They sail with our fleets. They fly with our eagles. They sleep with our martyred dead. The first requisite of honest candor, Mr. President, I respectfully suggest, is to relight this torch.

[63] Vandenberg to Baruch, February 15, 1945, Baruch MSS; Vandenberg to Joseph C. Grew, February 19, 1945, Vandenberg, ed., *Private Papers*, p. 150; Frank McNaughton to *Time* home office, February 16, 1945, McNaughton MSS. See also Byrnes to Roosevelt, February 17, 1945, Roosevelt MSS, OF 4675: "Crimea Conf." I. F. Stone feared that Vandenberg's hostility to the Polish settlement might impair Russian cooperation in the war against Japan: "To insist on perfectionism along the Pripet Marshes might mean payment in American lives on Pacific Islands. That would be a high price to pay for Polish megalomania and American domestic politics." ("This Is What We Voted For," *Nation*, CLX [February 17, 1945], 175.)

He then called his colleagues' attention to the Soviet Union's apparent determination to create a sphere of influence in Eastern Europe "contrary to our conception of what we thought we were fighting for." Rather surprisingly, Vandenberg found Russia's actions "perfectly understandable": it was "her insistent purpose never again to be at the mercy of another German tyranny." The USSR had legitimate reasons for doubting the ability of the future world organization to keep Germany disarmed, especially since there was still no assurance that the United States would join it. But why could not the United States, the Soviet Union, and Great Britain immediately sign a treaty which would "permanently, conclusively, and effectively" disarm Germany and Japan? Such a treaty, Vandenberg hoped, "would make postwar Soviet expansion as illogical as it would be unnecessary." [64]

The senator's hopeless addiction to purple prose obscured the point of his speech, however, while another remark, made almost as an aside, captured most of the attention:

I do not believe that any nation hereafter can immunize itself by its own exclusive action. . . . Our oceans have ceased to be moats which automatically protect our ramparts. Flesh and blood now compete unequally with winged steel. War has become an all-consuming juggernaut. . . . I want maximum American cooperation, consistent with legitimate American self-interest, with constitutional process and with collateral events which warrant it, to make the basic idea of Dumbarton Oaks succeed.

Coming from the Senate's most influential former isolationist this statement, befogged in rhetoric and shrouded in reservations though it was, caused advocates of international organization to stir attentively. Vandenberg had in fact been moving toward a repudiation of isolationism for some time, but this was his first public pronouncement on the subject. Internationalists jumped to applaud the address, which *Time* extravagantly called "the most important speech made by an American in World War II." Vandenberg himself later confessed that he had been "completely surprised by the nationwide attention which the speech precipitated." [65]

---

[64] *Congressional Record*, January 10, 1945, pp. 164–67. Vandenberg also proposed that when military necessity required unilateral decisions, these would be subject to later review by the world organization.

[65] *Congressional Record*, January 10, 1945, p. 166; *Time*, XLV (January 22, 1945),

The political significance of the speech did not escape Roosevelt. The following day he called members of the Senate Foreign Relations Committee, including Vandenberg, to the White House to inform them of his plans for the Big Three meeting. At a cabinet meeting later that day both Stimson and Byrnes praised the address, commenting that it offered great possibilities for the President. Roosevelt himself asked for fifty copies of the speech before leaving for Yalta. On his return, he announced the appointment of Arthur H. Vandenberg to the American delegation to the San Francisco Conference.[66]

Roosevelt's action placed Vandenberg in a dilemma. He could not accept this appointment without seeming to endorse the Yalta decision on Poland. He could not decline without endangering Senate approval of the United Nations Charter. Furthermore, Vandenberg feared that his refusal to serve might hurt the Republican Party by reviving old charges of isolationism: "It would have been just about equivalent to committing suicide in public." Senator Wheeler saw Vandenberg's predicament clearly: "He's got a lot of Poles in his state, and they certainly didn't make a good settlement for Poland. . . . He climbed way out on a limb in that security speech of his, and now he can't get back. He is sweating plenty. . . . He doesn't like it, but he'll have to go along now." Vandenberg finally decided to go to San Francisco, reserving the right, as he wrote the President, to suggest amendments to the proposed charter and to judge for himself whether he could support the final result. But as one of the senator's fellow delegates noticed, Vandenberg "seemed a little grouchy and suspicious of the whole business." [67]

15–16; Vandenberg to Fred S. Robie, July 8, 1948, Vandenberg, ed., *Private Papers,* pp. 139–40. For summaries of the public reaction to Vandenberg's speech, see *ibid.,* pp. 138–44; and Department of State, "Fortnightly Survey of American Opinion," No. 19, January 19, 1945. Vandenberg's prose style, though often obscure, was not without its usefulness, as Richard Rovere later noted: "Vandenberg can make a retreat sound like a call to arms, an evasion like a declaration of lofty principle." ("The Unassailable Vandenberg," *Harper's,* CXCVI [May, 1948], 395–96.)

[66] *Newsweek,* XXV (January 22, 1945), 38; Stimson notes of cabinet meeting, January 11, 1945, Stimson MSS, Box 418; Vandenberg to Robie, July 8, 1948, Vandenberg, ed., *Private Papers,* p. 140.

[67] Vandenberg to John Foster Dulles, February 17, 1945, Vandenberg, ed., *Private Papers,* p. 152; Vandenberg to H. G. Hogan, March 26, 1945, Vandenberg MSS; Frank McNaughton to *Time* home office, February 16, 1945, McNaughton MSS; Vandenberg to Roosevelt, February 15 and March 1, 1945, Vandenberg, ed., *Private Papers,* pp. 149, 153; Virginia Gildersleeve, *Many a Good Crusade,* p. 318. See also

Vandenberg explained his decision in a letter to Detroit Polish-American leader Frank Januszewski: "I could get no greater satisfaction out of anything more than from joining—aye, in leading—a public denunciation of Yalta and all its works as respects Poland." But Vandenberg doubted whether this would really help: "It would be a relatively simple matter to dynamite the new Peace League. . . . What would *that* do for Poland? It would simply leave Russia in complete possession of everything she wants. . . . There would be no hope left for justice except through World War Number Three immediately." Vandenberg believed he could accomplish more for Poland by seeking justice through the United Nations and by holding the Roosevelt Administration to "strict accountability for the kind of a Provisional Polish Government which we shall be parties to imposing on Poland." [68]

By making Vandenberg a delegate to the San Francisco Conference Roosevelt skillfully restrained the most dangerous potential critic of the Yalta agreements on Eastern Europe. This ensured that these distasteful but necessary concessions to the Soviet Union would not endanger American membership in the future United Nations. It is a measure of Roosevelt's achievement that the strongest criticism of the Yalta accords came, not over their tacit acquiescence in Soviet control of Eastern Europe, but over Roosevelt's secret commitment to give the Russians three votes in the United Nations General Assembly.[69] The President's clumsy handling of this matter overshadowed the adept way in which he "sugar-coated" the far more significant Yalta decisions on Eastern Europe.

Roosevelt's death on April 12, 1945, made Senate approval of the United Nations Charter certain. The *New Republic* wrote that "Franklin Roosevelt at rest at Hyde Park is a more powerful force for America's participation in a world organization than was President Roosevelt in the White House." Tributes to the dead President and speculation about the new one quickly replaced the atmosphere of distrust which had poisoned relations between the White House and Capitol Hill.

Vandenberg's comments on how his refusal to serve would hurt the Republican Party in letters to Howard C. Lawrence, February 20, 1945, and Frank Januszewski, May 15, 1945, Vandenberg MSS.

[68] Vandenberg to Januszewski, March 7, 1945, Vandenberg, ed., *Private Papers,* pp. 155–56.

[69] *Time,* XLV (April 9 and 16, 1945), 23–24, 19–20. See also Divine, *Second Chance,* pp. 272–76.

With the martyrdom of Roosevelt the cause of international organization became sacrosanct for all but the most unregenerate isolationists.[70]

VI

But just as this overwhelming domestic consensus in favor of world organization was forming, the international consensus necessary for its success seemed to be dissipating. Soviet actions in Eastern Europe during the latter part of February showed that Moscow's interpretation of the "democratic" guarantees written into the Yalta agreements differed drastically from the meaning assigned them by Western observers. Andrei Vishinsky, Soviet deputy commissar for foreign affairs, arrived in Bucharest demanding immediate installation of a new Rumanian government which would be more sympathetic to Moscow than the existing regime. When the king of Rumania hesitated, Vishinsky gave him two hours to comply and then stalked out, banging the door so hard that it cracked the plaster in the king's study. Simultaneously, in the Soviet capital, tripartite negotiations on implementing the Yalta Polish agreement were getting nowhere. Soviet Foreign Minister Molotov insisted repeatedly that members of the Lublin regime should form the basis of the new Polish provisional government, and refused to consider the inclusion of representatives from the London government-in-exile. Ambassador Harriman, his patience wearing thin, reported that Molotov was obviously under instructions "to give as little ground as possible in the direction of bringing in elements not under Soviet control and to fight every inch of the way." [71]

During March other disturbing events took place. The Anglo-American effort to negotiate at Berne for the surrender of German armies in Italy brought a reaction from Stalin bordering on hysteria. American military officials were receiving reports of harsh treatment from United States prisoners-of-war who had been liberated by the Russians. The So-

[70] *New Republic*, CXII (April 23, 1945), 539–40. See also Department of State, "Fortnightly Survey of American Opinion," No. 25, April 24, 1945; and I. F. Stone, "Farewell to F.D.R.," *Nation*, CLX (April 21, 1945), 437.

[71] Burton Y. Berry to Stettinius, February 28 and March 7, 1945, *FR: 1945*, V, 487–88, 502; Harriman to Stettinius, March 2, 1945, *ibid.*, p. 136. For the full documentation on the Polish and Rumanian situations, see *ibid.*, pp. 123–217, 470–524.

viet Union demanded that the Lublin Poles be invited to send delegates to the San Francisco Conference, despite the fact that their government had not yet been broadened in accord with the Yalta decisions. Late in March, Moscow announced that Molotov would not be attending the San Francisco meeting, a development which seemed to indicate waning Russian enthusiasm for an international organization. By April 2, Secretary of State Stettinius was warning his colleagues in the cabinet that a serious deterioration in relations with the Soviet Union had taken place.[72]

It is not clear to what extent President Roosevelt expected literal compliance with the Yalta agreements. When asked at a press conference whether Russian actions in Rumania were consistent with the Declaration on Liberated Europe, he brushed the question off: "O my God! Ask the State Department." But he later wrote Stalin that he could not understand why Rumanian developments should not come under the terms of that declaration. On March 11, Roosevelt cabled Churchill that "neither the Government nor the people of this country will support participation in a fraud or mere whitewash of the Lublin Government." Three weeks later he wired Stalin:

While it is true that the Lublin Government is to be reorganized and its members play a prominent role it is to be done in such a fashion as to bring into being a new Government. This point is clearly brought out in several places in the text of the agreement. I must make it quite plain to you that any such solution which would result in a thinly disguised continuance of the present Warsaw regime would be unacceptable and would cause the people of the United States to regard the Yalta agreement as having failed.

On the day before he died, however, Roosevelt was in a more conciliatory mood. He wrote Churchill: "I would minimize the general Soviet problem as much as possible, because these problems, in one form or another, seem to arise every day, and most of them straighten out." [73]

[72] Stimson Diary, March 16, 17, April 2, 4, 1945, Stimson MSS; Leahy, *I Was There*, pp. 385–94; Grew memorandum of a conversation with Soviet ambassador Gromyko, March 23, 1945, *FR: 1945*, I, 148; Grew to Roosevelt, March 23, 1945, *ibid.*, pp. 151–52; Roosevelt to Stalin, March 24, 1945, *ibid.*, p. 156; Forrestal Diary, April 2, 1945, Millis, ed., *Forrestal Diaries*, pp. 38–39. See also *Time*, XLV (April 9, 1945), 23; and *Newsweek*, XXV (April 16, 1945), 24.

[73] Roosevelt press conference, March 13, 1945, Roosevelt MSS, PPF 1-P, Vol. XXV; Roosevelt to Stalin, April 1, 1945, *FR: 1945*, V, 194–96; Roosevelt to Churchill, March 11, 1945, *ibid.*, p. 157, and April 11, 1945, *ibid.*, p. 210.

Roosevelt may well have expected the Russians to allow free elections in Poland and the rest of Eastern Europe. The habit of wartime collaboration was still alive, and the readiness of the Russians at Yalta to promise these elections had been encouraging. When it began to look as though Moscow was stalling, the President became concerned. He never wavered, however, in his insistence that governments installed in power along Russia's borders be "friendly" to the Soviet Union. F.D.R.'s superficial knowledge of Eastern Europe kept him from fully realizing the contradiction between freely elected and pro-Russian governments in that turbulent part of the world. It was like a labor-management conflict in the United States, he once told Polish Prime Minister Mikolajczyk: all that was necessary was an impartial mediator to prod the negotiations along.[74] But whatever his expectations, the President by his actions had led the American people to expect free elections in Eastern Europe, while at the same time leading the Russians to expect a free hand. The peculiar mixture of naïveté and realism which characterized Roosevelt's East European policy had created a painful dilemma, which it would now be up to Harry S. Truman to resolve.

[74] Ciechanowski, *Defeat in Victory*, pp. 299–300.

6

×××

Economic Relations:
Lend-Lease and the Russian Loan

From the purely economic point of view, prospects for postwar Soviet-American cooperation seemed encouraging during World War II. The United States had built up a massive industrial plant to produce war materials not only for itself but also for its allies. Reconversion to the production of consumer goods would be at best a painful process, and could be disastrous, for no one knew whether the American economy could maintain full employment in peacetime. The Soviet Union needed heavy industrial equipment, partly to rebuild its war-devastated economy, partly to satisfy its people's long denied desire for more consumer goods. Moscow could solve its reconstruction problems, it appeared, by placing massive orders for industrial equipment with American firms. Filling these orders would help the United States deal with its own reconversion problems and, in the process, would begin to integrate the Soviet Union into the multilateral system of world trade to which Washington attached such great importance. Both countries, it seemed, had a strong interest in promoting this most promising of economic partnerships.

But neither the Soviet Union nor the United States found it easy to divorce economics from politics. As the end of the war approached, American leaders became increasingly concerned about emerging areas of conflict with Russia—especially the problems of German reparations and self-determination in Eastern Europe. Moreover, Congress by this time had made it clear that it would not support American efforts to finance world reconstruction unless the United States obtained substantial benefits therefrom. Accordingly, the Roosevelt Administration decided early in 1945 that the advantages of withholding aid to Russia in hopes of extracting political concessions outweighed the economic gains to be derived from extending such assistance.

Although the Russians viewed American economic aid as an important part of their reconstruction program, they were never willing to sacrifice major political objectives to obtain it. An alternative though less desirable method of rebuilding Soviet industry did exist—the extraction of massive reparations from Germany while maintaining tight controls over the Russian consumer economy. Furthermore, Soviet ideologists believed Moscow would be doing the Americans a favor by accepting economic assistance. Anticipating a postwar depression in the United States brought on by the "internal contradictions" of capitalism, they expected to have American businessmen practically forcing unsold products upon the Russians, and hence saw little need to make the concessions which Washington demanded. Conflicting political goals thus overrode congruent economic interests to produce another of the irritants which led to the disintegration of the Grand Alliance.

I

A large postwar loan to the Soviet Union seemed the most efficient way for the United States to assist Russian reconstruction. Prewar imports from the USSR had never reached substantial levels, and would not come close to balancing the vast quantity of goods which the Russians would want after World War II. The Soviet Union possessed large gold reserves, but could not finance large purchases indefinitely in that manner. A long-term loan, however, would allow the Russians to meet their reconstruction needs at once, while gradually paying off the debt through increasing exports to the United States. By extending such a loan, Washington could ensure American businessmen the foreign market they would need to maintain full employment after the war. Late in 1943 the United States government informed the Russians, through both official and unofficial channels, that it was prepared to consider such a loan.

W. Averell Harriman, the new American ambassador in Moscow, strongly advocated postwar economic cooperation with the Soviet Union. Harriman's international banking firm had extended credits to the Soviet government in the 1920s, and Harriman himself had visited the country several times. He found the Russians to be "most meticulous" in meeting their financial commitments. In 1941, President Roosevelt had chosen Harriman to go to Moscow to help arrange for the extension of lend-lease aid. Shortly before his appointment as ambassador in October, 1943, Harriman told Roosevelt that the Soviet Union was depending on the United States for help in postwar reconstruction. At a press conference held after his arrival in Moscow, he stated that American assistance in rebuilding the Soviet economy deserved "the greatest possible consideration at this time." [1]

Harriman favored aiding Russia for two reasons. Like many other Americans, he expected the end of the war to bring a sharp rise in unemployment in the United States which might cause another depression. The production of heavy industrial equipment for the USSR could keep American factories operating at full pace for some time to come. But Harriman did not view aid to Russia solely in terms of its effect on the domestic economy. Moscow's intention to dominate Eastern Europe already worried him, and he regarded a postwar loan as one of the few means by which Washington could affect Russian actions in that part of the world. "Economic assistance," he wrote Secretary of State Hull early in 1944, "is one of the most effective weapons at our disposal to influence European political developments in the direction we desire and to avoid the development of a sphere of influence of the Soviet Union over Eastern Europe and the Balkans." [2]

Donald M. Nelson, chairman of the War Production Board, also raised the possibility of economic collaboration with Moscow during a

[1] W. Averell Harriman, "From Stalin to Kosygin: The Myths and the Realities," *Look*, XXXI (October 3, 1967), 55–62; Harriman to Roosevelt, July 5, 1943, *FR: Tehran*, p. 15; Harriman press conference, November 4, 1943, *FR: 1943*, III, 586–89. See also Harriman, *America and Russia in a Changing World*, pp. 2–7.

[2] Harriman to Hull, March 13, 1944, *FR: 1944*, IV, 951. See also *ibid.*, pp. 944–45, 1052–55. For Harriman's concern about the domestic economy, see *FR: 1943*, III, 586–89, 781–86, and *FR: 1944*, IV, 1032–35.

visit to the Soviet Union in October, 1943. Nelson told the Russian leaders that "a great future" existed in trade with America. The United States would have available after the war a vast surplus of industrial equipment which the Russians could employ to rebuild their economy, while the Soviet Union had raw materials which the United States could use. Mutual self-interest called for economic cooperation, Nelson argued, for the two economies so obviously complemented each other. Stalin agreed. In a long interview on October 16, he told Nelson that Russians liked Americans and their products, and wanted to import commodities from the United States after the war. The Soviet leader asked whether his government could purchase these goods on credit. Nelson, speaking strictly as an individual, replied that credit could probably be arranged, with initial repayments kept small until the Soviets had completed reconstruction. Stalin showed great interest in this idea, repeatedly and forcefully assuring Nelson that an American investment in Soviet reconstruction would be a sound one. Impressed by what he had heard, Nelson returned to tell the American people that Russia could be "an excellent source of business for America." [3]

At the Moscow Foreign Ministers' Conference that same month, Secretary of State Hull told the Russians that Americans desired "to cooperate fully in the rehabilitation of war damage in the U.S.S.R.," and suggested that the Russians begin negotiations on this subject with United States Embassy officials in Moscow as soon as possible. Early in November, Harriman brought up the matter with Anastas I. Mikoyan, Soviet commissar for foreign trade. Harriman asked the Russians to start thinking about what they would need to rebuild their economy, and mentioned the possibility of an American loan. "It would be in the self-interest of the United States," the ambassador pointed out, "to be able to afford full employment during the period of transition from wartime to peacetime economy." [4]

Harriman and President Roosevelt discussed aid to Russia at the Teheran Conference in December, 1943, but the President did not get a

[3] Nelson-Molotov conversation, October 12, 1943, Nelson-Stalin conversation, October 16, 1943, *FR: 1943,* III, 710–15; Donald M. Nelson, "What I Saw in Russia," *Collier's,* CXIII (January 29, 1944), 11 ff.

[4] Moscow Conference Document No. 36, "U.S. Proposal on Cooperation in the Rehabilitation of War Damage in the Soviet Union," *FR: 1943,* I, 739; Bohlen notes of Harriman-Mikoyan conversation, November 5, 1943, *ibid.,* pp. 781–86.

chance to bring up the matter with Stalin. He did authorize Harriman to continue his direct negotiations with the Russians. Harriman did not have to initiate discussions, however, for late in December Molotov, showing "the keenest interest in the matter," asked him what might be done about a postwar credit. One month later Mikoyan proposed to Harriman that the United States lend Russia one billion dollars, at an interest rate of one-half of 1 percent, with repayment to begin sixteen years after extension of the credit.[5] The Russians thus responded enthusiastically to the American offer to assist their reconstruction. Only at this point, however, did Washington begin to examine seriously the economic, legal, and political implications of extending such assistance.

II

Before the United States could extend reconstruction credits to the Soviet Union, it would have to devise some way to terminate the massive flow of war material already reaching the Russians under lend-lease. From the beginning of the war Soviet lend-lease shipments had enjoyed a unique status. At Roosevelt's insistence, American authorities accepted Russian aid requests at face value, without the close scrutiny given applications from other allies. Moreover, as the war drew to a close, lend-lease shipments to Russia were not cut back, as were those to other nations. From June of 1941 through June of 1943, the Soviet Union received more than four and a half million tons of equipment of all kinds from the United States. During the next twelve months, the period of the Third Lend-Lease Protocol, shipments exceeded five and a half million tons.[6]

The original lend-lease agreement with the Soviet Union, announced on November 4, 1941, called for repayment without interest beginning five years after the end of the war. On June 11, 1942, however, the United States canceled this arrangement and put Russian lend-lease on

[5] Roosevelt to Harriman, December 1, 1943, Roosevelt MSS, OF 220, Box 2; Harriman to Hopkins, January 4, 1944, *FR: 1944*, IV, 1032–35; Harriman to Hull and Stettinius, February 1, 1944, *ibid.*, pp. 1041–42.

[6] Herring, "Lend-Lease to Russia and the Origins of the Cold War," p. 95; Robert Huhn Jones, *The Roads to Russia: United States Lend-Lease to the Soviet Union,* Appendix A.

the same basis as British lend-lease, thus removing the formal requirement of repayment. Congress accepted this procedure to help America's
allies fight a common enemy, but, ever-sensitive to the dangers of pour-
ing resources down foreign "rat-holes," demanded that lend-lease supplies
not be used to support postwar reconstruction efforts. As Senator Vandenberg put it, lend-lease must not extend "1 minute or $1 into the
post-war period." Such a neat distinction would be difficult to make,
however, for many of the items shipped to Russia for military purposes
could also be used for reconstruction.[7]

Ambassador Harriman repeatedly asked the Russians to distinguish
clearly between goods actually needed to fight the war and material to
be used to rebuild the Soviet economy. He pointed out that although
President Roosevelt wanted to interpret the Lend-Lease Act broadly, he
could not do so because lend-lease would be an issue in the 1944 political campaign. In dispatches to Washington, Harriman warned that the
Soviets were already ordering more under lend-lease than they needed to
fight the war: "Unless we now begin to get at the least some knowledge
of the purposes for which they are using our shipments we lay ourselves
wide open to just criticism at home." [8]

Harriman proposed to solve this problem by having the United States
government lend the Russians enough money to obtain what they
needed for reconstruction. The Administration could then observe the
wishes of Congress by restricting lend-lease shipments to items of strictly
military utility. The ambassador suggested an initial credit of $500 mil-
lion, with repayment to take up to thirty years at an interest rate of 2 to
3 percent. Later on, larger credits could be granted. In addition to facilitating the orderly termination of lend-lease, Harriman expected the
credit to improve postwar political relations with Russia and to provide
"an outlet for American manufactured goods at the time our factories
and labor are released from war production." Harriman emphasized the
necessity of referring to this extension of money as a "credit" and not a
"loan." The Russians generally understood a loan to be granted without

[7] McNeill, *America, Britain, and Russia*, p. 24; Herring, "Lend-Lease to Russia," p.
102.
[8] Harriman-Mikoyan conversation, November 5, 1943, *FR: 1943*, III, 781–86; Harriman to Hopkins, January 7, 1944, *FR: 1944*, IV, 1032–35; Harriman to Hopkins,
January 15, 1944, *ibid.*, pp. 1039–40; Harriman to the President's Soviet Protocol
Committee, March 2, 1944, *ibid.*, pp. 1057–58.

restrictions on its use. In this case, Harriman recommended insisting that the money be spent only to purchase American manufactured products, raw materials, and services. Since there were many "undetermined questions" in political relations with the Soviet Union, he advised that Washington retain control of the unallocated balance of the credit at all times, refusing to fill Soviet orders if for any reason it seemed inadvisable to do so.[9]

The Administration found Harriman's proposal impractical because it could not extend reconstruction credits to the Soviet Union without some form of congressional authorization. The Export-Import Bank had general authority to make foreign loans without specific congressional approval, but the Johnson Act of 1934 categorically prohibited both government and private loans to the Soviet Union.[10] Even if the Johnson Act had not been on the books, an Export-Import Bank credit to Russia would have required special action by Congress because the bank had now virtually exhausted its allotted capital of $700 million. Harry Hopkins, who handled Russian lend-lease matters for President Roosevelt, informed Harriman early in February, 1944, that for these reasons the Administration preferred not to extend a separate reconstruction credit to the Russians at that time.

Hopkins recommended that the Russians continue to meet their reconstruction needs through lend-lease and agree to reimburse the United States for items of more than strictly military utility. This plan would ensure a steady flow of material useful for both the war and reconstruction, without necessitating an approach to Congress. If it failed, the United States could always revert to Harriman's proposal. Hull told Harriman that he would form a special interdepartmental committee "to study and coordinate" all matters relating to the possible future extension of reconstruction credits.[11]

Harriman reluctantly accepted the use of lend-lease machinery to cir-

[9] Harriman to Hopkins, January 7, 1944, *FR: 1944,* IV, 1032–35; Harriman to Hull and Stettinius, January 9, 1944, *ibid.,* pp. 1035–36; Harriman to Hull, Stettinius, and Hopkins, January 9, 1944, *ibid.,* pp. 1036–37.

[10] The Soviet government had never agreed to assume the debts to the United States of its predecessors, the Tsarist and Provisional governments. For negotiations on this matter, see *FR: The Soviet Union, 1933–1939,* pp. 161–91.

[11] Hopkins to Harriman, February 4, 1944, *FR: 1944,* IV, 1043–46; Hull to Harriman, February 8, 1944, *ibid.,* pp. 1047–48.

cumvent legal difficulties prohibiting direct aid to Soviet reconstruction, but he warned that this did not solve the problem. The Russians were planning a fifteen-year reconstruction program. Unless the American government could assure them of long-term credits in some form, they would not want to do business with the United States. Exports to the USSR were going to be vital in keeping American factories busy after the war. If the United States delayed extending credits, "we would then lose a competitive advantage in obtaining business for the time when it is most needed for the readjustment of our own war production program."

Furthermore, Harriman stressed using aid to the Soviet Union as a political weapon. Employed correctly, it could ensure that the Russians "play the international game with us in accordance with out standards." Harriman thought that Stalin would have to offer his people the prospect of rapid reconstruction in order to stay in power. A program of assistance to Russia which the United States could suspend at any time would be of "extreme value." Economic aid could also be used in Eastern Europe to prevent that region from falling under the domination of Moscow. To secure these political benefits, however, the United States would need a "well-forged" economic instrument. Vague promises to extend aid at some indefinite time in the future would only arouse suspicions in Moscow. Harriman pleaded with Hopkins not to let the question of aiding Russian reconstruction be bottled up in Hull's committee. He acknowledged the existence of difficulties in extending credits, but hoped that the economic and political advantages which he had mentioned might "offer ammunition for dealing with this aspect." [12]

Despite Harriman's reservations, the Roosevelt Administration stuck to its position. The Russians continued to satisfy their reconstruction needs through lend-lease, subject only to the condition that they reimburse the United States for material of more than military value.[13] This decision not to distinguish between lend-lease and reconstruction credits caused trouble later on when the Russians insisted on continuing this policy, while Congress, appalled by the prospect of reconstructing the world at the expense of the American taxpayer, demanded rigid separa-

[12] Harriman to Hopkins, February 13, 1944, *FR: 1944,* IV, 1052–53; Harriman to Hull and Stettinius, February 14, 1944, *ibid.,* pp. 1054–55.
[13] Stettinius and Leo T. Crowley to Roosevelt, March 6, 1944, *FR: 1944,* IV, 1059–60; Stettinius to Harriman, March 7, 1944, *ibid.,* pp. 1060–62.

tion. By the time Harriman's plan for a separate reconstruction credit was revived early in 1945, the political atmosphere was far less favorable to it than it had been in 1944.

III

The prospects for postwar Soviet-American trade would to a considerable extent determine the feasibility of a large American loan to the Soviet Union, for if imports from Russia failed to exceed exports, it would be difficult for the Russians to repay the loan in a reasonable length of time. Prewar trade figures were not encouraging. Between 1922 and 1938, exports to the USSR usually constituted between 1 and 2 percent of total American exports, and never exceeded 5 percent. Imports from the Soviet Union exceeded 1 percent of total imports only in 1938. The value of American exports to the Soviet Union fluctuated wildly from as high as $113.4 million in 1929 to as little as $8.9 million in 1933, averaging somewhat less than $50 million during the entire interwar period. American imports from the Soviet Union averaged only about $15 million annually.[14]

State Department officials felt pessimistic about the possibility of increasing imports from Russia. Elbridge Durbrow of the department's Division of European Affairs observed late in 1943 that, contrary to popular belief, the Russian and American economies were not complementary. The Soviet Union produced few goods which the United States could use. On the basis of anticipated trade figures, credits, if expected to be repaid within ten to twenty years, could not exceed $200 million. Hence, "extreme caution" should be taken to avoid giving false impressions regarding postwar trade opportunities with the Soviet Union. In April, 1944, the department received a report which predicted that after the war the United States would import from the Soviet Union only one-third of what it exported. A large American loan might increase American exports to that country for a time, but amortization and interest requirements would make it difficult for the Soviets to continue to

[14] Department of Commerce figures, cited in Ernest C. Ropes, "The Union of Soviet Socialist Republics as a Factor in World Trade," *World Economics,* II (October–December, 1944), 81.

take large American exports and still maintain a balance of payments equilibrium.[15]

Ambassador Harriman refused to admit that postwar American imports from the Soviet Union had to be so small. While he applauded the State Department's wish to deflate exaggerated optimism about trade with Russia, he called at the same time for a more positive program of stimulating imports "to the fullest extent possible." Russian requirements for American industrial equipment would be so great, Harriman felt, that trade between the two nations could advance significantly above prewar levels "provided we will adopt import policies that will make it possible." [16]

George F. Kennan, counselor of the embassy in Moscow, did not share his chief's optimism. Kennan regarded the problem of Russian foreign trade and credits as "simpler than people are apt to think." The Soviet Union would not depend on foreign trade in the postwar period and would not likely give up anything it considered vital to obtain such trade. Russia would accept credits from the West but would not be grateful for them, assuming that the nations extending them were acting in their own self-interest. Kennan worried that if a large portion of the American economy became dependent on Soviet trade orders, the Russians would not hesitate to exploit this dependence in ways detrimental to the United States.[17]

The Office of Strategic Services, surveying prospects for Russian-American economic relations in September, 1944, concluded that Soviet reconstruction would depend very little on foreign credit. A loan of $1 billion a year for the next three years would speed up rehabilitation of the Russian economy by no more than a few months. The rate of reconstruction would depend more on whether the Russians felt they had to maintain a large peacetime military establishment than on the availability of credits. Early in 1945 the State Department estimated that with-

[15] Durbrow memorandum, November 29, 1943, *FR: 1943,* III, 722–23; Report by the Interdepartmental Subcommittee on the Soviet Union of the Committee on Trade Agreements, "Aspects of Post-War Soviet Foreign Trade" (abstract), April, 1944, *FR: 1944,* IV, 959–60.

[16] Harriman to Hull, April 1, 1944, *FR: 1944,* IV, 958.

[17] Kennan memorandum, "Russia—Seven Years Later," September, 1944, printed in Kennan, *Memoirs,* pp. 503–31; Kennan to Harriman, December 3, 1944 [apparently misdated 1945], quoted *ibid.,* pp. 267–68.

out receiving foreign loans and through only limited use of its gold reserves the Soviet Union could, with the help of German reparations, regain its prewar level of capital investment by 1948. American credits would accelerate the process by only a matter of months. The Soviet Union, the department concluded, would therefore be able "to take a highly independent position in negotiations regarding foreign credits." [18]

Not all government officials concerned with Russian-American economic relations shared the pessimism of Kennan, the O.S.S., and the State Department. Ernest C. Ropes, chief of the Russian Unit of the Commerce Department's Bureau of Foreign and Domestic Commerce, foresaw a substantial postwar increase in American imports from the USSR. This would come about as a result of efforts by the United States to expand its world trade, and from the Soviet Union's natural desire to sell more in a market where it was making large purchases. Ropes acknowledged, however, that American imports from Russia would not come close to equaling exports, especially in the years immediately after the war. To make the purchases they wanted from the United States, the Russians would need credits running from ten to thirty years.

Ropes predicted that the Soviet Union would be a good credit risk. In lending money, one usually considered both the borrower's capacity and his willingness to repay. Russia's economic resources exceeded those of any other country, and its prewar reputation for meeting financial obligations had been excellent. "It would seem," Ropes concluded, "that the Soviet case is strong, and that the United States, to keep its war-expanded industry producing at a high rate in peace-time, could hardly find a means readier to its hand than to bid for Soviet business." [19]

The Treasury Department also rated the prospects for American imports from Russia higher than did the State Department. Treasury Secre-

[18] Summary prepared by Samuel Lubell in March, 1945, of an Office of Strategic Services study, "Russian Reconstruction and Postwar Foreign Trade Developments," September 9, 1944, Baruch MSS, "Selected Correspondence"; memorandum by Emilio G. Collado, January 4, 1945, *FR: 1945*, V, 938–40.

[19] Ropes, "The Union of Soviet Socialist Republics as a Factor in World Trade," pp. 85–86. Ropes retained his optimism about the benefits of a credit to Russia long after most people had given up hope. As late as the summer of 1946, after a trip to Russia, he was saying that the extension of a $1 billion credit to Russia would result in purchases by the Russians of $2 billion worth of American products. (*New York Times,* July 31, 1946.)

tary Henry Morgenthau, Jr., worried about the depletion of American natural resources, hoped to obtain strategic raw materials from the Soviet Union in return for a large, long-term loan. Early in 1944 he asked his assistant, Harry Dexter White, to estimate what quantities of mercury, manganese, chromium, and other strategic commodities the Soviet Union could produce and the United States could absorb. White predicted that the United States could import more than enough raw materials to allow the Russians to pay off a $5 billion loan in thirty years. The Russians could use this credit to purchase badly needed industrial and agricultural equipment from American firms. This arrangement would provide the United States with an important source of raw materials while at the same time guaranteeing a vast market for American industrial products.[20]

Although government agencies took a mixed view of the prospects for Soviet-American trade, American businessmen expressed fewer reservations. Concerned about finding postwar markets, they looked to the USSR as a new, virtually untapped field. Russia's massive reconstruction needs, they anticipated, would be met largely with American industrial equipment. Moreover, many businessmen believed that the Soviet government could not go on indefinitely denying its people a higher standard of living. Russia's masses would emerge from the war with an insatiable appetite for consumer goods, and while the Russian government might not want to import items directly from the United States, it would doubtless need to import the machines necessary to produce consumer goods for such a large market.

No one did more to propagate this point of view among businessmen than Eric Johnston, the dynamic young president of the United States Chamber of Commerce whom one admirer described as "the savior of his free-enterprise faith, the Luther of a business reformation." Johnston spent eight weeks in the Soviet Union in the summer of 1944. The Russians received him with the enthusiasm they reserved for prominent capitalists, allowing him to travel wherever he wanted and, in an unprecedented move, permitting reporters to accompany him. Johnston met with Foreign Trade Commissar Mikoyan and Foreign Minister Molotov,

[20] Blum, *Morgenthau Diaries: Years of War,* p. 304; White to Morgenthau, March 7, 1944, White MSS, Folder 23.

and on the evening of June 26, 1944, held a lengthy interview with Joseph Stalin.[21]

The interview started badly with Johnston suggesting that Stalin import American chain-store executives to improve Soviet distribution practices, while the Russian dictator drew wolves on his doodling pad and predicted a postwar depression in the United States. When the talk turned to economic relations with America, however, Stalin brightened. He proceeded to give Johnston the most complete account of Russia's postwar economic plans that any American had yet received. Stalin told Johnston that the Russians would import heavy industrial equipment, but not consumer goods. They would use some of this equipment to produce consumer goods themselves. Russia would not export manufactured products in large number, since these would be needed at home, but would export large quantities of raw materials. Stalin gave some hint of what would be demanded of the Russian economy when he told Johnston that steel production, then running about 10 to 12 million tons annually, would be increased to 60 million tons.

The Russian leader indicated that the Soviets wanted to purchase virtually unlimited quantities of American products, depending on what credit terms were extended. They would "pay promptly for everything, strictly in accordance with the terms of the contract." Listing possible Russian exports to the United States, Stalin asked: "Would you like manganese? We have quantities. We could give you chrome, platinum, copper, oil, tungsten. And then there's timber and pulp wood and furs. Perhaps you will want gold. . . . Most capitalistic countries want gold." Russia's requirements were so great, Stalin said, and its development so meager, that "I can foresee no time when we will have enough of anything." Ending the interview in a burst of good fellowship, the jovial autocrat told Johnston: "I like to do business with American businessmen. You fellows know what you want. Your word is good and, best of all, you stay in office a long time—just like we do over here. But a politician is here today and gone tomorrow, and then you have to make arrangements all over with a new set." [22]

[21] John Chamberlain, "Eric Johnston," *Life,* XVI (June 19, 1944), 97–98. For an account of Johnston's reception in the Soviet Union, see Harrison E. Salisbury, "Russia Beckons Big Business," *Collier's,* CXIV (September 2, 1944), 11 ff. On Johnston's meeting with Mikoyan and Molotov, see *FR: 1944,* IV, 967–68.

[22] Eric Johnston, "My Talk with Joseph Stalin," *Reader's Digest,* XLV (October,

Johnston reported to the members of the United States Chamber of Commerce that he found a growing sense of nationalism in Russia, a lessening of the traditional suspicion of foreigners, and, above all, a great desire for peace and the economic rehabilitation peace would bring: "Every top Communist leader with whom I discussed the problem talked about the need of raising the standard of living of the Russian people and the devoting of their resources as much as possible to that end after the war, particularly the production of consumer goods." The Russians greatly admired the United States, Johnston observed, especially its productive capacity. "They want to imitate America as far as possible, and that goes for the standard of living." Moscow would need long-term credits, either from private investors or from the United States government, but would constitute an excellent risk—credits to the Soviet Union would be as good as any in the postwar international field. The Russians would repay American credits with raw materials which the United States badly needed. By giving credit to the USSR the United States would not be aiding a future competitor—Russia "needs so much of almost every conceivable thing that I can foresee no period within our lifetime when Russia will be a competitor in the markets of the world with her produce." [23]

Johnston's conclusions were widely reported in business and financial publications and received a sympathetic hearing from American industrialists. A. M. Hamilton, foreign sales vice-president of the American Locomotive Company, described the Soviet Union as "potentially our greatest postwar customer." William L. Batt, vice-chairman of the War Production Board and president of S.K.F. Industries, wrote that "the problem of trade with Russia is easier of solution than the problem of trade with any other part of the world. The question is not likely to be, How much and how fast does Russia want our goods, but How fast and under what conditions are we able and willing to furnish them?" New York University's Institute of International Finance reported that under favorable conditions postwar Russian-American trade could surpass all previous records. The magazine *Industrial Marketing* called Russia

1944), 1–10. For Ambassador Harriman's somewhat more prosaic account of this meeting, see Harriman to Hull, June 30, 1944, *FR: 1944*, IV, 973–74.

[23] Report to the United States Chamber of Commerce, printed in *Export and Trade Shipper*, XLIX (July 31, 1944), 5–6. See also Eric Johnston, "A Business View of Russia," *Nation's Business*, XXXII (October, 1944), 21–22.

"without doubt the richest potential export market for American industrial equipment and products in the immediate and future postwar period." [24]

Fortune magazine reported in January, 1945, that some seven hundred American corporations had paid more than a quarter of a million dollars to place advertisements in a "Catalogue of American Engineering and Industry" which Russian representatives in New York were preparing to send to Soviet purchasing agencies. Predictions of postwar exports to Russia ran from $500 million to $5 billion, with most observers foreseeing exports of between $1 billion and $2 billion annually. The American-Russian Chamber of Commerce and the Chase National Bank were planning a public campaign to get the Johnson Act repealed so that private bankers could extend loans to Russia. Five other large banks were discussing the possibility of forming a combination to finance Russian trade. American bankers considered Russia an unusually good credit risk, oddly enough, because trade in the Soviet Union was a state monopoly. Funds would always be available to meet commitments. Since the Soviets could probably secure a loan from the United States government on more favorable terms than from private sources, however, most potential investors hesitated to act until Washington had decided what to do about a large reconstruction credit.[25]

Prospects for trade with the Soviet Union did not cause American businessmen to change their attitude toward Russia overnight. *Fortune*'s survey noted that major industrialists still felt vague anxieties about the dangers of communism, the emergence of Russia as the dominant military power in Europe and Asia, and the possibility that the USSR might in time become a major competitor for world markets. But, lacking confidence in the ability of their own economy to operate successfully in peacetime, leaders of the American business community could not help

[24] "What Business with Russia?" *Fortune,* XXXI (January, 1945), 153 ff.; William L. Batt, "Can We Do Business with Russia?" *Sales Management,* LV (October 15, 1945), 202; "The Prospects of Soviet-American Trade Relations," New York University Institute of International Finance, *Bulletin,* No. 139, August 27, 1945, p. 1; "Selling the Soviet," *Industrial Marketing,* XXX (July, 1945), 46 ff.

[25] "What Business with Russia?" pp. 153 ff.; "Russian-American Trade," *Index* [publication of the New York Trust Company], XXV (September, 1945), 62–72. On the security of Russia as a credit risk, see New York University Institute of International Finance, *Bulletin,* No. 139, August 27, 1945, p. 16; and William M. Mandel, "Russia—Our Biggest Postwar Market?" *Advertising and Selling,* XXXVII (May, 1944), 29 ff.

regarding with anticipation the advantages of helping the Russians attain that competitive position.[26]

Interestingly enough, both the Russian bid for a loan and the willingness of American businessmen to consider it were based on the belief that after the war the United States would undergo a serious depression. Current Marxist doctrine taught that internal contradictions would bring the capitalist system grinding to a halt soon after the war, and that in order to survive industries in the United States would have to seek new markets abroad.[27] Many American business leaders expected precisely the same thing, though for different reasons. They knew that the New Deal had not solved the problem of maintaining full employment in peacetime, and that after the artificial stimulus of military expenditures had ceased to operate, foreign markets might be the only means of avoiding another disastrous depression.[28] As it turned out, postwar economic developments in the United States proved both Marxist ideologues and American capitalists wrong. But before these events had had time to occur, political difficulties intervened to alter the whole framework in which the Russian loan had been discussed.

IV

American diplomats had never really divorced political considerations from the question of financing postwar reconstruction in the Soviet Union. Ambassador Harriman consistently regarded aid to Russia as "one of our principal levers for influencing political action compatible with our principles." [29] But during 1943 and 1944, most discussions of

[26] "What Business with Russia?" p. 204. An American Institute of Public Opinion poll, taken in August, 1945, found that by a majority of more than two to one business and professional leaders believed that the Russians could be trusted to cooperate with the United States after the war, a figure significantly higher than for other major occupation groups. (Cantril and Strunk, eds., *Public Opinion*, p. 371.)

[27] For convenient summaries of this point of view, see Leonard Schapiro, *The Communist Party of the Soviet Union*, pp. 532–33; and Ulam, *Expansion and Coexistence*, p. 410.

[28] William A. Williams, *The Tragedy of American Diplomacy*, pp. 217–18, 232–39; L. Gardner, *Economic Aspects of New Deal Diplomacy*, pp. 263–64, 282–83, 290–91.

[29] Harriman to Hull, March 13, 1944, *FR: 1944*, IV, 951. See also Harriman to Hull, September 20, 1944, *ibid.*, p. 997.

this subject had taken place within a primarily economic framework. The main benefit which Washington expected to receive from the proposed loan to Russia—full peacetime employment—was economic in nature, as were the principal factors impeding the extension of credits—the difficulty of ensuring repayment and the existence of legal restrictions on foreign lending. But by January of 1945, when the Russians again raised the question of a postwar loan, the atmosphere had changed. As the approach of victory exposed conflicts of interest with the Soviet Union, particularly in Eastern Europe and Germany, Washington officials came to feel that the political advantages of withholding the loan might well surpass the profits to be gained from extending it.

On January 3, 1945, Russian Foreign Minister Molotov told Harriman that if the United States would extend to the Soviet Union a $6 billion loan at an interest rate of $2\frac{1}{4}$ percent, the Soviet government would place large orders for capital equipment in the United States. Molotov pointedly reminded Harriman of "the repeated statements of American public figures" that such large orders would ease the American economy's transition from war to peace. Coming with no previous warning, the Russian "offer" surprised the American ambassador, who considered it "extraordinary both in form and substance." [30]

Nevertheless, Harriman advised the Department of State to disregard the unconventional form and unreasonable terms of Molotov's proposal, ascribing them to "ignorance of normal business procedures and the strange ideas of the Russians on how to get the best trade." The United States, he felt, should do everything it could through the extension of credits to help the Russians develop a sound economy. Friendly postwar relations would depend to some extent on American assistance in solving Russian reconstruction problems. Moreover, the sooner the Soviet government could provide a decent life for its people, the more tractable it would become. At the same time, the United States should make it quite clear to the Russians "that our willingness to cooperate with them . . . will depend upon their behavior in international matters." Washington should retain full control of any credits granted to Moscow in order to derive from them the maximum political advantages.[31]

[30] Harriman to Stettinius, January 4, 1945, *FR: 1945,* V, 942–44. Molotov proposed that the credit run for thirty years, with amortization to begin at the end of the ninth year.

[31] Harriman to Stettinius, January 6, 1945, *FR: 1945,* V, 945–47.

Meanwhile, and apparently coincidentally, Treasury Secretary Morgenthau was reviving his department's plan for extending credits to Russia. In a letter to Roosevelt early in January, he proposed giving the Russians a loan of $10 billion at 2 percent interest for the purchase of American products. The Russians would repay the loan mainly by exporting strategic raw materials, with amortization to extend over a period of thirty-five years.[32]

But Morgenthau encountered unsympathetic responses from both President Roosevelt and Secretary of State Stettinius when he talked this matter over with them on January 10, 1945. Roosevelt did not want to discuss credits with the Russians until after the forthcoming Yalta Conference, and seemed to favor using them as a device to extract concessions on other issues: "I think it's very important that we hold this back and don't give them any promises of finance until we get what we want." Later that day Morgenthau remarked to Stettinius that in dealing with the Russians one should offer the carrot and not the stick. Stettinius replied: "Henry, I don't think you'd feel that way if you knew all . . . if you had all the chips before you." On the following day Roosevelt told a group of senators that the loan might be a strong bargaining point to use in dealings with the Soviet Union, and that he had decided to take no action on the Russian request until he had talked to Stalin.[33]

The State Department now began to formulate a response to the suggestions of both the Russians and Morgenthau. Emilio G. Collado, chief of the Division of Financial and Monetary Affairs, did much to establish the department's position. Collado did not attempt to evaluate the wisdom of extending the loan itself, but emphasized the domestic political and economic difficulties it would entail. Congressmen would almost certainly balk at legislating credits for either the Soviet Union or

[32] Morgenthau to Roosevelt, January 1 and 10, 1945, *FR: 1945,* V, 937–38, 948–49. Morgenthau anticipated that, in addition to exporting raw materials to the United States, the Russians would repay the loan by exporting gold from their own reserves and dollars obtained from a favorable trade balance with the rest of the world, from the American tourist trade, and from the sale of some nonstrategic items to the United States.

[33] Morgenthau Diary, January 10, 1945, Blum, *Morgenthau Diaries: Years of War,* pp. 305–6; minutes, Secretary of State's Staff Committee meetings, January 12 and 19, 1945, Stettinius MSS, Box 235. According to Morgenthau, Stettinius actually prevented him from showing Roosevelt Harriman's telegram supporting the extension of a loan. Stettinius apparently did furnish Roosevelt with a summary of Harriman's views, however. See Stettinius to Roosevelt, January 8, 1945, *FR: 1945,* V, 947–48.

Great Britain. Morgenthau's plan to use the Russian loan to obtain stockpiles of strategic raw materials would not arouse enthusiasm on Capitol Hill, but would antagonize petroleum and mining interests. Consequently credits, if granted, would have to be extended through the Export-Import Bank, where special legislation would not be required. But this approach too would create problems, for Congress would have to extend the bank's lending authority before it could make a substantial loan. The lowest rate of interest which the bank could charge without discriminating against other borrowers was 4 percent, a rate almost twice what the Russians had proposed to pay. Collado admitted that a loan could benefit Soviet-American political relations, but thought that the economic boost it would give to American industry had been exaggerated.[34]

Other government officials raised additional objections. Leo T. Crowley, foreign economic administrator, thought that long-term credits would be an important element in Soviet-American relations, but pointed out that it would take some time to secure legislation to make credits possible. Elbridge Durbrow, chief of the State Department's Division of Eastern European Affairs, argued that the Soviet loan request was simply an attempt to secure lend-lease on a permanent basis. Edward S. Mason, deputy to Assistant Secretary of State William L. Clayton, warned that if the Russians were allowed to borrow money from the United States at exceptionally low interest rates, "it will have acted as a strong stimulus to state socialism, by enabling governments to undertake developmental investment on more favorable terms than those available to private investors." [35]

Determined to press for his proposal, Morgenthau forcefully argued that the United States should give a credit of $10 billion to the Russians immediately, without attaching conditions of any kind. In this way the United States could reassure the Soviets of its desire to live in peace after the war. Assistant Secretary of State Clayton, responding to Morgenthau's "impossible" proposal, summarized the arguments of his colleagues and then brought out into the open the political consideration at

[34] Memoranda by Collado, January 4 and 17, 1945, *FR: 1945,* V, 938–40, 956–60.

[35] Crowley to Stettinius, January 13, 1945, *FR: 1945,* V, 951–52; Durbrow to Clayton, January 11, 1945, *ibid.,* pp. 949–50; memorandum by Edward S. Mason, February 7, 1945, *ibid.,* pp. 973–75.

which Roosevelt and Stettinius had hinted: it would be harmful from the tactical point of view to grant such a large loan "and thus lose what appears to be the only concrete bargaining lever for use in connection with the many other political and economic problems which will arise between our two countries." [36]

The State Department on January 27, 1945, authorized the Moscow Embassy to inform the Russian government that

this Government is now studying ways and means of providing long-term credits for postwar projects. It will be some time before the necessary legislation can be enacted and a determination made with respect to the amounts which we can make available for this purpose. Until this can be done, no definite agreement can be formalized with respect to a credit for supplies of a purely post-war nature. It is the definite opinion of this Government that long-term postwar credits constitute an important element in the postwar relations between our two countries.

Summarizing the factors behind this decision in a telegram for Harriman, the department reiterated Collado's arguments that requests for specific congressional loan authorizations should be avoided, that the proposed interest rate would cause difficulties with the Export-Import Bank, and that the importation of Soviet raw materials would provoke opposition from petroleum and mining interests. Finally, "it would seem harmful at this time to offer such a large credit and lose what little bargaining exists in future credit extensions." The department asked that nothing more be done on this matter until Roosevelt had had a chance to discuss it with Stalin at Yalta. At the Big Three conference, however, the question of postwar credits received only passing attention from the foreign ministers. Churchill, Roosevelt, and Stalin apparently never got around to it.[37]

James Reston of the *New York Times* learned of the Russian request for a $6 billion loan sometime in January. Undersecretary of State Joseph C. Grew, whom Reston had asked for guidance on the story, said that he could make no comment, "but I would say, off-the-record and in

[36] Unsigned, undated memorandum, "Proposals Made by the Secretary of the Treasury to the Secretary of State Regarding Postwar Trade with the Soviet Union," *FR: 1945,* V, 961–63; Clayton memorandum of conversation with Morgenthau, January 25, 1945, *ibid.,* p. 966; Clayton to Stettinius, January 20, 1945, *ibid.,* pp. 964–66.

[37] Grew to Kennan, January 27, 1945, *FR: 1945,* V, 968–70; Grew to Harriman, January 26, 1945, *ibid.,* pp. 967–68; *FR: Yalta,* pp. 608–10.

a purely friendly way, that I advised him to go slow." Reston replied that the story was bound to break in two or three days and that his only wish was to present the whole picture. Grew remarked somewhat enigmatically that "there was no picture," and declined to elaborate his remarks. Two days later Reston's substantially accurate account of the Soviet loan request appeared on the front page of the *New York Times.* Reston concluded his story with the observation that "some members of the Administration [feel] that the present time is not propitious for discussing a post-war deal of this magnitude and it is said to be unlikely that it will be acted upon for some time." [38]

The Administration therefore postponed action for the second time on a Soviet loan request, evidently with the intention of extracting political concessions. Ironically, Treasury Secretary Morgenthau's simultaneous proposal probably stiffened State Department opposition to the idea. Top State Department officials still strongly resented Morgenthau's recent attempts to influence policy on Germany, and doubtless bristled automatically at this new Treasury incursion into diplomacy. When James F. Byrnes became secretary of state in July, 1945, he expressed the general departmental attitude by placing Morgenthau's proposal in the "Forgotten File," taking time only to muse that "our Treasury officials were not always the cold-hearted, glassy-eyed individuals all bankers are supposed to be." [39]

V

Meanwhile, the Administration's efforts to arrange for the orderly termination of lend-lease had collapsed, owing to the obstinacy of the Russians. During the spring of 1944, the United States government had proposed that the Soviet Union comply with congressional requirements by

---

[38] Grew memorandum of conversation with Reston, January 24, 1945, Grew MSS; *New York Times,* January 26, 1945.

[39] Byrnes, *All in One Lifetime,* p. 310. Thomas G. Paterson, "The Abortive American Loan to Russia and the Origins of the Cold War, 1943–1946," *Journal of American History,* LVI (June, 1969), 80–81, 91–92, implies that the Truman Administration was responsible for the decision to use the loan to secure political concessions from the Russians. Evidence cited above indicates that leading figures in the Roosevelt Administration supported this policy, however, and that the decision to implement it had been made by February, 1945.

providing reimbursement for lend-lease materials used in postwar reconstruction. The Roosevelt Administration offered to lend the Russians whatever amount of money was necessary to pay for these goods, at an interest rate of 2⅜ percent for thirty years. Moscow accepted the basic outline of this arrangement, but balked at the interest rate. Negotiations bogged down, and the Russians refused to sign the Fourth Lend-Lease Protocol, covering shipments of supplies from July of 1944 through June of 1945. This in no way impeded the flow of lend-lease goods to Russia, but it did delay agreement on how to distinguish between items of purely military value and those potentially useful for reconstruction.[40]

Both Roosevelt's advisers and congressional leaders were demanding with increasing regularity that such a distinction be made. Ambassador Harriman and General Deane repeatedly warned from Moscow that the Russians were taking advantage of American generosity by ordering more material under lend-lease than they needed to fight the war. *Newsweek* reported in August, 1944, that senators who had never criticized the use of lend-lease in wartime were now planning to oppose its use for reconstruction. Secretary of War Stimson pleaded with Roosevelt in October not to try to employ lend-lease supplies for postwar rehabilitation without securing new congressional authorization. Lauchlin Currie, one of Roosevelt's administrative assistants, warned him early in 1945 that "should the Russo-German war end and Russia *not* be at war with Japan, there will be great pressure from Congress and the press to cease lend-lease unless Russia goes to war with Japan." [41]

When the annual lend-lease extension bill came before the House of Representatives in March of 1945, Representative John Vorys, Republican of Ohio, introduced an amendment categorically prohibiting the use of lend-lease for postwar relief, rehabilitation, or reconstruction. Worried over congressional suspicions regarding the use of lend-lease after the

[40] For a convenient summary of negotiations on this subject during 1944, see John H. Fletcher to Collado and Clayton, January 17, 1945, *FR: 1945,* V, 954–56. The Russians finally signed the Fourth Protocol on April 17, 1945. (*Ibid.,* p. 997.)

[41] Herring, "Lend-Lease to Russia," pp. 96–98; *Newsweek,* XXIV (September 4, 1944), 19; Stimson Diary, October 13, 1944, quoted in Stimson and Bundy, *On Active Service,* pp. 592–93; Currie memorandum, drafted on November 14, 1944, sent to Roosevelt on January 19, 1945, Roosevelt MSS, PSF 57: "Crimea Conf." See also a memorandum by Harry Dexter White of a conversation between Stimson and Morgenthau, September 20, 1944, *FR: Yalta,* pp. 139–40; and Leahy, *I Was There,* pp. 320–21, 329.

war, the Roosevelt Administration decided not to oppose the Vorys Amendment, which had attracted considerable support from Republicans and some Democrats. Foreign Economic Administrator Crowley instead suggested a compromise which would forbid use of lend-lease for reconstruction but would allow recipient nations to obtain all goods contracted for provided they paid for what arrived after the end of the war. The Foreign Affairs Committee unanimously approved this arrangement, advising the full House of Representatives that such a clear expression of congressional intent would prevent future misunderstandings. Representative Karl Mundt told the House that "with this amendment added, there can be no post-war economic activities by Lend-Lease except through the most flagrant violation of the intent of Congress." The amended version of the lend-lease extension bill passed the House on March 13, 1945.[42]

The Foreign Economic Administration now recommended withdrawing the American proposal to let the Russians order reconstruction materials through the still unsigned Fourth Protocol. Instead the government should adopt a new policy, in line with the wishes of Congress, which would see to it that the Soviet Union did not receive significant amounts of heavy industrial equipment under lend-lease after the war. Ambassador Harriman approved this idea, pointing out that many of the arguments which a year earlier had caused him to recommend making American goods available for Russian rehabilitation were no longer present. On March 23, 1945, President Roosevelt officially approved the FEA's suggestion.[43]

When the Senate took up lend-lease extension early in April, it showed that it felt even more strongly than the House about the postwar uses of lend-lease. One group of senators regarded the Crowley-Vorys compromise as a clever loophole designed precisely to conceal the

[42] *Newsweek,* XXV (March 26, 1945), 46–48; *Congressional Record,* March 13, 1945, pp. 2120–21, 2124.

[43] Stettinius to Harriman, March 16, 1945, *FR: 1945,* V, 988; Harriman to Stettinius, March 20, 1945, *ibid.,* pp. 988–89; Grew and Crowley to Roosevelt, March 23, 1945, *ibid.,* p. 991. In his dispatch to Harriman Stettinius mentioned "recent discussions in Congress" as one reason why the Foreign Economic Administration was recommending this change of policy. Harriman, in his reply, expressed the hope that the Administration would continue to give the Russians "justifiable hopes" of working out an arrangement for a completely separate long-term reconstruction credit.

employment of lend-lease for reconstruction. Their attempt to remove this provision from the bill, thereby cutting off all lend-lease upon the termination of hostilities, failed on a 39-39 tie vote. On April 17, 1945, President Truman signed the amended lend-lease bill into law. The mood of Congress impressed itself vividly on the new Chief Executive. Truman regarded European reconstruction as a cause worthy of American assistance, but felt that this assistance should come through the Export-Import Bank. "If we undertook to use any Lend-Lease money for rehabilitation purposes we would open ourselves to Congressional criticism." [44]

Roosevelt's decision not to allow the Russians to obtain reconstruction materials through lend-lease, and his reluctance to discuss a postwar loan "until we get what we want," do not indicate that the President was about to give up his long-standing policy of cooperation with the Soviet Union at the time of his death. They do suggest, however, that recent developments—the Berne incident, the quarrel over German reparations, the Polish and Rumanian crises—had convinced him that appeals to "world opinion" or "high morality" alone would not move Stalin. In order to get the Russians to go along with the American postwar peace program, firm but friendly pressure would have to be applied, in much the same way that the United States had dealt with its British ally since 1941. Holding back aid to Russian reconstruction was one of the few means which Washington had of applying such pressure.[45] Roosevelt's successor in the White House went on to implement this policy, but in a manner far less tactful than the smooth and sophisticated squire of Hyde Park would have employed.

[44] *Congressional Record,* April 10, 1945, pp. 3246–47; Harry S. Truman, *Year of Decisions,* pp. 46, 98. See also Herring, "Lend-Lease to Russia," pp. 101–2, 104.

[45] For a more detailed discussion of the Roosevelt Administration's decision to apply economic pressure against the Russians, see George C. Herring, Jr., "Aid to Russia, 1941–1946: Strategy, Diplomacy, and the Origins of the Cold War," chapter 6.

7

Victory and Transition:
Harry S. Truman and the Russians

When Harry S. Truman became President of the United States on April 12, 1945, he had no intention of reversing Franklin D. Roosevelt's strategy of cooperation with the Soviet Union. It is true that as a senator from Missouri in June, 1941, he had delivered the snap judgment that Russia and Germany should be allowed to fight each other to the death, with the United States helping whichever side was losing. After Pearl Harbor, however, Truman loyally supported the Roosevelt Administration's foreign policy, a fact which made him an attractive candidate when F.D.R. began looking for a running-mate to replace Henry A. Wallace in 1944. The President failed to keep his new subordinate informed regarding diplomatic developments, but this characteristic negligence in no way lessened the new Chief Executive's determination, upon entering the White House, to work toward the goals his predecessor had set.[1]

The objectives of policy would remain the same, but Truman quickly made it clear that the manner of execution would not. Inexperienced in foreign affairs, yet determined to assert his authority,

[1] Truman, *Year of Decisions,* p. 12; Truman to Eleanor Roosevelt, May 31, 1947, and March 16, 1948, printed in William Hillman, *Mr. President,* pp. 51–52. See also Alfred Steinberg, *The Man from Missouri,* p. 186; and Jonathan Daniels, *The Man of Independence,* pp. 229, 258–59.

the new President sought to convey an impression of efficiency and decisiveness far removed from the lax and dilatory habits of F.D.R. Secretary of War Stimson immediately noticed the change:

It was a wonderful relief to preceding conferences with our former Chief to see the promptness and snappiness with which Truman took up each matter and decided it. There were no long drawn-out "soliloquies" from the President, and the whole conference was thoroughly businesslike so that we actually covered two or three more matters than we had expected to discuss.

Acting Secretary of State Grew wrote after a meeting with Truman early in May: "When I saw him today I had fourteen problems to take up with him and got through them in less than fifteen minutes with a clear directive on every one of them. You can imagine what a joy it is to deal with a man like that." But Truman's forthright approach to the problems of the presidency led him, during his first months in office, to make several hasty decisions on the basis of inadequate information.[2] These at times made it seem as if the new Chief Executive had decided to repudiate Roosevelt's "grand design."

By the time of Roosevelt's death Prime Minister Churchill and certain key American advisers—notably Harriman, Deane, Leahy, and James V. Forrestal, the new secretary of the navy—had developed strong doubts about the Soviet Union's willingness to cooperate with the United States after the war. Impressed, Truman at first accepted their recommendation that the only way to deal with the Russians was to take an unyielding stand, even if this meant straining the Grand Alliance. But strong countervailing forces kept the President from implementing this policy consistently during his first year in office. No warmonger, the new Chief Executive shrank from precipitating a third world conflict until all avenues of compromise had been explored. Knowledge that the American people still regarded the Russians as allies further inhibited Truman. Moreover, the President had promised to

[2] Stimson Diary, April 18, 1945, Stimson MSS; Grew to Cecil B. Lyon, May 2, 1945, Grew MSS, Box 122; Acheson, *Present at the Creation*, p. 731. Other early impressions of Truman's decisiveness appear in Albertson, *Roosevelt's Farmer*, p. 396; and Blum, *Morgenthau Diaries: Years of War*, p. 423. See also Herbert Feis, *Between War and Peace: The Potsdam Conference*, p. 160. In his memoirs, Truman listed Roosevelt's poor administrative methods as the one aspect of New Deal policy about which he had reservations. (*Year of Decisions*, pp. 12–13.) For an illuminating discussion of decision-making by Truman himself, see his *Mr. Citizen*, pp. 261–66.

carry out all the agreements Roosevelt had made with the Soviet Union, even though he doubted the wisdom of some of them. Former Roosevelt advisers like Hopkins, Davies, and Stimson, all opposed to any hasty confrontation with Moscow, remained influential during the early days of the Truman Administration. Finally, the new President himself came to view the leaders of the Soviet Union much as F.D.R. had seen them: as fellow "politicians" with whom "arrangements" could be made through personal diplomacy.[3]

The transfer of power at the White House, therefore, caused no overnight reversal of United States policy toward the Soviet Union, although Truman's abrasive personality may well have led the Russians to conclude, prematurely, that Roosevelt's goals had been abandoned. F.D.R. himself had expressed concern over Soviet behavior during the brief period between the Yalta Conference and his death, and had indicated, at least in his growing reluctance to aid Russian reconstruction, that he might be moving toward the tougher position several of his advisers had advocated. Truman relied more heavily on these counselors than did Roosevelt, and in his effort to appear decisive, probably accelerated the shift toward a firmer stance. But at the time he died Roosevelt had by no means given up hope of establishing friendly postwar relations with the Soviet Union, nor would Truman for some time to come.[4]

I

On the day after Roosevelt's death, Ambassador Harriman persuaded Stalin to reverse his earlier decision not to send Molotov to the San

[3] Truman, *Year of Decisions,* pp. 37, 70–72, 77–79; Truman to Stimson, July 7, 1950, printed in Hillman, *Mr. President,* p. 55; Daniels, *Man of Independence,* pp. 269–70, 285–86. See also Neumann, *After Victory,* pp. 163–65.

[4] The question of whether Truman reversed Roosevelt's Russian policy immediately after becoming President has caused much debate among historians. Works which stress the continuity of policy include Truman's own *Memoirs;* McNeill, *America, Britain, and Russia,* pp. 579–80; Feis, *Churchill, Roosevelt, Stalin,* pp. 596–600; and Kolko, *The Politics of War,* pp. 380–81. Accounts which argue that Truman reversed Roosevelt's policy include Elliott Roosevelt, *As He Saw It,* pp. xii–xiv; D. F. Fleming, *The Cold War and Its Origins, 1917–1960,* I, 265–69; Gar Alperovitz, *Atomic Diplomacy: Hiroshima and Potsdam,* pp. 12–13; Walter LaFeber, *America, Russia, and the Cold War, 1945–1967,* pp. 2, 21–22; Diane Shaver Clemens, *Yalta,* pp. 268–74; and Barton J. Bernstein, "American Foreign Policy and the Origins of the Cold War," in Bernstein, ed., *Politics and Policies of the Truman Administration,* p. 23.

Francisco Conference. The Soviet foreign minister agreed to stop in Washington to meet the new President of the United States before the conference opened on April 25.[5] This gave Truman less than two weeks to decide how he would deal with Russia, particularly on the crucial Polish issue. In line with his desire to continue Roosevelt's policies, Truman spent much of this time consulting with the late President's major advisers on Soviet affairs.

No one did more to shape Truman's views than Harriman himself. After spending more than a month in fruitless efforts to implement the Yalta agreement on Poland, the American ambassador to Moscow had grown deeply concerned regarding Soviet ambitions in Eastern Europe and, one week before Roosevelt's death, had summarized his conclusions in a lengthy cable to the State Department. The USSR had three basic objectives, Harriman wrote: cooperation with the United States and Great Britain in a world security organization; creation of a "unilateral security ring" through domination of the countries along Russia's western borders; and "penetration of other countries [by] Communist controlled parties . . . to create [a] political atmosphere favorable to Soviet policies." Washington had hoped that the success of the United Nations would convince Moscow that it did not need a sphere of influence in Eastern Europe, but it now appeared that the Russians intended to go ahead with their plans regardless of what the world organization did. Harriman believed that Stalin had interpreted acquiescent American attitudes on Eastern Europe as a sign of weakness, and had concluded that he could with impunity work his will there. Soviet-American relations would improve only when the British and Americans took a firmer and franker stand. The time had come when "we must by our actions in each individual case make it plain to the Soviet Government that they cannot expect our cooperation on terms laid down by them." [6]

Harriman had asked to come home for consultation before Roosevelt's death, and reached Washington in time to advise Truman at length prior to Molotov's arrival. In private conversations with the new President, he took an even blunter position than in his cables: Russian occupation of any country would resemble a "barbarian invasion"—one could expect not only Moscow's control of that nation's foreign policy

[5] Harriman to Stettinius, April 13, 1945, *FR: 1945,* I, 289–90; memorandum by Harry Hopkins, printed in Sherwood, *Roosevelt and Hopkins,* pp. 883–84.
[6] Harriman to Stettinius, April 6, 1945, *FR: 1945,* V, 821–24.

but the institution of secret police rule and the extinction of freedom of speech as well. Under these circumstances, the United States should reconsider its policy toward the Soviet Union. American acquiescence in Russian activities would have to stop; both sides would now have to make concessions. The Russians would not react violently to a firmer American policy, Harriman argued, because they still needed assistance from the United States to rebuild their war-shattered economy.[7]

Other presidential counselors echoed Harriman's call for a harder line with the Russians. Secretary of the Navy Forrestal, who had been reading Harriman's cables, warned Truman that Soviet actions in Poland were part of an over-all plan to take over Eastern Europe. The sooner the United States called a halt to this, the better. Bernard Baruch advised the President that he should observe American obligations strictly, but demand strongly that the Russians do the same. General Deane, who had returned to Washington shortly before Harriman, told Truman that timidity with the Soviet Union would achieve nothing; if the United States was right, it should be firm. Admiral Leahy admitted that the Yalta agreements on Poland might be open to variant interpretations, but thought that the United States should make its position clear. While it might not be possible to prevent Russian domination of Poland, the United States could at least try "to give to the reorganized Polish Government an external appearance of independence." [8]

Significant opposition to a toughening of policy toward the Soviet Union came only from the Secretary of War. Stimson had been shocked early in April to learn how far relations with Russia had deteriorated. Favoring firmness but opposing any show of temper, the Secretary resolved to use his influence to restrain those within the Administration who had expressed irritation with the Russians. Stimson sympathized with the Soviet desire to erect a protective ring of friendly states in Eastern Europe. The East European countries had never known democracy, he explained to Truman, and it seemed more important to continue cooperation with Russia than to break up the alliance over this issue.

[7] Bohlen memorandum of Truman-Harriman conversation, April 20, 1945, *FR: 1945*, V, 231–34.

[8] Forrestal Diary, April 23, 1945, Millis, ed., *The Forrestal Diaries*, p. 49; Baruch to Truman, April 20, 1945, Baruch MSS, "Selected Correspondence"; Bohlen memorandum of Truman meeting with advisers, April 23, 1945, *FR: 1945*, V, 255; Leahy, *I Was There*, p. 413.

The vehemence of anti-Russian feeling among Truman's advisers worried the Secretary of War. The bitterness of Harriman and Deane was to be expected because they had personally suffered discourtesies from the Russians for some time. But Forrestal's support for their views alarmed Stimson, and he noted regretfully that Truman himself "was evidently disappointed at my caution and advice." Only General Marshall, who still hoped to secure Russian assistance in the war against Japan, backed the Secretary of War. Stimson blamed the State Department for confronting Truman with such a crucial issue so early in his administration. The department should not have called the San Francisco Conference without first settling outstanding issues with the Russians. Now the disputes would become public. Opinion in the United States was "all churned up" and the department would probably feel compelled to force the American position through, a prospect which aroused in Stimson a feeling of "very great anxiety." [9]

Truman sided with the majority of his advisers who called for a stern response to Soviet actions in Eastern Europe. On April 17, after learning that the Russians intended to sign a treaty of mutual assistance with the Lublin Polish government, he resolved to "lay it on the line with Molotov." Admiral Leahy predicted on the 19th that "Molotov would be in for some blunt talking from the American side." Truman told Harriman on the 20th that he was not afraid of the Russians and that he intended to make no concessions to win their favor. He would not expect to get Moscow to accept 100 percent of what the United States proposed, but "we should be able to get 85 percent." Truman planned to tell Molotov "in words of one syllable" that unless the Russians observed the Yalta agreement on Poland, the Senate would never approve American membership in the United Nations.[10]

The new President's forthrightness came as a pleasant surprise to Harriman:

I had talked with Mr. Truman for only a few minutes when I began to realize that the man had a real grasp of the situation. What a surprise and relief this was! . . . I wanted . . . Molotov . . . to learn from the very highest source that we would not stand for any pushing around on the Polish ques-

[9] Stimson Diary, April 3, 23, 1945, Stimson MSS. See also Stimson and Bundy, *On Active Service*, pp. 605–11.

[10] Truman, *Year of Decisions*, pp. 49–50; Leahy, *I Was There*, p. 409; Bohlen memorandum, Truman-Harriman conversation, April 20, 1945, *FR: 1945*, V, 231–34.

tion. And I hoped the President would back me up. When I left that first conference with him that day, I knew that the President's mind didn't need any making up from me on that point.

Both Truman and Molotov went into their meeting on April 23 expecting the worst. The Soviet foreign minister told Joseph E. Davies a few hours before going to the White House that he feared Truman's unfamiliarity with the background of Big Three decisions might cause the new President to reverse Roosevelt's policy. At about the same time, Truman was telling a group of advisers that agreements with the Russians so far had been a one-way street. This could not continue. The United States was going to proceed with its plans for the San Francisco Conference, and if the Russians disapproved, "they could go to hell." [11]

At their meeting later that afternoon, Truman sharply reprimanded Molotov for Moscow's failure to carry out the Yalta decisions on Poland. An agreement had been made, and all that remained was for Stalin to keep his word. When Molotov tried to explain that the Soviet government was following what it considered to be the correct interpretation of the Yalta agreement, Truman cut him off. The United States wanted cooperation with the Soviet Union, he said, but not as a one-way proposition. "I have never been talked to like that in my life," Molotov huffed. Truman replied angrily: "Carry out your agreements and you won't get talked to like that." [12]

Truman's undiplomatic lecture to Molotov impressed Admiral Leahy, who thought that the Soviets would know after this meeting that the United States intended "to insist upon the declared right of all people to choose their own form of government." Senator Vandenberg, who heard of the encounter from Stettinius, considered it the best news in months: "F.D.R.'s appeasement of Russia is over." Truman himself was obviously pleased with his performance. He later told Davies:

I said [to Molotov] . . . that what we wanted was that you live up to your Yalta Agreement as to Poland. We will live up strictly to ours, and that is

[11] Cabell Phillips interview with Harriman, quoted in Phillips, *The Truman Presidency: History of a Triumphant Succession*, pp. 78–79; Davies Journal, April 23, 1945, Davies MSS, Box 16; Bohlen memorandum of Truman meeting with advisers, April 23, 1945, *FR: 1945*, V, 252–55.

[12] Truman, *Year of Decisions*, pp. 79–82. Bohlen's account of this meeting, in *FR: 1945*, V, 256–58, omits this last angry exchange.

exactly [what] I say to you now and there is no use discussing that further. I gave it to him straight "one-two to the jaw." I let him have it straight.

This tactic, Truman explained, was "the tough method. . . . Did I do right?" Davies, "gravely alarmed" by what he had heard, tried to tell the President "as tactfully as I could that 'he did wrong' as I saw the facts." [13]

There is little doubt that the Russians interpreted Truman's stormy interview with Molotov as evidence that the new administration had abandoned Roosevelt's policy of cooperation with the Soviet Union. The Soviets knew Roosevelt, Stalin had told Harriman in 1944, and could communicate with him. With Roosevelt alive, Molotov explained to Davies, the Soviet government had always had "full confidence" that differences could be worked out. Truman's belligerent attitude probably shocked the Russian foreign minister, convincing him that if only F.D.R. had lived, no confrontation over Eastern Europe would have taken place.[14] Such a view ignores the fact that Roosevelt himself had been deeply concerned before his death over what he regarded as Russian violations of the Yalta agreement. Moreover, Truman's tough rhetoric of April, 1945, was just that—rhetoric—and did not signify an end to American efforts to reach an accommodation with the Soviet Union.

The new Chief Executive probably thought he was carrying on Roosevelt's policies when he lectured Molotov on Moscow's failure to keep the

[13] Leahy, *I Was There,* p. 413; Vandenberg Diary, April 24, 1945, Vandenberg, ed., *Private Papers,* p. 176; Davies memorandum of conversation with Truman, April 30, 1945, Davies MSS, Box 16. After this discussion Davies wrote a personal letter to Molotov assuring him that "as you and the great Marshal Stalin come to know our frank President Truman better . . . a concert of action and purpose will be assured." (Davies to Molotov, May 2, 1945, Davies MSS, Box 16.) Jonathan Daniels, who interviewed Truman extensively about his early days in office, writes: "Perhaps not much was accomplished by that conference. . . . Afterwards he [Truman] realized that in some cases he had tried to learn too much too fast. There was very little time. . . ." (*Man of Independence,* pp. 269–70.) See also Harriman, *America and Russia,* p. 40.

[14] Harriman to Hull, June 30, 1944, *FR: 1944,* IV, 974; Davies Journal, April 23, 1945, Davies MSS, Box 16. One day after Truman's meeting with Molotov, Stalin cabled the new President: "Such conditions must be recognized unusual when two governments—those of the United States and Great Britain—beforehand settle with the Polish question in which the Soviet Union is first of all and most of all interested and put the government of the USSR in an unbearable position trying to dictate to it their demands." (Stalin to Truman, April 24, 1945, *FR: 1945,* V, 264.)

Yalta agreements. Anyone who had just succeeded to the presidency with as little advance preparation as Truman had would not likely have overruled such "experts" from the previous administration as Harriman, Deane, Forrestal, and Leahy. Determined to assert his authority by conveying the appearance of decisiveness, Truman assumed without hesitation the firm attitude they recommended. To a man of Truman's blunt, contentious personality, this tough policy must have seemed particularly congenial. But to view the new President's confrontation with Molotov as the opening move in a well-planned, long-range strategy for dealing with the Soviet Union is to presume a degree of foresight and consistency which simply was not present during the early days of the Truman Administration.[15]

"Getting tough with Russia" involved more than mere rhetoric. The American people would have to abandon certain recently acquired but strongly held assumptions: that there was no fundamental conflict of interest between the United States and the Soviet Union; that both nations could rely on the United Nations to guarantee their postwar security. "Getting tough with Russia" would also require Americans to depart from certain traditions which had always influenced their diplomacy: nonentanglement in the political affairs of Europe, and fear of a large-scale peacetime military establishment. Under the pressures of the Cold War Americans eventually did give up these assumptions and traditions, but this took time. Even in the unlikely event that in April, 1945, Truman was clear in his own mind on the need to reverse American policy toward the Soviet Union, public opinion would have significantly limited any moves in that direction for some time to come.

II

Truman also followed his predecessor's policy in the area of military strategy, but here the effect was to avoid conflict with the Soviet Union. Throughout the war, Roosevelt and his generals had employed the armed forces for the sole purpose of defeating the Axis, without regard to the political make-up of the postwar world. As the battle against Germany entered its last month, however, Prime Minister Churchill

[15] For a contrary view, see Alperovitz, *Atomic Diplomacy, passim.*

launched a vigorous challenge to this procedure, arguing that Eisenhower's troops should deploy themselves in such a way as to improve the West's bargaining position with the Russians. Simultaneously, Washington officials were beginning to question whether Soviet entry into the war against Japan was still worth the political price Roosevelt had promised to pay at Yalta. After consulting with his military advisers, Truman rejected both of these attempts to revise strategy in the light of political considerations, thus continuing another of the precedents Roosevelt had set.

Churchill's initiative originated shortly before F.D.R.'s death, when Eisenhower announced his intention not to try to take Berlin, but instead to halt his troops at the Elbe River. The General had several reasons for doing this. He wanted to reach agreement with Moscow on a clear line of demarcation which would prevent inadvertent clashes between the Red Army and Anglo-American forces as they drove toward each other across Germany. Moreover, a single thrust in the direction of Berlin might have exposed Eisenhower's flanks to attacks from the German army, or at least have allowed remnants of that force to escape to the "National Redoubt" which SHAEF intelligence believed Hitler was preparing in the Alps. Either situation would prolong the war, delaying the badly needed redeployment of American troops to the Pacific. Finally, Eisenhower's decision reflected the principle which American strategists had followed throughout the war: that military plans should aim at the destruction of enemy forces wherever they were, not at the capture of fixed geographical objectives.[16]

The British Prime Minister had objected to Eisenhower's decision, both on military and on political grounds. Berlin still retained a "high strategic importance," he wrote Roosevelt on April 1, 1945, if for no other reason than that the fall of Berlin would signal defeat to the German people. But even more significantly, if the Russians took Berlin "will not their impression that they have been the overwhelming contributor to our common victory be unduly imprinted in their minds, and may this not lead them into a mood which will raise grave and formidable difficulties in the future?" Roosevelt and the Joint Chiefs of Staff re-

---

[16] Stephen E. Ambrose, *Eisenhower and Berlin, 1945: The Decision to Halt at the Elbe,* chapters 3 and 4; Forrest C. Pogue, "The Decision to Halt at the Elbe," in Greenfield, ed., *Command Decisions,* pp. 479–92.

jected Churchill's argument. "Such psychological and political advantages as would result from the possible capture of Berlin ahead of the Russians," the Joint Chiefs noted on April 6, "should not override the imperative military consideration, which in our opinion is the destruction and dismemberment of the German armed forces." [17]

But even the decision to stop at the Elbe would leave Anglo-American forces deep within the occupation zone which the Big Three had previously assigned to the Soviet Union. On April 18, Churchill suggested to President Truman that Eisenhower's troops not withdraw from their advanced positions until certain concessions had been obtained from the Russians. The Prime Minister mentioned the need to secure Moscow's cooperation in establishing the four-power Allied Control Commission in Berlin, the fact that the British and American zones would need food from the primarily agricultural Soviet zone, and the apparent reluctance of the Russians to agree on occupation zones for Austria. After V-E Day, Churchill escalated his argument. Premature British and American withdrawal, he told Truman on May 11, would mean "the tide of Russian domination sweeping forward 120 miles on a front of 300 or 400 miles, . . . an event which, if it occurred, would be one of the most melancholy in history." The Anglo-Americans should not move their forces "until satisfied about Russian policies in Poland, Germany, and the Danube basin." One day later the Prime Minister used the phrase "iron curtain" for the first time to describe the division of Europe between the Russians and the West. By the end of May, the British were insisting that no withdrawals take place until "the whole question of the future relations of the two Governments with the Soviet Government in Europe" had been resolved. "Nothing really important has been settled

[17] Churchill to Roosevelt, April 1, 1945, printed in Churchill, *Triumph and Tragedy*, pp. 398–99; Joint Chiefs of Staff memorandum of April 6, 1945, quoted in Pogue, *The Supreme Command*, pp. 444–45. Roosevelt's reply to Churchill, drafted by Marshall, is summarized in Pogue, "The Decision to Halt at the Elbe," p. 485. Eisenhower wrote to Marshall on April 7: "I am the first to admit that a war is waged in pursuance of political aims, and if the Combined Chiefs of Staff should decide that the Allied effort to take Berlin outweighs purely military considerations in this theater, I would cheerfully readjust my plans and my thinking so as to carry out such an operation." (Eisenhower to Marshall, April 7, 1945, *Eisenhower Papers*, IV, 2592.) The tone of Eisenhower's dispatch, however, makes it clear that he did not expect such a drastic reversal of policy.

yet," Churchill warned Truman on June 4, "and you and I will have to bear great responsibility for the future." [18]

These increasingly importunate messages from London failed to impress American officials. The State Department opposed using the laboriously agreed-upon zonal boundaries as bargaining devices, arguing that this would retard rather than promote Russian cooperation in the occupation of Germany. General Eisenhower wrote with some asperity on April 23:

I do not quite understand why the Prime Minister has been so determined to intermingle political and military considerations in attempting to establish a procedure for the conduct of our own and Russian troops when a meeting takes place. My original recommendation . . . was a simple one and I thought provided a very sensible arrangement.

General Marshall agreed. Responding to a suggestion from Churchill that Eisenhower try to beat the Russians to Prague, Marshall wrote: "Personally and aside from all logistic, tactical, or strategic implications, I would be loath to hazard American lives for purely political purposes." Secretary of War Stimson warned in mid-May that the Russians would interpret any attempt to reverse the decision on zones as evidence that London and Washington had formed an alliance against them. This would make it impossible to work out any agreement on the quadripartite administration of Germany.[19]

When Russian, American, British, and French military commanders met in Berlin on June 5, 1945, to organize the four-power occupation of Germany, Marshal Zhukov made it clear that the Soviet Union would not allow the quadripartite control machinery to go into operation until all troops had been removed to their respective zones. Robert Murphy, political adviser to Eisenhower, informed the State Department that the Supreme Commander did not consider retention of American forces in the Soviet zone wise: "It is pretty obvious to all concerned that we really

[18] Churchill to Truman, April 18, 24, June 4, 1945, *FR: 1945,* III, 231–32, 240–41, 326; Churchill to Truman, May 11, 12, 1945, *FR: Potsdam,* I, 6–7, 9; British *aide-mémoire,* May 28, 1945, *FR: 1945,* III, 313.

[19] Stettinius to Leahy, April 21, 1945, *FR: 1945,* III, 235–36; Eisenhower to Marshall, April 23, 1945, quoted in Pogue, *The Supreme Command,* p. 486; memorandum by John J. McCloy of telephone conversation with Stimson, May 19, 1945, Stimson MSS, Box 421.

are desirous of removing our forces and that it is only a question of time
when we will inevitably do so." Harry Hopkins warned Truman on
June 8 that failure to withdraw Anglo-American troops into their assigned occupation zones "is certain to be misunderstood by Russia as
well as at home." Accordingly, Truman informed Churchill on June 11
that in view of these considerations, "I am unable to delay the withdrawal of American troops from the Soviet zone in order to use pressure
in the settlement of other problems." Churchill replied bitterly on the
14th: "Obviously we are obliged to conform to your decision. . . . I sincerely hope that your action will in the long run make for a lasting
peace in Europe." [20]

Truman later explained that although "politically we would have
been pleased to see our lines extend as far to the east as possible," there
were two reasons why he could not accept Churchill's proposal. Logistical considerations made it necessary to shift American troops from Europe to the Far East as quickly as possible, thus restricting opportunities
for challenging Russian policy in Europe. Moreover, Truman believed
that the best way to handle the Soviet Union was "to stick carefully to
our agreements and to try our best to make the Russians carry out their
agreements." The United States could hardly disregard the commitments
on occupation zones which Roosevelt had made, while at the same time
insisting that Moscow carry out to the letter the Yalta agreements on
Poland. Churchill, in retrospect, understood Truman's position well:

The case as presented to him so soon after his accession to power was
whether or not to depart from and in a sense repudiate the policy of the
American and British Governments agreed under his illustrious predecessor.
. . . His responsibility at this point was limited to deciding whether circumstances had changed so fundamentally that an entirely different procedure
should be adopted, with the likelihood of having to face accusations of

[20] Eisenhower to the Joint Chiefs of Staff, June 6, 1945, *FR: 1945*, III, 328–29;
Murphy to Stettinius, June 6, 1945, *ibid.*, p. 331; Hopkins to Truman, June 8, 1945,
ibid., p. 333; Truman to Churchill, June 11, 1945, *ibid.*, pp. 133–34; Churchill to
Truman, June 14, 1945, *ibid.*, pp. 134–35. Ironically, Stalin later requested a delay in
the redeployment of troops because the American and British zones in Berlin had not
yet been cleared of mines, and because Zhukov and other Soviet commanders had to
go to Moscow on June 24 to participate in a parade. (Stalin to Truman, June 16,
1945, *FR: 1945*, III, 137.) The actual withdrawal into occupation zones took place on
July 1.

breach of faith. Those who are only wise after the event should hold their peace.[21]

The new President demonstrated a similar reluctance to revise Roosevelt's military policies in the Far East. Shortly after entering the White House, Truman had advised both Soviet Foreign Minister Molotov and General Patrick J. Hurley, United States ambassador to China, that he would carry out the agreement Roosevelt had made at Yalta regarding Soviet entry into the war against Japan. For reasons of security, however, Chiang Kai-shek still had not been told of this arrangement, made largely at the expense of his country. This delay gave the State Department the opportunity to review the Yalta accord in the light of recent difficulties with the Russians in Eastern Europe. Hurley warned Truman on May 10 that Chiang would have to be informed of the Yalta agreement before long, since Russian military preparations in the Far East were becoming increasingly obvious. But the President, aware of the review his diplomatic advisers were undertaking, asked Hurley to delay telling Chiang for a while longer.[22]

Ambassador Harriman and Navy Secretary Forrestal had raised the need for a reevaluation of American political objectives in the Far East early in May. The time had arrived, Harriman told Forrestal on the 11th, "to come to a conclusion about the necessity for the early entrance of Russia into the Japanese war." The next day Harriman, Forrestal, Acting Secretary of State Grew, and Assistant Secretary of War John J. McCloy met to discuss, as Grew told Stettinius, "whether we were going to support what had been done at Yalta." As a result of this meeting, the State Department sent an official inquiry to the War and Navy departments asking: (1) whether military authorities considered Soviet entry into the Japanese war vital enough to preclude seeking Moscow's

[21] Truman, *Year of Decisions,* pp. 211, 214, 217; Churchill, *Triumph and Tragedy,* p. 487.

[22] Bohlen memorandum, Truman-Molotov conversation, April 22, 1945, *FR: 1945,* V, 236; Herbert Feis, *The China Tangle,* p. 283; Hurley to Truman, May 10, 1945, *FR: 1945,* VII, 865–68; Truman to Hurley, May 12, 1945, *ibid.,* p. 868. Hurley later maintained that Roosevelt had authorized him to seek a revision of the Yalta Far Eastern agreement, but the available evidence does not support this assertion. See, on this matter, Russell D. Buhite, "Patrick J. Hurley and the Yalta Far Eastern Agreement," *Pacific Historical Review,* XXXVII (August, 1968), 343–53.

agreement "to certain desirable political objectives in the Far East prior to such entry"; (2) whether "the Yalta decision in regard to Soviet political desires in the Far East [should] be reconsidered or carried into effect in whole or in part"; and (3) whether the Russians, provided they entered the war, should be given a role in the occupation of Japan. The additional political commitments which the department hoped to obtain from the Russians included a pledge to encourage Chinese Communist cooperation with Chiang Kai-shek, "unequivocal adherence of the Soviet Government to the Cairo Declaration regarding the return of Manchuria to Chinese sovereignty," establishment of a four-power trusteeship over Korea, and emergency landing rights for American commercial airplanes in the Kurile Islands.[23]

Military officials still considered Soviet participation in the Pacific War highly desirable, though not absolutely necessary for final victory over Japan. General Douglas MacArthur had told Forrestal in February, 1945, that Russian entry into the war would greatly facilitate an American invasion of the Japanese home islands by tying down the large Kwantung Army in Manchuria. Upon the recommendation of General Deane, the Joint Chiefs of Staff had decided early in April that the United States would not need air bases in Siberia, but they still agreed with MacArthur that a Soviet declaration of war would reduce American losses and help shorten the war. General Marshall noted later that month that the Russians had the capacity "to delay their entry into the Far Eastern war until we had done all the dirty work." The Army Chief of Staff hoped for Moscow's assistance "at a time when it would be helpful to us." Truman later recalled estimates from military experts that an invasion of Japan might cost half a million American casualties, hence "Russian entry into the war against Japan was highly important to us." [24]

The unknown factor which made it difficult to evaluate the need for

[23] Millis, ed., *The Forrestal Diaries,* pp. 52, 55–56; Grew memorandum of telephone conversation with Stettinius, May 12, 1945, Grew MSS; Grew to Forrestal and Stettinius, May 12, 1945, *FR: 1945,* VII, 869–70.

[24] Forrestal memorandum, conversation with MacArthur, February 28, 1945, Millis, ed., *The Forrestal Diaries,* p. 31; Deane, *The Strange Alliance,* pp. 262–68; Bohlen notes, Marshall meeting with Truman and other advisers, April 23, 1945, *FR: 1945,* V, 254; Truman, *Year of Decisions,* p. 265. See also Louis Morton, "Soviet Intervention in the War with Japan," *Foreign Affairs,* XL (July, 1962), 658.

Soviet military assistance in the Pacific, however, was the atomic bomb, upon which the United States and Great Britain had been working secretly since the beginning of the war. "These are vital questions and I am very glad the State Department has brought them up," Secretary of War Stimson noted on May 13; "the questions cut very deep and in my opinion are powerfully connected with our success with S-1 [the bomb]." Stimson at first wanted to take no position, suggesting that the United States simply stay out of arguments with the Russians until the bomb was ready. But the State Department pointed out that Truman had already agreed to meet Churchill and Stalin in Germany in July, and that the question of Russia's role in the Far East would have to be settled by then. "Over any such tangled wave of problems the S-1 secret would be dominant," the Secretary of War mused in his diary, "and yet we will not know until after that time probably, until after that meeting, whether this is a weapon in our hands or not. We think it will be shortly afterwards, but it seems a terrible thing to gamble with such big stakes in diplomacy without having your master card in your hand." The War Department therefore replied to the State Department's inquiry by noting that "Russian entry will have a profound military effect in that almost certainly it will materially shorten the war and thus save American lives." However, military officials continued to believe that the Russians would go to war with Japan when they got ready, regardless of what the United States did in the political field, and so expressed no objections to State Department efforts to seek additional clarification of the conditions for Soviet entry.[25]

Stalin gave the assurances the State Department wanted in a conversation with Harry Hopkins and Averell Harriman in Moscow on May 28, 1945. The Soviet Union would be ready to enter the war against Japan on August 8, he said, although the actual date would depend "on the execution of the agreement made at Yalta concerning Soviet desires." It would be necessary to have the Chinese accept Russia's political demands "in order to justify entry into the Pacific War in the eyes of the Soviet people." But at the same time, Stalin assured Hopkins and Harriman that the Soviet Union had no desire to challenge the American

[25] Stimson Diary, May 13, 14, 15, 1945, Stimson MSS; Stimson to Grew, May 21, 1945, *FR: 1945,* VII, 876–78. Forrestal associated the Navy Department with Stimson's conclusions. (Forrestal to Grew, May 21, 1945, *ibid.,* p. 878.)

"open door" policy in China, that Chiang Kai-shek's representatives, not the Chinese Communists, would be allowed to set up civil administration in parts of Manchuria liberated by the Red Army, and that while he, Stalin, knew little of the various Chinese leaders, he thought "Chiang Kai-shek was the best of the lot and would be the one to undertake the unification of China." The Russian leader also endorsed a four-power trusteeship for Korea.[26]

Reassured by these developments, Truman on June 9 instructed Hurley to tell Chiang Kai-shek about the Yalta Far Eastern agreement. On the same day he met with Dr. T. V. Soong, the foreign minister of China, and informed him that the United States was "definitely committed to the agreements reached by President Roosevelt." One week later, Truman reviewed plans for the invasion of Japan with his military advisers. General Marshall, speaking for the Joint Chiefs of Staff, stressed the advantages of Soviet participation as a means of containing Japanese troops in Manchuria and possibly shortening the war. "The impact of Russian entry on the already hopeless Japanese," he pointed out, "may well be the decisive action levering them into capitulation." Stimson agreed with Marshall but, having the atomic bomb firmly in mind, expressed hope "for some fruitful accomplishment by other means." Forrestal observed that there would still be time to reconsider the proposed military operations "in the light of subsequent events." Truman then approved the Joint Chiefs' strategy for the invasion of Japan, and announced that one of his major objectives at the forthcoming Big Three meeting would be "to get from Russia all the assistance in the war that was possible."[27]

Several years later, Truman summarized his attitude toward the Yalta Far Eastern agreement in a letter to Henry Stimson:

Some agreements were made early in 1943 [*sic*] to keep Russia in the war. Naturally if those agreements had been made after the surrender of Ger-

[26] Bohlen memorandum, Hopkins-Stalin conversation, May 28, 1945, *FR: 1945,* VII, 887–91. See also Hopkins' report to Truman of this conference, printed in Sherwood, *Roosevelt and Hopkins,* pp. 902–3.

[27] Truman to Hurley, June 9, 1945, *FR: 1945,* VII, 897–98; Grew memorandum, Truman-Soong conversation, June 9, 1945, *ibid.,* p. 896; Joint Chiefs of Staff minutes, meeting with Truman, Forrestal, McCloy, and Stimson, June 18, 1945, *FR: Potsdam,* I, 903–9. See also Truman, *Year of Decisions,* p. 265.

many and Japan they no doubt would have been arranged in a different manner. I made it my business to try to carry out agreements as they were made when the war was on—maybe that should not have been done but I would still follow that procedure because I believe when agreements are made they should be kept. That is not the policy of the Russian government.[28]

Truman's conduct of the war during the brief period of time between his accession to the presidency and the achievement of victory over Germany and Japan thus offers little evidence that the new Chief Executive had reversed his predecessor's policy of cooperation with the Soviet Union. As under Roosevelt, victory, not postwar political advantage, remained the primary goal of the American military effort right up to the moment of its attainment.

III

In the field of economic policy, the Roosevelt Administration in the months before F.D.R.'s death had toughened its position toward the Soviet Union. Prior to the Yalta Conference, the President had endorsed the State Department's decision to move slowly on extension of a postwar loan to the USSR. Roosevelt had taken a firm stand on reparations at the Big Three conference, indicating that the United States would not support the indiscriminate removal of German industrial equipment to rebuild the Soviet economy, and accepting only with the greatest reluctance the Russian figure of $20 billion "as a basis of negotiations" in the tripartite Reparations Commission. In March, the Administration had decided to terminate negotiations with Moscow on the use of lend-lease for reconstruction. Domestic considerations influenced the President's attitude in each of these cases: Congress had made it clear that it would not support reconstruction of foreign economies at the expense of the American taxpayer. But the Administration's political interests at home also fit in with a diplomatic tactic of increasing importance—the use of economic pressure to secure Soviet compliance with American plans for the postwar world.

[28] Truman to Stimson, July 7, 1950, quoted in Hillman, *Mr. President,* p. 55.

Ambassador Harriman demonstrated the relationship between reparations, lend-lease, and the postwar reconstruction loan in a series of telegrams sent to Washington during the week immediately preceding Roosevelt's death. "We now have ample proof," he noted on April 4, 1945,
"that the Soviet Government views all matters from the standpoint of
their own selfish interests":

The Soviet Government will end this war with the largest gold reserve of
any country except the United States, will have large quantities of Lend
Lease material and equipment not used or worn out in the war with which
to assist their reconstruction, will ruthlessly strip the enemy countries they
have occupied of everything they can move, will control the foreign trade of
countries under their domination as far as practicable to the benefit of the
Soviet Union, will use political and economic pressure on other countries including South America to force trade arrangements to their own advantage
and at the same time they will demand from us every form of aid and assistance which they think they can get.

If the United States was to protect its vital interests, Harriman concluded, it would have to adopt "a more positive policy of using our economic influence to further our broad political ideals." Washington
should continue to seek friendly relations with the Soviet Union, but on
a strictly *quid pro quo* basis. "This means tying our economic assistance
directly into our political problems with the Soviet Union." [29]

Harriman still favored extending a loan to Russia, but now regarded
it chiefly as a device for extracting political concessions. He believed that
the Russians, using their own resources, could regain their prewar level
of capital investment by 1948. They could not, however, carry out their
ambitious program of additional economic expansion without purchasing
American industrial equipment. The Soviet Union was weaker internally
than many people thought, he argued, therefore Washington could
safely attach political conditions to any Russian loan. The United States
should work first to meet the economic needs of its Western European
allies, and then allocate to the Russians whatever might be left. Moscow
deserved no special treatment in the matter, and Congress should not be
asked to authorize a special loan. The Administration should begin negotiations on the extension of credits through the Export-Import Bank.
"It would be inadvisable to give the Soviets the idea that we were cool-

[29] Harriman to Stettinius, April 4, 1945, *FR: 1945,* V, 817–20.

ing off on our desire to help." But at the same time "it would be quite satisfactory to have negotiations on the question of postwar credits drag along." [30]

The Soviet Union would also depend heavily on German reparations to achieve its program of postwar economic expansion. The United States should show sympathy for Moscow's position, Harriman wrote on April 3, but since the Russians had demonstrated little willingness to implement the Yalta decisions, "I . . . see no reason why we should show eagerness in expediting decisions on reparations, which is one subject to which the Soviet Government is most anxious to get us committed." The Red Army was already removing vast quantities of goods from Germany as it advanced toward Berlin, and there was no evidence that a reparations agreement would cause the Russians to show restraint in this regard. Delaying an agreement, however, might encourage them to cooperate in shipping food from their agricultural zone to the industrial areas which the Americans and British would occupy.[31]

On the matter of lend-lease, Harriman fully supported the Roosevelt Administration's decision not to allow the Russians to obtain reconstruction materials under the Fourth Protocol. There should be no Fifth Protocol, he argued. "Russian requests should be dealt with on a supply basis, and we should supply the absolute minimum requirements." The United States should continue to fill legitimate Russian military orders, especially for material to be used against Japan, but after V-E Day "the Soviet Union should have ample production to meet essential needs in many fields, and our shipments should be reduced accordingly." [32]

After becoming President, Truman read Harriman's cables carefully, and quickly indicated his support for the general policy which the am-

[30] Harriman to Stettinius, April 11, 1945, *FR: 1945*, V, 994–96; minutes of the Secretary of State's Staff Committee meeting, April 21, 1945, *ibid.*, p. 818; Bohlen memorandum, Harriman conversation with Truman, April 20, 1945, *ibid.*, p. 232; and Sulzberger, *A Long Row of Candles*, p. 256. Harriman's conclusion that the Soviet Union could regain its prewar level of capital investment by 1948 was based on a State Department estimate, forwarded to him on January 26, 1945. (*FR: 1945*, V, 939, 967.)

[31] Harriman to Stettinius, April 3, 1945, *FR: 1945*, III, 1186. See also Harriman to Stettinius, March 14, 1945, *ibid.*, pp. 1176–77; Harriman to Stettinius, April 4, 1945, *FR: 1945*, V, 817–18; and Harriman to Stettinius, April 6, 1945, *FR: 1945*, III, 1190–92.

[32] Harriman to Stettinius, March 20, 1945, *FR: 1945*, V, 988–89; minutes of the Secretary of State's Staff Committee meeting, April 21, 1945, *ibid.*, pp. 844–45.

bassador to Moscow had recommended. He intended to be "firm but fair," the new Chief Executive told Harriman on April 20; "the Soviet Union needed us more than we needed them." During his confrontation with Molotov three days later, Truman reminded the Soviet foreign minister that Congress would have to approve "any economic measures in the foreign field," and that it would not act without public support. He hoped "that the Soviet Government would keep these factors in mind." [33]

The Truman Administration bungled its first attempt to apply the policy which Harriman recommended, however. The ambassador suggested on May 9, 1945, that in view of Germany's surrender, the United States should begin curtailing lend-lease shipments to the Soviet Union. Supplies for possible use against Japan should continue to be sent, but the Administration should carefully scrutinize, "with a view to our own interests and policies," requests for other shipments. The American attitude should be one of firmness, Harriman stressed, "while avoiding any implication of a threat or any indication of political bargaining." Two days later Secretary of War Stimson found Truman "vigorously enthusiastic" about implementing "a more realistic policy" on Russian lend-lease, a position which the President said was "right down his alley." [34]

Undersecretary of State Grew and Foreign Economic Administrator Crowley, after consulting with the War and Navy departments and Ambassador Harriman, recommended to Truman on May 11 that he (1) continue lend-lease shipments destined for use against the Japanese as long as Soviet entry into the Far Eastern war was anticipated; (2) continue to ship supplies needed to complete work on industrial plants already under construction; (3) cut off all other lend-lease shipments to the Soviet Union as soon as physically practicable. No new lend-lease

[33] Bohlen memorandum, Truman-Harriman conversation, April 20, 1945, *FR: 1945*, V, 232; Bohlen memorandum, Truman-Molotov conversation, April 23, 1945, *ibid.*, pp. 256–57. Harriman later recalled: "Although he had only been in office for less than a week, he [Truman] had read all the papers regarding Yalta, the telegrams that I had sent; and the messages that President Roosevelt had sent to Stalin, and the replies. He was thoroughly briefed." (Remarks by Harriman at a ceremony commemorating the 25th anniversary of Truman's accession to the presidency, April 11, 1970, Harry S. Truman Library, Independence, Missouri.) See also Phillips, *The Truman Presidency*, p. 79; and Harriman, *America and Russia*, p. 40.

[34] Stettinius to Grew, May 9, 1945, *FR: 1945*, V, 998; Stimson Diary, May 11, 1945, Stimson MSS.

protocol should be negotiated to replace the one which would expire on June 30. Instead the Administration should consider Soviet requests for aid "on the basis of reasonably accurate information regarding the essentiality of Soviet military supply requirements and in the light of all competing demands for supplies in the changing military situation." After listening to the explanations of Grew and Crowley, Truman approved their proposal.[35]

But Crowley interpreted the lend-lease curtailment directive far more literally than Truman or Harriman had intended. Acting on the assumption that the new policy was "when in doubt hold," instead of "when in doubt give," Foreign Economic Administration representatives on the Soviet Protocol Committee insisted that ships containing Russian lend-lease material not destined for use in the Far East should turn around and return to port. Harriman later described himself as having been "taken aback" by this development. Truman, who had never intended to cut off supplies already on the way to the Soviet Union, quickly countermanded the turn-around order. But the diplomatic damage had been done. Through a bureaucratic blunder the Truman Administration did precisely what Harriman had sought to avoid: it gave Moscow the impression that it was trying to extract political concessions through a crude form of economic pressure.[36]

[35] Grew and Crowley to Truman, May 11, 1945, *FR: 1945,* V, 999–1000; Truman to Grew and Crowley, May 11, 1945, *ibid.,* p. 1000. Before delivering this recommendation to the White House, Crowley emphasized to Grew the necessity of making sure that Truman thoroughly understood what he was signing and "that he will back us up and keep everyone else out of it." Crowley expected trouble from the Russians, and "he did not want them to be running all over town looking for help." (Grew memorandum of conversation with Crowley, May 11, 1945, *ibid.,* p. 999*n.*) In his memoirs, Truman maintains erroneously that Grew and Crowley got him to sign the lend-lease termination order on May 8, without informing him of its contents. (*Year of Decisions,* pp. 227–29.)

[36] Herring, "Lend-Lease to Russia and the Origins of the Cold War," pp. 106–8; Leighton and Coakley, *Global Logistics, 1943–45,* pp. 695–96; Feis, *Between War and Peace,* p. 27. Herring notes that "the hard line on Soviet lend-lease taken by Crowley and the Foreign Economic Administration seems to have stemmed more from a rigid legalism than from Russophobia. During the congressional hearings on the extension of lend-lease, Crowley had made unequivocal commitments that lend-lease was to be used only to prosecute the war. Imbued with an extremely narrow concept of executive authority and not concerned with the diplomatic impact of his actions, he waged an unrelenting battle to honor these commitments." ("Lend-Lease to Russia," p. 108.)

Stalin told Harry Hopkins at the end of May that the United States had every right to terminate the flow of lend-lease to the Soviet Union, but that the abrupt manner in which aid had been cut off was "unfortunate and even brutal." If Washington's reluctance to continue lend-lease shipments was intended to pressure the Russians, Stalin said, it was a mistake. Accommodations could be arranged if the Americans approached the Russians on a friendly basis, but reprisals would only have the opposite effect. Hopkins tried to assure Stalin that the order to unload ships bound for Russia had been an error, that the United States had no intention of using lend-lease to force concessions from the Russians. Stalin's bitterness, however, remained unassuaged.[37]

Meanwhile the Truman Administration, in line with Harriman's suggestions, was taking its time about beginning talks with the Russians on reparations. Molotov discussed the issue at San Francisco on May 7 with Harriman and Edwin W. Pauley, Truman's newly appointed representative to the Allied Reparations Commission. The Russians wanted to know, Molotov said, when Pauley and his delegation planned to leave for Moscow, since the Soviet government "attached the greatest importance to the work of the Reparations Commission and hoped it would soon get started." Harriman pointed out that the United States and Great Britain wanted France to have a place on the commission, since that country had been given an occupation zone in Germany, but that the Russians had refused to agree to this without admitting Poland and Yugoslavia as well. Molotov suggested that it might expedite matters to return to the original Yalta formula of a strictly tripartite organization. Pauley expressed a desire to begin negotiations as soon as possible, but noted reports that the Russians were already removing from their zone German industrial equipment which might fall under the category of reparations. The British and Americans, he insisted, had carefully avoided this practice. Molotov asserted that the Red Army had taken only what it needed for prosecution of the war, and that he assumed American commanders were doing the same thing in the parts of Germany they occupied.[38]

[37] Bohlen notes, Hopkins-Stalin conversation, May 27, 1945, quoted in Sherwood, *Roosevelt and Hopkins,* pp. 894–97.

[38] Bohlen memorandum, Molotov-Pauley-Harriman conversation, May 7, 1945, *FR: 1945,* III, 1208–10. Roosevelt had originally named Isador Lubin to represent the

Shortly after this conversation, the State Department announced that Pauley and a thirty-man delegation would arrive in Moscow to begin negotiations early in June, after first surveying conditions in Germany. This news alarmed George F. Kennan, who was in charge of the American Embassy in Moscow during Harriman's absence in the United States. If Pauley and his delegation expected to work out a rational agreement with the Russians after careful study, Kennan warned Harriman, they were in for a disappointment:

[Russian] demands will be formulated among themselves, on the basis of considerations which will never be revealed to us, but which will certainly be political rather than economic. Any efforts on the part of foreign delegations to pull discussion down to a basis of economic equalities will be met with repetitious orations about what the Germans did to Russia. In the end, it will come down to a simple horse trade. How much are we going to make available to the Russians from our zones, and what price are we going to demand for it?

The United States, Kennan argued, would not need thirty experts to drive a bargain of this sort. But Harriman, who had seen Pauley's orders, was able to reassure his anxious subordinate: "We have nothing to worry about in regard to the size of the reparations delegation . . . Mr. Pauley's instructions are very firm and while we may not reach any agreement I have no fears about us giving in." [39]

Harriman was right. Pauley's directive, as approved by Truman on May 18, placed primary emphasis on the need to maintain the German economy intact, even if this meant restricting reparations shipments to Russia. While removals from existing facilities would inevitably lower the German standard of living, they "should be held within such limits as to leave the German people with sufficient means to provide a minimum subsistence . . . without sustained outside relief." Remaining in-

---

United States on the Reparations Commission, but Truman replaced him with Pauley, treasurer of the Democratic National Committee and a personal friend, because "I felt that the position required a tough bargainer, someone who could be as tough as Molotov." Lubin had been replaced, Truman told Henry Morgenthau, Jr., because "I don't think he is a big enough man." Lubin did agree to remain on the commission as Pauley's associate, however. (Truman, *Year of Decisions*, p. 308; Blum, *Morgenthau Diaries: Years of War*, p. 453.) For negotiations regarding composition of the Reparations Commission, see *FR: 1945*, III, 1177–97.

[39] Grew to Kennan, May 13, 1945, *FR: 1945*, III, 1211; Kennan to Harriman, May 14, 1945, *ibid.*, pp. 1211–13; Harriman to Kennan, May 20, 1945, *ibid.*, p. 1213n.

dustrial production would be used first to provide for the basic needs of the German people and to pay for essential imports, and only then as reparations. No plan could be approved which would "put the United States in a position where it will have to assume responsibility for sustained relief to the German people." [40]

"Germany would have to be fed," Truman later explained, "and I was determined to see that it would not once again be charity . . . from us that fed her." In maintaining this position, the President had no intention of denying reparations to the Soviet Union. Like Roosevelt, however, he sought some means of limiting excessive removals, so that the United States would not once more find itself obliged to prop up Germany's economy while the Germans produced reparations for Washington's former allies. He also hoped to make it clear to the Russians that they could not expect massive shipments of equipment from the industrialized Western zones without committing themselves to help feed the people of that area.[41]

Harriman's suggestions also helped to clarify Washington's thinking with regard to a postwar loan to the Soviet Union. Emilio G. Collado, director of the State Department's Office of Financial and Development Policy, recommended in April that after conclusion of the San Francisco Conference the Administration should begin making legislative arrangements to permit an Export-Import Bank loan to Russia "if political conditions are favorable." The loan would be not $6 billion, as the Russians had proposed, but $1 billion. The interest rate would be in accord with the bank's regular rates, roughly double the Soviet proposal of 2¼ percent. On June 2, 1945, Grew informed Harriman that the Administration would soon ask Congress to expand the Export-Import Bank's lending authority, setting aside $1 billion for the Soviet Union "if events so warrant." [42]

In mid-July, Foreign Economic Administrator Crowley asked Congress to raise the bank's loan ceiling from $700 million to $3.5 billion, and to repeal the Johnson Act's prohibition on loans to defaulting gov-

[40] "Instructions for the United States Representative on the Allied Commission on Reparations," May 18, 1945, *FR: 1945,* III, 1222–27.

[41] Truman, *Year of Decisions,* p. 308.

[42] Collado to Stettinius and Clayton, April 19, 1945, *FR: 1945,* V, 997–98; Grew to Harriman, June 2, 1945, *ibid.,* pp. 1011–12.

ernments. In answer to a question from Senator Robert A. Taft, Crowley acknowledged that between $700 million and $1 billion of the new lending authority would be tentatively allocated for a loan to the Soviet Union. Taft criticized the Administration request as an attempt to circumvent congressional prohibitions on the use of lend-lease for reconstruction, while Representative Everett M. Dirksen tried unsuccessfully to amend the bill to deny credits to any nation which refused to follow the principles of the Atlantic Charter. "I do not want a single American dollar to undo the work of a single American GI who is sleeping in a little cemetery in some far-off country," Dirksen proclaimed. The bill easily passed Congress after only brief debate, however, and Truman signed it into law on July 31, 1945.[43]

The Truman Administration could now lend up to $1 billion to the Soviet Union through the Export-Import Bank, without precipitating an embarrassing debate in Congress. Whether the Administration would actually use this authority, however, depended upon the course of Soviet-American relations. The loan to Russia, originally conceived of as a device to ensure economic prosperity at home, had now become a weapon in the growing political rivalry with Moscow. Things had changed, *Fortune* magazine observed, since Eric Johnston's trip to the Soviet Union in 1944. American economists now worried less about providing full employment after the war. The West European market for American products had greatly exceeded expectations. But most important were changes in the political climate: Moscow's actions in Eastern Europe had "frittered away Russia's enormous store of goodwill in this country." Until these "profound political difficulties" were resolved, the loan to Russia should remain in abeyance.[44]

Truman's foreign economic policy reflected the unique position in which Americans found themselves at the end of World War II. The United States had emerged from the war with a greatly expanded industrial plant at a time when all of the world's other major powers had

[43] *New York Times,* July 18, 1945; *Congressional Record,* July 13 and 20, 1945, pp. 7535–48, 7827–41; Export-Import Bank, *Semiannual Report to Congress for the Period July-December, 1945,* p. 9.

[44] *Fortune,* XXXII (July, 1945), 110. See also Herbert Feis, "Political Aspects of Foreign Loans," *Foreign Affairs,* XXIII (July, 1945), 609–19; and William Henry Chamberlin, "Can We Do Business with Stalin?" *American Mercury,* LXI (August, 1945), 194–201.

suffered serious economic losses. Many influential Americans believed that Washington could take advantage of this situation by using reconstruction assistance to shape political developments in the postwar world to its liking. "Let us not forget," Bernard Baruch reminded Truman in June, 1945, "that it is on the productive capacity of America that all countries must rely for the comforts—even the necessities—that a modern world will demand. We have the mass production and the know-how. Without us the rest of the world cannot recuperate; it cannot rebuild, feed, house or clothe itself." [45] Although Roosevelt might have handled matters like lend-lease termination more gracefully, it seems unlikely that he could have resisted the opportunity presented by this unusual situation any more than Truman did.

But Washington's effort to employ economic power for political purposes rested on two shaky assumptions: first, that other countries needed reconstruction aid so badly that they would accept whatever political conditions the United States imposed; and second, that Congress and the American taxpayer, both yearning for a return to fiscal normalcy, would appropriate the large sums of money required to finance such assistance. Events of late 1945 and early 1946 would make it clear that, in the case of the Soviet Union, neither of these assumptions could be taken for granted.

IV

The United Nations Conference on International Organization opened in a blare of publicity at San Francisco on April 25, 1945. This meeting, for which so many Americans held such high hopes, had the ironic effect of aggravating rather than alleviating international tensions, for it revealed to the public the full extent of the differences between Russia and the West. Yet at the same time it stimulated a reconsideration of policy toward the Soviet Union within the Truman Administration which led to a renewed effort to settle problems with Moscow through personal diplomacy.

Acrimony rather than harmony seemed the keynote during the early

[45] Baruch to Truman, June 8, 1945, Baruch MSS, "Memoranda—President Truman."

sessions at San Francisco. Molotov refused to accept the custom that the head of the host nation's delegation serve as chairman, and had to be put off with a compromise. Two days after the conference opened the Russian foreign minister asked for the admission of representatives from the Lublin Polish government, arguing that they deserved a place at San Francisco because under the Yalta agreement their group was to form the basis of the new provisional government in Warsaw. Senator Arthur H. Vandenberg, the leading Republican on the American delegation, virtually ordered Secretary of State Stettinius to reject Molotov's proposal at once and in public. Stettinius instantly complied. Vandenberg wrote in his diary that had the Lublin Poles been admitted, "it would have wrecked *any* chance of American approval of the work of the Conference." Tensions increased further on May 4, 1945, when the Soviet government acknowledged that it had arrested sixteen Polish underground leaders after having promised them safe conduct to come to Moscow to discuss broadening the Lublin regime. "This is bad business," Vandenberg noted. "If it should develop that the 16 are dead—?????" [46]

These developments caused genuine concern among Americans who had up to this time generally sympathized with the Russian point of view. In a series of editorial comments from April through June the *New Republic,* for example, criticized Moscow's refusal to reorganize the Lublin Polish government, arguing that the Yalta agreement itself had been a compromise and that no further compromises should be necessary. The Soviet Union seemed to be acting more to safeguard its own interests than from a desire to make the United Nations work. While this was to be expected in view of recent Russian history, it could have a most unfortunate effect upon public opinion in the United States. Senate ratification of the United Nations Charter might well depend on what the Russians did in Poland. Soviet diplomats would have to play "a slightly more subtle game than in the past few months if the immense store of good will which they have won . . . is not to be frittered away." Incidents such as the arrest of the sixteen underground leaders, the *New Republic* thought, demonstrated either ignorance of, or contempt for, the role of public opinion in the West. "TRB" commented that "at times it

[46] Vandenberg Diary, April 25, 27, May 4, 1945, Vandenberg, ed., *Private Papers,* pp. 177–78, 181, 185–86.

has seemed that the Soviet leaders were trying to throw away Washington's good will." [47]

But not all observers blamed the Russians for the disagreements at San Francisco. Many felt the United States to be just as reluctant to entrust its security to the new world organization. In order to maintain inter-American unity, Stettinius felt he had to invite Argentina to the conference. Molotov objected to admitting a state which had been sympathetic to the Nazis while Poland was still excluded from the world organization, but the Secretary of State insisted on marshaling the votes of the Latin American countries to push through the United States position. This led *Time* to comment that Washington was playing "a straight power game" in Latin America "as amoral as Russia's game in Eastern Europe," a judgment which seemed confirmed later in May when Senator Vandenberg successfully demanded that the Monroe Doctrine be exempted from the jurisdiction of the Security Council. "I think that it's not asking too much to have our little region over here," Secretary of War Stimson commented, "if she [Russia] is going to take these steps . . . of building up friendly protectorates around her." [48]

More alarming than these actions, however, were indications that the United States was using the San Francisco Conference as a platform from which to denounce the Russians. I.F. Stone brooded in the *Nation* that "too many members of the American delegation conceive this as a conference for the organization of an anti-Soviet bloc under our leadership." Writing in the *New Republic,* Thomas F. Reynolds asserted that the American delegation had missed no opportunity "to throw rocks in private at the Soviet hobgoblin." The editors of the *New Republic* feared that a "bitter anti-Soviet bloc in the State Department" was influencing Stettinius, and called for Truman to remove these officials from their posts. The most disturbing development to come out of San Francisco, Vera Micheles Dean observed, "was the tendency to believe that a conflict between the United States and Russia is becoming inevitable." In a private conversation with State Department officials, Raymond

[47] *New Republic,* CXII (April 9, 1945), 463; (April 30, 1945), 573, 612–14; (May 7, 1945), 630–31; (May 21, 1945), 708; (June 4, 1945), 771–72.

[48] *Time,* XLV (May 14, 1945), 38; Vandenberg to Stettinius, May 5, 1945, Vandenberg MSS; transcript of telephone conversation between Stimson and John J. McCloy, May 8, 1945, Stimson MSS, Box 420.

Gram Swing, a prominent liberal newscaster, charged that the United States representatives at San Francisco were "engaged in building up a logical record which would give us a clear and unarguable *casus belli* in a war which never ought to occur and which clearly could be avoided." [49]

There did seem to be some basis for these charges. Ambassador Harriman had flown to San Francisco immediately after Truman's interview with Molotov for the specific purpose "of making everyone understand that the Soviets . . . were not going to live up to their post-war agreements." Harriman met with members of the American delegation on the day the conference opened. Calling attention to Russian attempts "to chisel, by bluff, pressure, and other unscrupulous methods to get what they wish," he charged that Moscow wanted "as much domination over Eastern Europe as possible." While the United States could not go to war with the Soviet Union, it should do everything it could to impede Russian moves in Eastern Europe. During his stay in San Francisco, Harriman held several off-the-record press conferences in which he warned darkly of Soviet intentions. His blunt statements caused several reporters, among them Swing, to walk out, accusing the ambassador to the Soviet Union of being a "warmonger." [50]

Senator Vandenberg, the most influential member of the American delegation, had come to San Francisco determined to halt what he considered to be appeasement of the Russians. The Yalta agreements on Poland had been hard for the Michigan senator to swallow, but he knew the American people would not go to war with Russia to change them. The only other alternative was to use the San Francisco Conference to

---

[49] I. F. Stone, "Anti-Russian Undertow," *Nation,* CLX (May 12, 1945), 534–35; Thomas F. Reynolds, "The U.S.A. at San Francisco," *New Republic,* CXII (June 11, 1945), 810; *New Republic,* CXII (June 4, 1945), 771–72; *Time,* XLV (June 11, 1945), 24; Archibald MacLeish memorandum of conversation with Swing, May 21, 1945, Department of State records, 711.61/5-2245.

[50] Interview with Harriman, July 16, 1966, John Foster Dulles Oral History Collection; record of the 16th meeting of the American delegation to the San Francisco Conference, April 25, 1945, *FR: 1945,* I, 389–90; Charles J. V. Murphy, "W. Averell Harriman," *Life,* XXI (December 30, 1946), 64; Harriman, *America and Russia,* p. 42; MacLeish memorandum of conversation with Swing, May 21, 1945, Department of State records, 711.61/5-2245. See also MacLeish to Joseph C. Grew, May 26, 1945, *ibid.,* 711.61/5-2645 CS/A; Cox Diary, April 26, 1945, Cox MSS; and Curtis D. MacDougall, *Gideon's Army,* I, 23.

turn world opinion against the Soviet Union: "I have great hope that
we can here mobilize the conscience of mankind against the aggressor of
tomorrow. It may not prevent World War No. 3 someday. But if it fails
it will at least unite civilization against the new aggressor. That achievement seems to me to be of priceless value." Vandenberg liberally laced
the diary he kept during the conference with belligerent expressions of
hostility toward the Russians ("we should stand our ground against these
Russian demands and *quit appeasing Stalin and Molotov*"), and left San
Francisco convinced that the only way to deal with the Russians was to
make no concessions. The lesson of San Francisco was that "we can get
along with Russia *if and when* we can convince Russia that *we mean
what we say.*" Vandenberg told a group of Republican senators after returning to Washington that the main requirement for dealing with Russia was "having a mind of our own and sticking to it." He wrote his
wife shortly after the Senate ratified the United Nations Charter that, in
the final analysis, the success of the world organization would depend
"on Russia and whether we have *guts* enough to make her behave." [51]

John Foster Dulles, who acted as an adviser to the American delegation, shared many of Vandenberg's suspicions. Dulles doubted the ability
of the world organization to keep the peace, and believed that the Russians had ulterior motives for joining it. They might, he felt, be planning to use the international body as an instrument for exercising power
outside their sphere of influence. Worried that the United Nations could
someday become a Russian tool, Dulles told Vandenberg that the United
States should not join it without first securing the right of withdrawal.[52]

Officials in Washington, preoccupied with worry over Eastern Europe,
lend-lease, reparations, and the use of the atomic bomb, found the
proceedings in San Francisco increasingly irrelevant. To Secretary of

[51] Vandenberg to Frank Januszewski, May 15, 1945, Vandenberg MSS; Vandenberg
Diary, April 27, June 7, 1945, Vandenberg, ed., *Private Papers*, pp. 182, 208; Harold
H. Burton Diary, July 10, 1945, Burton MSS, Box 138; Vandenberg to Mrs. Vanden-
berg, undated, Vandenberg, ed., *Private Papers*, pp. 218–19.

[52] Forrestal Diary, April 9, 1945, Millis, ed., *The Forrestal Diaries*, pp. 41–42; record of the 33d meeting of the American delegation to the San Francisco Conference,
May 8, 1945, *FR: 1945*, I, 644; Vandenberg Diary, May 19, 1945, Vandenberg, ed.,
Private Papers, pp. 194–95. On Dulles' reservations about the United Nations see also
the interviews with Robert D. Murphy, May 19, 1965, and Andrew Cordier, February
1, 1967, Dulles Oral History Collection; and Dulles to Vandenberg, July 10, 1945,
Vandenberg MSS.

War Stimson, the situation seemed "unreal," with the delegates "babbling on as if there were no . . . great issues pending." Acting Secretary of State Joseph Grew felt that the United Nations "will be incapable of preserving peace and security" because the right of veto in the Security Council would prevent collective action against "the one certain future enemy, Soviet Russia." Russian actions in Eastern Europe had already demonstrated the kind of "world pattern" Moscow sought to create. The Russians would soon attempt to expand their influence through the rest of Europe, the Near East, and the Far East. "A future war with Soviet Russia," Grew concluded bleakly, "is as certain as anything in this world." [53]

Joseph E. Davies wrote to James F. Byrnes on May 10 that "the Russian situation . . . is deteriorating so rapidly that it is frightening." Justice Felix Frankfurter expressed concern about growing anti-Russian sentiment within the government in two conversations with Davies later that month. Deputy Foreign Economic Administrator Oscar Cox was so worried over the disturbing diplomatic situation that he set to work on an elaborate analysis of Soviet-American relations designed to show that no reason for conflict between the two nations existed. Assistant Secretary of State Archibald MacLeish warned on May 22 that "explicit reference to the possibility of a war with Russia is becoming more common in the American press from day to day." On the same day, former Undersecretary of State Sumner Welles charged publicly that "in five short weeks since the death of President Roosevelt the policy which he so painstakingly carried out has been changed. Our Government now appears to the Russians as the spearhead of an apparent bloc of the western nations opposed to the Soviet Union." [54]

Fears that the Truman Administration had reversed Roosevelt's policy toward the Soviet Union turned out to be premature, as Harry Hopkins' trip to Moscow soon showed. But the public Russian-American confron-

[53] Stimson Diary, May 15, 1945, Stimson MSS; Grew memorandum of May 19, 1945, quoted in Joseph C. Grew, *Turbulent Era: A Diplomatic Record of Forty Years, 1904–1945*, II, 1445–46.

[54] Davies to Byrnes, May 10, 1945, Davies Diary, May 13 and 18, 1945, Davies MSS, Boxes 16 and 17; Cox Diary, May 12–29, 1945, Cox MSS; MacLeish memorandum of conversation with Swing, May 22, 1945, Department of State records, 711.61/5-2245; Welles radio broadcast, May 22, 1945, reprinted in the *Congressional Record*, 1945 appendix, pp. A2507–A2508.

tation at San Francisco had two effects which were significant for the future: It exposed prominent Republicans like Dulles and Vandenberg to the frustrations of dealing with the Russians. Both men came away from the experience convinced that the only way to negotiate with Moscow was to take a firm position and avoid compromise. It also made clear to the American people the depth and extent of the divisions which separated the Soviet Union and the United States. Opinion polls showed that by the middle of May, 1945, the number of Americans who doubted Russia's willingness to cooperate with the United States after the war had risen to 38 percent of those questioned, the highest figure since March of 1942. Even more significantly, Americans for the first time attributed the difficulties in inter-Allied relations more to the Soviet Union than to Great Britain. As late as February, 1945, a majority of those dissatisfied with the extent of Big Three cooperation had held Britain responsible. But San Francisco shifted the blame to Russia, where it would stay for the rest of the Cold War.[55]

V

The striking deterioration in relations with Russia which took place in the month following Roosevelt's death left the new President deeply worried. Truman still used belligerent rhetoric in discussing the USSR. Early in May he told Elmer Benson, acting chairman of the National Citizens' Political Action Committee, that the Russians were "like bulls in a china shop. . . . We've got to teach them how to behave." But when Benson protested that there would be no peace unless Americans learned to get along with the Soviet Union, Truman admitted: "That is right." On May 13, Joseph E. Davies found the President "much disturbed" over the Russian problem. Molotov had apparently gone to San Francisco "to make trouble," Truman charged, and the newspapers— "these damn sheets"—were making it worse. But when Davies attributed much of the tension at San Francisco to the anti-Soviet bias of

[55] American Institute of Public Opinion poll of May 15, 1945, cited in Cantril and Strunk, eds., *Public Opinion,* pp. 370–71; Department of State, "Fortnightly Survey of American Opinion," No. 28, June 9, 1945; Almond, *The American People and Foreign Policy,* p. 96. For the February, 1945, survey, see Grew to Roosevelt, February 24, 1945, Roosevelt MSS, PSF 29: "State Department."

American officials, Truman agreed that such hostility existed and promised to change the situation. Davies left a memorandum with the President which argued that "it is . . . wrong to assume that 'tough' language is the only language they [the Russians] can understand." [56]

Truman at this time thought highly enough of Davies to entrust him later that month with a delicate mission to London to explain American policy to Winston Churchill, whose anti-Russian fulminations had become increasingly strident in recent weeks. Davies told the British Prime Minister that the President was "gravely concerned" over growing differences with the Soviet Union, many of which had sprung, Truman believed, from conflicting interpretations of the Yalta agreements:

The President's position was that every agreement made by President Roosevelt would be scrupulously supported by him. If there were differences of opinion as to what these agreements were, he wanted them cleared up. If new decisions were required for continued unity, he wanted clear understandings as to the terms. The U.S. would then fulfill these obligations, and he would confidently expect the same from associated governments.

Like Roosevelt, Truman believed that only continued Big Three unity could guarantee lasting peace. The President later acknowledged that Davies had represented his position with "accuracy" and "exceptional skill." [57]

By now Truman had accepted a proposal from Churchill for another Big Three meeting, but insisted that he could not leave the United States until July because of pressing domestic problems.[58] Ambassador

[56] MacDougall, *Gideon's Army*, I, 23; Davies memorandum of conversation with Truman, May 13, 1945, Davies MSS, Box 16; Davies to Truman, May 12, 1945, *ibid.*

[57] Davies report to Truman on conversations with Churchill, June 12, 1945, *FR: Potsdam*, I, 64–65; Truman, *Year of Decisions*, p. 261. Some confusion did arise over the plans for the Big Three meeting. Davies gave Churchill the impression that Truman wanted to meet Stalin first at a separate location, in order to avoid the impression of "ganging up" on the Russians. Churchill took violent exception to this. Truman later argued that he had only intended to suggest individual personal contacts at the proposed Big Three meeting, not a separate bilateral conference. On this matter, see *ibid.*, pp. 260–62; Churchill, *Triumph and Tragedy*, pp. 492–96; and Feis, *Between War and Peace*, pp. 124–27. Davies also took it upon himself to give the Prime Minister a lengthy exposition of his own personal views, including the suggestion that Churchill might now regret his decision to support Stalin instead of Hitler during the war. (*FR: Potsdam*, I, 73.)

[58] For messages regarding the timing of the Big Three conference, see *FR: Potsdam*, I, 3–20. According to Davies, Truman told him on May 21 that he had delayed the

Harriman objected to the delay, arguing that Soviet-American relations constituted "the number one problem affecting the future of the world" and that the two countries "were getting farther and farther apart." The President held to his timetable, however, prompting Harriman to suggest sending Harry Hopkins to Moscow at once to try to settle outstanding difficulties. Truman had previously considered this possibility, and after checking with Hopkins informed Stalin on May 19 that Roosevelt's former confidant would accompany Harriman back to the Soviet Union.[59]

By sending Hopkins to Moscow, Truman clearly demonstrated his desire to continue Roosevelt's Russian policy. "I want peace and I am willing to work hard for it," the President wrote in the diary which he sporadically kept during his early days in the White House; "to have a reasonably lasting peace, the three great powers must be able to trust each other." On the next day, Truman told Stettinius that he was confident that "Harry would be able to straighten things out with Stalin. He stated that. . . . the Hopkins Mission was going to unravel a great many things and that by the time he met with the Big Three . . . most of our troubles would be out of the way." Truman instructed Hopkins to "make it clear to Uncle Joe Stalin that I knew what I wanted—and that I intended to get—peace for the world for at least 90 years." The United States, Hopkins was to say, had no territorial ambitions or ulterior motives in Eastern Europe or anywhere else in the world, but when it made commitments it planned to keep them, and expected other nations to do the same. Truman left Hopkins free, he later wrote, "to use diplomatic language or a baseball bat if he thought that was the proper

Big Three meeting until after the first test of the atomic bomb, scheduled for mid-July. The President made a similar statement to Stimson on June 6. (Davies Diary, May 21, 1945, Davies MSS, Box 17; Stimson memorandum of conversation with Truman, June 6, 1945, Stimson MSS, Box 421.) But Truman explained to other advisers who knew about the bomb that he was postponing the meeting until he could finish work on the budget. (*FR: Potsdam,* I, 11, 13.) The question of whether the bomb influenced Truman's timing thus remains inconclusive. For two conflicting interpretations on this matter, see Alperovitz, *Atomic Diplomacy,* chapter 3; and Kolko, *Politics of War,* pp. 421–22.

[59] Grew memorandum, Truman-Harriman conversation, May 15, 1945, *FR: Potsdam,* I, 13–14; Truman to Stalin, May 19, 1945, *ibid.,* pp. 21–22. For the origins of the Hopkins mission, see Sherwood, *Roosevelt and Hopkins,* pp. 885–87; and Truman, *Year of Decisions,* pp. 257–58.

approach." But the President was well aware of Hopkins' sympathetic attitude toward the Russians, and by choosing him to undertake this mission ensured that the approach would be conciliatory.[60]

At their first meeting on May 26, Hopkins frankly told Stalin that within the past six weeks a serious deterioration in American opinion of Russia had occurred. Disaffection had developed not among the small minority who had always been hostile to the USSR but among "the very people who had supported to the hilt Roosevelt's policy of cooperation with the Soviet Union." This situation was very dangerous because it placed limitations on Truman's freedom of action: "Without the support of public opinion and particularly of the supporters of President Roosevelt it would be very difficult for President Truman to carry forward President Roosevelt's policy." Hopkins went on to explain the reasons for this feeling of alarm in the United States. He told Stalin that the "cardinal basis" of Roosevelt's foreign policy had been the assumption that both the United States and the Soviet Union had worldwide interests. At Yalta the two countries had come close to settling the outstanding issues between them. But because of the failure to carry out the Yalta agreement on Poland, public opinion in the United States had become upset. A series of events, unimportant in themselves, had left Americans bewildered at the Big Three's inability to agree.

At this point Stalin interrupted Hopkins to say that the Soviet Union wanted to have a friendly Poland, but that the British wanted to revive the old *cordon sanitaire.* Hopkins replied emphatically that the United States had no such intention; that Americans "would desire a Poland friendly to the Soviet Union and in fact desired to see friendly countries all along the Soviet borders." Stalin commented that if this was so, then it would be easy to reach an agreement on Poland.[61]

Hopkins explained that Poland was a symbol of American ability to work with the Soviet Union. The United States had no special interests in Poland and would recognize any government which the Polish people would accept and which was friendly to the Soviet Union. What upset

[60] Truman Diary, May 22, 1945, printed in Hillman, *Mr. President,* p. 116; Stettinius calendar notes, May 23, 1945, Stettinius Papers, Box 245; Truman, *Year of Decisions,* p. 258.

[61] Bohlen notes, Hopkins-Stalin meeting of May 26, 1945, quoted in Sherwood, *Roosevelt and Hopkins,* pp. 889–90.

the people and the government of the United States was the unilateral
action which the Russians and the Lublin Poles had taken in Poland.
Something would have to be done to calm this concern. If the American
people were to abandon isolationism, "our people must believe that they
are joining their power with that of the Soviet Union and Great Britain
in the promotion of international peace and the well being of human-
ity."

Stalin replied with a frank exposition of the Russian view on Poland.
He told Hopkins that twice within the last twenty-five years the Germans had invaded Russia through Poland. The Poles had either been too
weak to resist or had let the Germans through because they hated the
Russians so much. Polish weakness and hostility had hurt Russia in the
past; Russia had a vital interest in seeing to it that Poland was strong
and friendly in the future. Stalin admitted taking unilateral actions in
Poland, but said that this had been done for military reasons, not from
any desire to exclude the Soviet Union's allies from participation in postwar Polish affairs. The Russian leader then proposed a practical solution
of the problem. The present Warsaw government would form the basis
of the future Polish Provisional Government of National Unity, but representatives from other Polish groups who were friendly to both the Allies and the Russians could have four or five out of the eighteen or
twenty ministries in the government.[62]

Hopkins relayed this information to Washington, and by June 6 was
able to tell Stalin that Truman had agreed. The President and his advisers did not regard this solution of the Polish problem as final. Ambassador Harriman warned Truman on the 8th:

I am afraid Stalin does not and never will fully understand our interest in a
free Poland as a matter of principle. He is a realist in all of his actions, and
it is hard for him to appreciate our faith in abstract principles. It is difficult
for him to understand why we should want to interfere with Soviet policy in
a country like Poland, which he considers so important to Russia's security,
unless we have some ulterior motive.

But Truman's willingness to accept Stalin's offer marked a realization on
his part of something Roosevelt had found out earlier: given the realities

[62] Bohlen notes, Hopkins-Stalin meeting of May 27, 1945, quoted *ibid.,* pp.
899–901.

of the situation in Eastern Europe, the best the United States could hope for was that world opinion would force the Soviet-dominated Polish provisional government to hold free elections. In time, Truman even came to sound like Roosevelt when he discussed Poland. He told Dr. T. V. Soong later in June that he wanted the Polish question settled "in such a manner as to insure tranquility and stability." At Potsdam the following month, the President reminded Stalin: "There are six million Poles in the United States. A free election in Poland reported to the United States by a free press would make it easier to deal with these . . . people." But the Hopkins-Stalin agreement in no way altered the balance of power in Poland. The most that could be said for the new government in Warsaw, *Time* observed, "was that in forming it Russia had paid lip service to the Yalta pledges, and given the U.S. and Britain a chance to save face." [63]

If Stalin drove a hard bargain on Poland, however, he proved to be most accommodating on the other matters which Hopkins and Harriman took up with him. Russia would enter the war against Japan as promised, Stalin assured the Americans, and would scrupulously observe the independence of China. The Allied Control Council for Germany would begin work as quickly as possible, with Marshal Zhukov serving as the Soviet representative. The Russian leader indicated that he would be glad to meet Truman and Churchill in the vicinity of Berlin in mid-July. Near the end of Hopkins' stay in Moscow, Stalin cooperatively agreed to the American position on voting in the United Nations Security Council, thus breaking a deadlock which had threatened to wreck the work of the San Francisco Conference. "There has been a very pleasant yielding on the part of the Russians to some of the things in which we are interested," Truman told a press conference on June 13. "I think if we keep our heads and be patient, we will arrive at a conclusion; be-

[63] Harriman to Truman, June 8, 1945, *FR: Potsdam*, I, 61; Grew memorandum of Truman-Soong conversation, June 14, 1945, *FR: 1945*, VII, 902; minutes, 5th plenary meeting, Potsdam, July 21, 1945, *FR: Potsdam*, II, 206; *Time*, XLVI (July 16, 1945), 14. See also Truman, *Year of Decisions*, pp. 263–64; McNeill, *America, Britain, and Russia*, p. 591; and Byrnes, *Speaking Frankly*, p. 65. Admiral Leahy later noted: "The chief concern of Truman, as had been the case with Roosevelt, was to see that the Poles got a democratic government representing the majority of the inhabitants. Adding to the interest of America was the large and vocal group of Polish Americans who were important politically." (*I Was There*, p. 467.)

cause the Russians are just as anxious to get along with us as we are with them. And I think they have showed it very conclusively in these last negotiations." [64]

VI

The Hopkins-Stalin compromise settled the controversy over Poland for the time being, leaving Germany as the major issue facing the Big Three when they met at Potsdam in July.[65] United States plans for the occupation of Germany had been in a state of flux at the time of Roosevelt's death, with the State Department pushing a reparations program which looked toward revival of the German economy, while the Army prepared to implement JCS 1067, which still incorporated Morgenthau's punitive scheme of institutionalized chaos. But developments between April and July forced American officials to resolve the ambiguity of their German policy once and for all in favor of rehabilitation rather than repression.

The inadequacies of JCS 1067 became painfully apparent once military government authorities began trying to put it into effect. Confronted with the prospect of starving Germans, General Lucius D. Clay, military governor for the United States zone, quickly saw the illogic of prohibiting a resumption of industrial activity. Lewis Douglas, Clay's financial adviser, complained in amazement: "This thing was assembled by economic idiots! It makes no sense to forbid the most skilled workers in Europe from producing as much as they can for a continent which is desperately short of everything!" Unable to get Washington to undertake still another revision of JCS 1067, Douglas resigned in protest. Clay remained, taking advantage of loopholes in the directive to mitigate its more punitive provisions.[66]

Furthermore, Washington officials were becoming convinced that economic chaos, whether in Germany or in Europe as a whole, could only benefit the Soviet Union. In a conversation with Secretary of War Stim-

[64] Truman press conference of June 13, 1945, *Truman Public Papers, 1945*, p. 123. See also Sherwood, *Roosevelt and Hopkins*, pp. 891, 901–3, 907–8, 910–12.

[65] McNeill, *America, Britain, and Russia*, pp. 590–91.

[66] Clay, *Decision in Germany*, pp. 16–19; Murphy, *Diplomat among Warriors*, p. 251.

son on May 13, former President Herbert Hoover advocated a return to his World War I tactic of fighting communism by shipping food to starving Europeans. Three days later Stimson warned Truman of the importance of keeping Western Europe "from being driven to revolution or Communism by famine." But the Secretary of War pointed out that the rehabilitation of liberated Europe could not be separated from the problem of Germany, a subject on which there had already been too much "emotional thinking." Proposals such as Morgenthau's for keeping the Germans hungry would be a "grave mistake":

Punish her war criminals in full measure. Deprive her permanently of her weapons, her General Staff, and perhaps her entire army. Guard her governmental action until the Nazi educated generation has passed from the stage —admittedly a long job. But do not deprive her of the means of building up ultimately a contented Germany interested in following non-militaristic methods of civilization. . . . It is to the interest of the whole world that they [the Germans] should not be driven by stress of hardship into a non-democratic and necessarily predatory habit of life.

Navy Secretary Forrestal had come to similar conclusions. Germany had to be denied the capacity to make war, he wrote on May 14, but "to ignore the existence of 75 or 80 millions of vigorous and industrious people or to assume that they will not join with Russia if no other outlet is afforded them I think is closing our eyes to reality." [67]

Truman needed no convincing. Although he had signed the revised version of JCS 1067, knowing that occupation authorities needed some kind of directive, the new President made it clear that he would not oppose modification of the document's harsher provisions. Truman relied more heavily on State Department advice than Roosevelt had, while at the same time the War Department, under the influence of Stimson and Clay, was beginning to back away from Morgenthau's ideas. Although the new Chief Executive treated the Treasury Secretary courteously, dif-

[67] Stimson memorandum of conversation with Hoover, May 13, 1945, Stimson MSS, Box 421; Stimson to Truman, May 16, 1945, *ibid.;* Forrestal to Senator Homer Ferguson, May 14, 1945, Millis, ed., *The Forrestal Diaries,* p. 57. See also Hoover to Stimson, May 15, 1945, Stimson MSS, Box 421. The rigid ban which JCS 1067 imposed on political parties in the American zone also caused concern in the State Department and among occupation authorities for fear it would strengthen underground activity by German communists. See *FR: 1945,* III, 944, 949, 951; *FR: Potsdam,* I, 438, 472–73, 489, II, 774–75.

ferences between them soon became obvious. Truman asked Morgenthau to delay publication of his plan for Germany until after the Potsdam Conference: "I have got to see Stalin and Churchill, and when I do I want . . . all the cards in my hand, and the plan on Germany is one of them. I don't want to play my hand before I see them." In a conversation with State Department officials on May 10, the President said that he "entirely disagreed" with Morgenthau's recommendation that synthetic oil plants in Germany be destroyed. Later that month, Truman rebuked the Treasury Secretary for questioning the need to go through elaborate legal procedures in dealing with Nazi war criminals: "Even the Russians want to give them a trial." Early in July, just before leaving for Potsdam, the President finally asked for Morgenthau's resignation. In retrospect, Truman acknowledged that he had always opposed the Morgenthau Plan. It would have been "an act of revenge," he argued, "and too many peace treaties had been based on that spirit." [68]

But the Administration's decision in favor of rehabilitation made it all the more important to work out an agreement with the Soviet Union on reparations. If the Russians were given free rein to take what they wanted, they would strip the industrialized areas of western Germany, producing the economic chaos which Washington wanted to avoid. But if the Russians did not obtain a satisfactory reparations settlement, they might deny badly needed food shipments from their zone to the West, making it necessary for the British and Americans to launch a costly import program to ward off starvation. Hence, Washington officials sought an arrangement whereby they could control the flow of reparations to the Soviet Union without provoking reprisals. As Stimson told Truman: "We must find some way of persuading Russia to play ball." [69]

On July 3, 1945, three days before his departure for Potsdam, Truman

[68] Blum, *Morgenthau Diaries: Years of War,* pp. 451–52, 459–68; Grew memorandum of conversation with Truman, May 10, 1945, *FR: 1945,* III, 509; Truman, *Year of Decisions,* pp. 235–36. Truman says that he asked for Morgenthau's resignation after the Treasury Secretary demanded to be taken to Potsdam. Morgenthau's diary account, however, indicates that he only expressed regret that no Treasury representatives would be present at the Big Three conference and that he himself proposed his resignation. (Truman, *Year of Decisions,* p. 327; Blum, *Morgenthau Diaries: Years of War,* pp. 465–66.)

[69] Potsdam briefing book paper, "Policy Toward Germany," *FR: Potsdam,* I, 440–41; Stimson to Truman, May 16, 1945, Stimson MSS, Box 421.

named James F. Byrnes to replace Stettinius as secretary of state. Byrnes had attended the Yalta Conference at Roosevelt's request, but otherwise had little diplomatic experience. He did have an impressive domestic record, however, having served in both houses of Congress, on the Supreme Court, and as director of the Office of War Mobilization and Reconversion. The new Secretary of State looked forward to applying the negotiating techniques he had found useful in these jobs to the problems of foreign affairs. Truman and Byrnes had one overriding objective at Potsdam: they wanted to clear up remaining wartime problems so that United States military and economic responsibilities in Europe could be terminated as quickly as possible. Both men were able practitioners of the art of politics, acutely sensitive to the American public's desire for a return to normalcy at home and abroad. Both tended to look upon the Russians as fellow politicians, with whom a deal could be arranged.[70]

Soviet actions prior to Potsdam made it clear that Moscow would drive a hard bargain. The Russians had already systematically stripped the areas they occupied of heavy industry, railroad rolling stock, agricultural implements, and even furnishings from houses, but argued that these goods came under the category of "war booty" rather than reparations. Simultaneously, the Soviet Union had unilaterally turned over a large section of its occupation zone to the Poles, causing an exodus into the remainder of Germany of several million displaced Germans while reducing the area from which food for the Anglo-American zones could be made available. The Allies had agreed at Yalta that Poland should receive "substantial accessions of territory" from Germany to compensate for land taken by the Soviet Union, but London and Washington considered the boundary which the Russians assigned to the Poles—the line of the Oder and Western Neisse rivers—as running much too far to the west.[71]

Meanwhile the Reparations Commission, meeting in Moscow, had made no progress toward resolving that complex issue. The Russians

[70] McNeill, *America, Britain, and Russia,* pp. 611–12, 622; Daniels, *Man of Independence,* pp. 285–86; Welles, *Seven Decisions That Shaped History,* pp. 207–9.

[71] Potsdam briefing book paper, "Suggested United States Policy Regarding Poland," June 29, 1945, *FR: Potsdam,* I, 743–47. For Russian war booty removals, see Kennan to Stettinius, April 27 and May 3, 1945, *FR: 1945,* III, 1200, 1203–5.

continued to accord first priority to the removal of a fixed amount of goods and services from Germany—$20 billion, the figure accepted "as a basis for discussion" at Yalta, of which half would go the Soviet Union—regardless of what this would do to the German standard of living. The Americans, fearing economic collapse, continued to insist on the "first charge" principle, which would allow the extraction of reparations only after imports essential to maintain the German economy had been paid for. "It was clear to us," General Clay later wrote, "that for many months to come German production would not suffice to keep the German people alive, and that the use of any part of it for reparations would mean that once again the United States would be not only supporting Germany but also paying the bill for reparations." [72]

Determined not to repeat the post-World War I experience, Truman and Byrnes took a firm stand on reparations throughout the conference. "There was one pitfall I intended to avoid," Truman later recalled; "we did not intend to pay, under any circumstances, the reparations bill for Europe." The Secretary of State repeatedly stressed that "there will be no reparations until imports in the American zone are paid for. There can be no discussion of this matter." Convinced that the Russian position on war booty and the Polish-German border precluded any over-all arrangement on reparations which the Americans could accept, Byrnes proposed that each occupying power simply take what it wanted from its own zone. Since the Anglo-American zones contained the bulk of German heavy industry, Byrnes offered to give the Russians a certain percentage of what could be spared from these areas, and to exchange a further amount in return for food shipments from the Soviet zone. [73]

The Russians, still hoping for commitment to a fixed sum, did not like this proposal. A percentage of an undetermined amount, Molotov pointed out, meant very little. To compensate for war booty removals and the transfer of part of eastern Germany to Poland, the Soviet foreign minister offered to reduce the total reparations bill which the Russians sought, but Byrnes and Truman refused. They did offer to accept the Oder–Western Neisse line, pending final determination by the peace conference, if Moscow would agree to the American position on

[72] Clay, *Decision in Germany*, p. 38. Discussions in the Reparations Commission are covered in *FR: Potsdam*, I, 510–54.

[73] Truman, *Year of Decisions*, p. 323; minutes, 6th foreign ministers' meeting, July 23, 1945, *FR: Potsdam*, II, 279–80. See also *ibid.*, pp. 274–75, 295–98, 450–52, 471–76.

reparations. Faced with the alternative of getting no reparations from the Western zones at all, the Russians reluctantly went along with this bargain. The final protocol provided that reparations claims of each victor would be met by removals from the territory each occupied, but that in addition the Russians would receive from the Anglo-American zones 10 percent "of such industrial capital equipment as is unnecessary for the German peace economy." The Soviet Union would get another 15 percent of such material from the West in exchange for an equivalent value of food, coal, or other commodities from the Russian zone.[74]

Once the United States had decided to rehabilitate Germany, it could not agree to Moscow's demand for a guaranteed amount of reparations without placing unacceptable burdens on the American taxpayer. The compromise Byrnes arranged at Potsdam allowed the Soviet Union shipments of industrial equipment from the Western zones, but placed British and American officials in a position to control the flow of these goods through the "first charge" principle. At the same time, it obligated the Russians to help feed the American and British zones by sending food from the East. This arrangement promoted American economic interests but still left room for continued cooperation with the Soviet Union. By increasing the authority of the zonal commanders at the expense of the Allied Control Council, however, the Potsdam agreement undermined the principle of a unified Germany for which proponents of rehabilitation had long fought. Molotov realized this at once. Would not Byrnes's proposal, he asked, "mean that each country would have a free hand in their own zones and would act entirely independent of the others?" [75] But the President and his secretary of state, preoccupied with their immediate goal of minimizing American responsibilities in Europe, failed to see or chose to ignore the long-range implications of their own policy.

On other issues, Potsdam produced mixed results. The Russians agreed readily enough to the establishment of a Council of Foreign Ministers which would begin work on peace treaties with former Axis satellites. Efforts by the Americans to secure a stronger Soviet commitment to the Yalta Declaration on Liberated Europe failed, however, as the Russians insisted on equating the situation in Eastern Europe with that in Italy

[74] *FR: Potsdam,* II, 296–97, 473, 480, 512–14, 1485–86.
[75] Bohlen minutes, Byrnes-Molotov conversation, July 27, 1945, *FR: Potsdam,* II, 450.

and Greece. Stalin did renew his promise to enter the war against Japan, and cooperatively provided the Americans with news of peace feelers from Tokyo. A series of other matters, including the disposition of Italian colonies, revision of the Montreux Convention on the Black Sea straits, troop withdrawals from Iran, and an American proposal for the internationalization of inland waterways, were referred to the new Council of Foreign Ministers for future consideration.[76]

American officials left Potsdam with ambivalent feelings regarding the possibilities of future cooperation with the Soviet Union. Admiral Leahy noted that the British and Americans had been forced to accept many unilateral actions taken by the Russians since Yalta, but rejoiced that Truman had "stood up to Stalin in a manner calculated to warm the heart of every patriotic American" by refusing to be "bulldozed into any reparations agreement that would repeat the history of World War I." Byrnes believed that the concessions that had been made reflected the realities of the situation in Europe, and that his "horsetrade" on reparations and the Polish boundary question had left the way open for further negotiations at the foreign ministers' level. General Clay anticipated no serious difficulties in working with the Russians in Germany: "They know what they *want* and it is always easy to do business with those who do know their own desires." [77]

But the police-state atmosphere of the Soviet zone, together with painfully obvious evidence of looting, repelled the Americans. Secretary of War Stimson described the Russian attitude on war booty as "rather oriental," while Reparations Commissioner Pauley termed it "organized vandalism." Harriman pictured Russia as "a vacuum into which all movable goods would be sucked," and commented that "Hitler's greatest crime was that his actions had resulted in opening the gates of Eastern Europe to Asia." Joseph E. Davies, always a sensitive barometer of anti-Russian sentiment, noted that "the hostility to Russia is bitter and surprisingly open—considering that we are here to compose and secure peace":

There is constant repetition of the whispered suggestions of how ruthless the Russian Army had been in looting and shipping back vast quantities of ev-

[76] Potsdam protocol, August 1, 1945, *FR: Potsdam,* II, 1478–98.

[77] Leahy, *I Was There,* pp. 497–98; George Curry, *James F. Byrnes,* p. 125; Clay to Baruch, August 8, 1945, Baruch MSS, "Selected Correspondence."

erything from cattle to plumbing fixtures. . . . The atmosphere is poisoned with it. The French are carrying everything, including the kitchen stove, out of their territory. Our own soldiers and even some members of this delegation are "liberating" things from this area. But the criticisms are leveled only against the Soviets.

Davies worried that the President was "surrounded by forces actively hostile to the Russians, even to the point of destroying Big Three unity." [78]

But Truman took a more balanced view than many of his advisers. "Joe," he explained to Davies, "I am trying my best to save peace and to follow out Roosevelt's plans. . . . Jim Byrnes knows that, too, and is doing all he possibly can." The President found the tenacious bargaining tactics of the Russians frustrating—"on a number of occasions I felt like blowing the roof off the palace"—but thought he understood and could deal with the Soviet dictator: "Stalin is as near like Tom Pendergast as any man I know," the former senator from Missouri later commented. The Russians were negotiating from weakness rather than strength, Truman believed, because "a dictatorship is the hardest thing in God's world to hold together." While Stalin might want to dominate the world, he would likely find himself more concerned in future years with the problem of remaining in power. Moreover, Russian aggressiveness was based in part upon expectations of a postwar depression in the United States, a development which Truman hoped to avoid. According to one close observer, Truman after Potsdam approached the problem of dealing with Russia in the manner of a typical Middle American "who believed without contradiction in loving his neighbor and steadily watching him at the same time." Stalin was "an S.O.B.," the President told his startled companions on the voyage home, but then he added affably: "I guess he thinks I'm one too." [79]

[78] Stimson to Truman, July 22, 1945, *FR: Potsdam,* II, 808–9; Pauley to Byrnes, July 27, 1945, *ibid.,* p. 889; Forrestal Diary, July 29, 1945, Millis, ed., *The Forrestal Diaries,* pp. 79–80; Davies Diary, July 15, 16, 19, 21, 1945, Davies MSS, Box 18.

[79] Davies Diary, July 16, 1945, Davies MSS, Box 18; Truman, *Year of Decisions,* pp. 369, 411–12; Murphy, *Diplomat among Warriors,* pp. 278–79; Forrestal Diary, July 28, 1945, Millis, ed., *The Forrestal Diaries,* p. 78; Daniels, *Man of Independence,* pp. 276, 278–79, 285–86; Fletcher Knebel and Charles W. Bailey II, *No High Ground,* pp. 1–2. Daniels believes that Truman reached his conclusions about the weaknesses of dictatorships from having watched the operations of the Pendergast machine in Kansas City. (*Man of Independence,* p. 285.)

8

※※

The Impotence of Omnipotence:
American Diplomacy, the Atomic Bomb,
and the Postwar World

Knowledge that the United States had successfully tested the first atomic bomb on July 16, 1945, probably made the difficulties of dealing with the Russians at Potsdam seem less than overwhelming to the President. News of the secret explosion in the New Mexico desert had greatly cheered Truman and his advisers, contributing to their firm stand on German reparations and to their declining interest in securing Russian military assistance against Japan. American officials had anxiously debated whether to tell Stalin about the bomb before its use. Their conclusion, reported to the President by Secretary of War Stimson, had been to inform the Russians but to give them as little additional information as possible. Truman carried out this recommendation on July 24, casually telling the Soviet leader that the United States had developed a powerful new weapon. The President did not go into details, and Stalin simply expressed the hope that the device would be used on the Japanese.[1]

[1] Stimson Diary, July 3, 1945, Stimson MSS; minutes, meeting of the Combined Policy Committee, July 4, 1945, *FR: 1945,* II, 13; Truman, *Year of Decisions,* p. 416; Byrnes, *Speaking Frankly,* p. 263; Churchill, *Triumph and Tragedy,* pp. 572–73. For the effect news of the successful test had on American and British negotiators at Pots-

The possibility of employing the bomb to shorten the war had long been taken for granted by American and British political leaders. Roosevelt and Churchill had agreed as early as September, 1944, that if the weapon was ready in time it might, "after mature considerations," be put to use against the Japanese. Actually, F.D.R.'s position was less equivocal than the tone of this document indicates. Stimson later wrote that "at no time, from 1941 to 1945, did I ever hear it suggested by the President, or by any other responsible member of the government, that atomic energy should not be used in the war." Admiral Leahy thought that "FDR would have used it in a minute to prove that he had not wasted two billion dollars." Churchill concurred: "There was unanimous, automatic, unquestioned agreement around our table; nor did I ever hear the slightest suggestion that we should do otherwise." President Truman's attitude was equally clear: "I regarded the bomb as a military weapon and never had any doubt that it should be used." Throughout the war Anglo-American military strategy had been to seek victory as quickly as possible through technology, not manpower. The decision to drop the bomb marked the logical culmination of that effort.[2]

But the bomb had more than purely military implications. American possession of this revolutionary new weapon drastically altered the post-war balance of power, making it at least technically feasible for the United States to impose its will upon the rest of the world. "God Almighty in His infinite wisdom [has] dropped the atomic bomb in our lap," Senator Edwin C. Johnson of Colorado proclaimed in November, 1945; now for the first time the United States, "with vision and guts and plenty of atomic bombs, . . . [could] compel mankind to adopt the policy of lasting peace . . . or be burned to a crisp." No responsible official in the Truman Administration wanted to go that far, but the President and his advisers did expect that the American nuclear monopoly would

---

dam, see the Stimson Diary, July 16–19, 21–22, 24, 30, 1945, Stimson MSS; and the Davies Diary, July 28, 1945, Davies MSS, Box 19.

[2] Roosevelt-Churchill *aide-mémoire*, September 19, 1944, printed in Gowing, *Britain and Atomic Energy*, p. 447; Henry L. Stimson, "The Decision to Use the Atomic Bomb," *Harper's*, CXCIV (February, 1947), 98; Leahy interview with Jonathan Daniels, quoted in Daniels, *Man of Independence*, p. 281; Churchill, *Triumph and Tragedy*, p. 546; Truman, *Year of Decisions*, p. 419. See also Walter Smith Schoenberger, *Decision of Destiny*, pp. 44–47. For Anglo-American military strategy, see chapter 3.

improve the West's bargaining position with the Soviet Union. In particular, they anticipated that in return for agreeing to turn control of the bomb over to an international agency, they might secure political concessions from the Russians in Eastern Europe and elsewhere.[3]

These hopes were frustrated, however, for "atomic diplomacy" proved to be a surprisingly ineffective means of securing American objectives. The new weapon must have impressed Kremlin leaders—they apparently ordered a quick acceleration of their own bomb development program—but they carefully avoided any outward signs of concern.[4] The Soviet position on Eastern Europe became increasingly rigid after August, 1945, while Russian diplomats showed only the most casual interest in American plans to place control of atomic weapons in the hands of the United Nations. Washington officials had no intention of actually using the bomb to compel Moscow's cooperation, and they had devised no clear strategy for employing the weapon's potential power as a bargaining instrument on specific issues. Moreover, with the end of the war Congress began to reassert its authority over the conduct of foreign affairs, severely restricting the Administration's freedom of action not only in the field of international control but also in more conventional areas of military and economic policy. As a result, American leaders found it just as difficult, if not more so, to shape external developments to their liking after the bombs fell on Hiroshima and Nagasaki than they had before these awesome events had taken place.

[3] *Congressional Record,* November 28, 1945, pp. 11085–86; Truman, *Year of Decisions,* p. 87; Stimson memorandum of conversation with Truman, June 6, 1945, Stimson MSS, Box 421; Davies Diary, July 28–29, 1945, Davies MSS, Box 19. See also Daniels, *Man of Independence,* p. 266; and Herbert Feis, *The Atomic Bomb and the End of World War II,* pp. 194–95. Gar Alperovitz has argued that American officials did not regard use of the bomb as necessary to bring about Japan's surrender, but dropped it because "a combat demonstration was needed to convince the Russians to accept the American plan for a stable peace." (*Atomic Diplomacy,* p. 240.) Alperovitz fails to show conclusively that policy-makers at the time believed a Japanese surrender to be imminent, however, nor does he consider the domestic criticisms Truman and his advisers would have faced had they allowed the war to continue after the bomb had become available. Moreover, Alperovitz's account rests on the questionable assumption that Truman had, upon coming into office, decided to reverse Roosevelt's policy of cooperation with the Soviet Union. (On this point, see chapter 7.) For an effective critique of Alperovitz by a fellow revisionist, see Kolko, *Politics of War,* pp. 421–22, 538–43.

[4] On this point, see Ulam, *Expansion and Coexistence,* pp. 415–17.

I

The use of atomic energy for military purposes created special problems for a nation which prided itself on reaching decisions democratically. Public knowledge of the issues had always been regarded, accurately or inaccurately, as a prerequisite for successful operation of the American political system. But nuclear energy was a totally new field which only a tiny minority of Americans could understand. The process of educating the public would take time and, because of the forbiddingly technical nature of the subject, could never be thorough. Government officials could not wait for the people to become informed before deciding what to do with the new weapon, yet constitutionally they could not exclude them, or their representatives in Congress, from the policy-making process. Many national leaders themselves did not fully understand the problems they were now called upon to resolve. Hence, the formulation of United States policy on the control of atomic energy took place in an atmosphere of uncertainty, confusion, and ignorance.

The Truman Administration began considering the diplomatic implications of atomic energy shortly after Japan surrendered. Two alternatives confronted Washington officials: the United States could retain its monopoly over the bomb as long as possible, or it could turn over its weapons to an international authority on the condition that future nuclear powers do the same. Since most experts agreed that the American monopoly would be temporary, [5] the first approach threatened to precipitate a dangerous armaments race with the Soviet Union. International control, while it might prevent such a contest, involved risking American security by giving the nation's most powerful weapon to an unproven world body whose successful operation would depend in large measure upon the attitude of Moscow. Congressional fears to the contrary notwithstanding, the Truman Administration never seriously con-

[5] Scientists who had constructed the bomb pointed out that the weapon had evolved from the application of widely known scientific laws, and that given time any major industrial nation, including the Soviet Union, could emulate the American achievement. Alice Kimball Smith, *A Peril and a Hope: The Scientists' Movement in America, 1945–47,* provides a detailed discussion of the views of the atomic scientists. See also James B. Conant, *My Several Lives: Memoirs of a Social Inventor,* pp. 490–91.

templated giving the "secret" of the bomb directly to the Russians. But by the end of 1945, it had chosen to work for international control, and to seek the cooperation of the Soviet Union in that effort.

No man did more to set the stage for discussions within the government on this subject than Henry L. Stimson, who, as secretary of war, had supervised the Manhattan Project from the beginning. Despite his advanced age and varied duties, Stimson avoided a narrowly military approach to the bomb and, during 1945, brooded deeply over how the new weapon would affect American foreign policy. He told Truman that "development of this weapon has placed a certain moral responsibility upon us which we cannot shirk." [6]

In general, the Secretary of War accepted the scientists' view that atomic energy should be placed under international control. What concerned him was the possibility that the totalitarian nature of the Soviet regime might make it impossible for any outside agency to keep Russian nuclear development under surveillance. Internal pressures would eventually force a liberalization of Stalin's dictatorship, Stimson believed, and for a time he toyed with the idea of denying the Russians information about the bomb until these changes had taken place.[7] But by September, 1945, he had decided that the United States should make at least one direct and immediate effort to work out an international control agreement with Moscow.

The Secretary of War had concluded, upon reflection, that "any demand by us for an internal change in Russia as a condition of sharing in the atomic weapon would be so resented that it would make the objective we have in view less probable." If the United States did not approach the Russians with a plan for cooperation, "a secret armament race of a rather desperate character" might break out. Stimson granted that such an initiative might permit Soviet scientists to speed up their own bomb construction program, but "if we fail to approach them now

[6] Stimson to Truman, April 25, 1945, quoted in Stimson and Bundy, On Active Service, p. 636.

[7] As early as August, 1944, Stimson had referred cryptically to the necessity of bringing Russia "into the fold of Christian civilization" and to "possible use of S1 [the atomic bomb] to accomplish this." (Stimson notes for a conversation with Roosevelt, dated August 23, 1944, Stimson MSS, Box 413.) See also Stimson to Truman, "Reflections on the Basic Problems Which Confront Us," July 19, 1945, FR: Potsdam, II, 1155–57.

and merely continue to negotiate with them, having this weapon rather ostentatiously on our hip, their suspicions and their distrust of our purposes and motives will increase." The Secretary of War recommended that the United States, after consultation with its collaborators in the bomb project, Great Britain and Canada, make a direct proposal to the Soviet Union for a mutual halt in further bomb construction. Existing weapons would be impounded, and an international agreement would be obtained forbidding the use of atomic energy for military purposes.[8]

Stimson's recommendations received a mixed reception inside the military establishment. Robert P. Patterson, Stimson's successor as secretary of war, agreed that a direct approach to the Russians should be made. Patterson felt that the United States could not count on retaining its atomic monopoly for more than four years. All efforts should therefore be directed toward preventing a nuclear armaments race, "even though we now have and probably would continue for some time to have the military advantage of a start in such a contest." An expression of caution, however, came from Patterson's counterpart in the Navy Department, James V. Forrestal. Knowledge of the bomb construction process was the property of the American people, Forrestal warned, and

until we are very sure that it is the sense of the people to make disposition of this knowledge even to our Allies it seems to me that it is a step that should be considered most carefully and taken only after complete study and reflection so that the charge may never be levelled that it was done on impulse.

Forrestal worried about whether the United States could trust the Russians, who were, he felt, "Oriental" in their thinking. Washington should not rely on the honesty of the Kremlin leaders "until we have a longer record of experience with them on the validity of engagements, not from an expedient but from a moral point of view." The Secretary of the Navy favored having the United Nations appoint the United States as "the trustee of all information regarding the atomic bomb." In return Washington would agree to use the weapon only according to directions from the world organization.[9]

[8] Stimson to Truman, September 11, 1945, *FR: 1945,* II, 40–44.

[9] Stimson Diary, September 17, 1945, Stimson MSS; Patterson to Truman, September 26, 1945, *FR: 1945,* II, 54–55; Forrestal memorandum, September 21, 1945, Forrestal MSS, Box 100; Forrestal to Truman, October 1, 1945, *ibid.,* Box 2. See also Millis, ed., *The Forrestal Diaries,* pp. 94–96; and Truman, *Year of Decisions,* p. 526.

Like Forrestal, the Joint Chiefs of Staff expressed reservations. They admitted that the basic principles by which the bomb had been built were widely known, but noted that certain technical and manufacturing processes were still secret. Release of this information could only accelerate the armaments race. Until the major powers had agreed to settle their differences, the United States should insist on retaining the secret of these processes. Admiral William D. Leahy, who as Chief of Staff to the President served as the principal liaison officer between the Pentagon and the White House, also advised against giving up any secrets regarding bomb manufacture, and called for a program to keep the United States ahead of other nations which were trying to develop nuclear weapons. Those who thought international control could prevent use of the bomb were, in Leahy's view, simply uninformed.[10]

Stimson's proposals also evoked a mixed reaction from the men who had developed the bomb. Reflecting the attitude of the atomic scientists, Vannevar Bush, director of the Office of Scientific Research and Development, pointed out that Stimson had not suggested giving up the secret of the bomb: "that secret resides principally in the details of construction of the bombs themselves, and in the manufacturing processes." All that Stimson had recommended was to make known basic scientific knowledge which could not be kept confidential. Russia might well benefit more from this exchange of information than would the United States, but at least Washington would know, based on whether or not Moscow reciprocated, whether it could trust the Soviet Union.[11]

But Major General Leslie R. Groves, who had directed the Manhattan Project for the War Department, strongly criticized the idea of exchanging information with the Soviet Union. Groves viewed with skepticism the atomic scientists' statements that the Russians could build a bomb in four or five years, noting irritably that "the more they talk the shorter the time seems to get." He felt that the United States should retain control of nuclear weapons "until all of the other nations of the world are as anxious for peace as we are. And by 'anxious for peace,' I mean in the heart and not by speech or signature in a treaty which they do not in-

[10] Joint Chiefs of Staff memorandum to Truman, date not given, quoted in Truman, *Year of Decisions*, pp. 527–28; Leahy Diary, October 17, 1945, Leahy MSS.

[11] Bush to Truman, September 25, 1945, quoted in Truman, *Year of Decisions*, p. 527, and summarized in Hewlett and Anderson, *The New World*, p. 421.

tend to honor." Basically, Groves believed, the question was "whether we want to work to the bone to support other nations in luxury while they have long week-ends." [12]

Secretary of State James F. Byrnes also resisted any immediate move toward international control because he hoped the American monopoly over the bomb might make the Russians easier to deal with. As early as April, 1945, Byrnes had predicted to Truman that with exclusive possession of atomic weapons the United States would be able to dictate its own terms at the end of the war. In August, he had told J. Robert Oppenheimer, head of the Los Alamos scientific laboratories, that an international agreement to control nuclear energy was not practical in the near future. Instead Oppenheimer and his "gang" should proceed at full speed to develop a hydrogen weapon. Byrnes thought that too much emphasis had been placed on the views of the scientists in discussing international control. Although he admired their achievement in developing the bomb, he felt that they were no better informed than he on the question of whether to share knowledge of it with other countries. Inspection was the key: if the United States did not feel it could trust other nations to open their facilities to inspection, then it should not relinquish information on methods for manufacturing the bomb. The Secretary of State believed that the American monopoly would last, not from four to five years, as the scientists estimated, but from seven to ten years, and opposed doing anything to shorten its duration.[13]

Undersecretary of State Dean Acheson differed strongly with his chief on this issue. In a memorandum to Truman written while Byrnes was attending the London Foreign Ministers' Conference in September, 1945, Acheson emphasized the scientists' conclusion that "what we know [about] the bomb is not a secret which we can keep to ourselves."

[12] *New York Times*, September 22 and November 8, 1945. In his memoirs, Groves claimed that he "wholeheartedly concurred" with Stimson's proposal of September 11, 1945. (*Now It Can Be Told*, p. 408.) Groves's statements at the time do not support this assertion, however.

[13] Truman, *Year of Decisions*, p. 87; Oppenheimer to Stimson, August 17, 1945, quoted in Hewlett and Anderson, *The New World*, p. 417; Stettinius calendar notes, September 28, 1945, Stettinius MSS, Box 247; minutes of the meeting of the Secretaries of State, War, and Navy, October 16, 1945, *FR: 1945*, II, 59–61; Forrestal Diary, October 16, 1945, Millis, ed., *The Forrestal Diaries*, p. 102; Byrnes, *Speaking Frankly*, pp. 261–65.

There could be little doubt that the Russians were working on nuclear weapons:

The joint development of this discovery with the U.K. and Canada must appear to the Soviet Union to be unanswerable evidence of an Anglo-American combination against them. . . . It is impossible that a government as powerful and power conscious as the Soviet Government could fail to react vigorously to this situation. It must and will exert every energy to restore the loss of power which this situation has produced.

Acheson regarded a nuclear armaments race with Russia as futile because there could be no defense against the bomb, and use of it might destroy civilization. Under these circumstances, "the advantage of being ahead in such a race is nothing compared with not having the race." If the United States tried to proclaim itself sole trustee of the weapon, the Russians would regard this as nothing less than outright exclusion. The United States, Acheson concluded, would have to seek Soviet cooperation in some form of international control.

Acheson recognized that his suggestion might create political difficulties: "The public and Congress will be unprepared to accept a policy involving substantial disclosures to the Soviet Union." The Truman Administration could not wait, however, for public opinion to come around. Open debate of this issue would only exacerbate relations with Russia, making agreement more difficult to obtain, and in turn further inflaming domestic opposition. The United States would have to find a way to assure the Russians that they were not being kept from the secret of atomic energy, while at the same time educating the American people to the fact that this secret would not keep.[14]

Evidence of how fragile the United States nuclear monopoly was became painfully clear on September 30, 1945, when Canadian Prime Minister William L. Mackenzie King informed the President that Ottawa officials had uncovered an elaborate Russian espionage network, operating in both Canada and the United States, which had already transmitted an undetermined amount of information about the atomic bomb to the Soviet Union. Truman showed little surprise at this news, and advised against doing anything "which might result in premature action in any direction." Several weeks later the President explained to

[14] Acheson to Truman, September 25, 1945, *FR: 1945*, II, 48–50. See also Acheson, *Present at the Creation*, pp. 123–25.

Stettinius that, although the Russians were clearly working on a bomb, he was not as concerned as Mackenzie King. There was no "precious secret" which the United States could withhold from other countries. The American monopoly would last for from four to ten years. Washington would have to use that time to work out an international agreement to control atomic energy in the interests of world peace. Eventually American bombs would be turned over to the United Nations Security Council; nuclear weapons would be outlawed, just as the use of poison gas had been. The international control of atomic bombs was "the Number One problem of the world at the present moment," but Truman was confident that "we would in time come to some intelligent solution." [15]

The President's October 3 message to Congress on both the domestic and the international aspects of atomic energy represented a compromise between the conflicting points of view his advisers had expressed. "The essential theoretical knowledge upon which the discovery is based is widely known," he pointed out. Other nations would in time produce atomic bombs. Under these circumstances, the only alternative to "a desperate armaments race which might well end in disaster" was an agreement between all potential atomic powers to renounce the use of the bomb for military purposes. Accordingly, Truman announced that he would soon begin negotiations with Britain and Canada, and later with other nations, in an effort to work out such an arrangement. He did not, however, accept Stimson's proposal for an immediate approach to the Soviet Union.

The President's statement committed him to the principle of international control, but without going into detail about how such a control system might work. Anticipating congressional criticism, Truman pointedly emphasized that the forthcoming discussions would in no way reveal the manufacturing processes which had produced the bomb. He also promised to consult Congress fully as developments warranted, and to submit to it any agreements requiring congressional approval. "I should think he would be God damned glad to consult with Congress before negotiating agreements," Senator Vandenberg later growled to a reporter.

[15] J. W. Pickersgill and D. F. Forster, *The Mackenzie King Record, 1945–1946,* pp. 40–41; Stettinius calendar notes, October 22, 1945, Stettinius MSS, Box 247. For the Canadian spy case, see Pickersgill and Forster, *The Mackenzie King Record, 1945–1946,* chapters 2–4; and the *Report of the Royal Commission to Investigate Disclosures of Secret and Confidential Information to Unauthorized Persons, passim.*

"I wouldn't think any one human being would take the responsibility for settling this issue." [16]

II

Vandenberg's remark reflected a growing determination on the part of Congress, and particularly the Senate, to reassert its traditional authority over the formulation of foreign policy. For reasons of national security, legislators during the war had allowed the Chief Executive almost a free hand in dealing with other countries. Congressmen played a significant role only in drawing up plans for the United Nations, and then only at the invitation of the Roosevelt Administration.[17] But the wartime relationship between the White House and Capitol Hill was clearly an abnormal one, which legislators, at least, did not expect to continue after victory. Japan's surrender in August, 1945, signaled the gradual reemergence of Congress as a major influence on the making of foreign policy, and brought about a corresponding diminution in the freedom of action available to the Truman Administration.

The creation of a Special Senate Committee on Atomic Energy in October, 1945, made it clear that this was one field in which Congress would expect to influence policy. Most legislators reacted initially to news of the atomic bomb by asserting that the United States should not share the "secret" of its new weapon. Tom Connally, chairman of the Senate Foreign Relations Committee, suggested that the United Nations might be given a fleet of "atomic bombers" for use in keeping the peace, but opposed letting the world organization build bombs of its own. Richard Russell, another influential Senate Democrat, agreed: "I think we ought to keep the technical know-how to ourselves as long as possible." Vandenberg, now ranking Republican on the Foreign Relations Committee, called for retaining the American atomic monopoly until there was "absolute free and untrammeled right of intimate inspection

[16] Message to Congress of October 3, 1945, *Truman Public Papers, 1945,* pp. 362–66; Frank McNaughton to *Time* home office, October 6, 1945, McNaughton MSS. See also Truman to Tom Connally, September 24, 1945, quoted in Hillman, *Mr. President,* p. 49.

[17] Roland Young, *Congressional Politics in the Second World War,* pp. 146–48, 163–64; Westerfield, *Foreign Policy and Party Politics,* pp. 184–90, 203–12.

all around the globe." The Michigan Republican warned his colleagues: "There can be no dark corners in an atomic age."[18]

Some congressmen felt that the amount of money which the United States had spent on the bomb entitled it to at least a temporary monopoly. Representative Chester E. Merrow, Republican of New Hampshire, pointed out that the bomb had cost two and a half billion dollars: "Why anyone should desire to make available the knowledge we have acquired by our genius and our industry is beyond my comprehension." Senator Tom Stewart, a Tennessee Democrat, also stressed the high cost of the project: "We had to dig out the secret the hard way. . . . I want others to get the secret the hard way, as we found it."[19]

Fears of how other nations might use the bomb caused many legislators to oppose sharing knowledge of it. Senator Arthur Capper of Kansas wanted to know with certainty what Russia would do with atomic weapons before the United States released "this valuable military secret." Calling attention to Soviet intransigence, Representative Harold Knutson of Minnesota argued that until Moscow's intentions became clearer, "we had better keep the atomic-bomb secrets locked up in a burglar-proof vault." It would be "unthinkable," Senator Vandenberg proclaimed, to let Russia take the secret of atomic energy "behind its blackout curtain to do with it whatever Moscow pleases." American intentions with regard to the bomb aroused no such anxieties. Senator Connally observed that the bomb would be safe in the hands of the United States because "we shall never use it, except in the interest of world peace or our own necessary self-defense." Senator Raymond Willis of Indiana echoed Connally's views: "We know that we shall use atomic energy as an instrument of peace. We do not know what is in the minds of leaders of other nations."[20]

[18] Hewlett and Anderson, *The New World*, pp. 424, 435–36; *New York Times*, September 9 and 21, 1945; Vandenberg press statements of August 25, 1945, quoted in Vandenberg, ed., *Private Papers*, p. 221. Connally also favored leaving domestic control of atomic energy in the hands of the military: "I feared that by diverting control to civilians, information might leak out so other nations would learn things they shouldn't." (Tom Connally and Alfred Steinberg, *My Name Is Tom Connally*, p. 306.)

[19] *Congressional Record*, October 9, 18, 1945, pp. 9502, 9787–88.

[20] North American Newspaper Alliance telegraph poll, cited in the *New York Times*, September 29, 1945; Vandenberg to Edward A. Thompson, October 26, 1945, Vandenberg, ed., *Private Papers*, p. 223; *New York Times*, September 9, 1945; *Congressional Record*, October 4, 1945, p. 9407.

Some members of Congress eventually realized that the United States could not hope to retain a permanent monopoly over the bomb. Jerry Voorhis of California, who maintained contacts with the atomic scientists, told the House of Representatives that "if I believed for one moment that it were possible for the United States to keep the secret . . . that is what I would be for doing." But "those who really know" maintained unanimously that there was no secret to keep. Senator Vandenberg also gradually came around to this point of view: "All of our scientists, without exception, testify that any other nation can . . . in the course of the next few years . . . produce atomic bombs of their own whether we like or not." For this reason Vandenberg supported international control, after foolproof inspection systems had been devised. Other senators argued, however, that the head start which the United States enjoyed in bomb development would give it a permanent advantage over other nations. Senator Johnson of Colorado told the Senate: "We have the jump on the rest of the world in [the bomb's] development and use. That is the important thing. We should not fritter away that significant and tremendous advantage by surrendering its know-how and its formulas to anyone." "By the time they have discovered the secret," Senator Stewart of Tennessee asserted, "we shall . . . be too far ahead of them and they will be afraid to use the secret they have discovered." [21]

Congressional fears that the Truman Administration might share atomic bomb information with Russia reached a high point on September 22, 1945, when newspapers carried accounts of the previous day's cabinet meeting at which Secretary of Commerce Henry A. Wallace was reported to have advocated such a course of action. Despite subsequent denials from both Wallace and Truman, concern on Capitol Hill mounted. *Time* correspondent Frank McNaughton reported to his editors that "if the Truman Administration should give away the secret of the atomic bomb there would be hell to pay in Congress. Nothing the Administration might do could cause more trouble or so severely shake confidence as this one act." A quickly arranged telegraph poll of congressmen taken the following week supported McNaughton's conclusions: fifty-five out of sixty-one responding senators and representa-

[21] *Congressional Record,* September 12, October 18, November 28, 1945, pp. 8568–69, 9787–88, 11085–87; Vandenberg to L. F. Beckwith, November 13, 1945, Vandenberg, ed., *Private Papers,* p. 224.

tives unequivocally opposed sharing knowledge of the bomb with any country.[22]

Legislators on Capitol Hill reflected in general the attitudes of their constituents on the international control of atomic energy. Opinion polls showed that to a surprising extent Americans realized that their monopoly over the bomb would not last. A survey made in September, 1945, revealed that 82 percent of a national sample expected other nations to develop bombs of their own sooner or later. The same poll indicated, however, that 85 percent of those questioned wanted the United States to retain exclusive possession of the weapon as long as possible. International control evoked little support: a poll taken in August, 1945, and repeated two months later, showed that more than 70 percent of the public opposed turning nuclear weapons over to the United Nations.[23] Clearly the Truman Administration would have to overcome considerable skepticism on the part of Congress and the public if it was to implement its program of international control.

Congressional wariness on the subject of atomic energy grew largely out of a distrust of Russia that had increased substantially since the spring of 1945. Soviet behavior in Eastern Europe had alienated many Americans, as had the uncompromising position of Russian negotiators at San Francisco and Potsdam.[24] Simultaneously, evidence had begun to accumulate that the Kremlin might be embarking on a new crusade to organize world revolution. In April, Jacques Duclos, a leading French communist, had publicly attacked American party members for collaborating with nonrevolutionary elements during the war. The *Daily Worker,* the newspaper of the "nonpartisan" Communist Political Association, reprinted Duclos's criticisms, together with a contrite acknowledgment by Earl Browder of their validity. Shortly thereafter the association dissolved itself, becoming once more the Communist Party of the United States. Early in June, six people, including several State Department officials, were arrested for having leaked sensitive documents to the

[22] *New York Times,* September 22 and 24, 1945; McNaughton to *Time* home office, September 22, 1945, McNaughton MSS; North American Newspaper Alliance poll, cited in the *New York Times,* September 29, 1945.

[23] National Opinion Research Center poll of September, 1945, American Institute of Public Opinion polls of August 22 and October 3, 1945, cited in Cantril and Strunk, eds., *Public Opinion,* pp. 21–22. See also Department of State, "Fortnightly Survey of American Opinion," Nos. 34 and 36, September 6 and October 5, 1945.

[24] On this point, see chapter 7.

editors of the journal *Amerasia*. Only two of the six were prosecuted, and these received light fines, but the fact that the editor of *Amerasia* had been seen with Browder and the Soviet consul in New York led many observers to suspect espionage.[25]

The House Committee on Un-American Activities had seemed almost moribund after the decision of its chairman, Martin Dies of Texas, not to seek reelection in 1944. But when the Seventy-ninth Congress met early in January, 1945, John E. Rankin of Mississippi executed a smooth parliamentary maneuver which transformed the body into a permanent standing committee of the House, with broad investigative powers. The apparent shift in tactics by the international communist movement in the spring of 1945 gave the revived committee a tempting target, and in September it began its first postwar investigation of American communism. The committee wanted to find out, according to Representative Gerald W. Landis, "whether the Communists are still planning to destroy or overthrow the American system of government." Rankin, with a shrewd eye for publicity, added that the hearings would cover the Hollywood film industry: "Alien elements are at work out there to overthrow our Government by means of subtle propaganda in our movies." The inept broadsides of Rankin and his colleagues shed little light on the real relationship between the Kremlin and American communists, but they did publicize the possibility of internal subversion at a time when Soviet-American relations were rapidly deteriorating.[26]

[25] Walter Goodman, *The Committee: The Extraordinary Career of the House Committee on Un-American Activities*, pp. 175–76; Earl Latham, *The Communist Controversy in Washington*, pp. 203–16; U.S. Senate, Committee on the Judiciary, Subcommittee to Investigate the Administration of the Internal Security Act and Other Internal Security Laws, *The "Amerasia" Papers: A Clue to the Catastrophe of China, passim*. For the effect of the Duclos article on the American Communist Party, see Irving Howe and Louis Coser, *The American Communist Party: A Critical History (1919–1957)*, pp. 437–49; David Shannon, *The Decline of American Communism*, chapter 1; and Irving Ross, "It's Tough to Be a Communist," *Harper's*, CXCII (June, 1946), 533–36. Historians have differed sharply on the intent behind the Duclos article. See, for example, Schlesinger, "Origins of the Cold War," pp. 43–44, which argues that the article did signify a reversion to revolutionary tactics, and Kolko, *Politics of War*, pp. 441–42, which asserts that it did not. Whatever the purpose of the article, however, it is clear that observers in Washington interpreted it as an ominous shift in the party line.

[26] Goodman, *The Committee*, pp. 167–70, 176; *New York Times*, September 24, 1945.

Shortly after V-E Day, several other congressional committees began clamoring for the opportunity to investigate Russian-American relations by visiting the Soviet Union. Ambassador Harriman secured assurances from Molotov that such groups would be welcome, and at least three separate delegations of legislators made the trip during the late summer congressional recess. One of these groups, composed of seven members of the House Select Committee on Postwar Economic Policy and Planning, toured Russia and thirteen other European countries in an effort to decide what American policy should be regarding postwar loans to foreign governments. On September 14, 1945, this delegation, led by Committee Chairman William M. Colmer of Mississippi, enjoyed the distinction of a personal interview with Joseph Stalin.[27]

Colmer told the Soviet leader that his committee knew about the Russian desire for a loan from the United States. How, he wanted to know, would the Soviets use the money, how would they pay it back, and what could Washington expect in return? Stalin acknowledged that the Soviet Union had applied for a $6 billion loan some six months earlier, but had heard nothing from the United States since. The loan, he said, would be used to purchase American industrial equipment which the Soviets wanted for reconstruction, and would be repaid by exports of gold and various raw materials. Stalin expressed irritation about American inquisitiveness regarding repayment: Washington was talking freely about lending money to Chiang Kai-shek—surely the Soviet Union had greater capabilities of paying back a loan than did the Chinese. Colmer thought Stalin's answers "responsive although at times . . . evasive." The Soviet Union's police-state atmosphere shocked the Mississippi congressman and his colleagues, however, as did the strong fear of Russia which they encountered in surrounding countries. The delegation stopped off in London on its way home to report to Secretary of State

[27] Harriman to Stettinius, June 15, 1945, *FR: 1945*, V, 861–62. Also visiting Russia in September, 1945, were four members of the House Foreign Affairs Committee, investigating the need for aid under the United Nations Relief and Rehabilitation Administration, and Democratic Senator Claude Pepper of Florida, who went to Russia as a private citizen. The House Foreign Affairs Committee delegation report, not issued until May 31, 1946, is printed in *U.S. News,* XX (June 28, 1946), 63–70. On Pepper's visit, see his account, written for the North American Newspaper Alliance and printed in the *New York Times,* October 1, 1945; Kennan to Acheson, September 15, 1945, *FR: 1945,* V, 881–84; and *Time,* XLVI (October 1, 1945), 27.

Byrnes, and later conferred personally with President Truman. Before both men Colmer's group stressed the necessity "of stiffening our collective backbone in dealing with the Soviet Republic." [28]

The Colmer committee was willing to approve an American loan to the Soviet Union, but only if the Russians met certain conditions. They would have to disclose what proportion of total production they devoted to armaments. They would be required to reveal vital statistics on the operation of the Soviet economy, and to provide an opportunity to check the accuracy of these figures. The Soviet Union would have to give up the administration of relief for political purposes in Eastern Europe and disclose the terms of its trade treaties with the countries of this area. Within both the USSR and the East European countries under its control, the Kremlin would have to guarantee full protection of American property, the right to distribute American books, magazines, newspapers, and motion pictures, freedom of religion, freedom of the press, and free elections. Finally, the United States should insist upon "the fulfillment of Russia's political obligations on the same terms as those of other Governments. This includes the withdrawal of Russian occupation forces in accordance with the Potsdam agreements and the Yalta conference and other agreements." In short, Colmer and his colleagues demanded that, in return for an American loan, the Soviet Union reform its internal system of government and abandon the sphere of influence it had so carefully constructed in Eastern Europe. "Unless Russia reconverts her war machine to peace," Colmer asked, "why should we support it? It may mean business, but . . . it may not be good business." [29]

The Truman Administration still had not given up the idea of a loan

[28] Kennan to Acheson, September 15, 1945, *FR: 1945,* V, 881–84. See also a summary of notes taken by an unnamed member of the delegation and published in the *New York Times,* November 8, 1945; and Representative Colmer's own account of the interview, *Congressional Record,* August 2, 1946, pp. A4895–A4898. George F. Kennan, who served as interpreter for the delegation, recalls that one slightly intoxicated congressman went into the meeting with Stalin threatening loudly to "biff the old codger one in the nose." Much to Kennan's relief, however, the congressman "did nothing more disturbing than to leer and wink once or twice at the bewildered dictator." The incident, Kennan says, was one in a long series "that gradually bred in me a deep skepticism about the absolute value of people-to-people contacts for the improvement of international relations." (Kennan, *Memoirs,* pp. 276–77.)

[29] *New York Times,* November 12, 1945; Colmer address to a meeting of the National Industrial Conference Board, New York City, November 20, 1945, printed in the *Congressional Record,* November 26, 1945, pp. A5103–A5105.

to the Soviet Union; it simply sought to withhold economic assistance until the Kremlin made certain concessions in the political sphere. During the summer of 1945 Administration officials had secured from Congress an increase in the lending authority of the Export-Import Bank, so that a loan could be granted without precipitating a full-scale debate on Capitol Hill. This approach did not take the question completely out of the hands of legislators, however, for they could still make trouble for the Administration if they disapproved of the terms of the loan. Colmer's committee made it clear that, to satisfy Congress, the State Department would have to demand such sweeping political concessions as to make Moscow's rejection of the loan a foregone conclusion. Assistant Secretary of State Will Clayton explained to Ambassador Harriman late in November that the department had been "pursuing [a] policy of not encouraging active discussions and at present [the] matter is dormant." [30]

The net effect of the reassertion of congressional authority which took place in the fall of 1945 was to drive the Truman Administration toward a firmer Russian policy. Whether Congress would support the measures necessary to implement such a program, however, was open to doubt. Although the United States now had an atomic bomb, its conventional armed forces, after V-J Day, had begun to disappear. More than twelve million men and women had been on active duty in all branches of the services at the end of June, 1945. One year later this figure would drop to barely three million. By June of 1947, the number of military personnel would be down to one and a half million. Secretary of War Patterson and Navy Secretary Forrestal warned the cabinet as early as October 26, 1945, that the rapid pace of demobilization was threatening the American strategic position throughout the world. President Truman agreed: "So far as I was concerned, the program we were following was no longer demobilization—it was disintegration of our armed forces." [31]

[30] Clayton to Harriman, November 30, 1945, *FR: 1945,* V, 1048. See also Herring, "Aid to Russia, 1941–1946," chapter 9.

[31] U.S. Bureau of Census, *Historical Statistics of the United States, Colonial Times to 1957,* p. 736; Truman, *Year of Decisions,* p. 509. Adam B. Ulam suggests that American fears regarding the strategic impact of demobilization may have been exaggerated. Apparently the Soviet Union also demobilized rapidly after World War II. (*Expansion and Coexistence,* p. 414).

But Truman could do little to resist demands to "bring the boys home." Congressmen found their mailboxes filled with letters from wives calling for the quick return of their husbands, often accompanied by baby pictures and even baby shoes. At one point a group of furious war wives literally besieged General Eisenhower in a congressman's office on Capitol Hill where he had gone to testify on demobilization. Servicemen in the Far East stamped home-bound mail with the legend "No Boats No Votes," an obvious reference to possible retaliation in the 1946 congressional elections if the release of troops did not speed up. In January of 1946, riots broke out at several overseas military installations to protest the slow pace of demobilization. "The President has shown a lot of guts in many matters," former Undersecretary of State Joseph Grew wrote to a friend, "but if you can persuade him to stop demobilization, with all its political implications, you're a bigger man than I am." [32]

Prospects that Congress would approve Administration plans for a postwar military establishment seemed dim. In October, 1945, Truman called for the continuation of selective service and the institution of universal military training, a program which would require a year of training for all physically-fit eighteen-year-old men. Both proposals aroused strong opposition in a nation which had never before known permanent conscription in peacetime. Moreover, with the war over many Americans hoped for relief from the crushing burden of taxation which a large military program would require. By December, 1945, *Newsweek*'s editors saw little chance that Congress would extend the draft past its May 15, 1946, deadline, while "only dramatically menacing world developments" appeared likely to secure passage of universal military training. James Reston noted early in 1946 that those congressmen who shouted loudest for a tough anti-Russian policy were the least willing to vote the money and the manpower necessary to implement such a policy.[33]

In assuming this contradictory stance, legislators were merely reflecting the views of their constituents, most of whom wanted the government to "get tough with Russia" while at the same time bringing back the low taxes and volunteer military forces of the prewar period. Not for

[32] R. Alton Lee, "The Army 'Mutiny' of 1946," *Journal of American History*, LIII (December, 1966), 555–71; *Newsweek*, XXVII (February 4, 1946), 55–57; Grew to Barrett Wendell, November 16, 1945, Grew MSS, Box 123.

[33] Truman, *Year of Decisions*, pp. 510–11; *Newsweek*, XXVII (January 7, 1946), 16; *New York Times*, March 17, 1946.

some time would Americans realize that they could not have both. This attitude on the part of Congress and the public left the Truman Administration in an awkward position: further compromises with the Russians were sure to be politically unpopular, yet strategically the nation was in no condition to resist the Kremlin's next moves. Under these circumstances it is not surprising that, despite their atomic monopoly, American officials felt very little freedom to maneuver as they turned to the problem of postwar relations with the Soviet Union.

III

The first postwar confrontation with Russia came in September, 1945, when the foreign ministers of the United States, the USSR, Great Britain, France, and China met in London to draw up peace treaties for Finland, Hungary, Rumania, and Bulgaria, all former German satellites. American diplomats had not sought to challenge Russian control of these countries as long as the war was on, but after Germany's surrender they expected free elections to be held in accordance with the Yalta Declaration on Liberated Europe. Moscow seemed willing to tolerate democratic procedures in Finland and possibly Hungary, but American observers in Bucharest and Sofia accused Soviet occupying forces of trying to set up puppet governments in Rumania and Bulgaria. Truman expressed concern over these reports, and late in the summer of 1945 began an effort to secure Russian compliance with the agreement made at Yalta.[34]

State Department officials realized that the United States lacked the power to influence directly events in Rumania and Bulgaria, but hoped that by delaying the signature of peace treaties and withholding diplomatic recognition they could force implementation of the Yalta accord. Truman and Byrnes endorsed this strategy, and at Potsdam made it clear to the Russians that the United States would not recognize or make

[34] Joseph C. Grew memorandum of a conversation between Truman and Arthur Bliss Lane, June 4, 1945, quoted in Grew, *Turbulent Era*, II, 1464–65. For reports from American observers in Rumania and Bulgaria, see *ibid.*, pp. 1454–55; and *FR: Potsdam*, I, 357–432. News that the Russians were seizing American-owned industrial equipment in Eastern Europe as reparations intensified the Administration's concern. (*Ibid.*, pp. 420–32.)

peace with the former German satellites in Eastern Europe until their governments had been reorganized and until American press and radio correspondents had been admitted. Byrnes told Molotov that "we would, frankly, always be suspicious of elections in countries where our representatives are not free to move about and where the press cannot report freely." Truman promised Stalin that "when Hungary, Rumania, and Bulgaria were set up on a basis where we could have free access to them, we would recognize them but not sooner." [35]

Information that the atomic bomb would soon be ready contributed to the Administration's decision to press for self-determination in the Balkans. Byrnes explained to Joseph E. Davies at Potsdam that "the New Mexico situation [the first successful test of the bomb] had given us great power, and that in the final analysis, it would control." Late in August, the Secretary of State told John J. McCloy that he intended to go to the London Foreign Ministers' Conference with the implied threat of the bomb in his pocket, and on September 4 Stimson recorded in his diary a similar conversation with Byrnes: "His mind is full of his problem with the coming meeting of the foreign ministers and he looks to having the presence of the bomb in his pocket, so to speak, as a great weapon." The Secretary of State begged Stimson to keep the President from even mentioning the possibility of international control until after the London meeting.[36]

Byrnes's hope that American possession of the bomb would make the Russians more manageable was quickly frustrated, however, for at London Molotov proved to be more stubborn than ever. The Soviet foreign minister reiterated the bid Stalin had made at Potsdam for Russian control of former Italian colonies in Africa. He also accused the Americans of supporting anti-Russian elements in Eastern Europe, and asserted that the regimes in Rumania and Bulgaria were more representative than the British-sponsored government of Greece. When Byrnes argued that

[35] Potsdam briefing book paper, "Recommended Policy on the Question of Establishing Diplomatic Relations and Concluding Peace Treaties with the Former Axis Satellite States," June 29, 1945, *FR: Potsdam,* I, 357–62; Llewellyn E. Thompson minutes, 5th foreign ministers' meeting, July 22, 1945, *ibid.,* II, 231; Thompson minutes, 8th plenary meeting, July 24, 1945, *ibid.,* II, 359.

[36] Davies Journal, July 29, 1945, Davies MSS, Box 19; Stimson Diary, August 12–September 4, 1945, Stimson MSS; minutes of the meeting of the Secretaries of State, War, and Navy, October 10, 1945, *FR: 1945,* II, 55–56.

American correspondents had been allowed into Greece but had been kept out of Rumania and Bulgaria, Molotov neatly parried: "Apparently in Greece the correspondents were happy, but the people were not; whereas in Rumania the people were happy, but the correspondents were not." The USSR, Molotov added, considered the feelings of the people more important than those of the correspondents. The Soviet diplomat made Moscow's position clear: unless the British and Americans accepted Russian terms for peace treaties in Eastern Europe, he would not accept the Anglo-American draft terminating hostilities with Italy.

Byrnes patiently tried to reason with Molotov in a series of private meetings. The long dispute over Poland, he explained, had made the American people sensitive to the need for strict observance of the Yalta agreements. Americans knew that Moscow had imposed a subservient regime on Rumania, and that neither in that country nor in Bulgaria could American newsmen travel freely. The Secretary of State asked Molotov to look at the problem from his point of view: If he did sign treaties with Bucharest and Sofia, they would have to go before the Senate. How, the senators would wonder, did Byrnes know that regimes in those countries had popular support? The Secretary of State would have to reply that, because of the exclusion of American correspondents, he knew little about these governments. The Senate would then probably reject the treaties. Byrnes assured Molotov that the United States did not want unfriendly governments along Russia's border. But neither did it want unrepresentative regimes which would violate the Yalta Declaration on Liberated Europe. Could not coalitions be formed which would be friendly to the Russians and at the same time representative? If this could be done, it would be greeted with joy in the United States and would permit Byrnes to support the Soviet position as he wished to do.[37]

The Soviet foreign minister remained unmoved. In an apparent attempt to improve his bargaining position, he called on September 22 for the exclusion of France and China from further discussion of the satellite peace treaties, arguing that their participation up to this point had violated instructions agreed upon by the Big Three at Potsdam. Two days later, Molotov demanded establishment of an Allied Control Council in Japan, composed of representatives from the United States, the Soviet

[37] Bohlen minutes, Byrnes-Molotov conversations, September 16 and 19, 1945, *FR: 1945*, II, 194–201, 243–47.

Union, Great Britain, and China, to supervise the policies of General Douglas MacArthur and the American occupation forces. Byrnes refused to give in on either of these points, and after a futile appeal to Stalin by Truman, the conference broke up early in October with Big Three unity in serious disarray. The foreign ministers could not even agree on a public communiqué.[38]

The failure of the London Conference left Byrnes surprised and disappointed. Publicly he maintained a conciliatory posture: the experience of London, he told a national radio audience shortly after his return, had shown "the hard reality that none of us can expect to write the peace in our own way." But in private, the Secretary of State bitterly accused Moscow of duplicity: "The Russians were welching on all the agreements reached at Potsdam and at Yalta." Stalin's word was worth little, Byrnes warned his cabinet colleagues:

Though they had a formal treaty of non-aggression with Japan the Russians, as far back as Yalta, were making definite plans for their attack upon Japan. . . . Stalin and Molotov would probably be insulted today if you implied that they had intended to keep their solemn treaty with Hitler. By implication of the same process of reasoning, it would not be wise for us to rely on their word today.

There was no question, the Secretary of State told his predecessor, Stettinius,

but that we were facing a new Russia, totally different than the Russia we dealt with a year ago. As long as they needed us in the War and we were giving them supplies we had a satisfactory relationship but now that the War was over they were taking an aggressive attitude and stand on political and territorial questions that was indefensible.

[38] *FR: 1945*, II, 313–15, 328–29, 331, 334, 336–39, 357–58. The United States had rebuffed an earlier Russian bid for a role in the occupation of Japan, made at the time of that country's surrender in August, 1945. On this episode, see Herbert Feis, *Contest over Japan*, pp. 15–17, 19–20; Deane, *The Strange Alliance*, pp. 278–79; and Truman, *Year of Decisions*, pp. 412, 430–32, 440–44. In his memoirs, Byrnes states that Molotov brought up the question of Japan in a private meeting on September 22, before discussing the matter of French and Chinese participation in negotiating the satellite peace treaties. (*Speaking Frankly*, p. 102.) Feis has concluded from this that the Russians were mainly interested in the Japanese question and brought up the exclusion of France and China only after Byrnes had avoided discussion of it. (*Contest over Japan*, p. 42.) But the official American records of the conference, cited above, contain no indication that Japan was discussed prior to September 24.

What the Russians really wanted, Byrnes thought, were uranium deposits in the Belgian Congo; hence Molotov's interest in the Italian colonies of Libya and Tripolitania. The Soviet foreign minister had been "insufferable," the Secretary of State told Joseph Davies; he was "almost ashamed" for having taken what he did from Molotov. If the Senate ever found out how the Russians had behaved at London, the situation would become "very much worse." [39]

But members of the Senate Foreign Relations Committee strongly applauded Byrnes's refusal to compromise when he appeared before them on October 8. The only question in the minds of the senators seemed to be whether the Secretary had been tough enough with the Russians, and whether he intended to continue this policy in the future. Similarly John Foster Dulles, who had attended the London Conference as a Republican observer, praised Byrnes's decision to "stand firm for basic principles." Professions of wartime unity had been nothing more than "soothing syrup," Dulles argued; it was no longer necessary, nor was it healthy, to hide the fact that fundamental differences now existed between the United States and the Soviet Union.[40]

The London Conference demonstrated clearly that simple possession of an atomic bomb had not made the United States omnipotent in its dealings with Moscow—the Russians seemed almost to go out of their way to show that they had not been impressed. Byrnes had no intention of actually threatening use of the bomb to force concessions from the Russians, but he had hoped to hold back an American commitment to the international control of atomic energy until the Soviet Union agreed to a European peace settlement which Washington could accept.[41] Molotov's studied intransigence at London, however, raised doubts as to

[39] Byrnes radio address of October 5, 1945, *Department of State Bulletin*, XIII (October 7, 1945), 507; Stettinius calendar notes, September 12, 1945, Stettinius MSS, Box 247; minutes of a meeting of the Secretaries of State, War, and Navy, October 16, 1945, *FR: 1945*, II, 59–61; Stettinius calendar notes, September 28, 1945, Stettinius MSS, Box 247; Davies notes of conversation with Byrnes, October 9, 1945, Davies MSS, Box 22. See also Millis, ed., *The Forrestal Diaries*, pp. 102–3.

[40] *New York Times*, October 7, 9, 1945; *Time*, XLVI (October 15, 1945), 21; Curry, *Byrnes*, p. 157. See also James Reston's column in the *New York Times*, October 14, 1945.

[41] Stettinius calendar notes, September 28, 1945, Stettinius MSS, Box 247; minutes of the meeting of the Secretaries of State, War, and Navy, October 10, 1945, *FR: 1945*, II, 55–57.

whether the Russians were interested in signing peace treaties on any terms but their own. Moreover, Truman's October 3, 1945, message to Congress on atomic energy, made without consulting the absent Secretary of State, had undercut Byrnes's bargaining strategy by endorsing international control long before any European peace agreements were in sight.

Truman's decision to commit the United States to the principle of international control worried the Secretary of State. Molotov, he told Patterson and Forrestal, might now insist on taking up the issue of atomic energy before concluding peace treaties with the defeated German satellites. Besides, not enough yet was known about technical aspects of the problem to draw up a workable control scheme. Public ventilation of the subject would only intensify pressure, both at home and abroad, for the United States to relinquish control of the bomb too soon. Accordingly Byrnes planned to "plead with the President not to push the question of consultation." [42]

But the President had already backed away from the full implications of his October 3 message. In a press conference on the 8th, he distinguished between the scientific principles which had been applied to build the bomb and the actual technical processes of construction: "So far as the scientific knowledge is concerned, all the scientists [in the world] know the answer, but how to put it to work practically is our secret. . . . If they catch up with us on that, they will have to do it on their own hook, just as we did." Truman's first major postwar speech on foreign policy, delivered in New York on October 27, 1945, suggested that the world might be better off if the bomb remained in American hands:

In our possession of this weapon, as in our possession of other new weapons, there is no threat to any nation. The world, which has seen the United States in two great recent wars, knows that full well. The possession in our hands of this new power of destruction we regard as a sacred trust. Because of our love of peace, the thoughtful people of the world know that that trust will not be violated, that it will be faithfully executed.

This address led the editors of the *Nation* to comment that Truman had assumed the ambitious task of conducting American foreign policy si-

[42] *Ibid.*, p. 56.

multaneously according to the principles of Theodore Roosevelt and St. Francis of Assisi.[43]

Writing to a close friend early in November, Forrestal explained that the President simply had not yet committed himself firmly on the subject of international control: "Until the Russians indicate that they are willing to play on a basis of reciprocal confidence it is very difficult to establish the basis for negotiations." Forrestal felt that Truman was "passionately desirous" of making peace as soon as possible, but was at the same time reluctant to relinquish an element of American power which might help shape the final settlement.[44]

The President's emphasis on exclusive possession of the bomb, together with his apparent delay in formulating a policy on international control, stimulated considerable criticism from liberal observers. Radio commentator Raymond Gram Swing, who had close ties with the atomic scientists, charged as early as October 12 that Truman was seeking security through "the power to kill rather than . . . the power to reason," and called on public opinion and Congress to force a repudiation of this policy. Mrs. Franklin D. Roosevelt wondered publicly how "we can hold this secret and expect others to trust us when we, apparently, do not trust anyone else." J. Robert Oppenheimer told Byrnes that negotiations with the Russians on international control should not be delayed any further. Byrnes replied gruffly that the Administration, not the scientists, would handle diplomatic questions.[45]

But Truman was also coming under pressure from the British and Canadians, with whom he had promised to discuss international control. On October 16, Prime Minister Clement Attlee reported strong sentiment in Parliament for a statement on atomic energy. Attlee offered to delay until he could consult with Truman, but warned that he could not

[43] *Truman Public Papers: 1945*, pp. 381–82, 437; *Nation*, CLXI (November 3, 1945), 445. Truman does *not* quote this portion of his October 27 speech in *Year of Decisions*, pp. 537–38.

[44] Forrestal to E. Palmer Hoyt, November 1, 1945, Forrestal MSS, Box 63.

[45] Swing radio broadcast of October 12, 1945, Swing MSS, Box 28; *Time*, XLVI (October 22, 1945), 22; Byrnes account of conversation with Oppenheimer, minutes of a meeting of the Secretaries of State, War, and Navy, October 23, 1945, *FR: 1945*, II, 61–62. A State Department survey of editorial opinion noted that the President's press conference statement on October 8 had received "severe criticism and demands for reconsideration . . . from a large number of editors and commentators." ("Fortnightly Survey of American Opinion," No. 37, October 19, 1945).

postpone comment indefinitely. The first full session of the United Nations General Assembly was to take place in London in January, 1946. The success of this meeting might be jeopardized if no policy on international control had been agreed upon. Attlee offered to come to Washington as soon as possible with Canadian Prime Minister Mackenzie King to begin negotiations. In his October 27 address, Truman mentioned once again the possibility of talks with the British and Canadians, and three days later announced that Attlee and Mackenzie King would arrive early in November.[46]

Nevertheless, Truman and Byrnes still dragged their feet in formulating a policy to be put forth in these negotiations. Several times during October Secretary of War Patterson prodded Byrnes without result to begin work on this matter, and on November 1 he expressed his anxieties in a formal letter to the Secretary of State. Patterson also communicated his concern to Vannevar Bush, who asked to see Byrnes on November 3. From this meeting Bush learned to his dismay that "there was no organization for the meeting, no agenda being prepared, and no American plan in form to present." The Secretary of State then surprised Bush by asking him to formulate such a plan. Pulling his wits together, Bush spent the weekend drawing up suggestions for the negotiations and on November 5, five days before Attlee and Mackenzie King were due to arrive, presented his ideas to Byrnes.[47]

The basic American objective, Bush wrote, was to avoid an atomic arms race which could lead to a future war. The major difficulty involved was the suspicious attitude of the Soviet government. The solution was "to make the agreements in such manner that it will be in Russia's interest to keep them." Bush advocated proposing to the Russians a series of steps, to each of which the Soviet Union would be asked to conform. First, the Russians would be invited to join with the British and

[46] Attlee to Truman, October 16, 1945, *FR: 1945*, II, 58–59; *Truman Public Papers: 1945*, pp. 437, 453. For a summary of the British attitude toward international control, see Hewlett and Anderson, *The New World*, pp. 456–58.

[47] Minutes of the meeting of the Secretaries of State, War, and Navy, October 16 and 23, 1945, *FR: 1945*, II, 59–62; Patterson to Byrnes, November 1, 1945, cited in Hewlett and Anderson, *The New World*, p. 459; memorandum by Captain R. Gordon Arneson on "Negotiations with the British and Canadians, November 1–November 16, 1945," April 17, 1946, *FR: 1945*, II, 63–69; Bush to Stimson, November 13, 1945, Stimson MSS, Box 427. See also Vannevar Bush, *Pieces of the Action*, pp. 296–97.

the Americans to create, under the auspices of the United Nations General Assembly, an organization to disseminate scientific information in all fields, including atomic fission. This would cost the United States nothing because most of this scientific information would be available to the Russians anyway. It would, however, serve as a test of Moscow's intentions. The second step would involve formation of a United Nations Commission of Inspection which would have the right to inspect any scientific laboratory in any country engaging in atomic research. The commission would assume its functions gradually, so that the United States would not immediately have to expose the operations of its atomic plants. After the inspection system had been perfected, all nations would agree as a third step to stockpile materials capable of atomic fission, releasing them for peaceful purposes only. The Commission of Inspection would report any diversion of fissionable material to the production of weapons. Until the full plan went into effect, the United States would continue to produce material necessary to make bombs, but would promise the world not to assemble actual weapons. After the inspection system had begun to operate, other nations would be invited to inspect this American stockpile of fissionable material.[48]

President Truman endorsed these proposals on November 7 apparently because, as Bush noted, they constituted the only plan the Administration had. In the process of drafting the formal document, however, the State Department added one additional step providing for safeguards to protect states which complied with the agreement. As finally approved by Truman, Attlee, and Mackenzie King on November 15, 1945, the agreement called for establishment of a United Nations commission which would work

(a) for extending between all nations the exchange of basic scientific information for peaceful ends;

(b) for control of atomic energy to the extent necessary to ensure its use only for peaceful purposes;

(c) for the elimination from national armaments of atomic weapons and of all other major weapons adaptable to mass destruction;

(d) for effective safeguards by way of inspection and other means to

[48] Bush to Byrnes, November 5, 1945, *FR: 1945,* II, 69–73; Bush and Groves to Byrnes, November 9, 1945, *ibid.,* p. 74.

protect complying states against the hazards of violations and evasions.

The accord specified that "the work of the Commission should proceed by separate stages, the successful completion of one of which will develop the necessary confidence of the world before the next stage is undertaken." [49]

The Truman-Attlee-King agreement was a cautious plan which did not, as Bush repeatedly pointed out, provide for any premature relinquishment of the American atomic monopoly. The international control system would go into effect gradually, one step at a time, a feature of the plan which would cause confusion later on because the State Department had made the institution of safeguards the last step in the process. If at any time the Russians failed to complete a step to American satisfaction, the United States could drop out. All in all Bush approved of the plan, although the slipshod method in which policy had been formulated appalled him: "I have never participated in anything that was so completely unorganized or so irregular," he wrote to Stimson. "I have had experiences in the past week that would make a chapter in 'Alice in Wonderland.' " [50]

The improvised nature of the Truman-Attlee-King accord made it impossible for the Administration to consult congressional leaders until only a few minutes before the agreement was publicly announced. Senator Robert La Follette had warned Admiral Leahy two days earlier that the members of the Senate Foreign Relations Committee resented their exclusion from the policy-making process. Now the two leading members of that committee, Connally and Vandenberg, reacted with considerable irritation, even to the extreme point of refusing to pose for pictures with Truman, Attlee, and Mackenzie King. Connally told Byrnes that he and Truman had no authority to promise to share information on atomic energy without consulting Congress. Vandenberg returned to the Senate and made a long-planned speech on the "iron curtain" in which he emphasized pointedly that it was in the Congress "where a basic and unavoidable share of the responsibility for these fateful decisions inevitably resides and where it is going to stay." [51]

[49] Bush to Stimson, November 13, 1945, Stimson MSS, Box 427; Hewlett and Anderson, *The New World*, pp. 461–65; *Truman Public Papers: 1945*, pp. 472–75.

[50] Bush to Stimson, November 13, 1945, Stimson MSS, Box 427.

[51] Leahy Diary, November 13, 1945, Leahy MSS; Vandenberg, ed., *Private Papers*,

The manner in which the Truman Administration handled the issue of international control illustrated the confused state of policy-making in Washington in the fall of 1945. In the belief that American possession of the bomb would make the Russians easier to deal with, Byrnes had opposed even discussing the subject until after a general European peace settlement. But Truman, under pressure from the atomic scientists and advisers like Stimson and Acheson, publicly endorsed international control without consulting the Secretary of State. Byrnes did manage to delay formulation of a specific control proposal for a time, but could not do so indefinitely because of the President's earlier public statement. Meanwhile no one had consulted Congress, whose leaders, suspicious from the beginnning of international control, had come to believe that the Administration was about to give the bomb away. Actually the views of the President, the Secretary of State, and congressional leaders were not far apart. All would likely have agreed with Truman when he told Joseph Davies in September, 1945:

When we get down to cases, is any one of the Big Powers—are we, going to give up these locks and bolts which are necessary to protect our house . . . against possible outlaw attack . . . , until experience and good judgment say that the community is sufficiently stable and decent, and the police force sufficiently reliable to do that job for us [?] Clearly we are not. Nor are the Soviets. Nor is any country if it can help itself.[52]

But confusion over tactics obscured agreement regarding goals, so that by the end of 1945 a serious conflict had developed between the State Department and Congress over the international control of atomic energy.

IV

Shortly after the conclusion of the London Conference, James Reston observed that two schools of thought on how to handle Russia now existed within the government, based on contradictory perceptions of Moscow's intentions. One group of policy-makers had virtually written off the pos-

---

pp. 226–27; *Newsweek,* XXVI (November 26, 1945), 34; *Congressional Record,* November 15, 1945, pp. 10696–99.

[52] Davies notes of conversation with Truman, September 18, 1945, Davies MSS, Box 22.

sibility of settling outstanding issues, arguing that the Kremlin was firmly committed to a program of unlimited expansion. Further concessions would only whet Stalin's appetite; the United States and its Western European allies should begin pooling their military and economic resources if the Russian dictator's ambitions were to be thwarted and the world balance of power restored. These officials applauded Byrnes's hard line at London as a step in the right direction. But a second group within the government held that the Soviet Union still shared with the United States a common interest in establishing a world security system which would prevent future wars. They admitted that serious disagreements had arisen, but felt that these could be overcome if both sides showed a willingness to negotiate and compromise. This more optimistic group did not condone Soviet behavior in Eastern Europe, but questioned whether the Kremlin could realistically be expected to relax its control over that part of the world while the United States continued to oppose Russian participation in the occupation of Japan and in the administration of former Italian colonies in Africa.[53]

Much of the confusion which surrounded the formulation of American policy in the fall of 1945 stemmed from the fact that the Truman Administration had not yet committed itself to either point of view. Congressional leaders and most military officials had, by this time, begun to advocate a firmer approach to Moscow. Members of the Senate Foreign Relations Committee had given Byrnes a warm reception on his return from London, and Navy Secretary Forrestal was advising the President to speak out publicly against the Russians in order to counteract growing pressure for demobilization. Truman himself seemed to be moving toward a tough line. In his Navy Day address on October 27 the President announced that while in some cases it might not be possible to prevent forcible imposition of an unrepresentative regime on an unwilling people, the United States would never recognize any such government.[54]

But Truman had not, at this time, given up hope of reaching an accommodation with the Russians. In a long private conversation with

[53] *New York Times,* September 30, October 14, 1945.
[54] *New York Times,* October 9, 1945; *Newsweek,* XXVI (October 22, 1945), 30; Forrestal Diary, October 16, 1945, Millis, ed., *The Forrestal Diaries,* pp. 101–2; Truman speech of October 27, 1945, *Truman Public Papers: 1945,* pp. 431–38.

Stettinius five days earlier, the President had observed that cooperation with Moscow during the war had been based solely on military necessity. Now, with victory achieved, "it was inevitable that we should have real difficulties but we should not take them too seriously." The breakdown of the London Conference had not upset Truman: "This was almost bound to happen at the end of the war. . . . It was perhaps better to [have it] happen out in the open at this stage." Serious differences existed between Russia and the United States, but the President hoped "that we could work them out amicably if we gave ourselves time." The United Nations could play an important role in this process, and so could personal diplomacy. Stalin, Truman commented, was "a moderating influence in the present Russian government. . . . It would be a real catastrophe if Stalin should die at the present time." Truman believed that the USSR, like the United States, was having serious postwar internal problems, and that "this might explain some of the things that they had been doing." [55]

Byrnes, too, was having second thoughts about the tough policy he had followed at the London Foreign Ministers' Conference. Even before departing for home, he had announced American willingness to recognize the government of Hungary pending the holding of free elections, and to consider Moscow's request for establishment of an Allied Control Council in Japan. He had heard criticism "from all sides" of Washington's refusal to allow its allies to participate in the occupation of Japan, he commented: "We were going off in a unilateral way as the Russians were going off in the Balkans." On October 9, shortly after arriving back in Washington, the Secretary of State told Davies that the United States had compromised on Poland, Finland, and Hungary, and would try to do the same thing on Rumania and Bulgaria. The next day he announced the dispatch to those two countries of a delegation headed by Mark Ethridge, publisher of the *Louisville Courier-Journal,* to check on the accuracy of State Department reports regarding Russian activities. The Secretary of State opposed Forrestal's suggestion that Truman publicly condemn Soviet policy, arguing that this would be an unnecessarily provocative move, and viewed as "a revelation" news from Ambassador Harriman late in October that Stalin really was upset over American

[55] C. P. Noyes notes, Truman-Stettinius conversation, October 22, 1945, Stettinius calendar notes, Stettinius MSS, Box 247.

policy in Japan. On October 31, four days after Truman's bellicose Navy Day speech, the Secretary of State told a New York audience that while the people of Eastern Europe should have the right to choose their own forms of government, the Soviet Union did have legitimate security interests there. The United States, he promised, would never support anti-Russian movements in that part of the world.[56]

Late in November, Byrnes proposed another meeting of the Big Three foreign ministers, to take place in Moscow before Christmas. The Secretary of State had found it difficult to press for more authority for American representatives in Rumania and Bulgaria while denying Russian requests for a role in the occupation of Japan, and was now prepared to arrange a compromise even over the objections of General MacArthur, the Supreme Allied Commander. Moreover, he realized that as long as the Rumanian and Bulgarian peace treaties remained unsigned, the Russians would have an excuse to keep troops in those countries. Byrnes had also concluded that Molotov himself had caused many of the procedural difficulties at London; by holding the new conference in Moscow the Secretary of State hoped to deal directly with Stalin, thus bypassing the obstinate Soviet foreign minister. The American attitude on the Balkans had not changed, Byrnes told British Foreign Secretary Ernest Bevin, but if the Russians agreed to talk about that issue "I should think that that would be evidence of their willingness to reach some compromise." Bevin, who could be obstinate himself, objected strongly to the proposed meeting and agreed to attend only after Byrnes threatened to go to Moscow without him.[57]

The Secretary of State had also altered his tactics for dealing with Moscow on the subject of atomic energy. Byrnes had originally planned

[56] Bohlen minutes, Byrnes-Molotov conversations, September 28 and 30, 1945, *FR: 1945,* II, 437, 489; Stettinius calendar notes, September 28, 1945, Stettinius MSS, Box 247; Davies memorandum of conversation with Byrnes, October 9, 1945, Davies MSS, Box 22; *New York Times,* October 11, 1945; Forrestal Diary, October 16, 1945, Millis, ed., *The Forrestal Diaries,* pp. 101–2; Byrnes, *Speaking Frankly,* p. 108; Byrnes speech of October 31, 1945, *Department of State Bulletin,* XIII (November 4, 1945), 709–11. For Harriman's talks with Stalin about Japan, see Feis, *Contest over Japan,* pp. 51–77. For the Ethridge Mission, see Mark Ethridge and C. E. Black, "Negotiating on the Balkans, 1945–1947," in Dennett and Johnson, eds., *Negotiating with the Russians,* pp. 184–203.

[57] Byrnes, *All in One Lifetime,* pp. 318–19; Byrnes, *Speaking Frankly,* pp. 108–9; Byrnes to Bevin, November 27 and 29, 1945, *FR: 1945,* II, 582–83, 588–89. See also Byrnes's memoranda of conversations with Lord Halifax, November 29, 1945, and with Michael Wright, December 4, 1945, *ibid.,* pp. 590–91, 593–95.

to present the Truman-Attlee-King proposal for international control at the first meeting of the United Nations General Assembly in January, 1946, without consulting the Russians in advance. But the atomic scientists and several of their prominent supporters in Congress argued that the matter should be discussed with the USSR prior to that time. Benjamin V. Cohen and Leo Pasvolsky, two of Byrnes's closest advisers, recommended a similar course of action, as did the British. Byrnes yielded to these pressures and, on November 27, advised Bevin that the Moscow negotiations would also deal with atomic energy. The Secretary of State then organized a committee of advisers, headed by Cohen and Pasvolsky, to decide what he should tell the Russians.[58]

The draft proposal which Byrnes's advisers worked out adopted the four basic steps toward international control mentioned in the Truman-Attlee-King agreement. It differed significantly from that document, however, by failing to make completion of one stage an absolute requirement for implementation of the next: "successful international action with respect to any phase of the problem is not necessarily a prerequisite for undertaking affirmative action with respect to other phases." [59] This change of wording was of great importance, for conceivably scientific and technical information regarding atomic energy might now be exchanged prior to the establishment of foolproof safeguards. It is unclear whether or not this modification represented an effort by State Department officials to improve the chances of Russian acceptance. What is clear, however, is that this new formula seriously undermined the acceptability of the proposal to the Congress of the United States.

On December 10, 1945, the Secretary of State called in key members of the Senate Foreign Relations and Atomic Energy committees to brief them on what he proposed to do at Moscow. The senators were still

[58] Cohen and Pasvolsky to Byrnes, November 24, 1945, cited in Hewlett and Anderson, *The New World,* p. 470; Byrnes to Bevin, November 27, 1945, *FR: 1945,* II, 582–83. See also Byrnes's memorandum of a conversation with Lord Halifax, November 29, 1945, *ibid.,* p. 590; and a British *aide-mémoire* of that date, *ibid.,* pp. 77–78. Byrnes had told a group of reporters on November 21 that he intended to go directly to the General Assembly meeting in January without consulting the Russians in advance. (*New York Times,* November 22, 1945.) For the views of the atomic scientists and their supporters in Congress, see *ibid.,* November 17, 1945; Hewlett and Anderson, *The New World,* p. 470; and Smith, *A Peril and a Hope,* pp. 222–24.

[59] "Draft Proposals on Atomic Energy for Submission to the Soviet Government," December 10, 1945, *FR: 1945,* II, 92–96.

angry over Byrnes's handling of the Truman-Attlee-King agreement and resented his failure to seek their advice earlier—one senator commented that the Foreign Relations Committee had been created to "consult" with the Executive, not to be "informed" of what it had already decided to do. But the senators' anger stemmed from more than this lapse of protocol. They strongly criticized the State Department's draft proposal on atomic energy for leaving open the possibility of exchanging information before the institution of safeguards. Senator Vandenberg warned that the Senate would oppose giving up any scientific data "unless and until the Soviets are prepared to be 'policed' by UNO." Any other course of action would be "sheer appeasement." Senator Connally asked whether the Secretary of State had not reversed the proper order of procedure—should he not seek safeguards before exchanging scientific information? Upon learning that Byrnes had invited Dr. James B. Conant to serve as a consultant on atomic energy at Moscow, the Texas senator snorted irritably at the folly of entrusting such delicate missions to "college professors." Byrnes received this outburst of senatorial ire without comment, and two days later left for the Soviet Union. Feeling that they had made little impression on the Secretary of State, the senators asked for a meeting with the President himself.[60]

Truman met with Connally, Vandenberg, and their colleagues on December 14, 1945, two days after Byrnes's departure for Moscow. The President appeared surprised to learn that the State Department's draft proposals would permit the exchange of scientific and technical information prior to the establishment of safeguards, but when the senators suggested that Byrnes be instructed by radio to change his plan, Truman remained noncommittal. Vandenberg noted that the senators had at least made their protest: "We shall hold the Executive Department responsible. It is our unanimous opinion that the Byrnes formula must be *stopped.*" [61]

[60] Vandenberg Diary, December 10, 1945, Vandenberg, ed., *Private Papers,* pp. 227–28; Connally and Steinberg, *My Name Is Tom Connally,* pp. 289–90; *New York Times,* December 20 and 29, 1945. As had been the case with the Truman-Attlee-King agreement, Byrnes's tardiness in consulting the Senate resulted more from his habit of leaving policy undecided until the latest possible moment than from a desire to bypass Capitol Hill. Conant's appointment was also a last-minute affair; see his *My Several Lives,* pp. 476–77.

[61] Vandenberg Diary, December 11, 1945 [misdated], Vandenberg, ed., *Private Papers,* p. 229.

But the President did not ignore the senators' criticisms. He quickly ordered Acting Secretary of State Acheson, who had attended the meeting, to cable a full account of it to Byrnes in Moscow. On December 17, the Secretary of State replied, maintaining that he had never intended to make possible the exchange of information without safeguards, and promising to follow the more strictly worded formula of the Truman-Attlee-King agreement. When news of the senators' confrontations with Truman and Byrnes leaked to the press on December 20, the President, now reassured, sent the Secretary of State an expression of confidence.[62]

Surprisingly enough, Byrnes had less trouble winning Russian acceptance of the American plan for a United Nations Atomic Energy Commission than he did in securing congressional approval. The Russians showed little apparent interest in the question at Moscow, and aside from asking that the commission report to the Security Council instead of to the General Assembly, suggested no changes in the American plan. The conferees agreed that the commission would, by separate stages, make proposals to exchange basic scientific information, limit the use of atomic and other weapons of mass destruction, and set up effective safeguards. Repeating the Truman-Attlee-King formula, the agreement provided that "the work of the Commission should proceed by separate stages, the successful completion of each of which will develop the necessary confidence of the world before the next stage is undertaken." [63]

Byrnes's chief objective at Moscow was to resolve the impasse over Rumania and Bulgaria, so that work on peace treaties with Germany's former satellites could begin. The Ethridge report, presented to Byrnes on December 7, 1945, offered little reason for optimism. It stated frankly that "constant and vigorous intrusion [by the Russians] into the

[62] Acheson to Byrnes, December 15, 1945, *FR: 1945*, II, 609–10; Byrnes to Acheson, December 17, 1945, *ibid.*, p. 609*n*; Acheson to Byrnes, December 21, 1945, *ibid.*, pp. 709–10; *New York Times*, December 20, 1945.

[63] Moscow Conference communiqué, December 27, 1945, *FR: 1945*, II, 822–24. A convenient summary of the negotiations on atomic energy at Moscow is in Hewlett and Anderson, *The New World*, pp. 475–76. Molotov seemed determined to minimize the importance of the bomb during the Moscow negotiations. He requested that the subject be moved from first to last place on the conference agenda, and took considerable delight in asking Conant whether he had an atomic bomb in his pocket. Stalin chided his foreign minister for his flippant attitude, however, and congratulated the American scientists on their "great invention." (Conant, *My Several Lives*, pp. 482–83; Byrnes, *All in One Lifetime*, pp. 336–37.)

internal affairs of these countries is so obvious to an impartial observer that Soviet denial of its existence can only be regarded as a reflection of the party line." The report noted that, according to present American policy, peace could come only if representative governments existed throughout Europe. To concede the Soviets a sphere of influence in Eastern Europe would only be to invite its extension. Unless the United States was prepared to abandon the Yalta Declaration on Liberated Europe, it should take steps to ensure its implementation. By the time the report reached him, however, Byrnes had decided to make another attempt at compromise with the Russians. For this reason he circulated the report privately, but refused to allow its publication.[64]

At Moscow, Byrnes and Molotov had no more luck in reaching an accord on Eastern Europe than they had had at London three months earlier. But the Secretary of State placed his main hope on a direct appeal to Stalin, and at his first meeting with the Russian leader on December 23 he secured the concessions he wanted. Stalin emphasized the Soviet Union's determination to have only friendly governments along its borders. He then conceded, however, that "perhaps the Bulgarian parliament could be advised to include some members of the loyal opposition in the new Government" and that "in the case of Rumania . . . it might be possible to make some changes . . . which would satisfy Mr. Byrnes." Byrnes jumped at the opportunity and rapidly worked out with Stalin an agreement calling for a three-power commission to go to Rumania and advise the government to take in two additional ministers. The Soviet government would itself propose a slight broadening of the Bulgarian regime.[65]

Stalin's concessions did nothing to weaken Russian influence in Eastern Europe—George F. Kennan aptly described them as "fig leaves of democratic procedure to hide the nakedness of Stalinist dictatorship." [66]

[64] "Summary Report on Soviet Policy in Rumania and Bulgaria," December 7, 1945, *FR: 1945*, V, 633–37; Ethridge and Black, "Negotiating on the Balkans," pp. 200–2.

[65] Record of the Byrnes-Stalin meeting of December 23, 1945, *FR: 1945*, II, 752–56. During this conversation Byrnes mentioned the Ethridge report, announcing that he might have to publish it if no accord was reached on Rumania and Bulgaria. Stalin replied that if this happened he would ask a Soviet journalist, Ilya Ehrenburg, to report publicly on conditions in those two countries. The Soviet leader assured Byrnes that Ehrenburg would be as "impartial" as Ethridge had been.

[66] Kennan, *Memoirs*, p. 284.

But the concessions had great symbolic importance for Byrnes. He could now say that the Russians had at least genuflected before the Yalta Declaration on Liberated Europe by agreeing to make the governments of Rumania and Bulgaria more representative, in much the same way that Stalin had bowed in the direction of the Yalta Polish agreement in May by agreeing to a token broadening of the Warsaw government. This would make it possible for Byrnes to justify extending diplomatic recognition to Rumania and Bulgaria, and to conclude peace treaties with them.

In return, the Secretary of State agreed to make token concessions on the issue of Japan. The United States would establish an "Allied Council," made up of representatives of the United States, the British Commonwealth, China, and the Soviet Union, which would consult with and advise General MacArthur on occupation measures. But this body was in no way comparable to the Allied Control Council in Germany— MacArthur was obliged to take its advice only if the "exigencies of the situation" permitted. The General himself was to decide when they did and when they did not. Just as the agreement on Eastern Europe allowed the Americans to save face while tacitly acknowledging Soviet control, so the Far Eastern accord allowed the Russians a token role in the occupation of Japan without in fact impairing American authority.[67]

The Moscow agreement indicated clearly that Byrnes had abandoned "atomic diplomacy." In order to secure any kind of agreement at all from the Russians, the Secretary of State had been forced to fall back upon the *quid pro quo* negotiating tactics he had employed at Potsdam. But the situation had changed profoundly since the summer of 1945: the critical manner in which leading Republicans and Democrats, as well as Truman himself, greeted Byrnes's efforts at Moscow indicated that compromise with the Soviet Union was no longer politically feasible. As a result, the United States government moved, during the first three months of 1946, into a fundamental reorientation of policy toward the Soviet Union.

[67] Moscow Conference communiqué, December 27, 1945, *FR: 1945*, II, 819. See also Feis, *Contest over Japan*, pp. 103–4.

9

Getting Tough with Russia:
The Reorientation of
American Policy, 1946

Byrnes felt that he had achieved much at Moscow. The Russians accepted his plan for a general peace conference and his list of states to be invited. The compromise arrangement on Rumania and Bulgaria, though vague, at least committed the Soviet Union on paper to the principle of self-determination. Stalin agreed to token participation in the occupation of Japan without challenging American control of that enterprise, and reiterated his recognition of Chiang Kai-shek's Nationalist government in China, a gesture which seemed especially significant just as General George C. Marshall was embarking on his mission to try to end the civil war there. Much to Byrnes's surprise, the Russians accepted without significant modification the American plan for a United Nations Atomic Energy Commission which would begin work on international control. The foreign ministers failed to reach agreement only on the question of when the Russians would withdraw their troops from northern Iran, which they had occupied during the war. Consequently, the Secretary of State returned to the United States "far happier" with the results of this meeting than with the outcome of the London Conference fifteen weeks earlier.[1]

But though the initial editorial reaction to Moscow was generally friendly, Byrnes quickly found himself under attack from leading Republicans and several of his own colleagues in the Truman Administration. Russian behavior over the past year had gradually convinced many Washington officials that Stalin had no interest in self-determination, the revival of world trade, or collective security. Only by negotiating with the Soviet Union from a position of strength, they felt, could the United States obtain the kind of peace settlement it wanted. Byrnes's refusal to compromise at London had pleased American advocates of a tough line, but they worried that at Moscow he had made concessions which the Russians could only interpret as a sign of weakness. Why, they asked, should the United States, sole possessor of the atomic bomb, continue to appease Moscow? [2]

This divergence over policy developed because of poor communication between the State Department, the White House, the Capitol Hill. Byrnes, overconfident of his abilities as a negotiator, had switched abruptly to more conciliatory tactics after the failure of the London Conference without giving congressional leaders or the President a clear idea of his intentions. Up to this point Truman, preoccupied with domestic problems, had allowed his secretary of state a free hand. But dissatisfaction with Byrnes's performance at Moscow forced the President to reassert his authority in the field of foreign affairs. Simultaneously, Republican leaders made it clear that any further compromises with the Soviet Union would cause them to launch a public attack on Administration policy. Byrnes, slowly realizing how far he had strayed from the prevailing mood in Washington, moved early in 1946 to repair his relations with the White House, Congress, and leading Republicans by reverting to a firmer position in his dealings with the Russians.

Confusion over Soviet intentions also contributed to the Truman Ad-

[1] Byrnes, *Speaking Frankly*, pp. 121–22. See also the *Washington Post*, December 26 and 28, 1945; and the Davies Diary, January 4, 1946, Davies MSS, Box 22.

[2] *Newsweek*, XXVII (January 7, 1946), 29; *Time*, XLVII (January 7, 1946), 19–20; Davies Diary, December 31, 1945, Davies MSS, Box 22. See also Byrnes, *All in One Lifetime*, p. 317; and the Department of State, "Fortnightly Survey of American Opinion," No. 42, January 8, 1946.

ministration's vacillating foreign policy. Without a convincing explanation of the motives underlying Russian behavior, Washington officials found it difficult to decide upon a consistent plan of action.[3] If Kremlin leaders were chiefly interested in guaranteeing Soviet security, opportunities still existed to resolve outstanding disputes. Truman had been operating on this assumption when he met Stalin at Potsdam, and Byrnes apparently adhered to it as late as December, 1945, in his talks with the Russians at Moscow. But other American officials were coming to feel that they had misjudged the Kremlin's policy: Soviet actions in Eastern Europe in 1945, together with the change in tactics by the international communist movement, convinced them that Moscow had embarked on a program of unlimited expansion which threatened the very survival of the United States and its Western allies. A series of alarming developments in February, 1946, lent credence to this view, as did a persuasive analysis of the relationship between ideology and Soviet diplomacy by George F. Kennan, the American chargé d'affaires in Moscow.

The convergence of these external and internal trends in late February and early March, 1946, produced a fundamental reorientation of United States policy toward the Soviet Union. Up to this time the Truman Administration, despite occasional outbursts of angry rhetoric, was still trying to resolve differences with Moscow through negotiation and compromise. In March, 1946, however, Administration officials began bringing their diplomacy into line with their rhetoric. From this time on American policy-makers regarded the Soviet Union not as an estranged ally but as a potential enemy, whose vital interests could not be recognized without endangering those of the United States. Truman and his advisers continued diplomatic contacts with the Russians, but they firmly resolved to offer no further concessions of the kind Byrnes had made at Moscow. The Secretary of State himself accurately described the new policy as one of "patience with firmness"; [4] in time it would come to be known by a less precise but more ominous term—"containment."

[3] On this point, see Joseph and Stewart Alsop, "We Have No Russian Policy," *Washington Post,* January 4, 1946.

[4] Curry, *Byrnes,* p. 210.

I

Truman's dissatisfaction with Byrnes's conduct of foreign policy had been growing for several months. Part of the difficulty was personal. According to one observer, Byrnes resented having been denied the Democratic vice-presidential nomination in 1944, and felt himself better qualified to occupy the White House than Truman. The President himself later acknowledged that he had chosen Byrnes to be secretary of state partly out of a sense of guilt over the 1944 episode. Whatever the reason for his appointment, Byrnes had clearly intended to be a strong secretary of state. As mobilization and reconversion director under Roosevelt, he had enjoyed virtually complete autonomy in organizing the wartime economy. This exceptional delegation of power, Truman believed, caused Byrnes to think that as secretary of state he could have a free hand in running foreign policy.[5]

During his first months in office, the Secretary of State showed an almost ostentatious desire to act as an independent agent. At the London Conference of Foreign Ministers, he refused to report back to the State Department. "Hell," he told the secretary of the American delegation, "I may tell the President sometime what happened, but I'm never going to tell the State Department about it." At the Moscow Conference in December, Byrnes remarked to Ambassador Harriman that he did not intend to send daily reports to Washington: "I don't trust the White House. It leaks. And I don't want any of this coming out in the papers until I get home." Byrnes did send Truman one direct dispatch from Moscow describing the progress of the meeting, but it gave the President little information he did not already have from the newspapers. Truman considered this an inadequate account from a cabinet member to the Chief Executive: "It was more like one partner in business telling the other that his business trip was progressing well and not to worry."[6]

[5] Daniels, *Man of Independence,* p. 308; Truman, *Year of Decisions,* pp. 546–47. See also Acheson, *Present at the Creation,* pp. 136–37.

[6] Interview with Theodore C. Achilles, Dulles Oral History Project; Cabell Phillips interview with Harriman, quoted in Phillips, *The Truman Presidency,* p. 148; Byrnes to Truman, December 24, 1945, *FR: 1945,* II, 760; Truman, *Year of Decisions,* p.

Byrnes's reputation as a compromiser also caused alarm among Administration advisers. Senator Tom Connally viewed his appointment as secretary of state with considerable skepticism because he felt that the South Carolinian was "devoted to expediency." The publisher of the *Army-Navy Journal* warned Truman's press secretary in December that Byrnes, overly anxious to reach agreements with the Russians, might make concessions of which the American people would not approve. Harriman developed strong doubts about Byrnes after the London Conference, and resolved never to accept another diplomatic post under him. Kennan, Harriman's counselor in the Soviet Union, observed Byrnes closely at Moscow and concluded that he had no fixed objectives: "His main purpose is to achieve some sort of an agreement, he doesn't much care what. The realities behind this agreement, since they concern only such people as Koreans, Rumanians, and Iranians, about whom he knows nothing, do not concern him. He wants an agreement for its political effect at home." When the Moscow decisions were announced, the United States mission staff in Rumania regarded them as a "sell-out," and for a time considered resigning en masse. The American ambassador in Italy, Alexander Kirk, told C. L. Sulzberger in the spring of 1946 that Byrnes was "awful" and had "given far too much away to the Russians." [7]

Admiral William D. Leahy, the crusty Chief of Staff to the Commander in Chief, criticized Byrnes with particular vehemence. One of the first of Truman's advisers to advocate a tough policy toward the Soviet Union, Leahy by the end of 1945 had come to regard almost anyone who would consider agreement with the Russians as an appeaser. Byrnes's efforts to settle the Chinese civil war by encouraging Chiang Kai-shek to bring communists into his government caused Leahy to wonder, in the privacy of his diary, whether the Secretary of State might not be under the influence of "communist" elements in the State Depart-

---

549. On Byrnes's administrative methods, see also Acheson, *Present at the Creation,* p. 163; *The Journals of David E. Lilienthal,* II, 159; and Feis, *Contest over Japan,* pp. 124–26.

[7] Connally and Steinberg, *My Name Is Tom Connally,* p. 289; John C. O'Laughlin to Charles G. Ross, December 18, 1945, Truman MSS, OF 386; Kennan Diary, December 19, 1945, quoted in Kennan, *Memoirs,* pp. 287–88. See also the Sulzberger Diary, January 24, 26, April 22, 1946, quoted in Sulzberger, *A Long Row of Candles,* pp. 292–93, 311.

ment. The Moscow agreement seemed to confirm his suspicions: both the State Department and the new Labor government in Britain, he wrote, were bowing before Russian demands in a manner resembling what Chamberlain had done at Munich.[8]

Truman himself had expressed concern over his secretary of state's attitude shortly before Byrnes left for Moscow. He was fond of Byrnes, the President told Joseph E. Davies, a mutual friend, but Byrnes was a "conniver." Truman expected to have to do some "conniving" himself "to get the boat steady." Davies attributed Truman's displeasure with Byrnes partly to the Secretary of State's carelessness about keeping the President informed, partly to indications that "someone had been needling him against Byrnes." At Truman's request, Davies saw Byrnes on December 11, but apparently failed to convey to the Secretary a full expression of the President's mood.[9]

Byrnes's decision to release the Moscow Conference communiqué before consulting the White House further irritated Truman, who awaited the Secretary's return from the Soviet Union in an angry mood. Upon landing in Washington on December 29, 1945, Byrnes instructed the State Department to arrange for a radio report to the nation. At the same time he asked the White House for an appointment with the President. Truman replied pointedly through his press secretary that Byrnes should see the Chief Executive before reporting to the nation. Accordingly, Byrnes met Truman that evening on the presidential yacht *Williamsburg*. Recollections differ as to precisely what took place. Truman recalled that he took Byrnes into a stateroom and complained about the Secretary's inadequate reporting of developments in Moscow. "I said it was shocking that a communiqué should be issued in Washington announcing a foreign-policy development of major importance that I had never heard of. I said I would not tolerate a repetition of such conduct."

Byrnes himself, however, remembered receiving criticism only from Admiral Leahy, not Truman. George Allen, director of the Reconstruc-

[8] Curry, *Byrnes,* p. 342; Leahy Diary, November 28, December 11, 26, 28, 1945, January 1, 1946, Leahy MSS. There is some evidence that Leahy deliberately leaked information critical of Byrnes to certain favored newspaper columnists. See the Davies Journal, January 28, February 5, 1946, Davies MSS; and Tristam Coffin, *Missouri Compromise,* pp. 40–41.

[9] Davies Journal, December 8 and 11, 1945, Davies MSS, Box 22. See also Murphy, *Diplomat among Warriors,* pp. 300–1.

tion Finance Corporation, was present on board the *Williamsburg* and recalled no evident bitterness between Truman and Byrnes. Allen did receive the clear impression, however, that Truman had decided "to put an end to the holdover policy of Russian appeasement." Another guest on the *Williamsburg,* Clark Clifford, remembered no particular hostility between the President and the Secretary of State but noted that "all through dinner Leahy, in a really effective and gentle manner to which Byrnes could not take exception, had the needle in him." Leahy himself recorded in his diary that he asked Byrnes repeatedly what benefits the United States got out of the Moscow agreement, but that Byrnes had been unable to tell him. Truman had shown great dissatisfaction with Byrnes before his arrival on the yacht, Leahy observed, but the Secretary of State had apparently managed for the time being to soothe the Chief Executive.[10]

Whatever Truman told Byrnes on board the *Williamsburg,* there is no doubt that the President disliked the Moscow agreement. As he went over the conference documents Byrnes had left with him, Truman later wrote, "it became abundantly clear to me that the successes of the Moscow conference were unreal." The President particularly objected to Byrnes's failure to secure concessions from the Russians on the international control of atomic energy and on the withdrawal of Russian troops from Iran. Truman brooded over these developments for a week, and then on January 5, 1946, called Byrnes to the White House for a reprimand. Reading from a memorandum written out in longhand, Truman told the Secretary of State that although he would like to delegate as much authority as possible to cabinet members, he did not intend to abdicate his right as President to make final decisions. For this reason, it was vital for Byrnes to keep the President constantly informed as to the course of diplomatic negotiations.

The President then launched into a violent attack on Russian policy. He had only that morning read the Ethridge report on conditions in Rumania and Bulgaria, and was determined not to recognize these two governments until their composition had been radically changed. He called for a vigorous American protest against Russian actions in Iran,

[10] Byrnes, *All in One Lifetime,* pp. 342–43; Truman, *Year of Decisions,* p. 550; Jonathan Daniels interviews with George Allen and Clark Clifford, cited in Daniels, *Man of Independence,* pp. 309–11; Leahy Diary, December 29, 1945, Leahy MSS. See also Acheson, *Present at the Creation,* p. 136. For the Moscow Conference communiqué, see the *Department of State Bulletin,* XIII (December 30, 1945), 1027–32.

which were "an outrage if I ever saw one." He charged that the Russians intended to invade Turkey and seize the Black Sea Straits. Truman did not think the United States should "play" at compromise any longer: "Unless Russia is faced with an iron fist and strong language another war is in the making. Only one language do they understand—'how many divisions have you?' . . . I'm tired of babying the Soviets." [11]

Truman's outburst at Byrnes stemmed from more than bruised pride over the Secretary's failure to consult him. It indicated clearly the President's growing determination to put into effect a firmer policy toward the Soviet Union. An arrangement whereby the Russians would convey the appearance of self-determination within their sphere of influence had seemed acceptable enough in Poland in May of 1945, but by December, when Byrnes agreed to similar compromises in Rumania and Bulgaria, public trust in Russian intentions had badly eroded. Opinion polls showed that at the time of Japan's surrender, 54 percent of a national sample had been willing to trust the Russians to cooperate with the United States in the postwar world. Two months later, following the failure of the London Conference, this figure had dropped to 44 percent. By the end of February, 1946, it would stand at 35 percent.[12]

For a man of his long experience in domestic affairs, Byrnes seemed oddly unaware of this progressive deterioration of faith in the good intentions of the Soviet Union. The praise he won for his firm stand at London apparently surprised him, as did the criticism he incurred for his compromises at Moscow.[13] Truman, however, fully realized the importance of this gradual shift in opinion, especially in view of increasingly ominous indications that Republicans might try to capitalize on it in the 1946 congressional elections. The wartime policy of conceding whatever

[11] Truman memorandum for conversation with Byrnes, January 5, 1946, Truman, *Year of Decisions*, pp. 551–52. Byrnes denied ever having read or listened to this memorandum. George Curry, Byrnes's biographer, suggests that Truman did not actually read the memorandum to Byrnes, but sought to express his concern in a less forceful manner. Byrnes himself did not take it as a reprimand, and claims that if he had read the document he would have resigned on the spot. (Curry, *Byrnes*, pp. 189–90.)

[12] American Institute of Public Opinion polls of August 8, October 17, 1945, and February 27, 1946, cited in Cantril and Strunk, eds., *Public Opinion*, p. 371. In each of these national samples, between 13 and 16 percent of those polled were undecided as to whether Russian cooperation could be expected.

[13] Byrnes, *All in One Lifetime*, p. 317; memorandum of a conversation between Byrnes and Georges Bidault, May 1, 1946, *FR: 1946*, II, 204.

was necessary to reach agreement with the Russians was no longer politically feasible; the President made it clear that the Secretary of State would have to accustom himself to a less conciliatory approach.

II

Between September of 1945 and March of 1946 Republican criticism of Administration diplomacy reached its greatest intensity since before Pearl Harbor. The bipartisan foreign policy which Roosevelt and Hull had so painstakingly constructed now seemed to be falling apart. Secretary of State Byrnes, who strongly supported bipartisanship, found himself under increasingly violent attack from prominent Republicans who had grown disenchanted with his Russian policy. Byrnes eventually succeeded in placating these Republican critics, just as he placated Truman and his other critics within the Administration. To do this, however, the Secretary had to repress his strong inclination to deal with the Kremlin in the same way that he had dealt with the United States Congress— by practicing the politics of compromise.

Initial indications of G.O.P. dissatisfaction came in October, 1945, when James Reston reported that "leading members of the Republican Party" resented Byrnes's failure to ask their advice before formulating diplomatic policy. Reston's story left little doubt that one of the party leaders to whom he referred was John Foster Dulles, the unofficial Republican spokesman on foreign affairs. In an effort to bolster bipartisanship, Byrnes had invited Dulles to serve on the American delegation to the London Foreign Ministers' Conference. The Secretary of State sought no suggestions in advance of the meeting, however, leading Dulles to conclude that his only function had been to place a Republican stamp of approval on policies already decided upon by the Administration. Dulles also objected to Byrnes's penchant for compromise and, according to the testimony of at least two observers, threatened to lead the Republican Party in a public attack on the Secretary of State if he yielded to Soviet demands.[14]

[14] *New York Times,* October 9, 1945; interviews with Carl W. McCardle and Theodore C. Achilles, Dulles Oral History Project. See also John Foster Dulles, *War or Peace,* pp. 29–30. In a conversation with Stettinius on October 1, 1945, Dulles said that he was "discouraged and unhappy" about the way the foreign ministers'

During the following months prominent G.O.P. leaders criticized Administration policy with increasing frequency. The Republican members of Congress issued a statement on December 5, 1945, calling for greater efforts to fulfill wartime pledges to small nations. Governor Dwight Green of Illinois told the Republican National Committee that the party should not hesitate to protest the "shameful betrayal of Poland." Senator Homer Capehart of Indiana grumbled that Byrnes's concessions at Moscow reminded him "of Chamberlain and his umbrella appeasement of Hitler." In January, 1946, House Minority Leader Joseph W. Martin proclaimed Republican opposition to "any betrayal of the small nations of the world in the making of the peace." [15]

The views of Senator Arthur H. Vandenburg of Michigan would, more than those of any other individual, determine the Republican position on policy toward the Soviet Union. Early in 1945 Vandenburg had strongly criticized the Yalta accords on Eastern Europe, but after President Roosevelt sent him to the San Francisco Conference, he formed a close working relationship with Secretary of State Stettinius and played a vital role in rallying Senate support for the United Nations Charter. Truman's decision to replace Stettinius with Byrnes threatened to undo the Administration's close ties with Vandenburg. The Michigan senator distrusted Byrnes because "his whole life has been a career of compromise." The South Carolinian had gained his great influence in the Senate and later with Roosevelt through his ability to conciliate, but Vandenberg's experience at San Francisco had taught him that the only way to deal with the Russians was to be firm and unyielding. Accordingly, as Arthur H. Vandenberg, Jr., observed, "the very quality for which Byrnes had been best known in the Senate was the one that Vandenberg feared might be Byrnes's undoing in the international political field." [16]

---

meeting had gone. While he expressed no direct criticism of Byrnes, Dulles did say that the Secretary of State was "extremely nervous, . . . tired out and exhausted, and facing this failure of his first mission on his own was getting under his skin." Dulles then praised the "nerve and guts" Stettinius had shown at San Francisco by risking a breakup of the conference rather than give in to Russian demands, and said that he was still telling all the Republicans about it. (Stettinius calendar notes, October 1, 1945, Stettinius MSS, Box 247.)

[15] *New York Times,* December 6, 1945; *Newsweek,* XXVI (December 17, 1945), 36; *Washington Post,* December 29, 1945; *New Republic,* CXIV (February 11, 1946), 172.

[16] Vandenberg to Mrs. Vandenberg, undated, Vandenberg, ed., *Private Papers,* p. 225; *ibid.,* p. 243.

Vandenberg also distrusted Byrnes because the new Secretary of State refused to ask his advice on foreign policy. Dean Acheson, who understood the Michigan senator well, observed that one could get Vandenberg to agree to almost anything provided only that one patiently consulted with him in advance. Byrnes's reluctance to perform this civility got him into as much trouble with Vandenberg as it did with Truman. The Secretary of State chose Dulles instead of Vandenberg to represent the Republican Party at London. Even worse, he repeatedly failed to seek the counsel of Vandenberg and other senators while formulating policy on the international control of atomic energy, a matter about which Vandenberg felt strongly. Consequently, the Michigan senator began the year 1946, in the words of his son and confidant, "with deep reservations . . . regarding the consistency and clear-sighted self-interest of our policy as practiced by Byrnes." [17]

In December of 1945, Truman asked both Vandenberg and Dulles to represent the Republican Party at the first meeting of the United Nations General Assembly, which was to take place in London the following month. Vandenberg wrote to Dulles that he did not want to go to London, but, he conceded, "it may be my duty to go along." Dubious about his ability to work with Byrnes, the Michigan senator reserved his right to resign from the delegation if he disagreed with the Administration's proposals on the international control of atomic energy. Privately he let it be known that he would come home sooner than anyone expected "if at London I collide with a Truman-Byrnes appeasement policy which I cannot stomach." [18]

Vandenberg did come close to resigning when he read the agreement on international control which Byrnes had made at Moscow. He explained to Senator Brien McMahon, a fellow member of the Senate Atomic Energy Committee:

It listed *four* stages for the work of the UNO Commission—"disclosures" FIRST and total "security" LAST. Then it said that "the work of the Com-

[17] Dean Acheson, *Sketches from Life of Men I have Known*, pp. 126–27; Vandenberg, ed., *Private Papers*, p. 237. Byrnes has said that he selected Dulles to go to London instead of Vandenberg because Dulles "had not been active in partisan politics." (Interview with James F. Byrnes, Dulles Oral History Project.) For Vandenberg's criticisms of Byrnes's policy on the international control of atomic energy, see chapter 8.

[18] Vandenberg to Dulles, December 19, 1945, and Truman, December 21, 1945, Vandenberg, ed., *Private Papers*, pp. 230, 232; Vandenberg to John W. Blodgett, December 24, 1945, Vandenberg MSS.

mission should proceed by separate stages" and that each "stage" should be completed before the next is undertaken. It seemed to me that this could be read in no other way than that the precise thing is to happen against which both *our* Committee and the Foreign Relations Committee is so earnestly opposed. I felt that I had no right to go to London, as a Senate spokesman, under any such instructions to promote any such objectives.

To another friend, Vandenberg described the Moscow communiqué as "one more typical American 'give away' on this subject." The senator communicated his displeasure to Acting Secretary of State Acheson, who quickly set up an appointment with the President on December 28.[19]

Truman and Acheson assured Vandenberg that the Moscow statement meant that adequate security arrangements would accompany each stage in the establishment of international control. With Truman's approval, Vandenberg issued a public statement making this point clear. These reassurances made it possible for the Michigan senator to accompany the American delegation to London: "Indeed," he wrote Senator McMahon, "the circumstances *now* probably *demand* that I go." Since a literal reading of the Moscow communiqué would not include Truman's qualifications, it was vital, in Vandenberg's view, that this document not be made the basis of the proposal to be presented to the General Assembly.[20]

At London, both Vandenberg and Dulles worried over the Secretary of State's apparent willingness to conciliate the Russians and exerted pressure on him to take harder positions. Vandenberg told *Newsweek* correspondent Edward Weintal: "Thank heavens that Jimmy Byrnes hates disagreements, because I don't know where I would be if he decided to continue this fight." *Newsweek* later reported Vandenberg's fear that the Secretary of State "might be tempted to yield on vital issues for harmony's sake." Eleanor Roosevelt, another American representative at London, wrote privately that "Secy. Byrnes is afraid of his own delegation." Byrnes returned from London deeply apprehensive about the future of bipartisanship. Dulles, he charged, had leaked to reporters the fact that there had been disagreement among the United States delegates. Vandenberg was upset over accusations from fellow Republicans

[19] Vandenberg to McMahon, January 2, 1946, and C. E. Hutchinson, December 29, 1945, Vandenberg MSS.
[20] *New York Times,* December 29, 1945; Leahy Diary, December 28, 1945, Leahy MSS; Vandenberg to McMahon, January 2, 1946, Vandenberg MSS.

that he had become an "appeaser" by working with Byrnes, and was also looking for a way out of bipartisan cooperation. "The fact had to be faced," the Secretary of State told his colleagues in the cabinet, "that Vandenberg's—and for that matter Dulles's—activities from now on could be viewed as being conducted on a political and partisan basis." [21]

Public statements which Dulles and Vandenberg made on their return from London gave Byrnes ample cause for concern. While Vandenberg expressed optimism regarding the new world organization's prospects, he criticized the timidity of American policy:

> The United States must not be a silent partner in this cooperative enterprise. It is our right and it is our duty to speak in these councils just as firmly and just as earnestly for ideals of justice and the fundamentals of freedom as it is for others in the UNO to assert their viewpoints. I hope to see the Government of the United States more firmly assert its moral leadership in these respects.

Stettinius later explained to Cordell Hull that "Van is pretty sore on not being taken into camp a little bit more, not only in London but in Washington too. He and Jimmy [Byrnes] are not getting on at all well. . . . Van . . . says collaboration at the present time is just being told about it the night before it goes into the newspaper." Dulles, in speeches at Princeton University and before the Foreign Policy Association in New York, complained that the Administration had chosen its delegation at the last minute and had given it no meaningful tasks to perform. Future delegations should be allowed time to develop policies which would be "realistic and significant and expressive of the righteous faith of the best of America." *Newsweek* reported late in February that both Vandenberg and Dulles were angry at Byrnes and might refuse to serve on any more delegations with him.[22]

James Reston, who had called attention to Republican discontent with Administration foreign policy in the fall of 1945, found it even

[21] Interview with Edward Weintal, Dulles Oral History Project; *Newsweek*, XXVII (January 21, 1946), 39–40; Eleanor Roosevelt to Bernard Baruch, January 16, 1946, Baruch MSS, "Selected Correspondence"; Forrestal Diary, January 29, 1946, Millis, ed., *The Forrestal Diaries*, p. 132. See also the Stettinius calendar notes, January 7, 1946, Stettinius MSS, Box 247.

[22] *New York Times*, February 17, 23, March 2, 1946; Stettinius calendar notes, March 1, 1946, Stettinius MSS, Box 247; *Newsweek*, XXVII (March 11, 1946), 19.

greater after the London United Nations meeting. Republicans objected, he noted, to Administration insistence that members of the American delegation carry out State Department policies, even though they had not been consulted on them in advance. But G.O.P. dissatisfaction grew out of substantive as well as procedural considerations: "Republicans seem to favor a bolder and what they believe would be a much more forthright policy of leadership in world affairs than the Administration is now following." The 1946 congressional elections were approaching. Republican leaders, scenting victory, had no desire to associate themselves with a policy of "appeasement" which might hurt them at the polls.[23]

Republican criticism reached a climax on February 27, 1946, when Vandenberg rose on the floor of the Senate to express his feelings. "What is Russia up to now?" he demanded:

We ask it in Manchuria. We ask it in Eastern Europe and the Dardanelles. . . . We ask it in the Baltic and the Balkans. We ask it in Poland. . . . We ask it in Japan. We ask it sometimes even in connection with events in our own United States. What is Russia up to now?

Vandenberg asserted that two rival ideologies, democracy and communism, now found themselves face to face. They could live together in harmony, but only

if the United States speaks as plainly upon all occasions as Russia does; if the United States just as vigorously sustains its own purposes and its ideals upon all occasions as Russia does; if we abandon this miserable fiction, often encouraged by our own fellow-travellers, that we somehow jeopardize the peace if our candor is as firm as Russia's always is; and if we assume a moral leadership which we have too frequently allowed to lapse.

The United States should draw a line, Vandenberg proclaimed, beyond which it would not compromise. Then it should make clear, through plain speaking, precisely where that line lay. "Where is right? Where is justice? There let America take her stand."

The Michigan senator praised the "sterling services" at London of his Democratic counterpart, Senator Connally, the "distinguished" conduct of the new American ambassador to the United Nations, Stettinius, the "sturdy" manner of British Foreign Secretary Bevin, the "able" perform-

[23] *New York Times,* February 26, 1946.

ance of French Foreign Minister Georges Bidault, and even the "brilliant" Soviet representative, Andrei Vishinsky, "one of the ablest statesmen I have ever seen in action." But he pointedly avoided any praise for Secretary of State Byrnes, an example, Arthur Krock noted, of "derogation by omission." When Vandenberg finished speaking, the Senate and the galleries stood and applauded, while a large group of colleagues lined up to shake his hand.[24]

Vandenberg's speech clearly served notice on the Truman Administration that if it continued the conciliatory policy which Byrnes had employed at Moscow and at the General Assembly meeting in London, it could not expect further support from the Republican Party. The prospect of congressional elections less than seven months away made this threat seem particularly ominous. What Vandenberg and his fellow Republicans did not know, however, was that the President and his advisers had already decided to implement the hard line which the G.O.P. had called for. An important new analysis of the influence of ideology on Soviet behavior had given Administration officials the rationale they needed for a "get tough with Russia" policy. At the moment Vandenberg was speaking, State Department speechwriters were placing the finishing touches on the first public statement of the Administration's new position.

III

American officials had been worrying about the relationship between communism and Soviet foreign policy for some time. Ambassador Harriman, who had never taken too seriously the abolition of the Comintern, reported as early as January, 1945, that the Russians were using local communist organizations as one means of extending their influence over neighboring countries, but he still interpreted this activity as an effort to ensure the security of the Soviet Union. By April of that year, however, Harriman had become convinced that ideology had replaced security as the chief determinant of Soviet policy. "The outward thrust of Commu-

[24] *Congressional Record*, February 27, 1946, pp. 1692–95. See also the *New York Times*, February 28 and March 1, 1946; and the *New Republic*, CXIV (March 11, 1946), 335–36.

nism [is] not dead," he told Navy Secretary Forrestal; "we might well have to face an ideological warfare just as vigorous and dangerous as Fascism or Nazism." [25]

The apparent abandonment of "popular front" tactics by the international communist movement alarmed government leaders, just as it did members of Congress. State Department officials attached great significance to Jacques Duclos's attack on the Communist Party of the United States, regarding it as clear evidence that Moscow had decided to resume its efforts to spread world revolution. In June of 1945, the department prepared a long report for President Truman on international communism. Taking note of recent developments in the French, Italian, and American parties, the analysis concluded that communism posed a serious challenge to the government of the United States. American communists could be expected to attack the Truman Administration for having abandoned Roosevelt's policies. Communists would attempt to gain confidential information by infiltrating sympathizers into sensitive government positions. Communist-inspired labor disputes would break out. In Europe, communists would attempt to impede the operations of American occupation forces. The report advised treating United States communists as an "un-American" fifth column group owing allegiance to a foreign power. It predicted that party members would try to portray any action taken against them as anti-Soviet, but argued that decisive moves against domestic subversion might actually improve relations with Russia by demonstrating "the inherent strength of this country." [26]

George F. Kennan warned from Moscow in July, 1945, that the abolition of the Comintern had in no way weakened Moscow's control over the international communist movement. Foreign communists had always demonstrated total loyalty to Moscow's orders, he maintained, even when these ran counter to the best interests of their own countries. Undersecretary of State Joseph Grew echoed Kennan's conclusions: "Evidence has been accumulating for some time that [the] Communist In-

[25] Harriman to Stettinius, January 10, 1945, *FR: Yalta*, pp. 450–51; Forrestal Diary, April 20, 1945, Millis, ed., *The Forrestal Diaries*, p. 47. See also Harriman to Stettinius, April 4, 1945, *FR: 1945*, V, 817–20.

[26] Memorandum by Raymond E. Murphy, special assistant to the Director of European Affairs, Department of State, on "Possible Resurrection of Communist International, Resumption of Extreme Leftist Activities, Possible Effect on United States," June 2, 1945, *FR: Potsdam*, I, 267–80. For the Duclos article, see chapter 8.

ternational is being reactivated on a regional basis." Communist parties throughout the world were taking advantage of the vacuum left by the defeat of Germany and inevitable postwar dislocations to win support for their cause. Absence of a direct link with Moscow only made their efforts more efficient. Secretary of State Byrnes suggested at Potsdam that differences in ideology between the Soviet Union and the United States were so pronounced that peaceful relations between the two countries might be impossible. Byrnes did not fully accept this pessimistic appraisal, as his subsequent behavior at Moscow made clear, but he was sufficiently concerned about the possibility of internal subversion to order a discreet purge of questionable elements within the Department of State in the fall of 1945.[27]

No one within the government took these indications of a revived communist movement more seriously than did James V. Forrestal, secretary of the navy. He wrote in May, 1945, that "we must face our diplomatic decisions from here on with the consciousness that half and maybe all of Europe might be communistic by the end of the next winter." One month later he told Harry Hopkins and Lord Halifax, the British ambassador, that the United States could work with the Russians only if they had given up their old intention of communizing the world. Forrestal clearly ascribed Soviet behavior to ideology, not to a desire for security. He pointed out to Senator Homer Ferguson that

the bolsheviks have the advantage over us of having a clear outline of economic philosophy, amounting almost to religion, which they believe is the only solution to the government of man. It is the Marxian dialectic; it is as incompatible with democracy as was Nazism or Fascism because it rests upon the willingness to apply force to gain the end, whether that force is applied externally or by internal commotion.

Forrestal noted that he had not had much time to think about this problem, but that someone within the government should be thinking about it.[28]

---

[27] Kennan to Byrnes, July 15, 1945, *FR: 1945,* V, 866–67; Grew to Kennan, July 25, 1945, *ibid.,* pp. 872–73; Walter Brown notes of a conversation with Byrnes, July 24, 1945, quoted in Curry, *Byrnes,* p. 345. For Byrnes's departmental "purge," see *ibid.,* pp. 140–44.

[28] Forrestal Diary, May 14 and June 30, 1945, Millis, ed., *The Forrestal Diaries,* pp. 57–58, 72; Forrestal to Ferguson, May 14, 1945, *ibid.,* p. 57. See also Arnold A. Rogow, *James Forrestal: A Study of Personality, Politics, and Policy,* chapter 4.

Toward the end of 1945, Forrestal commissioned Professor Edward F. Willett of Smith College to prepare a report on the relationship between communism and Soviet foreign policy. This was a vital topic, the Navy Secretary wrote Walter Lippmann, "because to me the fundamental question in respect to our relations with Russia is whether we are dealing with a nation or a religion." Willett's paper stated that the ultimate goals of communism were well known; what was not clear was whether the leaders of the Soviet Union still adhered to that doctrine. If they did not, then there was at least a possibility of settling outstanding differences. But if the Kremlin had firmly committed itself to communism, its objectives would be so diametrically opposed to those of the United States "as to make warfare between the two nations seem inevitable." Another of Forrestal's advisers argued that while the Russians might still give primary emphasis to maintaining their own security, it looked as though Stalin would not consider himself secure as long as capitalism survived anywhere in the world. "We are trying to preserve a world in which a capitalistic-democratic method can continue," Forrestal wrote early in 1946, "whereas if Russian adherence to truly Marxian dialectics continues their interest lies in a collapse of this system." [29]

On February 9, 1946, in Moscow, Joseph Stalin made a rare public speech in which he stressed the incompatibility of communism and capitalism. World War II had broken out, the Soviet leader asserted, because of the uneven rate of development in capitalist economies. War could have been avoided had some method existed for periodically redistributing raw materials and markets between nations according to need. No such method could exist, however, under capitalism. Stalin clearly implied that future wars were inevitable until the world economic system was reformed, that is, until communism supplanted capitalism as the prevailing form of economic organization. Emphasizing how rapid economic development under the Soviet Union's first three Five-Year Plans

[29] Memorandum by E. F. Willett on "Dialectical Materialism and Russian Objectives," January 14, 1946, Forrestal MSS, Box 17, "Russia study" folder; memorandum by Thomas B. Inglis on "Soviet Capabilities and Possible Intentions," January 21, 1946, *ibid.*, Box 24, "Russia" folder; Forrestal diary, January 2, 1946, Millis, ed., *The Forrestal Diaries*, p. 127. Forrestal circulated Willett's memorandum widely among government officials and such key nonofficial advisers as Walter Lippmann, Henry Luce, and Bernard Baruch. (*Ibid.*, p. 128; Vincent Davis, *Postwar Defense Policy and the U.S. Navy, 1943–1946*, pp. 221–22, 328.)

had made possible victory over Germany, he called for three postwar
Five-Year Plans, so that "our country [will] be insured against any
eventuality." [30]

Sympathetic American observers of the Soviet Union interpreted Stalin's speech as an attempt to rally support within his country for the
new Five-Year Plan. The Soviet dictator, they contended, had to stress
the existence of dangers from the outside world to justify to his people
the difficult sacrifices which the new plan would demand. Secretary of
Commerce Henry Wallace viewed the address as a friendly challenge to
prove that the American economic system could work without frequent
depressions.[31]

Most observers, however, agreed with *Time,* which described the
speech as "the most warlike pronouncement uttered by any top-rank
statesman since V-J Day." The Russians had abandoned the "soft" policy
they had followed during the war, the magazine asserted, and were now
returning to the slogans and tactics of world revolution. The *New York
Times* noted editorially that Stalin's address would disappoint those who
assumed that communism and capitalism could coexist peacefully in the
postwar period. Ambassador Harriman, arriving back in Washington at
the end of his three-year tour of duty in Moscow, told Admiral Leahy
that the primary objective of Soviet foreign policy was now to extend
communist ideology to other parts of the world. Even liberals like Eric
Sevareid and William O. Douglas saw ominous overtones in Stalin's
speech. Sevareid wrote in March:

The attitude of the American Communist Party . . . coupled with the line
taken by Communists in France, England, South American countries and
other places, . . . make it as clear as daylight that the comintern, formalized
or not, is back in effective operation. If you can brush aside Stalin's speech of
February 9, you are a braver man than I am.

Douglas told Forrestal simply that Stalin's speech constituted "the Declaration of World War III." Forrestal himself from this time on appar-

[30] *Vital Speeches,* XII (March 1, 1946), 300–4.
[31] *New Republic,* CXIV (February 18, 1946), 235–36; Raymond Gram Swing
broadcast of February 11, 1946, Swing MSS, Box 29; Department of State, "Fortnightly Survey of American Opinion," No. 45, February 26, 1946; *New York Times,*
February 20, 1946.

ently concluded that it would be impossible for democracy and communism to coexist.[32]

Stalin's February 9 address came at an extremely tense period in Soviet-American relations. Washington officials worried over the apparent determination of the Russian government to retain troops in Iran and Manchuria. In the United Nations Security Council the Soviet Union had just used its veto for the first time, not on a matter vital to its national security, but on a relatively minor issue connected with the presence of Anglo-French forces in Syria and Lebanon. On February 16, 1946, news of the Canadian spy case broke with the announcement from Ottawa of the arrest of twenty-two individuals on charges of trying to steal information on the atomic bomb for the Soviet Union. Several days later, FBI Director J. Edgar Hoover and General Leslie R. Groves admitted to a Senate committee that the Russians had obtained secret data on the bomb through the Canadian espionage operation.[33]

The Canadian spy case frightened Americans not only because it involved the atomic bomb but also because it seemed to indicate a link between Soviet espionage activities and the world communist movement. *Time* noted darkly that "there is no doubt that Russian Communism holds a peculiar attraction for some scientists and technicians." Representative John Rankin warned that the spy ring extended "throughout the United States and is working through various Communist front organizations," but that the House Un-American Activities Committee was on its trail. Admiral Leahy expressed the hope that the spy case would expose some of the communists who he believed had infiltrated the State Department. The Canadian incident greatly strengthened the

[32] *Time,* XLVII (February 18, 1946), 29–30; *New York Times,* February 11, 1946; Leahy Diary, February 21, 1946, Leahy MSS; Sevareid to Harry Snydermann, March 22, 1946, Sevareid MSS, Box 1; Forrestal Diary, February 17, 1946, Millis, ed., *The Forrestal Diaries,* pp. 134–35. For the State Department's reaction to Stalin's speech, see *FR: 1946,* VI, 695*n.*

[33] *New York Times,* February 17, 1946; Hewlett and Anderson, *The New World,* p. 501. The February 16 announcement had been stimulated, in part, by a Drew Pearson radio broadcast on February 3 which had revealed some details of the case. Canadian Prime Minister Mackenzie King believed that the Pearson account had been officially "inspired": "I may be wrong but I have a feeling that there is a desire at Washington that this information should get out." (Pickersgill and Forster, *The Mackenzie King Record, 1945–1946,* pp. 133–35.)

argument of those within and outside the Administration who had been calling for a firmer policy toward the Soviet Union. As the *New Republic* lamented, the episode played into the hands of "Army officers and reactionary Congressmen, whose entire answer to the atomic-bomb question is unlimited bomb production in this country and unlimited espionage in other countries." [34]

Two weeks after Stalin's speech, and one week after news of the spy case broke, there arrived at the State Department a long cable from George F. Kennan, the American chargé d'affaires in Moscow, analyzing the motives behind Soviet behavior. Kennan had developed strong feelings about communism while serving in the Moscow Embassy during the 1930s: "I was never able to accept or condone the stony-hearted fanaticism that was prepared to condemn . . . entire great bodies of people . . . for no other reason than that their members had been born into certain stations of life." Returning to Moscow to serve under Harriman in 1944, Kennan soon found himself at odds with the prevailing policy of cooperation with the Russians. Repeatedly he bombarded the State Department with unsolicited critical analyses of Soviet policy, couched in discursive literary language. These efforts made no impression whatsoever in Washington, if, indeed, they were ever read. By February of 1946, however, the mood had changed. Wartime collaboration had collapsed, and Ambassador Harriman was on his way home for good. Kennan, left in charge of the Moscow Embassy, was surprised to receive a cable from an exasperated State Department soliciting his opinion on why the Russians behaved the way they did.

"They had asked for it. Now, by God, they would have it." Kennan rapidly composed an eight-thousand-word telegram, "neatly divided, like an eighteenth-century Protestant sermon, into five separate parts," and sent it off to Washington. The Soviets, he wrote, saw the world as split into capitalist and socialist camps, between which there could be no peaceful coexistence. They would try to do everything possible to strengthen the socialist camp, while at the same time working to divide

[34] *Time,* XLVII (February 25, 1946), 25–26; *New York Times,* February 17, 1946; Leahy Diary, February 16, 1946, Leahy MSS; *New Republic,* CXIV (March 4, 1946), 299–300. Joseph E. Davies found himself very much alone when he argued that "Russia in self-defense has every moral right to seek atomic bomb secrets through military espionage if excluded from such information by her former fighting allies." (*New York Times,* February 19, 1946.)

and weaken capitalist nations. In time, capitalism would collapse because of its own internal contradictions and socialism would rise to take its place. Kennan emphasized that the Russians had not arrived at this analysis from an objective study of conditions outside the Soviet Union. Rather, it stemmed from the Kremlin leaders' need to justify their autocratic rule—a need Russian rulers had felt for centuries. For Stalin and his associates, Marxist ideology provided the justification

for the dictatorship without which they did not know how to rule, for cruelties they did not dare not to inflict, for sacrifices they felt bound to demand. Marxism is the fig leaf of their moral and intellectual respectability. Without it they would stand before history, at best, as only the last of that long succession of cruel and wasteful Russian rulers who have relentlessly forced their country on to ever new heights of military power in order to guarantee external security for their internally weak regime.

The implications of Kennan's analysis were ominous. If Soviet foreign policy was formulated not in response to what happened in the rest of the world but solely as a result of conditions within Russia, then no action of the United States, no matter how well intentioned, could bring about any diminution of hostility toward the West. The United States was confronted with "a political force committed fanatically to the belief that with [the] U.S. there can be no permanent modus vivendi, that it is desirable and necessary that the internal harmony of our society be broken, if Soviet power is to be secure." The Russians would try to achieve their objectives by increasing the power and influence of the Soviet state, while at the same time working through "an underground operating directorate of world communism, a concealed Comintern tightly coordinated and directed by Moscow." Under these circumstances only two courses of action remained to the United States: first, to resist as effectively as possible communist attempts, external and internal, to overthrow Western institutions; second, to wait for internal changes within the Soviet Union to produce some change in Russian policy.[35]

The reaction in Washington to this explanation of Soviet behavior was, in Kennan's words, "nothing less than sensational." President Truman read it, the State Department sent Kennan a message of commendation, and Secretary of the Navy Forrestal had it reproduced and made

[35] Kennan to Byrnes, February 22, 1946; *FR: 1946*, VI, 696–709. See also Kennan, *Memoirs*, pp. 68–69, 292–93.

required reading "for hundreds, if not thousands, of higher officers in the armed services." The telegram arrived just as pressures were converging from several sources to "get tough with Russia." Truman himself had done nothing to implement his resolution to "stop babying the Soviets" in the month and a half since his reprimand to Byrnes, but on February 20, 1946, he told Admiral Leahy that he was extremely unhappy with the existing policy of appeasing the Russians and was determined to assume a stronger position at once. Kennan's telegram of the 22d provided precisely the intellectual justification needed for this reorientation of policy.[36]

Kennan himself, writing in retrospect, recognized clearly the importance of the timing:

It was one of those moments when official Washington, whose states of receptivity . . . are . . . intricately imbedded in the subconscious . . . , was ready to receive a given message. . . . Six months earlier [it] would probably have been received in the Department of State with raised eyebrows and lips pursed in disapproval. Six months later, it would probably have sounded redundant, a sort of preaching to the convinced. . . . All this only goes to show that more important than the observable nature of external reality, when it comes to the determination of Washington's view of the world, is the subjective state of readiness on the part of Washington officialdom to recognize this or that feature of it.

The telegram, Kennan later admitted "with horrified amusement," read "like one of those primers put out by alarmed congressional committees or by the Daughters of the American Revolution, designed to arouse the citizenry to the dangers of the Communist conspiracy." [37] But at the time it proved persuasive enough, providing American officials with the intellectual framework they would employ in thinking about communism and Soviet foreign policy for the next two decades.

IV

The first public expression of the Administration's new policy came on February 28, 1946, in a speech which Byrnes delivered to the Over-

[36] Kennan, *Memoirs*, pp. 294–95; Leahy Diary, February 20, 21, 1946, Leahy MSS. For the reception of Kennan's telegram in Washington, see also Millis, ed., *The Forrestal Diaries*, pp. 135–40; Jones, *The Fifteen Weeks*, p. 133; and Lilienthal, *Journals*, II, 26.

[37] Kennan, *Memoirs*, pp. 294–95.

seas Press Club in New York. Americans had welcomed the Soviet Union into the family of nations as a power second to none, the Secretary of State pointed out:

We have approved many adjustments in her favor and, in the process, resolved many serious doubts in her favor. . . . Despite the differences in our way of life, our people admire and respect our Allies and wish to continue to be friends and partners in a world of expanding freedom and rising standards of living. But in the interest of world peace and in the interest of our common and traditional friendship we must make it plain that the United States intends to defend the [United Nations] Charter.

Through that document the major nations of the world had pledged themselves to renounce aggression. "We will not and we cannot stand aloof if force or the threat of force is used contrary to the purposes and principles of the Charter." No nation had the right to station troops on the territory of another sovereign state without its consent. No nation had the right to prolong unnecessarily the making of peace. No nation had the right to seize enemy property before reparations agreements had been made. The United States did not regard the status quo as sacrosanct, but it could not overlook "a unilateral gnawing away at the status quo." Byrnes concluded in a manner reminiscent of Theodore Roosevelt: "If we are to be a great power we must act as a great power, not only in order to ensure our own security but in order to preserve the peace of the world." [38]

Since it came only one day after Vandenberg's strong Senate speech attacking Administration foreign policy, many observers regarded Byrnes's address as nothing more than a hastily written reply to the Michigan senator. Irreverent reporters quickly dubbed it the "Second Vandenberg Concerto." Arthur Krock commented that the barbs Republican leaders had been aiming at the State Department had clearly had their intended effect. Vandenberg himself did not hesitate to claim credit for the Secretary of State's new position. Early in April he admitted to Hamilton Fish Armstrong that he had been "partially responsible" for Byrnes's speech. The Secretary of State had been "loitering around Munich" but was now "on the march." By July, the senator was writing that "almost everybody . . . concedes to me the *major influence* in *changing* the American attitude from 'appeasement' to *firm resistance.*"

[38] *Department of State Bulletin*, XIV (March 10, 1946), 355–58.

A year later, Vandenberg would look back to his own address as a crucial turning point:

At London . . . I was completely dissatisfied with our complacency in the presence of Soviet truculence. You may recall that I made a vigorous speech on the floor of the Senate immediately upon my return. Thereafter, former Secretary of State Byrnes sharply shifted his official position and I am bound to testify that during the remainder of his term he vigorously resisted any such "appeasement" and firmly stood his ground in behalf of American rights and American ideals.[39]

Republican pressure undoubtedly did influence the Secretary of State's new position. Even if Byrnes did not revise his address at the last moment, as he later claimed, Vandenberg's remarks on the floor of the Senate made it possible for the Secretary to speak with far greater confidence of getting a favorable response. But to see Byrnes's February 28 address merely as an oratorical gesture designed to placate Arthur H. Vandenberg is to underrate considerably its significance. This was the first open manifestation of the tougher Russian policy toward which the Truman Administration had been moving since the Moscow Conference. It also offered an important indication that Byrnes had resolved his differences with critics inside the Administration over the conduct of foreign affairs. The calm but uncompromising tone of the Secretary's remarks reflected a policy whose time, in the view of American leaders, had clearly come. "Perhaps the most significant thing about this forceful address," Anne O'Hare McCormick concluded, "is that he [Byrnes] thought it was what the country wanted and was waiting to hear." [40]

Less than a week after Byrnes spoke, Winston Churchill, former Brit-

[39] *Time,* XLVII (March 11, 1946), 19; *Newsweek,* XXVII (March 21, 1946), 35; *New York Times,* March 2, 1946; Vandenberg to Armstrong, April 2, 1946, Frank Januszewski, July 27, 1946, and H. W. Smith, March 6, 1947, Vandenberg MSS.

[40] *New York Times,* March 2, 1946. Byrnes later denied having revised his speech to take into account Vandenberg's criticisms. He explained that he had avoided taking a strong stand prior to this time because he had been worried about the weaknesses of the armed forces. "I thought it wise not to voice publicly my concern when we had only a twig with which to defend ourselves." But after hearing a report from General Eisenhower on the progress of Army reorganization, Byrnes felt he could safely speak. (Byrnes, *All in One Lifetime,* p. 349.) Truman told Stettinius on February 28 that Vandenberg had found out in advance about Byrnes's speech, and had arranged to give his own address on the floor of the Senate one day earlier. (Stettinius calendar notes, February 28, 1946, Stettinius MSS, Box 247.)

ish prime minister and now a private citizen, introduced the phrase "iron curtain" to the world in a speech at Fulton, Missouri. Truman himself lent tacit endorsement to Churchill's March 5, 1946, message by accompanying him to Missouri and personally introducing him to the Fulton audience. Administration officials later denied that the President had had any advance knowledge of what the British statesman proposed to say, but in fact Churchill had carefully cleared his address with the White House several weeks in advance, and both Truman and Byrnes had read the final draft of the speech prior to its delivery. Far from being a surprise, the harshly anti-Soviet Fulton address was very likely, as *Time* suggested, a "magnificent trial balloon" designed to test the American public's response to the Administration's new "get tough with Russia" policy.[41]

Churchill had arrived in the United States in January, 1946, to begin a long Florida vacation. At Truman's request he agreed to speak at Fulton in March, and as early as February 10 flew to Washington to tell the President what he planned to say. News that the President planned to introduce the former prime minister caused some concern among Administration advisers. Robert Hannegan, chairman of the Democratic National Committee, warned Joseph Davies that Truman's presence on the platform might be construed as an endorsement of whatever Churchill said. Davies went directly to the President on February 11, advising him to be sure to ask to see Churchill's text in advance. Truman blandly replied that this would not be necessary, since the speech would only be "the usual 'hands across the sea' stuff." [42]

The British leader continued to keep Administration officials fully informed of his progress in drafting the Fulton speech. Secretary of State Byrnes and his friend Bernard Baruch flew to Florida to see Churchill on February 17, and there heard an outline of the proposed address. When

[41] *Time,* XLVII (March 18, 1946), 19. For subsequent disclaimers of responsibility by the Administration, see Truman's press conference of March 8, 1946, *Truman Public Papers: 1945,* p. 145; and the statement by Press Secretary Charles G. Ross, *New York Times,* March 19, 1946.

[42] Leahy Diary, February 10, 1946, Leahy MSS; Davies Journal, February 11, 1946, Davies MSS, Box 23. See also Lord Halifax to Henry L. Stimson, February 13, 1946, Stimson MSS, Box 429. For background on the Fulton speech, see Jeremy K. Ward, "Winston Churchill and the 'Iron Curtain' Speech," *The History Teacher,* I (January, 1968), 5 ff.

Churchill came through Washington on his way to Fulton, he gave "dress rehearsals" of the speech to both Byrnes and Admiral Leahy. Churchill sent Truman a copy of his comments before they left Washington, but the President, anticipating criticism from the Russians, decided not to look at it so that he could truthfully say he had not read the speech prior to its delivery. Byrnes did, however, give the President a full summary of the address. Later, on the train, Truman changed his mind and actually read the speech, remarking according to Churchill that "it was admirable and would do nothing but good though it would make a stir." [43]

The Fulton address painted a much gloomier picture of the state of international affairs than that to which Americans had been accustomed:

From Stettin in the Baltic to Triest in the Adriatic, an iron curtain has descended across the Continent. Behind that line lie all the capitals of the ancient states of central and eastern Europe. Warsaw, Berlin, Prague, Vienna, Budapest, Belgrade, Bucharest and Sofia, all these famous cities and the populations around them lie in the Soviet sphere and all are subject in one form or another, not only to Soviet influence but to a very high and increasing measure of control from Moscow.

The Soviet Union, Churchill asserted, did not want war. But the Russians did want "the fruits of war and the indefinite expansion of their power and doctrines." No one could know with certainty what were the limits of these "expansive and proselytizing tendencies." Western powers could not hope to preserve peace by allowing Moscow free rein: "From what I have seen of our Russian friends . . . I am convinced that there is nothing they admire so much as strength, and there is nothing for which they have less respect than for military weakness." The United Nations offered the best hope for peace. But Churchill cautioned that the world organization itself would be ineffective unless there developed a "fraternal association of the English-speaking peoples." [44]

[43] *New York Times,* February 18, 1946; Byrnes, *All in One Lifetime,* p. 349; Leahy Diary, March 3, 1946, Leahy MSS; Francis Williams, *A Prime Minister Remembers: The War and Post-War Memoirs of the Rt. Hon. Earl Attlee,* pp. 162–63.

[44] *Vital Speeches,* XII (March 15, 1946), 329–32. The actual phrase, "iron curtain," was not new. Churchill had used the term in a telegram to Truman on May 12, 1945 (see Churchill, *Triumph and Tragedy,* pp. 489–90), and Senator Vandenberg had used it in a Senate speech (*Congressional Record,* November 15, 1945, pp. 10696–99).

Churchill confused the issue by coupling his frank analysis of Soviet policy with his call for what most observers regarded as an Anglo-American alliance. Senators Claude Pepper, Harley M. Kilgore, and Glen Taylor issued a joint statement on March 6 accusing the British leader of being unable to free his thinking "from the roll of the drums and the flutter of the flag of Empire." Churchill's "fraternal association," they argued, would "cut the throat" of the United Nations. Mrs. Franklin D. Roosevelt publicly chided her late husband's wartime associate for implying that the English-speaking peoples could get along "without the far greater number of people who are not English-speaking." When Churchill made his next public address in New York on March 15, pickets appeared outside his hotel chanting "Winnie, Winnie, go away, UNO is here to stay!" and "Don't be a ninny for imperialist Winnie!" The State Department at the last minute advised Undersecretary of State Acheson to absent himself from the proceedings so that his presence would not imply official approval of what Churchill said.[45]

Most observers, however, still regarded the Fulton address as a public expression of what the Administration thought privately. Ernest K. Lindley pointed out that government officials, speaking strictly off-the-record, generally applauded Churchill's speech as something which badly needed to be said.[46] There is no reason to question the accuracy of this view. The criticism directed at the Administration's "magnificent trial balloon" did not weaken Truman's resolve to reorient American policy toward the Soviet Union. It simply indicated that while the American people were anxious to "get tough with Russia," they were not yet fully prepared to accept the responsibilities, in the form of closer ties with Britain and other noncommunist nations, which "getting tough" entailed.

If the oratorical efforts of Byrnes and Churchill left any doubt regarding the Administration's new attitude toward the Soviet Union, the manner in which it handled the Iranian crisis of March, 1946, quickly

---

[45] Taylor-Kilgore-Pepper press release, March 6, 1946, copy in the Theodore Francis Green MSS, Box 414, "Foreign Relations Legislation" file; *New York Times,* March 15, 1946; Acheson, *Sketches from Life,* p. 62. For reaction to the Fulton address, see also the *New York Times,* March 6 and 7, 1946; *Time,* XLVII (March 25, 1946), 19; *Newsweek,* XXVII (March 25, 1946), 28; and the Department of State, "Fortnightly Survey of American Opinion," No. 47, March 20, 1946.

[46] *Newsweek,* XXVII (March 10, 1946), 29–30, 36.

resolved them. Early in 1942, Great Britain and the Soviet Union had moved troops into Iran to keep that strategically located and oil-rich country from falling into the hands of the Axis. Both Allies agreed to respect the independence and territorial integrity of Iran and to withdraw their forces six months after the termination of hostilities, an understanding which they reaffirmed at Teheran in 1943, and again at the foreign ministers' conference in September, 1945. Reports reaching London and Washington during the final months of 1945, however, raised fears that the Russians might try to annex the province of Azerbaijan to the Soviet Union, with the intention of bringing all of Iran into Moscow's sphere of influence once the British had withdrawn. Attempts to elicit reassurance on this point from the Kremlin proved unavailing— Stalin told Byrnes at Moscow that if Soviet forces were pulled out Iranian saboteurs might try to blow up the Baku oil fields—and on January 19, 1946, the Iranian government with the tacit approval of the United States placed the question of Azerbaijan before the United Nations Security Council.[47]

At first, Byrnes rejected suggestions that the United States issue a public statement on the situation for fear this "might imply that we have already formed a fixed opinion with regard to the merits of the case." But when the March 2, 1946, deadline for withdrawing foreign troops from Iran passed without any Soviet moves to evacuate Azerbaijan, the Secretary of State adopted a tougher approach. On March 5, the same day Churchill spoke at Fulton, he dispatched a stiff note to Moscow calling for the immediate removal of Soviet forces from Iranian soil. The Secretary then took the unusual step of releasing the substance of this note to the press, without waiting for the Russian reply.[48]

The week which followed was an extremely tense one—*Newsweek* found the atmosphere reminiscent of the fall of 1938, when the Munich crisis was at its height. Early on the morning of March 6, 1946, the State Department received word from its vice-consul in Azerbaijan, Robert Rossow, Jr., that "exceptionally heavy Soviet troop movements" were taking place, not toward the Russian border, but in the direction of Tur-

[47] *FR: 1945,* VIII, 388–522; *FR: 1946,* VII, 289–304. See also the minutes of the Byrnes-Stalin conversation of December 19, 1945, *FR: 1945,* II, 685.

[48] Byrnes to Wallace Murray, January 28, 1946, *FR: 1946,* VII, 317; Byrnes to Molotov, March 5, 1946, *ibid.,* pp. 340–42; *New York Times,* March 6, 1946.

key, Iraq, and the Iranian capital, Teheran. Byrnes, upon hearing of these developments, exclaimed angrily that the Russians now seemed to be adding military invasion to their political subversion in Iran. A Foreign Service officer who showed Byrnes the alleged troop movements on a map recalls that the Secretary beat one fist into the other and announced: "Now we'll give it to them with both barrels." Noting that the Russians had not yet replied to the department's March 5 note, Byrnes and his advisers decided to dispatch a stronger telegram to Moscow asking the reason for these military maneuvers. When, by March 12, no answer had been received, the department released to the press news that Russian tanks were moving on Teheran. Apparently stung by the unwanted publicity, TASS, the Soviet news agency, three days later issued a statement denying these reports "absolutely." [49]

Throughout this period bilateral negotiations between the Russian and Iranian governments had been going on, first in Moscow, then in Teheran, in accordance with a Security Council resolution of January 30. Despite this, the Iranians, with the strong encouragement of the United States, insisted on submitting the issue of Soviet troop movements to the Council, which was due to meet again in New York on March 25. The Russians objected to this procedure, letting the Iranians know privately that they would regard such a move as an "unfriendly" act. On the day the Council met, however, TASS announced that the USSR had promised to pull all troops out of Azerbaijan within five or six weeks. Andrei Gromyko, Russian representative at the United Nations, requested that in view of this accord the Iranian matter be withdrawn from the Security Council agenda. Byrnes refused, arguing that the Iranians had not confirmed the Soviet agreement or made clear whether the Russians expected anything in return. On March 27, after the Council had voted to leave the matter on the agenda, Gromyko angrily and dramatically walked out of the chamber. One week later, however, the

[49] *Newsweek,* XXVII (March 25, 1946), 24; Rossow to Byrnes, March 5, 1946 (received in Washington on March 6), *FR: 1946,* VII, 340; memorandum by Edwin M. Wright, "Events Relative to the Azarbaijan Issue—March, 1946," August 16, 1965, *ibid.,* pp. 346–48; Byrnes to Molotov, March 8, 1946, *ibid.,* p. 348; *New York Times,* March 13, 1946; Kennan to Byrnes, March 15, 1946, *FR: 1946,* VII, 356. James Reston observed later in March that the department had almost certainly exaggerated the seriousness of these Russian troop movements. (*New York Times,* March 20, 1946.)

Soviet and Iranian governments announced a formal agreement calling for the withdrawal of Soviet troops by early May and recognizing Iranian sovereignty over Azerbaijan.[50]

Byrnes's decision to push the Iranian issue through the Security Council, even after the Russians had indicated their willingness to withdraw troops from Iran, stemmed chiefly from domestic considerations: the Secretary of State wanted to make clear to his critics at home that the United States had abandoned the politics of appeasement once and for all. Benjamin V. Cohen, Byrnes's close associate, explained the situation to Molotov at the Paris Foreign Ministers' Conference later in April:

> Mr. Cohen made the point that, whereas before a public event such as the retention of Soviet troops, beyond the treaty date, in Iran had occurred, it was possible to attempt privately to arrange matters in dispute, but that once a public event such as in this case had occurred, the issue had to be met in the light of public opinion, and it was impossible then to settle such things on the basis of any deal.

Byrnes himself told French Foreign Minister Georges Bidault that he "had been very much impressed with the way opinion had rallied behind the American position during the discussions of the Iranian question in the Security Council." Soviet popularity in the United States had been "completely dissipated" by Moscow's behavior. The Secretary of State acknowledged that recently he had been subjected to considerable criticism for yielding too much to the Russians. "This period, however, had passed and American opinion was no longer disposed to make concessions on important questions." [51]

V

The period of late February and early March, 1946, marked a decisive turning point in American policy toward the Soviet Union. Prior to this

[50] *FR: 1946*, VII, 322–415. The April 4 agreement granted the Russians 51 percent of the shares in a joint Iranian-Soviet oil company, but the Iranian parliament later refused to ratify this agreement. (Herbert Feis, *From Trust to Terror*, p. 85.)

[51] Bohlen notes, conversation between Byrnes, Cohen, and Molotov, April 28, 1946, *FR: 1946*, VII, 442; Bohlen notes, Byrnes-Bidault conversation, May 1, 1946, *ibid.*, II, 204.

time, Washington officials had frequently resisted Russian demands, but not on a consistent basis. As late as December, 1945, Byrnes was still operating on the assumption that Russia and the United States shared a common interest in settling outstanding difficulties. But by March of 1946, widespread criticism of "appeasement" had made it clear to the Truman Administration that further compromises with Moscow would mean political disaster at home. Simultaneously Soviet behavior, together with Kennan's persuasive analysis of it, convinced Washington officials that Stalin and his associates were ideological zealots who viewed conflict with the West as necessary to attain their objectives. Byrnes's Overseas Press Club speech, Churchill's Fulton address, and the State Department's firm handling of the Iranian crisis meant that American officials had gone as far as they could go in seeking a settlement with Moscow: negotiations would continue, but from now on all the concessions would have to come from the other side.[52]

Contemporary observers clearly saw the period as a pivotal one. A State Department survey of editorial opinion noted that the speeches of Vandenberg, Byrnes, and Churchill were widely regarded as constituting "a turning point in American policy toward Russia," and had produced a public reaction "of unprecedented magnitude." The *New Republic*'s "TRB," always a sensitive interpreter of the Washington mood, observed that judicious men within the government, whom no one could accuse of being Russophobes, now expected a major confrontation with Moscow. Foreign Service officer C. Burke Elbrick wrote privately to Arthur Bliss Lane, the American ambassador in Warsaw: "You will have noted a general toughening in the official attitude not only toward our Polish friends but, what is more important, toward the originator of many of our present difficulties and misunderstandings. We all hope that it will produce fruit." Elmer Davis told his radio audience that people who had been demanding a firmer policy toward Russia were now getting what they had asked for.[53]

[52] Assistant Secretary of State James C. Dunn wrote Byrnes in April that "the basic objectives of the Russians on the one hand and the British, French and ourselves on the other . . . are at present so divergent that the possibility of reaching agreement lies chiefly in the hope that the Russians may feel it essential to improve their relations with the British and ourselves and their world standing." (Dunn to Byrnes, April 18, 1946, *FR: 1946,* II, 72.)

[53] Department of State, "Fortnightly Survey of American Opinion," No. 47, March

The increasing popularity of Secretary of State Byrnes also indicated that a change in policy had taken place—as Byrnes moved toward a tougher position he regained much of the support he had lost through his earlier conciliatory approaches to Moscow. Admiral Leahy now denied recurring rumors that he had tried to have Byrnes fired, and assured the Secretary of State of his friendship. Averell Harriman told C. L. Sulzberger in April that Byrnes had increased in stature and was "a much stronger man now." James Reston and Arthur Krock noted that the Iranian crisis had greatly increased Byrnes's prestige; no one could now assert, Krock commented, that the Secretary of State was "a trader and a compromiser who will always take the easiest way out of a difficulty." Bernard Baruch, whom Truman had just named to represent the United States on the United Nations Atomic Energy Commission, congratulated Byrnes on his performance in the Security Council with an elaborately mixed biblical metaphor: "You proved yourself a David in meeting the Goliath of disintegration at the first UNO meeting. . . . Let us not fear the Philistines of whom Samson slew a thousand with the jawbone of an ass. There are bigger asses and bigger jawbones now than in those days." [54]

Another clear sign of the Administration's new policy was the alarm generated among the dwindling number of prominent Americans who still sympathized with the Russians. Joseph E. Davies wrote to Cordell Hull on March 17 that the past year's deterioration of Big Three unity had been nothing short of "tragic." Davies noted that since the Moscow Conference members of the Senate had been demanding that Byrnes take a firmer line, and that the Secretary of State had now yielded to this pressure. Senator Claude Pepper of Florida interpreted recent Russian actions as resulting not from expansive tendencies within the Soviet Union but from fear of a hostile Anglo-American coalition. Former Interior Secretary Harold Ickes publicly implied that the Truman Adminis-

20, 1946; *New Republic,* CXIV (March 18, 1946), 382; Elbrick to Lane, March 11, 1946, Lane MSS; Davis radio broadcast, March 5, 1946, Davis MSS, Box 13. See also *Newsweek,* XXVII (April 8 and 15, 1946), 16, 20.

[54] Leahy Diary, March 13, 18, 1946, Leahy MSS; Sulzberger Diary, April 22, 1946, quoted in Sulzberger, *A Long Row of Candles,* p. 311; *New York Times,* April 7, 1946; Baruch to Byrnes, March 31, 1946, Baruch MSS, "Selected Correspondence." See also *Newsweek,* XXVII (April 29, 1946), 16; and *U.S. News,* XX (May 3, 1946), 54.

tration had abandoned President Roosevelt's policy of cooperation with Russia. James Roosevelt, the late President's son, questioned whether Truman had made a real effort to represent the Kremlin's point of view to the American people. Secretary of Commerce Henry A. Wallace sent a letter to Truman on March 14 advocating a wholly new approach to the Russians, stressing the possibility of economic collaboration. Several days later Wallace proclaimed publicly that the United States and Great Britain could not "try to strut around the world and tell people where to get off." [55]

But an opinion poll taken in mid-March demonstrated with emphatic clarity that the American public was no longer prepared to accept the views of Wallace and other Russophiles: 71 percent of those polled disapproved of the policy the Soviet Union was following in world affairs; only 7 percent expressed approval. Sixty percent of the same sample thought the United States was being "too soft" in its relations with Moscow; only 3 percent felt Washington's approach was "too tough." [56] Truman and Byrnes could thus count on solid public support as they moved to implement their new policy of "patience with firmness"; whether Americans would willingly assume the costs of this policy over a long period of time remained, however, very much in doubt.

[55] Davies to Hull, March 17, 1946, Davies Journal, March 25, 1946, Davies MSS, Box 23; *New York Times,* March 21, 15, 19, 1946. Wallace's March 14 letter is printed in Truman, *Year of Decisions,* pp. 555–56.

[56] American Institute of Public Opinion poll of March 13, 1946, cited in Cantril and Strunk, eds., *Public Opinion,* pp. 963, 1060. The exact questions asked in this poll were: "In general, do you approve or disapprove of the policy Russia is following in world affairs?" Approve, 7 percent; disapprove, 71 percent; no opinion, 22 percent. "Do you think the United States is being too soft or too tough in its policy toward Russia?" Too soft, 60 percent; too tough, 3 percent; all right, 21 percent; no opinion, 16 percent.

10

To the Truman Doctrine:
Implementing the New Policy

By stressing the importance of internal influences on Soviet diplomacy, Kennan's "long telegram" of February 22, 1946, provided Washington officials with a convincing rationale for the "get tough with Russia" policy toward which they had already been moving. Further concessions to Moscow would be futile, Kennan argued; the Stalinist regime would always remain hostile because it depended upon the existence of foreign threats to maintain its domestic authority. "Nothing short of complete disarmament, delivery of our air and naval forces to Russia and resigning of powers of government to American Communists" would come close to alleviating Russian distrust, and even then the Kremlin would probably "smell a trap and would continue to harbor the most baleful misgivings." Suspicion, Kennan noted in March, "is an integral part of [the] Soviet system, and will not yield entirely to any form of rational persuasion or assurance." [1]

The Truman Administration's handling of the Iranian crisis showed its acceptance of Kennan's analysis: throughout the rest of 1946 the United States made no concessions of significance to the Soviet Union.

---

[1] Kennan to Byrnes, March 20, 1946, *FR: 1946,* VI, 723. For the "long telegram," see chapter 9.

In the Mediterranean, Washington employed a vigorous demonstration of gunboat diplomacy to turn back an apparent Soviet bid for the Dardanelles. In Germany, United States officials began moving toward tacit dismemberment rather than see that country unified under Moscow's control. At the United Nations, American diplomats decided that the risk of a nuclear arms race was preferable to the adoption of a less-than-foolproof scheme for the international control of atomic energy. At the seemingly interminable meetings of the Council of Foreign Ministers in Paris and New York, and at the larger but less important Paris Peace Conference, Byrnes, with Connally and Vandenberg at his side, stubbornly resisted Soviet demands. With the extension of a $3.75 billion loan to Great Britain, the Truman Administration committed itself to the principle of using American resources to rebuild Western Europe, not so much for the traditional objective of reviving world trade, though this goal remained important, but for the more urgent purpose of alleviating social and economic conditions which might breed communism.

But although most Americans supported the Administration's determination to take a firm stand, few seemed willing to make the sacrifices necessary to implement this policy. Pressure for instant demobilization continued, raising doubts as to whether the Pentagon could maintain the military strength necessary to back up a tougher diplomatic strategy. Popular demands for the abolition of wartime taxes and economic controls made it clear that the government would have difficulty in financing aid to nations threatened by communism. The hostile response to Churchill's Fulton address and the British loan revealed that a substantial number of Americans still indulged in old-fashioned Anglophobia, a luxury ill-suited to a nation seeking to rally the forces of the West against Soviet expansionism. "Getting tough with Russia" involved responsibilities as well as rhetoric, and government leaders could not hope to accomplish their objectives without educating the American people to that fact.

The Truman Doctrine, proclaimed in March, 1947, represented a deliberate effort by the Administration to do this. By portraying the Soviet-American conflict as a clash between two mutually irreconcilable ideologies, the President and his advisers managed to shock Congress and the public into providing the support necessary to implement a tough policy. But in the process they trapped themselves in a new cycle of rhetoric and response which in years to come would significantly restrict the Administration's flexibility in dealing with Moscow.

I

After the events of February and March, 1946, it became increasingly difficult for American officials to continue viewing Soviet behavior solely in terms of a search for security. Kennan's emphasis on the ideological determinants of Kremlin policy, together with Stalin's February 9 speech and Russian belligerence in Iran, strongly reinforced the judgment of those who believed that Moscow sought to impose communism on as much of the world as possible. Those who had not previously held this view now began to find it more and more persuasive. Simultaneously, successful resolution of the Iranian crisis convinced virtually all Washington policy-makers that Byrnes's policy of "patience with firmness" offered the only sure means of countering the Soviet challenge without resort to war.

Members of the military establishment found Kennan's analysis especially persuasive. "We are dealing not only with Russia as a national entity," Forrestal told Winston Churchill on March 10, "but with the expanding power of Russia under Peter the Great plus the additional missionary force of a religion." In April, the Navy Secretary warned that "the Commies are working their heads off in France, the Balkans, Japan and anywhere else where they happen to have access." General Lucius D. Clay, military governor of the United States zone in Germany, admitted to Forrestal that Stalin's February speech had caused him to reassess his previous opinion that the Russians did not want a war. Lieutenant General John R. Hodge, commander of American forces in Korea, wrote Secretary of War Robert Patterson in November that "there can be no question but as to the world-wide push of Communism with the main all-out effort now directed against the United States." Patterson himself observed in the summer of 1947 that he had once thought the Russians had abandoned the idea of an inevitable struggle between capitalism and communism, "but apparently it is still part of the creed." [2]

[2] Forrestal Diary, March 10 and July 16, 1946, Millis, ed., *The Forrestal Diaries,* pp. 144, 182; Forrestal to Clarence Dillon, April 11, 1946, *ibid.,* p. 153; Hodge to

American diplomats in the Soviet Union expressed similar views. Late in May, 1946, General Walter Bedell Smith, the new United States ambassador in Moscow, quoted with apparent approval a British Foreign Office analysis of Russian intentions which asserted that the Kremlin had set no limits to its objectives in Europe. Elbridge Durbrow, Kennan's replacement as chargé d'affaires in Moscow, reported in the fall of 1946 that the Russians were trying to accomplish what they had been unable to achieve after World War I: "namely, [to] extend their control and introduce their type of Marxian political and economic system as far as possible" while the Red Army was occupying Eastern Europe and the Balkans. "In [the] event of another world war, which according to their continually emphasized Marxian theory is inevitable, they hope to be strong enough to extend their system yet further." John Paton Davies, first secretary of the Moscow Embassy, wrote Ambassador Smith in November that "the political philosophy of the men who rule Russia, despite its confusing tactical flexibility, is as intolerant and dogmatic as that which motivated the zealots of Islam or the Inquisition in Spain." [3]

Members of the press quickly sensed the increasing emphasis policymakers were placing on ideology. Joseph and Stewart Alsop reported as early as February 28, 1946, that Washington now feared Soviet commitment "to a policy of unlimited expansion." In March, C. L. Sulzberger noted a consensus among diplomatic observers that most Kremlin officials now believed in the incompatibility of communism and capitalism, though some thought Stalin himself had not yet firmly embraced this doctrine. James Reston observed in May that, in the view of Washington officials, the Soviet Union was "using its economic, political and military power to support Communist elements all over Europe." By September, *Newsweek* was reporting flatly: "U.S. officials in the best position to judge fear they have confirmation that the Soviet Government has

---

Patterson, November 5, 1946, Patterson MSS, Box 20; Patterson to Palmer Hoyt, June 23, 1947, *ibid.* Other expressions of concern over the ideological orientation of Soviet foreign policy can be found in a memorandum by Vice-Admiral Forrest P. Sherman, March 17, 1946, Forrestal MSS, Box 17; Forrestal's speech to the Pittsburgh Foreign Policy Association, April 29, 1946, quoted in Millis, ed., *The Forrestal Diaries,* p. 155; and the Leahy Diary, May 7, 1946, Leahy MSS.

[3] Smith to Byrnes, May 31, 1946, *FR: 1946,* VI, 758; Durbrow to Byrnes, October 31, 1946, *ibid.,* p. 797; Davies to Smith, November 18, 1946, *ibid.,* p. 806.

made up its mind that capitalism must be destroyed if Communism is to live." [4]

Perhaps the most influential unofficial analysis of how communism influenced Soviet foreign policy came from John Foster Dulles, still the Republican Party's chief spokesman on international affairs. After brooding over the matter for some time, Dulles, by the spring of 1946, had become convinced that ideological influences governed Russian behavior. Accepting an invitation from Henry Luce to use *Life* magazine as a forum for his views, Dulles wrote a widely quoted article that argued:

The foreign policy of the Soviet Union is world wide in scope. Its goal is to have governments everywhere which accept the basic doctrine of the Soviet Communist Party and which suppress political and religious thinking which runs counter to these doctrines. Thereby the Soviet Union would achieve world-wide harmony—a *Pax Sovietica.*

In Dulles' view, Stalin's *Problems of Leninism* was to communism what Hitler's *Mein Kampf* had been to fascism: a program for unlimited expansion which world statesmen could ignore only at their peril. Dulles accepted the Soviet threat optimistically, agreeing with Arnold Toynbee that without periodic challenges, civilizations decayed and passed away. Strong military power, together with an effective demonstration of American ideals in action, would, he felt, wean the world's uncommitted peoples away from the appeal of communism. Dulles' argument received wide attention and a generally favorable response.[5]

The growing tendency to view Moscow's actions as motivated chiefly by ideology soon had its effect on the public at large. Wartime opinion polls had indicated that most Americans, particularly those well in-

---

[4] *Washington Post,* March 1, 1946; *New York Times,* March 24 and May 6, 1946; *Newsweek,* XXVIII (September 9, 1946), 27.

[5] Louis L. Gerson, *John Foster Dulles,* pp. 44–51; John Foster Dulles, "Thoughts on Soviet Foreign Policy and What to Do about It," *Life,* XX (June 3 and 10, 1946), 113–26, 118–30; Dulles to Joseph Barnes, January 31, 1947, Dulles MSS. See also Dulles' speech prepared for delivery at the College of the City of New York, June 19, 1946, *Vital Speeches,* XII (July 15, 1946), 593–95; *New York Times,* September 9, 1946; and Dulles to James P. Warburg, September 16, 1946, Dulles MSS. Luce in 1965 described his relationship with Dulles as follows: "I would say that between 1944 and 1953, when he became Secretary of State, my main connection with him was as an editor with a very special writer. We chose him to express. . . . Well, I won't put it quite that way. He had ideas that he wanted to give expression to, and they very much coincided with the general ideas that we had here." (Interview with Luce, July 28, 1965, Dulles Oral History Project.)

formed about Russia, regarded security from future attack as the main goal of Stalin's foreign policy. A *Fortune* poll taken as late as September, 1945, revealed that only 25 percent of the sample expected the Russians to try to spread communism into Eastern Europe. A similar survey made in July, 1946, however, showed that more than half of those polled now believed that the Kremlin wanted to dominate as much of the world as possible. Subsequent polls consistently demonstrated that approximately two out of three Americans held this view. Unlike the wartime situation, levels of information about Russia seemed to make no difference in determining attitudes on this point: most Americans now viewed the Soviet Union as a dictatorship irrevocably committed to the forcible imposition of communism wherever it did not already exist.[6]

In the summer of 1946, President Truman directed his special counsel, Clark M. Clifford, to compile a comprehensive report on American relations with the Soviet Union. The resulting hundred-thousand-word document, prepared after consultations with the Secretaries of State, War, and Navy, the Joint Chiefs of Staff, the Attorney General, the Director of Central Intelligence, and other top Administration officials, drew heavily on Kennan's analysis by stressing the influence of ideology on Russian diplomacy: "The key to an understanding of current Soviet foreign policy . . . is the realization that Soviet leaders adhere to the Marxian theory of ultimate destruction of capitalist states by communist states." Kremlin leaders did not want an immediate confrontation with the West, but they apparently did regard an eventual war with the United States and other capitalist countries as inevitable:

They are increasing their military power and the sphere of Soviet influence in preparation for the "inevitable" conflict, and they are trying to weaken and subvert their potential opponents by every means at their disposal. So long as these men adhere to these beliefs, it is highly dangerous to conclude that hope of international peace lies only in "accord," "mutual understanding," or "solidarity" with the Soviet Union.

Concessions to the Russians would only have the effect "of raising Soviet hopes and increasing Soviet demands." If Moscow refused to cooperate with the United States, "we should be prepared to join with the British

[6] Almond, *The American People and Foreign Policy,* pp. 94–95; M. Brewster Smith, "The Personal Setting of Public Opinions: A Study of Attitudes Toward Russia," *Public Opinion Quarterly,* XI (Winter, 1947–48), 514–15. For wartime attitudes on the relationship of ideology to Soviet foreign policy, see chapter 2.

and other Western countries in an attempt to build up a world of our own . . . recogniz[ing] the Soviet orbit as a distinct entity with which conflict is not predestined but with which we cannot pursue common aims."

Americans would have to face the fact, the memorandum continued, that Stalin might at any time provoke war in order to expand the territory under communist control or to weaken potential capitalist opponents. Washington should be prepared "to resist vigorously and successfully any efforts of the U.S.S.R. to expand into areas vital to American security." Only through maintenance of a strong military establishment could this be done:

The language of military power is the only language which disciples of power politics understand. The United States must use that language in order that Soviet leaders will realize that our government is determined to uphold the interests of its citizens and the rights of small nations. Compromise and concessions are considered, by the Soviets, to be evidences of weakness and they are encouraged by our "retreats" to make new and greater demands.

If necessary, the United States should even be prepared "to wage atomic and biological warfare." The Clifford report concluded that the objective of American policy should be to convince leaders of the Soviet Union that war between communism and capitalism was not inevitable: "It is our hope that they will change their minds and work out with us a fair and equitable settlement when they realize that we are too strong to be beaten and too determined to be frightened." [7]

Ironically, Kennan himself did not believe that the Soviet Union sought world revolution. In his view, Marxist-Leninist ideology was simply a crude means of justifying a repressive regime, not a blueprint for unlimited expansion. A Soviet invasion of Western Europe seemed highly unlikely to Kennan; indeed, he felt that the Russians would have difficulty in retaining control of their East European satellites. In October, 1946, he wrote:

I think it is a mistake to say that the Soviet leaders wish to establish a *Communist* form of government in the ring of states surrounding the Soviet

[7] "American Relations with the Soviet Union," a report prepared by Clark M. Clifford and submitted to Truman on September 24, 1946, printed in Arthur Krock, *Memoirs: Sixty Years on the Firing Line,* Appendix A, pp. 431, 476–78, 482. Clifford's assistant, George M. Elsey, actually drafted most of the report. (Elsey memorandum on "L'Affaire Wallace," September 17, 1946, Elsey MSS, Box 105.)

Union on the west and south. What they do wish to do is to establish in those states governments *amenable to their own influence and authority.* The main thing is that these governments should follow Moscow's leadership. . . . In certain countries which are already extensively under Soviet influence, as for example Poland, there has been as yet no effort to establish what we might call a Communist form of government. There have indeed been efforts—and very important and successful ones—to carry out in those countries social and economic reforms designed to ease the maintenance there of permanent communist-inspired dictatorships. But this is not a Communist form of government. It should always be borne in mind that for the Communist leaders, power is the main thing. Form is a secondary consideration.

Kennan did not, however, make this distinction clear in his "long telegram" of February, 1946, or in a highly publicized elaboration of that dispatch, the famous "X" article which appeared in *Foreign Affairs* in July, 1947.[8] His lack of clarity had the effect, therefore, of confirming the growing suspicion in Washington that Stalin, like Hitler, would not stop until he dominated the entire world.

II

The Administration's new policy of "patience with firmness," described in the Clifford memorandum, manifested itself clearly in relations with the Soviet Union during the rest of 1946. Secretary of State Byrnes exhibited ample reserves of both qualities during the long series of international conferences held throughout the summer and fall to write peace treaties for Italy, Hungary, Bulgaria, Rumania, and Finland. The Council of Foreign Ministers met in two sessions in Páris from April through July to draft the treaties. From July to October, representatives from all of the World War II allies gathered in the French capital to consider the drafts which the Big Four had agreed upon. Following this, the foreign ministers met again in New York in November to put the treaties in final form, a process completed early in December. Throughout the lengthy wrangle over the "minor" peace treaties, Byrnes adhered tena-

---

[8] Kennan, *Memoirs,* pp. 247–51; Kennan to Admiral Harry Hill, October 7, 1946, copy in Forrestal MSS, Box 70; Mr. "X," "The Sources of Soviet Conduct," *Foreign Affairs,* XXV (July, 1947), 566–82. For an account of the circumstances surrounding publication of the "X" article, see Kennan, *Memoirs,* pp. 354–67.

ciously to the American position, forcing the Russians to make most of the concessions.[9]

The Secretary of State carefully sought bipartisan support at every stage of this process. Taking literally Senator Vandenberg's desire to be in on the "takeoffs" of American foreign policy as well as the "crash landings," Byrnes saw to it that he and Senator Connally were included in the American delegation to each of these conferences. This took the senators out of the country in a year when both faced reelection, but Connally had no significant opposition in Texas, and the Administration offered no encouragement to Vandenberg's weak Democratic opponent in Michigan. Vandenberg and Connally soon became bored with the proceedings since every speech had to be repeated in several different languages—Byrnes observed with amusement that both senators became experts at drawing "futuristic" doodles during these periods—but their presence was important to the Secretary of State in securing domestic backing for his policies. The two senators strongly reinforced Byrnes's determination to make no further compromises with the Russians. Byrnes also saw to it that his policy of toughness with Russia attracted wide attention. Beginning with the Iranian discussions in March, the Secretary of State kept correspondents informed on an off-the-record basis of the American position on all pending issues. He also continued to report frequently and at length to the American people by radio on his diplomatic activities, making no effort to conceal disagreements with Moscow.[10]

[9] The Council of Foreign Ministers' meetings in Paris and New York are covered in *FR: 1946*, Vol. II, *passim*. For the Paris Peace Conference, see *ibid.*, Vols. III, IV, *passim;* and Harold Nicolson's literate assessment, "Peacemaking at Paris: Success, Failure or Farce?" *Foreign Affairs*, XXV (January, 1947), 190–203. These negotiations are conveniently summarized in Curry, *Byrnes,* chapters 7–9. Byrnes did agree to two concessions on the Italian peace treaty: the Russians would be allowed to take $100 million in reparations from Italy, and Trieste would be placed under United Nations rather than Italian control. These arrangements in no way diminished Anglo-American predominance in Italy, however, and gave the Russians substantially less than what they had originally demanded. On this point, see Feis, *From Trust to Terror,* pp. 121–25.

[10] Vandenberg, ed., *Private Papers,* pp. 230, 309; Byrnes, *Speaking Frankly,* pp. 151, 236, 250–51. See also Westerfield, *Foreign Policy and Party Politics,* pp. 213–14; and Byrnes's radio addresses of May 20, July 15, and October 19, 1946, *Department of State Bulletin,* XIV (June 2, 1946), 950–54, XV (July 28 and October 27, 1946), 167–72, 739–43.

But the tedious deliberations in Paris and New York were largely a sideshow: the important developments in Soviet-American relations during the remainder of 1946 took place in Germany, where efforts to implement the Potsdam Agreement had broken down; in the United Nations, where the American plan for the international control of atomic energy was under discussion; and in the Near East, where the Russians seemed to be launching a new expansionist campaign. The principle of "patience with firmness" governed the Administration's handling of each of these situations.

Washington's position on the postwar treatment of Germany had become clear by the time of the Potsdam Conference in July, 1945: the United States would support the demilitarization, denazification, and deindustrialization of the former Reich, but not to the point of causing an economic collapse which might impair prospects for European recovery and impose a heavy relief burden on American taxpayers. For this reason, Byrnes had adamantly opposed Soviet demands for a fixed amount of reparations, arguing that removals should be limited to whatever percentage of German resources was not needed to maintain a minimal standard of living. A compromise arrangement had finally been worked out whereby the Russians agreed to satisfy their reparations requirements by removals from their own zone, plus 10 percent of whatever capital equipment from other zones was "unnecessary for the German peace economy." In addition, the Soviet Union would get another 15 percent of such material from the West in return for an equivalent value of food, coal, or other commodities from the Russian zone. The four-power Allied Control Council, working under principles established by the Allied Reparations Commission, would decide how much capital equipment could be spared from the Western zones for reparations shipments, both to the Soviet Union and to other claimants, subject to the final approval of the zonal commander from whose territory the material was taken.[11]

American diplomats did not regard this agreement as sanctioning the dismemberment of Germany. The Potsdam protocol explicitly provided that, as long as the occupation lasted, that country would be treated as an economic unit. No German government would be formed for the pres-

[11] Potsdam Conference protocol, August 1, 1945, *FR: Potsdam*, II, 1481–87. For background on the Potsdam Agreement, see chapter 7.

ent, but "certain essential central German administrative departments" would be established to handle finance, transportation, communications, foreign trade, and industry on a nationwide basis. In addition, Washington officials interpreted the agreement to mean that the occupying powers would have to work out a uniform formula for reparations removals from all zones; otherwise, as Reparations Commissioner Pauley noted, discrepancies from zone to zone would create wide differences in standards of living, thus violating the principle of economic unity. State Department experts realized that in practice it might be easier to administer the three Western zones as a unit than to agree on common policies with the Russians, but they felt that the effort to achieve four-power control should at least be made.[12]

As it turned out, however, the chief opposition to treating Germany as an economic unit came not from the Russians but from the French. France's role in the occupation of Germany was anomalous: French representatives had taken no part in the Potsdam deliberations, but at Yalta five months earlier the Big Three had agreed to give France an occupation zone and a seat on the Allied Control Council. This placed the Paris government in a position to veto implementation of whatever parts of the Potsdam protocol it did not like. General de Gaulle, reflecting French fears of a resurgent Germany, very strongly disliked the agreement's emphasis on economic unity and called for detachment of the Rhineland and the Ruhr. If the Allies opposed him, de Gaulle let it be known, France would have to protect itself by vetoing restoration of the centralized German administrative agencies provided for in the Potsdam accord. "It is a matter of life and death for us," he told American Ambassador Jefferson Caffery; "for you, one interesting question among many others." [13]

Throughout the last half of 1945, American officials regarded France

[12] *FR: Potsdam,* II, 1483–84; Pauley to Clay, August 11, 1945, *FR: 1945,* III, 1251–53; Clayton and Collado to Willard Thorp, August 16, 1945, *FR: Potsdam,* II, 938–40.

[13] Caffery to Byrnes, November 3, 1945, *FR: 1945,* III, 890–91. See also *ibid.,* pp. 842–45, 869–71, 878; Eisenhower to Marshall, October 13, 1945, Eisenhower MSS, 1916–52, Box 73; Clay, *Decision in Germany,* p. 39; Murphy, *Diplomat among Warriors,* p. 287; and McNeill, *America, Britain, and Russia,* p. 627. John Gimbel, *The American Occupation of Germany: Politics and the Military, 1945–1949,* chapters 1–4, strongly emphasizes the importance of the French attitude.

as the major obstacle to a settlement of the German question, but by the end of February, 1946, growing concern over Russian intentions forced them to view the problem in broader terms. Robert Murphy, General Clay's political adviser in Germany, warned on February 24 that the Soviet Union might be using the delay in implementing the Potsdam Agreement to solidify its position in eastern Germany, with the idea of later calling for a unified Reich under Russian auspices. Continued French recalcitrance could well play into Moscow's hands. Murphy thought it odd that the German Communist Party was opposing internationalization of the Ruhr while French Communists were supporting it, and raised the possibility that both groups might be following orders from Moscow. Centralized German economic agencies would have at least partially broken down zonal boundaries, he pointed out, making it difficult for the Russians to continue running their zone on a unilateral basis. If the French continued to resist economic unification, Murphy suggested, Washington should consider temporarily withholding cooperation in other fields until a more favorable attitude developed.[14]

Murphy's analysis arrived in Washington three days after Kennan's "long telegram," just as United States officials were undertaking their fundamental reevaluation of policy toward the Soviet Union. H. Freeman Matthews, director of the State Department's Office of European Affairs, forwarded Murphy's dispatch to Byrnes, noting that it added to the economic reasons for establishing central German administrative agencies "a compelling political reason for overcoming French obstruction, viz., that the Soviet Government and the German Communist Party are making effective capital out of the present impasse by becoming the champions of German unity." The department also sent Murphy's message to Kennan in Moscow, asking for his observations.[15]

Kennan agreed that the Russians welcomed French resistance to central German agencies. There could be no doubt, he asserted, that Maurice Thorez, leader of the French Communist Party, was acting "as [a] Moscow stooge." But Kennan warned that German economic unity

[14] Murphy to Byrnes, February 24, 1946, *FR: 1946*, V, 505–7. See also Patterson to Byrnes, February 25, 1946, summarized in Byrnes to Murphy, March 12, 1946, *ibid.*, pp. 524–25; Murphy to Forrestal, March 18, 1946, Forrestal MSS, Box 101; and Murphy to Byrnes, March 19, 1946, *FR: 1946*, V, 527–28.

[15] Matthews to Byrnes, February 28, 1946, *FR: 1946*, V, 508; Byrnes to Kennan, February 27, 1946, cited *ibid.*, p. 516*n*.

would not necessarily weaken the Soviet position: the Russians would agree to central agencies only if they thought they could control them, and this could lead to the eventual communization of the entire country. The real problem in Germany, Kennan contended, was the economic chaos wrought by the Russians' amputation of territory east of the Oder-Neisse line. When the Americans and British agreed to this at Potsdam, they destroyed whatever possibility existed for a unified and sovereign Germany "fitted constructively into [the] pattern of western European life." Under the circumstances, there were only two alternatives:

(1) to leave [the] remainder of Germany nominally united but extensively vulnerable to Soviet political penetration and influence or (2) to carry to its logical conclusion the process of partition which was begun in the east and to endeavor to rescue [the] western zones of Germany by walling them off against eastern penetration and integrating them into [the] international pattern of western Europe rather than into a united Germany.[16]

Kennan's analysis pinpointed the delicate and perplexing situation confronting American officials in Germany early in 1946. French opposition to German economic unity threatened not only to make the division of that country permanent but to place upon the United States the burden of supporting the food-deficient Western zones. But centralized German agencies, as Kennan pointed out, could fall under Russian control, giving Moscow an opportunity to dominate all Germany. Compared to this, a permanently divided Reich seemed the lesser of two evils. The United States could hardly commit itself to either centralization or dismemberment until Stalin's goals became clearer. But Washington did launch a series of diplomatic initiatives in the spring of 1946 designed to smoke out Russian intentions in Germany, while leaving open the possibility of moving in either direction.

On April 29, 1946, Byrnes proposed to the Council of Foreign Ministers, meeting in Paris, a four-power treaty guaranteeing the disarmament of Germany for the next twenty-five years. Senator Vandenberg had originally suggested such a pact in January, 1945, as a means of convincing the Russians that they did not have to take over Eastern Europe in order to gain security from future attack. Administration officials had

[16] Kennan to Byrnes, March 6, 1946, *FR: 1946*, V, 516–20. See also Kennan to Carmel Offie, May 10, 1946, *ibid.*, pp. 555–56.

considered the idea off and on during the summer of 1945, and Byrnes had casually mentioned it to the Russians at both London and Moscow. The Secretary of State decided to push the four-power accord at Paris as a test of Soviet objectives in Germany. He explained to Molotov that "frankly, there were many people in the United States who were unable to understand the exact aim of the Soviet Union—whether it was a search for security or expansionism. Such a treaty as had been proposed and also the similar treaty suggested for Japan he had felt would effectively take care of the question of security." Vandenberg, who was attending the Paris Conference as a member of the American delegation, put the matter more bluntly in his diary: "If and when Molotov finally refuses this offer, he will confess that he wants *expansion* and not 'security.' . . . Then moral conscience all around the globe can face and assess the realities—and prepare for the consequences." [17]

Four days after Byrnes made his proposal in Paris, General Clay announced the suspension of further reparations shipments from the American zone until the four occupying powers agreed to treat Germany as an economic unit. This action was aimed in part at the French, whose stubborn resistance to central German agencies had delayed economic unification. But American officials now viewed their difficulties with France in the larger context of deteriorating relations with the Soviet Union: Stalin, they felt, had been surreptitiously supporting the French stand all along because it allowed him to remain committed to the principle of a unified Germany while operating his zone on a unilateral basis. These suspicions seemed confirmed early in April when Soviet representatives on the Allied Control Council had proclaimed their unwillingness to implement a common import-export program for all of Ger-

[17] Bohlen memorandum, Byrnes-Molotov conversation, April 28, 1946, *FR: 1946*, II, 146–47; Vandenberg Diary, April 29, 1946, Vandenberg, ed., *Private Papers*, p. 268. For background on the four-power treaty, see Vandenberg's speech in the *Congressional Record*, January 10, 1945, pp. 164–67; Grenville Clark to Truman, June 2, 1945, copy in Hopkins MSS, Box 331; *FR: Potsdam*, I, 162–63, 450–52; *FR: 1945*, II, 267–68, III, 527–31; Byrnes, *Speaking Frankly*, pp. 171–76. The text of the proposed treaty is in *FR: 1946*, II, 190–93. An unidentified member of the American delegation at Paris—possibly Vandenberg—explained the strategy behind Byrnes's proposal as follows: "If they [the Russians] are sincere in their intentions toward the rest of the world, they must sign. If they are not and refuse to sign, it will make them appear an outlaw nation before the eyes of the world." (*New York Times*, April 30, 1946.)

many until reparations deliveries had been completed. Clay's order to halt removals from the American zone would, as Undersecretary of State Acheson explained, "put Soviet protestations of loyalty to Potsdam to [the] final test and fix blame for [the] breach of Potsdam on [the] Soviets in case they fail to meet this test." [18]

Moscow's response to these initiatives did nothing to relieve American suspicions. After a delay of two months, Molotov on July 9 rejected Byrnes's proposed treaty on the grounds that demilitarization could not be guaranteed until all reparations deliveries had been completed. The Soviet foreign minister then revived the original Russian demand for a fixed sum of $10 billion, to which, he claimed, Roosevelt had agreed at Yalta, and vigorously condemned the "unlawful" action of General Clay in halting removals from the American zone. On the following day Molotov came out against detachment of the Ruhr from Germany, blandly disclaiming any Russian intention to stand in the way of the "rightful aspirations" of the German people or to wreck their economy. American officials regarded this contradictory series of statements as a blatant attempt to extract maximum reparations while at the same time posing as a defender of German economic unity. Byrnes now became convinced that the Russians would never allow implementation of the Potsdam accords, and from this time on moved toward the concept of a divided Germany as the only alternative to a Russian-dominated Reich.[19]

After careful consultation with the President, congressional leaders, and military and diplomatic advisers, the Secretary of State announced a

[18] Acheson to Byrnes, May 9, 1946, *FR: 1946*, V, 549. For background on Clay's decision, see Murphy to Byrnes, April 4, 10, and May 6, 1946, *ibid.*, pp. 547–48. Clay's order terminating reparations shipments has been the source of some confusion. Clay himself, writing in retrospect, pictured it as a move designed to force the Russians to comply with the Potsdam Agreement (*Decision in Germany*, pp. 120–25), an interpretation subsequently stressed by William H. McNeill (*America, Britain, and Russia*, p. 726). John Gimbel, on the basis of American military government records, argues that Clay's decision at the time was directed primarily at the French, and came to be viewed as an anti-Russian move only after the Cold War had developed. (*The American Occupation of Germany*, pp. 56–61.) Department of State records unavailable when Gimbel was writing his book make it clear, however, that American officials at that time saw the move primarily as a means of testing Russian commitment to the principle of German economic unity, and that they viewed difficulties with France in the light of the emerging Soviet-American confrontation. (*FR: 1946*, V, 549–56.)

[19] Molotov statements of July 9 and 10, 1946, *FR: 1946*, II, 842–47, 869–73. See also Byrnes, *Speaking Frankly*, pp. 179–81.

new United States policy on Germany in a speech delivered at Stuttgart on September 6, 1946. Byrnes reiterated American support for the principle of economic unity, but added this significant qualification: "If complete unification cannot be secured, we shall do everything in our power to secure maximum possible unification." Repeating an offer made at the Paris Foreign Ministers' Conference in July, Byrnes expressed willingness to merge the American zone economically with any or all other zones. He also endorsed movement toward political unification by calling for establishment of a German provisional government. The Secretary of State made it clear, however, that Washington would not tolerate a unified Germany under Soviet control: "We do not want Germany to become the satellite of any power." Hence, "as long as there is an occupation army in Germany, American armed forces will be part of that occupation army." [20]

Byrnes's Stuttgart speech represented an important reversal of the American position on Germany. Since the early days of World War II, State Department planners had fought tenaciously for the principle of economic unity, defending it successfully against Morgenthau and other advocates of vengeance. But the reorientation of policy toward Russia early in 1946 threw new light on the German question: American diplomats gradually came to realize that unification could pose serious dangers if it brought about an expansion of Soviet power. Since the Russians had made it clear that they would permit a consolidation of zones only on their terms, Washington officials decided to accept the division of Germany as the least distasteful of several unpalatable alternatives. Byrnes had called the Russians' bluff in Germany, Truman explained to Joseph Davies several days after the Stuttgart address; now "Britain and the United States would have to go along without them." [21]

The President and his advisers also had to confront unpalatable alternatives in dealing with atomic energy. Policy-makers in this field hoped to devise a scientifically sound method for detecting clandestine rearmament which would be flexible enough to overcome Soviet suspicions, yet sufficiently rigorous to ward off congressional criticism. The task proved to be an impossible one. As distrust of Russia grew during 1946, the Ad-

[20] *Department of State Bulletin,* XV (September 15, 1946), 496–501.
[21] Davies memorandum of conversation with Truman, September 10, 1946, Davies MSS, Box 24.

ministration began to shape its policy, not according to what the Russians might accept, but in terms of what Congress would not condemn. Just as Washington had come to favor a divided Germany to the prospect of a unified Reich under Soviet control, so it came to prefer the risk of a nuclear arms race to the possibility that an imperfect control system might endanger American security.

Early in January, 1946, Secretary of State Byrnes had appointed a committee headed by Undersecretary of State Acheson to draw up specific proposals on international control which the United States could place before the United Nations Atomic Energy Commission. Acheson's group in turn recruited a board of consultants under the direction of David E. Lilienthal, chairman of the Tennessee Valley Authority, to sift workable recommendations from the masses of technical data available. The consultants' task, Lilienthal wrote in his journal, was "to develop a position, based on facts not now known by our political officers, that will 'work,' and have a good chance of being accepted, especially by Russia." [22]

The Acheson-Lilienthal report recommended establishment under the United Nations of an international "Atomic Development Authority" which would, after a worldwide survey of raw materials, assume control of all highly concentrated uranium and thorium deposits. The authority would make its resources available for peaceful purposes only. Any unapproved use of fissionable materials by a particular nation would be regarded as a danger signal, giving other countries sufficient time to prepare themselves for possible attack. Under the plan the United States reserved for itself the decision as to when or whether to stop manufacturing atomic bombs of its own. Byrnes submitted the report to President Truman on March 21, 1946, and, after a series of inadvertent leaks, formally released it to the public on March 28.[23]

In an effort to make the Acheson-Lilienthal recommendations more palatable to a skeptical Congress, Truman and Byrnes decided to entrust Bernard M. Baruch with the task of presenting the American proposal to the United Nations. Baruch, then seventy-six, was a native of South

[22] Hewlett and Anderson, *The New World*, pp. 531–34; Lilienthal Journal, January 24, 1946, *Lilienthal Journals*, II, 14.

[23] Hewlett and Anderson, *The New World*, pp. 540–58; Acheson, *Present at the Creation*, pp. 151–54.

Carolina who by the age of thirty had made himself a millionaire through cagey stock market investments. After serving as chairman of the War Industries Board in World War I, he devoted much of his energy to financing favorite politicians, an activity which understandably made him popular in Congress, and to nurturing carefully his public image as a park-bench philosopher and adviser to presidents. David Lilienthal described him in 1944 as "a shrewd, smart, and experienced old boy. . . . He likes to have his finger in all the pies, working by remote control, so that if things go wrong he doesn't have to take the responsibility. And about the vainest old man I have ever seen." Baruch's appointment astonished and disappointed the technical experts who had helped prepare the Acheson-Lilienthal report, but Truman and Byrnes clearly expected the septuagenarian's great prestige to enhance the plan's political acceptability.[24]

Baruch surprised Administration officials, however, by demanding the right to make changes in the Acheson-Lilienthal proposal before presenting it to the United Nations. The report was "pretty close" to government policy, he complained to Truman on March 26, yet he had had no hand in formulating it. When reporters outside the White House questioned him on the document, Baruch ostentatiously turned off his hearing aid. Both Truman and Byrnes went out of their way to assure him that the Acheson-Lilienthal recommendation was not the final United States position, and that Baruch and his own staff would have opportunities to make their views known. Baruch chose as his advisers not the scientists who had helped to prepare the report but a group of Wall Street bankers who knew little of the intricacies of atomic energy.[25]

Since the proposed international control agency would derive its authority from the Security Council, Baruch feared that any permanent member of the Council could veto its action. Therefore, he felt, use of the veto should be prohibited when the Security Council was considering

[24] "Bernard M. Baruch," *Current Biography, 1950,* pp. 14–17; Lilienthal Journal, February 13, 1944, *Lilienthal Journals,* I, 625. For the reaction to Baruch's appointment, see *ibid.,* II, 30; and Acheson, *Present at the Creation,* p. 154.

[25] Baruch to Truman, March 26, 1946, printed in Truman, *Years of Trial and Hope,* pp. 8–9; Byrnes to Baruch, April 19, 1946, *ibid.,* pp. 9–10; Hewlett and Anderson, *The New World,* pp. 556–58. Truman charged in his memoirs that Baruch's main concern was to see that he received sufficient public recognition.

atomic energy matters. Defenders of the Acheson-Lilienthal report replied that this suggestion could only lessen the chances of Soviet acceptance, while contributing nothing to American security. Any nation which tried to veto Security Council action in this field, they argued, would automatically be presumed guilty of secretly building atomic bombs. By threatening to resign, however, Baruch forced Truman and Byrnes to accept his point of view. Having employed Baruch in order to take advantage of his personal prestige, the Administration felt it could not dismiss him without undermining the credibility of the whole "get tough with Russia" campaign. Baruch's appointment was "the worst mistake I have ever made," Byrnes confided to Acheson, "but we can't fire him now, not with all the other trouble." [26]

On June 14, 1946, Baruch presented the American proposal on international control to the United Nations in characteristically apocalyptic language ("We are here to make a choice between the quick and the dead"). The plan followed the main outlines of the Acheson-Lilienthal report except for Baruch's insistence on exempting the Atomic Development Authority from the Security Council veto. The Russian delegate, Andrei Gromyko, immediately attacked Baruch's proposal as an attempt to undermine big-power unity in the Security Council, and suggested instead the immediate destruction of all atomic weapons. The United States rejected the Russian plan because of its failure to provide safeguards. Debate dragged on until December 30, 1946, when the United Nations Atomic Energy Commission adopted the Baruch Plan by a 10–0 vote, with the Soviet Union and Poland abstaining. This merely transferred the dispute to the Security Council, where the Russian veto prevented adoption of the United States proposal.[27]

The Soviet Union's rejection of the Baruch Plan came as no great surprise to American officials. Ambassador Walter Bedell Smith had warned from Moscow as early as April, 1946, that the Russians had no interest in a workable international control system and were counting

---

[26] Draft by Fred Searls of Baruch letter to Byrnes, March 31, 1946, Baruch MSS, United Nations Atomic Energy Commission file, section 1; Baruch memoranda of conversations with Byrnes and Truman, June 7, 1946, *ibid.;* Baruch, *The Public Years,* pp. 346–47; Lilienthal Journal, June 13, December 29, 1946, *Lilienthal Journals,* II, 59, 124–25.

[27] For an extended summary of the United Nations debate on atomic energy, see Hewlett and Anderson, *The New World,* pp. 576–618.

on producing their own bombs, relying in the meantime on domestic political constraints within the United States to keep the Truman Administration from employing "atomic blackmail." The only control system which Moscow would accept, Smith argued, would be one which furnished Soviet scientists with full technical data on the making of bombs, with no restrictions as to the use of such information.[28] Neither the Acheson-Lilienthal report nor the final proposal which Baruch made to the United Nations came anywhere close to meeting this requirement; both provided that until the control plan went into effect, the United States would retain its monopoly over nuclear weapons. Hence, Baruch's insistence on abolishing the veto almost certainly did not, in itself, wreck prospects for international control.

The real problem was that American leaders, by the summer of 1946, simply were no longer willing to trust the Russians. "We should not under any circumstances throw away our gun," Truman told Baruch, "until we are sure that the rest of the world can't arm against us." Even former Secretary of War Henry L. Stimson, who had originally proposed seeking a control agreement with the Soviet Union, had by this time changed his mind. "The time has passed for handling the bomb in the way I suggested to the President last summer," he wrote to Baruch in June. By September, Stimson was telling Forrestal that the United States should not delay in making as many "atomic missiles" as possible. Baruch himself showed little disappointment over the Russian attitude. "If we have made every effort to reach an agreement," he commented in August, "we can then face a break with a clear conscience." Above all, there could be no compromise: "This problem [is] far too important to do any trading about." [29] As in the case of Germany, the United States would still seek a settlement with the Russians on the international control of atomic energy, but only on American terms. If the Russians failed to accept these, Washington was prepared to face with equanimity the prospect of a divided world.

[28] Smith to Byrnes, April 28, 1946, *FR: 1946,* VI, 749.

[29] Truman to Baruch, July 10, 1946, quoted in Truman, *Years of Trial and Hope,* p. 11; Stimson to Baruch, June 18, 1946, Stimson MSS, Box 432; Forrestal Diary, September 11, 1946, Millis, ed., *The Forrestal Diaries,* pp. 199–200; Baruch comments at a meeting of the United States and Canadian delegations to the United Nations Atomic Energy Commission, August 1, 1946, Baruch MSS, United Nations Atomic Energy Commission file, section 1.

The outbreak of a new crisis in the eastern Mediterranean in August, 1946, made clear the extent of Washington's commitment to an uncompromising policy. On August 7, the Russians requested a revision of the Montreux Convention to allow for joint Turkish-Soviet defense of the Dardanelles. American officials viewed this move as the culmination of a long effort by Moscow to establish naval bases in Turkey, a development which they feared might make that country a Soviet satellite. Edwin C. Wilson, the United States ambassador in Ankara, warned the State Department that if Turkey fell under Russian control, the way would be open for a Soviet advance into the Persian Gulf and the Suez Canal area. "Once this happens [the] fat is in the fire again." [30]

Washington officials agreed. Truman's top military and diplomatic advisers concluded that the Soviet note clearly reflected a desire to dominate Turkey, and that if Moscow succeeded, it would be "extremely difficult, if not impossible" for the United States to keep the Russians from gaining control of Greece and all of the Near and Middle East. Only the conviction that the United States was prepared to use force would deter the Kremlin: "The time has come when we must decide that we shall resist with all means at our disposal any Soviet aggression." At a meeting on August 15, Truman endorsed this conclusion with such alacrity that General Eisenhower, then Army Chief of Staff, politely asked whether the Chief Executive realized that this position could lead to war if the Russians did not back down. Truman surprised Eisenhower by delivering a brief but impressive lecture on the strategic significance of the Black Sea straits, leaving no doubt that he understood fully the ominous implications of the memorandum he had just approved. The Administration strongly encouraged the Turks to resist the Russian demands and, to back them up, dispatched units of the American fleet to the eastern Mediterranean. One month later Secretary Forrestal announced that the Navy would henceforth maintain a permanent presence in that part of the world.[31]

[30] Wilson to Byrnes, August 12, 1946, *FR: 1946*, VII, 837. For the Russian note of August 7, 1946, see *ibid.*, pp. 827–29. For background on the growing American concern about the Soviet ambitions in the Near East, see the comprehensive memorandum by Loy W. Henderson, head of the State Department's Office of Near Eastern Affairs, dated December 28, 1945, *ibid.*, pp. 1–6.

[31] Acheson to Byrnes, August 15, 1946, *FR: 1946*, VII, 840–42. See also the Forrestal Diary, August 15 and September 30, 1946, Millis, ed., *The Forrestal Diaries,*

In face of these maneuvers, the Russians dropped their demands for bases in the Dardanelles, thus averting a major confrontation. The episode was significant, though, for it showed that the Truman Administration was now willing to risk war if necessary in order to block further Soviet expansion. Washington officials now agreed, for the most part, on the need for a firm policy. Whether the American people were prepared to make the sacrifices necessary to carry out such a policy, however, was another question. Forrestal worried that the nation's armed forces lacked the strength to sustain the President's position, and called for a campaign to arouse an apathetic public to the dangers of the situation. Clark Clifford's September, 1946, memorandum made the same point: "Only a well-informed public will support the stern policies which Soviet activities make imperative and which the United States government must adopt." [32] Implementation of the strategy of "containment" had already begun, but the Truman Administration still faced the task of persuading the American people to bear the burdens which this course of action would entail.

III

The Truman Administration's new policy of toughness toward Russia underwent two internal challenges during the summer and fall of 1946, both launched by groups which had not yet accommodated themselves fully to the realities of the postwar international environment. A dwindling band of popular front liberals, convinced that Roosevelt's policy of cooperation with the Soviet Union still offered the best hope for world peace, vigorously condemned Truman's uncompromising stand. A far larger group of Americans, though they favored firmness with Moscow, threatened to deprive the Administration of the means to carry out such a policy by calling for a return to the military and economic practices of

pp. 192, 211; Truman, *Years of Trial and Hope*, p. 97; Acheson, *Present at the Creation*, pp. 195–96; and Phillips, *The Truman Presidency*, pp. 170–71. In a conversation on August 20, 1946, Acheson assured Lord Inverchapel, the British ambassador, that the Administration regarded the Turkish crisis with the utmost seriousness and was prepared to go to war if necessary to defend the Turks. (*FR: 1946*, VII, 849–50.)

[32] Forrestal Diary, August 15 and 23, 1946, Millis, ed., *The Forrestal Diaries*, pp. 192, 196–97; Clifford memorandum quoted in Krock, *Memoirs*, p. 482.

pre-World War II isolationism. Both challenges had to be overcome before the Administration could begin to devise long-range plans to counteract what it saw as the Soviet "menace."

American liberals found themselves torn between conflicting impulses in reacting to the new "get tough with Russia" policy. Many of them still operated under the assumption that fascism represented the only significant threat to American democracy, and found it difficult to criticize a nation like the Soviet Union which had fought Hitler so effectively. While few liberals tried to defend Russian behavior in Eastern Europe and the Near East, they detected little difference between these actions and the British imperialism which Truman had apparently endorsed by joining Churchill at Fulton. Molotov's refusal to sign Byrnes's twenty-five-year German disarmament pact puzzled liberals, however, as did Moscow's rejection of the Baruch Plan. Moreover, a few influential liberals had begun to worry that American communists might try to infiltrate their movement in order to promote the Kremlin's interests. As a result, liberal opinion regarding Russia was in a state of flux in the summer of 1946.[33]

Since the death of Roosevelt, Henry A. Wallace, formerly secretary of agriculture and vice-president, now secretary of commerce, had emerged as the most influential single leader of the liberal community. Despite his position in the cabinet, Wallace did not hesitate to speak out on foreign policy. In a series of public statements during the spring of 1946, he criticized Churchill's Fulton address, warned of the dangers of an atomic armaments race, and, to the extreme irritation of Secretary of State Byrnes, called for dismantling an American military base in Iceland. The Secretary of Commerce also sent two confidential letters to Truman, one of them twelve pages long, arguing that the Russians had justifiable reasons for fearing the United States and advocating new approaches to Moscow by liberalizing the Baruch Plan and extending a loan to promote Soviet-American trade. Truman ignored the first letter

[33] Alonzo L. Hamby, "Henry A. Wallace, the Liberals, and Soviet-American Relations," *Review of Politics,* XXX (April, 1968), 154–57; Hamby, "Harry S. Truman and American Liberalism, 1945–1948" (unpublished Ph.D. dissertation, University of Missouri, 1965), pp. 85–87, 107–8; James Reston in the *New York Times,* May 6, 1946; Alfred Baker Lewis to James Loeb, Jr., and Reinhold Niebuhr, April 16, 1946, Niebuhr MSS, Box 12; Loeb letter to the editor, *New Republic,* CXIV (May 13, 1946), 699.

and sent only a perfunctory reply to the second one. At this point, late in the summer of 1946, Wallace resolved to resign from the cabinet following the November election, but in the meantime he agreed to campaign for the Democratic Party. His first speech, on foreign policy, was scheduled before a joint meeting of the National Citizens Political Action Committee and the Independent Citizens Committee of the Arts, Sciences, and Professions at Madison Square Garden on the night of September 12, 1946.[34]

Stripped of its rhetoric, Wallace's address was an uncharacteristically realistic plea for recognition that the world was now divided into political spheres of influence: "We should recognize that we have no more business in the *political* affairs of Eastern Europe than Russia has in the *political* affairs of Latin America, Western Europe and the United States." Wallace did express the hope that there could still be an open door for trade throughout the world, including Eastern Europe. Economic contacts, in his view, could lessen tensions which political divisions had created. The Secretary of Commerce sternly lectured both the British and the Russians: London should give up its "imperialistic" policies, while Moscow "should stop teaching that [its] form of communism must, by force if necessary, ultimately triumph over democratic capitalism." Both countries, he argued, could learn a lesson from Roosevelt's Good Neighbor policy. Ironically, in view of subsequent events, Wallace's predominantly left-wing audience hissed and booed his critical comments about Russia, and the *Daily Worker* at first strongly condemned his position.[35]

The rhetoric in Wallace's speech attracted more attention than its substance, however, for in what seemed to be a direct slap at Administration policy, he proclaimed: "We are reckoning with a force which cannot be handled successfully by a 'Get tough with Russia' policy. 'Getting tough' never bought anything real and lasting—whether for schoolyard bullies or businessmen or world powers. The tougher we get,

[34] Hamby, "Harry S. Truman," pp. 19–21; Hamby, "Henry A. Wallace," pp. 157–59; Truman, *Year of Decisions*, pp. 555–57. For Byrnes's irritation regarding Wallace's statements, see Millis, ed., *The Forrestal Diaries*, pp. 154–55; and Vandenberg, ed., *Private Papers*, p. 266.

[35] The text of Wallace's speech is in *Vital Speeches*, XII (October 1, 1946), 738–41. On reaction to the speech, see the *New York Times*, September 13, 1946; and Hamby, "Henry A. Wallace," p. 160.

the tougher the Russians will get." Then came the shocker: "Just two days ago, when President Truman read these words, he said that they represented the policy of his administration." Reaction was sharp and instantaneous. The next day Arthur Krock listed at least six points on which Wallace's speech conflicted with Truman's foreign policy. *New York Times* correspondent Harold Callendar reported from the Paris Peace Conference that Wallace's address had "cut the ground from under the foreign policy that Mr. Byrnes had labored for a year to develop." Senator Vandenberg rumbled ominously that Republicans could only cooperate "with one Secretary of State at a time." [36]

Truman's efforts to explain the situation only compounded the confusion. Wallace had shown the President a copy of his speech on September 10, emphasizing its critical remarks about Russia. Truman, after a cursory scanning of the text, had made no objections. In a press conference on the 12th, the President had told reporters who had seen Wallace's prepared text that the policies advocated by the Secretary of Commerce and the Secretary of State were "exactly in line." Two days after the Madison Square Garden address, Truman tried to quiet growing criticism by issuing a "clarifying" statement maintaining that he had approved Wallace's right to give the speech, but not the content of it. On September 16, Wallace proclaimed his intention to make further statements on foreign policy. This provoked Secretary of State Byrnes, still in Paris, into threatening immediate resignation unless Truman muzzled Wallace. After further hesitation, the President on September 20 announced that he had asked the Secretary of Commerce to resign.[37]

The Truman-Wallace-Byrnes imbroglio was an important test of the Administration's commitment to its new policy of toughness with Russia. Still the leader of the liberal wing of the Democratic Party, Wallace was no ordinary cabinet member. By firing him, Truman cut the last of his tenuous ties to the liberals less than two months before the congres-

[36] *Vital Speeches*, XII (October 1, 1946), 739; *New York Times*, September 13, 15, 1946.

[37] A full account of the events of September 12–20, 1946, is in Curry, *Byrnes*, pp. 253–72, but see also Schapsmeier, *Prophet in Politics*, chapter 10; Truman, *Year of Decisions*, pp. 557–60; Byrnes, *All in One Lifetime*, pp. 370–76; Millis, ed., *The Forrestal Diaries*, pp. 206–10; Acheson, *Present at the Creation*, pp. 190–92; and Phillips, *The Truman Presidency*, pp. 148–52.

sional elections. But the alternative would have been not simply the resignation of Byrnes as secretary of state. Keeping Wallace on would have alienated Vandenberg and brought about the collapse of bipartisan unity on foreign policy. It would have given Republicans a magnificent opportunity to base their fall campaign on the charge that Democrats were "soft" on communism. It would also have meant repudiating a course of action which Truman himself strongly believed to be right. Angering liberals by removing Wallace was the lesser evil, hence it is not surprising that the President acted as he did.

The other major internal challenge to Truman's diplomatic strategy grew out of a surprisingly tenacious strain of isolationism which still affected the thinking of a large number of Americans and their representatives in Congress. These people believed, or at least hoped, that the United States could return to the small military establishment and low taxes of the prewar period without significantly endangering national security. Unlike the Wallace situation, the threat which this attitude posed to the Administration's "get tough with Russia" policy was much too deeply rooted to be blunted by the simple expedient of firing a member of the cabinet.

Demands for immediate demobilization had continued to intensify throughout the first part of 1946. Top civilian and military officials tried to counteract this pressure by launching a public campaign for retention of the draft and universal military training. President Truman told the nation in April that it would be "a tragic breach of national duty and international faith" if the American people failed to accept the responsibilities of leadership which went with their position as the strongest country in the world. The Administration did manage to secure an extension of the Selective Service Act in June, but one year later Congress allowed the draft to expire completely. Meanwhile, a potent combination of religious, pacifist, educational, farm, and labor organizations kept the proposal for universal military training from ever receiving serious consideration. "It looks as if Congress is determined to disarm us," Elmer Davis wrote to Bernard Baruch, "whether anybody else disarms or not." Not until Americans had suffered the repeated shocks of the Czechoslovak coup, the Berlin blockade, the Soviet atomic bomb, the fall of China, and the Korean War would they bring themselves to accept a large peacetime military establishment as a normal state of affairs.[38]

The Administration also had to overcome isolationist tendencies in the field of economics before it could implement a policy of containment. The war had left vast areas of the world devastated. Government leaders knew that the economies of these regions could not revive without outside help, which only the United States could provide. Failure to furnish this assistance would not only damage the American economy by leaving the United States with few foreign markets; it would also breed conditions in those countries which would promote the spread of communism. President Truman summarized the arguments for American foreign economic aid as follows:

We shall help because we know that we ourselves cannot enjoy prosperity in a world of economic stagnation. We shall help because economic distress, anywhere in the world, is a fertile breeding ground for violent political upheaval. And we shall help because we feel it is right to lend a hand to our friends and allies who are recovering from wounds inflicted by our common enemy.[39]

Whether the American people would be willing to provide such assistance, however, was very much in doubt. Traditional distrust of foreigners still existed, compounded by the memory that only Finland among America's former allies had not defaulted on its World War I debts. Having generously furnished lend-lease to fight the common enemy in World War II, Americans, yearning for normalcy, found it difficult to see why they should do more.

The Administration's lengthy fight to secure congressional approval of a $3.75 billion loan to Great Britain during the first half of 1946 made this attitude painfully obvious. Opposition to the loan stemmed from a variety of sources: old-fashioned Anglophobia, fear that the loan would support socialism or imperialism, doubt as to whether the British would repay the loan, Zionist opposition to British policy in Palestine, suspicion that the loan would set a precedent for assistance to other countries, especially Russia. In a series of public speeches Undersecretary of State

---

[38] Truman Army Day speech, April 6, 1946, *Truman Public Papers: 1946*, p. 186; Davis to Baruch, May 20, 1946, Baruch MSS, UNAEC file, section 1: "Atomic Energy: Miscellaneous Suggestions" folder. See also Samuel P. Huntington, *The Common Defense: Strategic Programs in National Politics*, pp. 33–64.

[39] Truman speech of April 6, 1946, *Truman Public Papers: 1946*, p. 189.

Acheson repeatedly tried to picture the loan as part of a larger situation—the necessity to revive world trade—but without much success. In the end Congress approved the loan chiefly because the Administration said it was necessary to fight communism.[40]

Acheson described the dilemma facing American policy-makers in a little-noticed speech to the Associated Harvard Clubs in Boston on June 4, 1946. The most important task in conducting American foreign policy, he maintained, was "focusing the will of 140,000,000 people on problems beyond our shores . . . [when] people are focusing on 140,- 000,000 other things." This problem had greatly contributed to American difficulties in asserting moral, military, and economic leadership in the postwar world:

[It lies] at the root of the hysteria which has wrought such havoc with our armed services, and continues to do so. [It lies] at the root, also, of the difficulty which we have in using our great economic power, in our own interest, to hasten recovery in other countries along lines which are essential to our own system. . . . The slogans "Bring the boys home!" and "Don't be Santa Claus!" are not among our more gifted or thoughtful contributions to the creation of a free and tranquil world.

Americans were not well prepared for world leadership: "We believe that any problem can be solved with a little ingenuity and without inconvenience to the folks at large." The problems of the postwar world were not like this. "[For] all our lives the danger, the uncertainty, the need for alertness, for effort, for discipline will be upon us. . . . We are in for it and the only real question is whether we shall know it soon enough."[41]

The outcome of the November, 1946, congressional elections further discouraged those who had hoped for a more cooperative attitude toward foreign policy questions on Capitol Hill. Taking advantage of a combi-

[40] *Newsweek,* XXVII (February 11, 1946), 20; Vandenberg, ed., *Private Papers,* pp. 230–31; *Department of State Bulletin,* XIV (March 31, May 5, 26, 1946), 511–14, 759–60, 893–94, 914; Frank McNaughton to *Time* home office, July 13, 1946, McNaughton MSS; *Congressional Record,* July 13, 1946, p. 8915. The fight over the British loan killed whatever slim chances still remained that the Administration might grant a loan to the Soviet Union. On this point see George F. Luthringer to Clayton, May 23, 1946, *FR: 1946,* VI, 842–43; John H. Crider in the *New York Times,* July 21, 1946; and Herring, "Aid to Russia, 1941–1946," chapter 9.

[41] *Department of State Bulletin,* XIV (June 16, 1946), 1045–47.

nation of circumstances—accumulated grievances after thirteen years of Democratic rule, the trauma of reconversion to a peacetime economy, lack of firm leadership from the White House, recurrent labor troubles, the meat shortage, the Wallace affair—Republicans gained control of both the Senate and the House of Representatives for the first time since 1930. The G.O.P. victory initially did not seem to threaten the bipartisan foreign policy which Truman and Byrnes had worked out with Vandenberg. The Michigan senator, who now became chairman of the Senate Foreign Relations Committee and president *pro tempore* of the Senate, continued to speak for Republicans on foreign affairs while Senator Robert A. Taft of Ohio, whose inclinations lay in a more isolationist direction than Vandenberg's, deliberately concentrated on domestic matters. It quickly became clear, however, that external and internal problems could not be so neatly divided: the conservative domestic program of Taft and Speaker of the House Joseph W. Martin posed a clear threat to the internationalist foreign policy which Vandenberg and the Administration supported.[42]

Republican candidates had campaigned in 1946 on a platform pledging to reduce income taxes by 20 percent, cut government spending, and raise tariffs. When the Eightieth Congress convened in January, 1947, G.O.P. leaders made it clear that they intended to fulfill these promises. But across-the-board tax cuts, spending reductions, and tariff increases seemed likely to undermine the foundations of Administration foreign policy, now based on the principles of maintaining sufficient military force to counter overt Soviet aggression, while at the same time extending economic aid to nations threatened by communism from within. Republican pledges, if implemented, would limit the Administration's ability to put its new Russian policy into effect.[43]

President Truman asked the Eightieth Congress on January 10, 1947, for $37.7 billion to finance government operations for the fiscal year beginning July 1, of which $11.2 billion was to go for national defense. But on February 14, the Joint Congressional Committee on the Legislative Budget recommended a budget ceiling of $31.5 billion. This involved cutting appropriations for the Army by $1 billion, the Navy by

[42] Vandenberg, ed., *Private Papers,* pp. 318–19; Ernest K. Lindley, "Republican Dividing Line," *Newsweek,* XXIX (March 3, 1947), 26.

[43] Jones, *The Fifteen Weeks,* pp. 90–91, 96–97.

$750 million, and the Army's overseas relief program for occupied countries by $500 million. General George C. Marshall, who had recently replaced Byrnes as secretary of state, warned that conditions in occupied countries would become "impossible" if Congress approved these budget cuts. Navy Secretary Forrestal thought that they would make the Navy "practically immobile and impotent." Secretary of War Patterson wrote former Secretary of State Byrnes that the proposed Republican action would mean "that we will travel again the same old road, disarming while the other major powers remain armed." [44]

The House of Representatives accepted the Joint Committee's recommendation for a budget slash of $6 billion, but in the Senate, largely through the influence of Vandenberg, the reduction was kept to $4.5 billion. In the resulting conference committee, the Senate's wishes prevailed, and a budget of $34.7 billion was approved. Vandenberg also succeeded in staving off Republican efforts to raise tariffs, but only in return for a concession from the State Department allowing the United States to withdraw from any reciprocal trade agreement which threatened to harm a domestic industry.[45]

The determination of conservative Republicans to cut the budget regardless of what effect this might have on Administration foreign policy worried many Washington observers. Senator Henry Cabot Lodge compared the approach of his G.O.P. colleagues to that of "a man wielding a meat ax in a dark room [who] might cut off his own head." Vandenberg suggested that Republican behavior might present to the world a picture of "Uncle Sam with a chip on each shoulder and both arms in a sling." Ernest K. Lindley charged in *Newsweek* that through "myopia, ignorance, and indifference" conservative Republicans, many of them vociferous critics of Russia, were "lending the Kremlin the greatest aid and comfort." Columnist Joseph Alsop put the matter even more bluntly: "The world is about to blow up in our faces, and the damned fools in Congress behave as though there was nothing worse to worry about than their richer constituents' difficulty in paying their taxes." [46]

[44] *Newsweek,* XXIX (February 24, 1947), 26; Jones, *The Fifteen Weeks,* pp. 90–91; Patterson to Byrnes, February 11, 1947, Patterson MSS, Box 18.

[45] Jones, *The Fifteen Weeks,* pp. 91, 96–99; *Newsweek,* XXIX (February 17, 1947), 26.

[46] Jones, *The Fifteen Weeks,* p. 91; *Newsweek,* XXIX (March 3, 1947), 25–26; Alsop to Martin Sommers, February 25, 1947, Alsop MSS, Box 1.

But in their push for economy at all costs, Republicans in Congress reflected the wishes of a substantial number of Americans who hoped that peace would bring a return to small government, low taxes, and noninvolvement in events overseas. The depth of this feeling indicated that the Truman Administration still had far to go in educating the American people to the responsibilities of world leadership. No one was more aware of this than Joseph M. Jones, of the State Department's Office of Public Affairs. Late in February he sent a memorandum to Assistant Secretary of State William Benton emphasizing how the concessions Congress had extracted from the Administration would increase the difficulty of dealing with the constantly-worsening world economic crisis:

I think we must admit the conclusion that Congress and the people of this country are not sufficiently aware of the character and dimensions of the crisis that impends, and of the measures that must be taken in terms of relief, loans, gifts, constructive development programs and liberal trade policies—all of these on a scale hitherto unimagined—if disaster is to be avoided. . . . The State Department knows. Congress and the people do not know.

Jones called for an immediate program "to inform the people and convince the Congress adequately with respect to today's crisis." Such a program should involve a "grave, frank, statesmanlike appeal to the people" in which "the danger should be described fully and the cost of both action and inaction estimated." [47] During the next two weeks, to Jones's astonishment and pleasure, a combination of unexpected developments caused the Administration to embark on precisely the kind of campaign which he had recommended.

IV

Despite gloomy developments on the domestic and international fronts, morale in the Truman Administration and the Department of State was surprisingly high early in 1947. The Republican victory had a

---

[47] Jones to Benton, February 26, 1947, Jones MSS. Interestingly enough, Jones at this time felt that Secretary of State Marshall, not President Truman, should make the appeal to the country because Marshall "is the only one in the Government with the prestige to make a deep impression." Jones favored having Marshall make a personal appearance before Congress "with tremendous advance build-up."

strangely invigorating effect on Truman, who later told Jonathan Daniels that "the Eightieth Congress was the luckiest thing that ever happened to me." Shortly after the elections, Truman had won a major victory by forcing the capitulation of John L. Lewis in an acrimonious labor dispute. By February, 1947, Joseph Alsop perceived "a complete change of atmosphere at the White House." He noted that "ever since the Lewis crisis, the President has grown surer and surer of himself. He no longer moans to every visitor that he doesn't want the job and never did. On the contrary, he spent two hours with Bob Hannegan yesterday planning on how to get it again." Alsop also observed that Truman now greatly enjoyed "diplomatic receptions and other such occasions of unalloyed horror, taking the utmost delight in the odd spectacle of himself in a White Tie and Tails pumphandling the great—or at any rate the conspicuous." [48]

Morale had also greatly improved in the Department of State with the resignation of Byrnes as secretary of state in January, 1947, and the appointment of General Marshall to replace him. Byrnes's reluctance to consult subordinates, together with his lax administrative methods and his long absences from the country, had kept him from forming close working relationships with career officers in the department. As one department malcontent complained: "The State Department fiddles while Byrnes roams." Marshall, on the other hand, insisted on orderly staff procedures and placed far more responsibility for policy-making on subordinates than Byrnes or previous secretaries had done. Undersecretary of State Acheson was particularly pleased with the change, as David Lilienthal observed in March, 1947:

Dean spent a good deal of time bubbling over with his enthusiasm, rapture almost, about General Marshall. . . . To work with him is such a joy that he can hardly talk about anything else. I am delighted with this, for Jimmy Byrnes' erratic and often thoughtless (as well as sometimes just plain inept) administrative and other ideas had about driven Dean crazy. Marshall . . . has made a new man of Dean, and this is a good thing for the country right now.

The effect of Marshall's appointment, Joseph Jones later recalled, "was felt from top to bottom and called forth a great surge of ideas and constructive effort." [49] The new sense of purpose which invigorated both the White House and the State Department contributed significantly to the speed and decisiveness with which these institutions responded to the crisis, late in February, 1947, caused by the abrupt British withdrawal from Greece and Turkey.

The British government officially informed the State Department on February 21, 1947, that because of internal economic difficulties it would have to suspend economic and military aid to Greece and Turkey as of March 31. The situation in Turkey posed no immediate danger, but in Greece a communist-led guerrilla movement, supplied from Yugoslavia, Bulgaria, and Albania and feeding on the economic distress wrought by years of war and government ineptitude, threatened to move into the power vacuum left by the British withdrawal. The State Department regarded these guerrillas as "an instrument of Soviet policy," and worried that if they came to power in Greece a "domino" effect would propel Turkey, Iran, and possibly even Italy and France into a Russian sphere of influence. The only alternative seemed to be immediate and massive American economic and military aid to prop up the sagging Greek regime. By February 26, the President and the Secretaries of State, War, and Navy had all agreed that such aid should be given. Their problem now was to convince an increasingly economy-minded Congress to undertake this new and expensive commitment.[50]

On February 27, President Truman invited a bipartisan group of congressional leaders to the White House for a briefing on the Greek crisis. Secretary of State Marshall described the reasons why the British had withdrawn aid from Greece and Turkey, the danger that these areas might fall under Soviet domination, and the decision which the executive branch had reached on the necessity for American assistance. Mar-

[49] Jones, *The Fifteen Weeks,* pp. 105–7; Graham H. Stuart, *The Department of State,* pp. 425, 440; Lilienthal Journal, March 9, 1947, *Lilienthal Journals,* II, 158–59. On Marshall's working methods, see Jones, *The Fifteen Weeks,* pp. 106–10; Acheson, *Sketches from Life,* pp. 147–66; Kennan, *Memoirs,* pp. 345–47; and Robert H. Ferrell, *George C. Marshall,* pp. 17–20, 49–54.

[50] Jones, *The Fifteen Weeks,* pp. 3–8, 129–38; "Background Memorandum on Greece," March 3, 1947, Jones MSS; Acheson, *Present at the Creation,* pp. 217–19. See also the "Memorandum Regarding Greece" prepared by the State Department's Office of Near Eastern and African Affairs, October 21, 1946, *FR: 1946,* VII, 240–45. For background on the Greek civil war, see Stephen G. Xydis, *Greece and the Great Powers, 1944–1947;* and Edgar O'Ballance, *The Greek Civil War, 1944–1949.*

shall's dry, laconic presentation failed to impress the suspicious congressmen, who began muttering darkly about "pulling British chestnuts out of the fire." At this point, Dean Acheson asked for permission to speak. The Undersecretary of State painted a vivid picture of a world divided between irreconcilable ideologies, a situation unparalleled since the days of Rome and Carthage. The Soviet Union, he asserted, was trying to impose its ideology on as much of the world as possible. A victory for communism in Greece, Turkey, Iran, or any of the other countries of the Near East and Mediterranean region could lead rapidly to the collapse of pro-Western governments throughout Europe. Russian control over two-thirds of the world's surface and three-fourths of its population would make American security precarious indeed. Therefore, aid to Greece and Turkey was not simply a matter of rescuing British chestnuts, it was a sober and realistic effort to protect the security of the United States by strengthening the ability of free people to resist communist aggression and subversion.

Acheson's speech understandably left the congressmen somewhat awed. After a brief period of silence, Vandenberg announced that since the country clearly faced a serious crisis, he would support the Administration's request for aid to Greece and Turkey provided the President personally put the situation before Congress and the people in the same terms which Acheson had just employed. The other congressmen present registered no objections, and the meeting broke up with the tacit understanding that congressional leaders would support aid to Greece and Turkey if the Administration explained clearly that this aid was necessary to prevent the further expansion of communism.[51]

With Vandenberg's injunction clearly in mind, Marshall and Acheson set the State Department to work to draft a speech for Truman to give to Congress. The chief information officers of the State, War, and Navy departments met on February 28 to consider the most effective manner in which to present the decision to aid Greece and Turkey. Out of this meeting came a working paper which defined the problem confronting the Administration as follows:

[51] The most complete account of the February 27, 1947, meeting is in Jones, *The Fifteen Weeks*, pp. 138–42, but see also Vandenberg, ed., *Private Papers*, pp. 338–39; Truman, *Years of Trial and Hope*, pp. 103–4; Acheson, *Present at the Creation*, p. 219; and Xydis, *Greece and the Great Powers*, pp. 478–80.

1. To make possible the formulation of intelligent opinions by the American people on the problems created by the present situation in Greece through the furnishing of full and frank information by the government.
2. To portray the world conflict between free and totalitarian or imposed forms of government.
3. To bring about an understanding by the American people of the world strategic situation.

The paper recommended that Truman proclaim it to be "basic United States policy" to "support free peoples who are resisting attempted subjugation by armed minorities or by outside pressures." It concluded with an extensive set of suggestions for off-the-record press conferences, written material, radio discussions, magazine and feature articles, and public speaking programs through which the department's new policy could be presented to the people.[52]

A few officials objected to having the President make such a sweeping commitment. White House administrative assistant George Elsey noted that "there has been no overt action in the immediate past by the U.S.S.R. which serves as an adequate pretext for [an] 'All-out' speech. The situation in Greece is relatively 'abstract'; there have been other instances—Iran, for example—where the occasion more adequately justified such a speech." The heavy ideological emphasis of the State Department's draft appalled George Kennan, whose "long telegram" of February, 1946, had done so much to make the Administration think in ideological terms. Although Kennan supported aid to Greece and Turkey, he objected to placing it "in the framework of a universal policy rather than in that of a specific decision addressed to a specific set of circumstances." Kennan had always perceived keenly the limitations which domestic considerations imposed on the conduct of foreign relations, but he was surprisingly blind to the difficulties of overriding these limitations in order to implement an unpopular policy. The Truman speech was, in fact, aimed more toward the American public than toward the world; it was, as Clark Clifford put it, "the opening gun in a campaign to bring people up to [the] realization that the war isn't over by any means." The domestic situation had made it clear, in the words of one of the information officers present at the February 28 meeting, that "the

[52] Jones, *The Fifteen Weeks,* pp. 150–53; State-War-Navy Coordinating Committee Subcommittee on Information Paper, "Information Program on United States Aid to Greece," submitted to Acheson on March 4, 1947, Jones MSS.

only way we can sell the public on our new policy is by emphasizing the necessity of holding the line: communism vs. democracy should be the major theme." [53]

It was. When Truman came before Congress on March 12, 1947, to ask for aid to Greece and Turkey, he made the ideological confrontation between the Soviet Union and the United States the central focus of his remarks:

At the present moment in world history nearly every nation must choose between alternative ways of life. The choice is too often not a free one.

One way of life is based upon the will of the majority, and is distinguished by free institutions, representative government, free elections, guaranties of individual liberty, freedom of speech and religion, and freedom from political oppression.

The second way of life is based upon the will of a minority forcibly imposed upon the majority. It relies upon terror and oppression, a controlled press and radio, fixed elections, and the suppression of personal freedoms.

I believe that it must be the policy of the United States to support free people who are resisting attempted subjugation by armed minorities or by outside pressures.[54]

The Truman Doctrine constituted a form of shock therapy: it was a last-ditch effort by the Administration to prod Congress and the American people into accepting the responsibilities of the world leadership which one year earlier, largely in response to public opinion, Washington officials had assumed by deciding to "get tough with Russia."

Kennan's fears to the contrary notwithstanding, the Truman Administration never intended to commit itself to help victims of communist aggression anywhere in the world. Acheson explained to the Senate Foreign Relations Committee on March 24, 1947, that aid to Greece and Turkey would not set a precedent for subsequent American policy, and that all requests for assistance in the future would be evaluated individually in terms of "whether the country in question really needs assistance, whether its request is consistent with American foreign policy, whether the request for assistance is sincere, and whether assistance by the United States would be effective in meeting the problems of that

[53] Elsey to Clifford, March 8, 1947, Elsey MSS, Box 17; Kennan, *Memoirs*, pp. 314–15, 319–20; Clifford statement quoted by Elsey in a handwritten memorandum dated March 9, 1947, Elsey MSS, Box 17; Jones, *The Fifteen Weeks*, pp. 151, 154–55.

[54] *Truman Public Papers: 1947*, pp. 178–79.

country." [55] The Administration's reluctance to support Chiang Kai-shek against the Chinese Communists showed that it took Acheson's qualification seriously, as did Washington's failure to contest the communist takeover in Czechoslovakia in 1948.[56]

But the fall of China and the Korean War, together with the domestic onslaught of McCarthyism, would make it politically impossible for Truman and his successors to continue making such fine distinctions in formulating American policy. By presenting aid to Greece and Turkey in terms of an ideological conflict between two ways of life, Washington officials encouraged a simplistic view of the Cold War which was, in time, to imprison American diplomacy in an ideological straitjacket almost as confining as that which restricted Soviet foreign policy. Trapped in their own rhetoric, leaders of the United States found it difficult to respond to the conciliatory gestures which emanated from the Kremlin following Stalin's death and, through their inflexibility, may well have contributed to the perpetuation of the Cold War.

[55] Statement of March 24, 1947, quoted in Jones, *The Fifteen Weeks,* p. 190. See also the State Department Policy Planning Staff memorandum of May 23, 1947, quoted *ibid.,* pp. 251–52.

[56] On this point, see Seyom Brown, *The Faces of Power,* p. 17.

11

〉〉〈〈〈

Conclusion:
The United States and the
Origins of the Cold War

American leaders did not want a Cold War, but they wanted insecurity even less. By early 1946, President Truman and his advisers had reluctantly concluded that recent actions of the Soviet Union endangered the security of the United States. This decision grew out of a complex of internal and external pressures, all filtered through the perceptions and preconceptions of the men who made American foreign policy. In order to understand how they came to this conclusion, it is necessary to view the situation as they saw it, not as it appears today in the cold, but not always clear, light of historical hindsight.[1]

World War II had produced a revolution in United States foreign policy. Prior to that conflict, most Americans believed that their country could best protect itself by minimizing political entanglements overseas. Events of 1939–40 persuaded leaders of the Roosevelt Administration that they had been wrong; Pearl Harbor convinced remaining skeptics. From then on, American policy-makers would seek security through involvement, not isolation: to prevent new wars, they believed, the whole

[1] On this point, see Robert F. Berkhofer, Jr., *A Behavioral Approach to Historical Analysis,* pp. 32–45.

system of relations between nations would have to be reformed. Assuming that only their country had the power and influence to carry out this task, United States officials set to work, even before formal entry into the war, to plan a peace settlement which would accomplish such a reformation.

Lessons of the past greatly influenced Washington's vision of the future. Determined to avoid mistakes which, in their view, had caused World War II, American planners sought to disarm defeated enemies, give peoples of the world the right to shape their own future, revive world trade, and replace the League of Nations with a new and more effective collective security organization. But without victory over the Axis, the United States would never have the opportunity to implement its plan for peace. Given the realities of the military situation, victory depended upon cooperation with the Soviet Union, an ally whose commitment to American postwar ideals was, at best, questionable.

Kremlin leaders, too, looked to the past in planning for the future, but their very different experiences led them to conclusions not always congruent with those of their American allies. For Stalin, the key to peace was simple: keep Russia strong and Germany weak. The Soviet dictator enthusiastically applauded American insistence on unconditional surrender, questioning only the wisdom of making this policy public. He showed little interest in Washington's plans for collective security, the reduction of tariff barriers, and reform of the world monetary system. Self-determination in Eastern Europe, however, he would not allow: the region was vital to Soviet security, but the people who lived there were bitterly anti-Russian. Nor could Stalin view with equanimity Allied efforts, also growing out of lessons of the past, to limit reparations removals from Germany. These two conflicts—Eastern Europe and Germany—became major areas of contention in the emerging Cold War.

Moscow's position would not have seemed so alarming to American officials, however, had it not been for the Soviet Union's continued commitment to an ideology dedicated to the overthrow of capitalism throughout the world. Hopes that the United States might cooperate successfully with the USSR after the war had been based on the belief, encouraged by Stalin himself, that the Kremlin had given up its former goal of exporting communism. Soviet expansion into Eastern Europe in 1944 and 1945, together with the apparent abandonment of popular front tactics by the world communist movement, caused Western observers to fear that they had been misled. Just at the moment of victory over the Axis, the old specter of world revolution reappeared.

It seems likely that Washington policy-makers mistook Stalin's determination to ensure Russian security through spheres of influence for a renewed effort to spread communism outside the borders of the Soviet Union. The Russians did not immediately impose communist regimes on all the countries they occupied after the war, and Stalin showed notoriously little interest in promoting the fortunes of communist parties in areas beyond his control.[2] But the Soviet leader failed to make the limited nature of his objectives clear. Having just defeated one dictator thought to have had unlimited ambitions, Americans could not regard the emergence of another without the strongest feelings of apprehension and anger.

Nor did they see any reason to acquiesce timidly in what Stalin seemed to be doing. The United States had come out of the war with a monopoly over the world's most powerful weapon, the atomic bomb, and a near-monopoly over the productive facilities which could make possible quick rehabilitation of war-shattered economies. Convinced that technology had given them the means to shape the postwar order to their liking,[3] Washington officials assumed that these instruments would leave the Russians no choice but to comply with American peace plans. Attempts to extract concessions from Moscow in return for a loan failed, however, when the Soviet Union turned to German reparations to meet its reconstruction needs. The Russians also refused to be impressed by

[2] Historians, revisionist and nonrevisionist, now generally agree on the limited nature of Stalin's objectives. See, for example, Ulam, *Expansion and Coexistence,* pp. 403–4, 420–23; McNeill, *America, Britain, and Russia,* pp. 316, 406, 408, 476; Fleming, *The Cold War and Its Origins,* I, 252–62; Kolko, *Politics of War,* pp. 618–23; LaFeber, *America, Russia and the Cold War, 1945–1967,* pp. 17, 23; Louis J. Halle, *The Cold War as History,* pp. 11, 17, 46; Deutscher, *Ironies of History,* pp. 151–56; Schlesinger, "Origins of the Cold War," p. 36; and Starobin, "Origins of the Cold War: The Communist Dimension," pp. 686–88. But in 1947 the distinguished historian William L. Langer was writing: "We can see clearly now that it was a mistake to believe that the Bolsheviks had given up the idea of world revolution. . . . Europe and the world have been freed of the Nazi menace only to be confronted with the specter of Communist control." ("Political Problems of a Coalition," *Foreign Affairs,* XXVI [October, 1947], 88.)

[3] On this point, see Sir Denis Brogan, "The Illusion of American Omnipotence," *Harper's,* CCV (December, 1952), 21–28.

the atomic bomb, leaving the Truman Administration with the choice of actually using it, or returning to *quid pro quo* bargaining. American omnipotence turned out to be an illusion because Washington policy-makers failed to devise strategies for applying their newly gained power effectively in practical diplomacy.

Frustrated in their efforts to work out an acceptable settlement with the USSR, under severe pressure from Congress and the public to make no further compromises, American leaders embarked on a new Russian policy during the first months of 1946. Henceforth, expansionist moves by the Kremlin would be resisted, even at the risk of war. Negotiations would continue, but future concessions would have to come from Moscow. Meanwhile, the United States would begin rebuilding its military forces, now badly depleted by demobilization, and would launch an ambitious program of economic assistance to nations threatened by communism. Administration officials found it necessary to exaggerate the Soviet ideological challenge in order to win support for these projects from parsimonious legislators, but there can be no doubt that the President and his advisers regarded the danger as a serious one. Nor can there be any question that the general principle of "getting tough with Russia" evoked overwhelming public approval: a generation seared by the memory of Munich would not tolerate appeasement, however unpleasant the alternatives might be.

It is easy for historians, writing a quarter of a century later, to suggest ways in which the United States might have avoided, or at least lessened, the dangers of a postwar confrontation with the Soviet Union. President Roosevelt could have eased Russia's military burden by launching a second front in Europe in 1942 or 1943. He could have explicitly exempted Eastern Europe from provisions of the Atlantic Charter, thereby recognizing the Soviet sphere of influence in that part of the world. American officials could have aided in the massive task of repairing Russian war damage by granting a generous reconstruction loan, and by allowing extensive reparations removals from Germany. Finally, the United States could have attempted to allay Soviet distrust by voluntarily relinquishing its monopoly over the atomic bomb.

But these were not viable alternatives at the time. A premature second front would have greatly increased American casualties and might have weakened support for the war effort. Recognition of the Soviet position in Eastern Europe would have aroused opposition in the Senate to American membership in the United Nations, and might have endangered Roosevelt's reelection prospects. Economic concessions to the Russians, in the form of either a reconstruction loan or a more flexible attitude on reparations, would have evoked a storm of protest from a Congress still largely isolationist in its approach to foreign aid. A decision to give up the atomic bomb would have so alienated the American people and their representatives on Capitol Hill as to impair the very functioning of the government. Policy-makers operate within a certain range of acceptable options, but they, not historians, define degrees of acceptability. It is surely uncharitable, if not unjust, to condemn officials for rejecting courses of action which, to them, seemed intolerable.

A fairer approach is to ask why policy-makers defined their alternatives so narrowly. Important recent work by revisionist historians suggests that requirements of the economic system may have limited the options open to American officials in seeking an accommodation with Russia. Leaders of the United States had become convinced, revisionists assert, that survival of the capitalist system at home required the unlimited expansion of American economic influence overseas. For this reason, the United States could not recognize legitimate Soviet interests in Eastern Europe, Germany, or elsewhere. By calling for an international "open door" policy, Washington had projected its interests on a worldwide scale. The real or imagined threat of communism anywhere endangered these interests, and had to be contained.[4]

Revisionists are correct in emphasizing the importance of internal constraints, but they have defined them too narrowly: by focusing so heavily on economics, they neglect the profound impact of the domestic political system on the conduct of American foreign policy. The Constitution did, after all, give the public and their representatives on Capitol

[4] This interpretation was originally put forward by William A. Williams in *The Tragedy of American Diplomacy*. Important extensions and elaborations of Williams' thesis include Gardner, *Economic Aspects of New Deal Diplomacy* and *Architects of Illusion*; Kolko, *Politics of War*; LaFeber, *America, Russia, and the Cold War*, especially chapters 1 and 2; Gar Alperovitz, *Cold War Essays*, especially pp. 75–121; David Horowitz, *Free World Colossus*; and the essays on foreign policy in Barton J. Bernstein, ed., *Politics and Policies of the Truman Administration*. Revisionists are by no means in agreement on all aspects of the debate surrounding the origins of the Cold War, but they do all accept the basic elements of the Williams thesis.

Hill at least a negative influence in this field, and while these influences may not have determined the specific direction of diplomatic initiatives, they did impose definite limitations on how far policy-makers could go. The delay in opening the second front, nonrecognition of Moscow's sphere of influence in Eastern Europe, the denial of economic aid to Russia, and the decision to retain control of the atomic bomb can all be explained far more plausibly by citing the Administration's need to maintain popular support for its policies rather than by dwelling upon requirements of the economic order.

One might, of course, argue that the political system reflected the economic substructure, and that American officials were merely unwitting tools of capitalism, but it is difficult to justify this assumption without resorting to the highly questionable techniques of economic determinism.[5] At times, it seems as if revisionists do employ this approach— they frequently take literally only statements of economic interest, disregarding as irrelevant whatever other explanations policy-makers gave for their actions. But the revisionists are not consistent in their economic determinism. Carried to its logical conclusion, that view of history would seem to indicate that the Cold War was an irrepressible conflict between two diametrically opposed ideologies; a clash for which individuals, presumably puppets of these systems, could bear no responsibility. Revisionists do not see the Cold War that way. They assert that the United States, because of its military and economic superiority over the Soviet Union, could have accepted Moscow's postwar demands without endangering American security. Because it did not, they hold leaders of the United States responsible for the way in which the Cold War developed, if not for the Cold War itself.[6] This places revisionists in the odd posi-

[5] For three recent critiques of economic determinism, see Berkhofer, *Behavioral Approach to Historical Analysis*, pp. 56–57; David Hackett Fischer, *Historians' Fallacies: Toward a Logic of Historical Thought*, pp. 74–78; and Richard Hofstadter's essay on Charles Beard in *The Progressive Historians*, especially pp. 244–45.

[6] Gardner, *Architects of Illusion*, pp. x–xi; Horowitz, *Free World Colossus*, pp. 19–20. See also Gardner's comment in Lloyd C. Gardner, Arthur M. Schlesinger, Jr., and Hans J. Morgenthau, *Origins of the Cold War*, p. 109. The most thorough critique of Cold War revisionism is Charles S. Maier, "Revisionism and the Interpretation of Cold War Origins," *Perspectives in American History*, IV (1970), 313–47; but see also Paul Seabury, "Cold War Origins," *Journal of Contemporary History*, III (January, 1968), 169–82; Daniel M. Smith, "The New Left and the Cold War," *University of Denver Quarterly*, Winter, 1970, pp. 78–88; Christopher Lasch, "The Cold War, Revisited and Re-Visioned," *New York Times Magazine*, January 14, 1968, es-

tion of employing a single-cause explanation of human behavior, yet criticizing the subjects they deal with for not liberating themselves from the mechanistic framework which they, as historians, have imposed.

But even if, as the revisionists suggest, American officials had enjoyed a completely free hand in seeking a settlement with the Soviet Union, it seems unlikely that they would have succeeded. Accomplishment of this task required not only conciliatory actions by Washington but a receptive attitude on the part of Moscow. The latter simply did not exist. Traditional distrust of foreigners, combined with ideological differences, would have militated against a relationship of mutual trust with the United States regardless of who ruled Russia. Stalin's paranoia, together with the bureaucracy of institutionalized suspicion with which he surrounded himself, made the situation much worse. Information on the internal workings of the Soviet government during this period is still sparse, but sufficient evidence exists to confirm the accuracy of Kennan's 1946 conclusion that Russian hostility sprang chiefly from internal sources not susceptible to gestures of conciliation from the West.[7]

Historians have debated at length the question of who caused the Cold War,[8] but without shedding much light on the subject. Too often they view that event exclusively as a series of actions by one side and re-

---

pecially p. 59; and Henry Pachter, "Revisionist Historians and the Cold War," in Irving Howe, ed., *Beyond the New Left*, pp. 166–91. My own reservations about Cold War revisionism were more fully expressed in "Domestic Influences on American Policy Toward the Soviet Union, 1941–1947," a paper delivered at the 1970 annual convention of the American Historical Association.

[7] Kennan to Byrnes, March 20, 1946, *FR: 1946*, V, 723. See also Schlesinger, "Origins of the Cold War," pp. 46–50; and Ulam, *Expansion and Coexistence*, p. 399. Recently published memoirs by Soviet diplomatic and military officials depict vividly the almost pathological suspicion with which Stalin treated his own associates. A valuable compilation of translated excerpts is Seweryn Bialer, compiler, *Stalin and His Generals: Soviet Military Memoirs of World War II*. See also Svetlana Alliluyeva, *Twenty Letters to a Friend;* Milovan Djilas, *Conversations with Stalin;* Harrison E. Salisbury, *The 900 Days: The Siege of Leningrad;* and, if we may assume its authenticity, Nikita S. Khrushchev, *Khrushchev Remembers*. But no one has more effectively portrayed Stalin's personality and the effect it had on the Soviet bureaucracy than Alexander I. Solzhenitsyn in his novel *The First Circle*.

[8] Thomas G. Paterson, ed., *The Origins of the Cold War*, provides the most useful introduction to this debate, but see also Norman A. Graebner, "Cold War Origins and the Continuing Debate: A Review of Recent Literature," *Journal of Conflict Resolution*, XIII (March, 1969), 123–32; and Robert W. Sellen, "Origins of the Cold War: An Historiographical Survey," *West Georgia College Studies in the Social Sciences*, IX (June, 1970), 57–98.

actions by the other. In fact, policy-makers in both the United States and the Soviet Union were constantly weighing each other's intentions, as they perceived them, and modifying their own courses of action accordingly. In addition, officials in Washington and Moscow brought to the task of policy formulation a variety of preconceptions, shaped by personality, ideology, political pressures, even ignorance and irrationality, all of which influenced their behavior. Once this complex interaction of stimulus and response is taken into account, it becomes clear that neither side can bear sole responsibility for the onset of the Cold War.

But neither should the conflict be seen as irrepressible, if for no other reason than the methodological impossibility of "proving" inevitability in history.[9] The power vacuum in central Europe caused by Germany's collapse made a Russian-American confrontation likely; it did not make it inevitable. Men as well as circumstances make foreign policy, and through such drastic expedients as war, appeasement, or resignation, policy-makers can always alter difficult situations in which they find themselves. One may legitimately ask why they do not choose to go this far, but to view their actions as predetermined by blind, impersonal "forces" is to deny the complexity and particularity of human behavior, not to mention the ever-present possibility of accident. The Cold War is too complicated an event to be discussed in terms of either national guilt or the determinism of inevitability.

If one must assign responsibility for the Cold War, the most meaningful way to proceed is to ask which side had the greater opportunity to accommodate itself, at least in part, to the other's position, given the range of alternatives as they appeared at the time. Revisionists have argued that American policy-makers possessed greater freedom of action, but their view ignores the constraints imposed by domestic politics. Little is known even today about how Stalin defined his options, but it does seem safe to say that the very nature of the Soviet system afforded him a larger selection of alternatives than were open to leaders of the United States. The Russian dictator was immune from pressures of Congress, public opinion, or the press. Even ideology did not restrict him: Stalin was the master of communist doctrine, not a prisoner of it, and could modify or suspend Marxism-Leninism whenever it suited him to do so.[10]

[9] Fischer, *Historians' Fallacies*, pp. 12–13.
[10] Schlesinger, "Origins of the Cold War," p. 48; Starobin, "Origins of the Cold War," p. 683.

This is not to say that Stalin wanted a Cold War—he had every reason to avoid one. But his absolute powers did give him more chances to surmount the internal restraints on his policy than were available to his democratic counterparts in the West.

The Cold War grew out of a complicated interaction of external and internal developments inside both the United States and the Soviet Union. The external situation—circumstances beyond the control of either power—left Americans and Russians facing one another across prostrated Europe at the end of World War II. Internal influences in the Soviet Union—the search for security, the role of ideology, massive postwar reconstruction needs, the personality of Stalin—together with those in the United States—the ideal of self-determination, fear of communism, the illusion of omnipotence fostered by American economic strength and the atomic bomb—made the resulting confrontation a hostile one. Leaders of both superpowers sought peace, but in doing so yielded to considerations which, while they did not precipitate war, made a resolution of differences impossible.

BIBLIOGRAPHY

Archives and Manuscript Collections

Alsop, Joseph W., and Stewart Alsop. Library of Congress.
Baruch, Bernard M. Princeton University Library.
Burton, Harold H. Library of Congress.
Clapper, Raymond. Library of Congress.
Clayton, William L. Harry S. Truman Library.
—— Rice University Library.
Clifford, Clark M. Harry S. Truman Library.
Connally, Tom. Library of Congress.
Cox, Oscar. Franklin D. Roosevelt Library.
Coy, Wayne. Franklin D. Roosevelt Library.
Davies, Joseph E. Library of Congress.
Davis, Elmer. Library of Congress.
Democratic National Committee Records. Franklin D. Roosevelt Library.
—— Harry S. Truman Library.
Dulles, John Foster. Princeton University Library.
Eisenhower, Dwight D. Dwight D. Eisenhower Library.
Elsey, George M. Harry S. Truman Library.
Fahy, Charles. Franklin D. Roosevelt Library.
Fischer, Louis. Franklin D. Roosevelt Library.
Forrestal, James V. Princeton University Library.
Green, Theodore Francis. Library of Congress.
Grew, Joseph C. Houghton Library, Harvard University.
Hopkins, Harry L. Franklin D. Roosevelt Library.
Hull, Cordell. Library of Congress.
Hurley, Patrick J. University of Oklahoma Library.

Jones, Jesse H. Library of Congress.
Jones, Joseph M. Harry S. Truman Library.
Kilgore, Harley M. Franklin D. Roosevelt Library.
Lane, Arthur Bliss. Yale University Library.
Leahy, William D. Library of Congress.
Long, Breckinridge. Library of Congress.
McNaughton, Frank. Harry S. Truman Library.
Maverick, Maury. University of Texas Library.
Morgenthau, Henry, Jr. Franklin D. Roosevelt Library.
Niebuhr, Reinhold. Library of Congress.
Patterson, Robert P. Library of Congress.
Roosevelt, Franklin D. Franklin D. Roosevelt Library.
Rosenman, Samuel I. Franklin D. Roosevelt Library.
—— Harry S. Truman Library.
Ross, Charles G. Harry S. Truman Library.
Sevareid, Eric. Library of Congress.
Simmons, David E. University of Texas Library.
Snyder, John W. Harry S. Truman Library.
Steinhardt, Laurence A. Library of Congress.
Stettinius, Edward R., Jr. University of Virginia Library.
Stimson, Henry L. Yale University Library.
Swing, Raymond Gram. Library of Congress.
Thomas, Elbert H. Franklin D. Roosevelt Library.
Truman, Harry S. Harry S. Truman Library.
U.S. Department of State Archives, 1943–45. Record Group 59, National Archives.
Vandenberg, Arthur H. William L. Clements Library, University of Michigan.
Villard, Oswald Garrison. Houghton Library, Harvard University.
White, Harry Dexter. Princeton University Library.
White, Wallace H. Library of Congress.

Other Unpublished Material

Diebold, William, Jr. "What Shall Germany Pay? The New Reparations Problem," in the mimeographed Council on Foreign Relations series, "American Interests in the War and the Peace," April, 1944.
Dobney, Frederick John. "The Papers of Will Clayton." Ph. D. dissertation, Rice University, 1970.
Dulles, John Foster. Oral History Collection, Princeton University Library.
Eckes, Alfred E. "Bretton Woods: America's New Deal for an Open World." Ph. D. dissertation, University of Texas, 1969.
Gaddis, John Lewis. "Domestic Influences on American Policy Toward the So-

viet Union, 1941–1947." Paper delivered at the 1970 annual convention of the American Historical Association.

—— "The United States and the Origins of the Cold War, 1943–1946." Ph. D. dissertation, University of Texas, 1968.

Hamby, Alonzo L. "Harry S. Truman and American Liberalism, 1945–1948." Ph. D. dissertation, University of Missouri, 1965.

Harriman, W. Averell. Remarks at a ceremony commemorating the twenty-fifth anniversary of Harry S. Truman's accession to the presidency, April 11, 1970. Harry S. Truman Library, Independence, Missouri (mimeographed).

Hartmann, Susan M. "President Truman and the 80th Congress." Manuscript in the author's possession.

Herring, George C., Jr. "Aid to Russia, 1941–46: Strategy, Diplomacy, and the Origins of the Cold War." Manuscript in the author's possession.

Maddux, Thomas R. "American Relations with the Soviet Union, 1933–1941." Ph. D. dissertation, University of Michigan, 1969.

Mazza, Sister Mary Assumpta. "A Survey of Changing Attitudes Toward the Soviet Union as Reflected in American Periodicals: 1942–1949." Ph. D. dissertation, St. John's University, 1957.

Sellen, Albert R. "Congressional Opinion of Soviet-American Relations, 1945–1950." Ph.D. dissertation, University of Chicago, 1954.

Street, Karl W. "Harry S. Truman: His Role as Legislative Leader, 1945–1948." Ph.D. dissertation, University of Texas, 1963.

Sylwester, Harold J. "American Public Reaction to Communist Expansion: From Yalta to NATO." Ph.D. dissertation, University of Kansas, 1969.

Theoharis, Athan. "The Yalta Myths: An Issue in American Politics, 1945–1955." Ph.D. dissertation, University of Chicago, 1965.

U.S. Department of State. "Fortnightly Survey of American Opinion," 1944–47. Office of Policy Guidance, Bureau of Public Affairs, Department of State.

Official Documents

Canada. *Report of the Royal Commission to Investigate Disclosures of Secret and Confidential Information to Unauthorized Persons.* Ottawa, 1946.

Correspondence Between the Chairman of the Council of Ministers of the U.S.S.R. and the Presidents of the U.S.A. and the Prime Ministers of Great Britain During the Great Patriotic War of 1941–1945. 2 vols. Moscow, 1957.

Documents on American Foreign Relations. Vols. II–IX (1939–47). Boston and Princeton, 1940–49.

Public Papers of the Presidents: Harry S. Truman, 1945–1947. Washington, D.C., 1961–63.

U.S. Bureau of the Census. *Historical Statistics of the United States, Colonial Times to 1957.* Washington, D.C., 1960.

U.S. Congress. *Congressional Record.* 78th through 80th Congresses.

U.S. Department of State. *Department of State Bulletin.* Vols. IV–XVI (1941–47).

—— *Foreign Relations of the United States:* Annual volumes, 1941–46. Washington, D.C., 1958–70.

—— *Foreign Relations of the United States: The Conference of Berlin (The Potsdam Conference), 1945.* 2 vols. Washington, D.C., 1960.

—— *Foreign Relations of the United States: The Conferences at Cairo and Tehran, 1943.* Washington, D.C., 1961.

—— *Foreign Relations of the United States: The Conferences at Malta and Yalta, 1945.* Washington, D.C., 1955.

—— *Foreign Relations of the United States: The Conferences at Washington, 1941–1942, and Casablanca, 1943.* Washington, D.C., 1968.

—— *Foreign Relations of the United States: The Conferences at Washington and Quebec, 1943.* Washington, D.C., 1970.

—— *Foreign Relations of the United States: The Soviet Union, 1933–1939.* Washington, D.C., 1952.

U.S. Export-Import Bank. *Semiannual Report to Congress for the Period July-December, 1945.* Washington, D.C., 1946.

U.S. Senate. Committee on the Judiciary. Subcommittee to Investigate the Administration of the Internal Security Act and Other Internal Security Laws. *The "Amerasia" Papers: A Clue to the Catastrophe of China.* 2 vols. Washington, D.C., 1970.

Newspapers and Periodicals

Life, 1941–47.
Nation, 1943–47.
New Republic, 1943–47.
New York Times, 1941–47.
Newsweek, 1943–47.
Time, 1943–47.
U.S. News, 1943–47.
Washington Post, 1945–46.

Books

Acheson, Dean. *Present at the Creation: My Years in the State Department.* New York, 1969.

—— *Sketches from Life of Men I have Known.* New York, 1961.

Adler, Selig. *The Isolationist Impulse: Its Twentieth Century Reaction.* New York, 1957.

Agee, James. *Agee on Film: Reviews and Comments.* Boston, 1958.

Albertson, Dean. *Roosevelt's Farmer: Claude R. Wickard in the New Deal.* New York, 1961.

Alliluyeva, Svetlana. *Twenty Letters to a Friend.* Translated by Priscilla J. McMillan. New York, 1967.

Almond, Gabriel A. *The American People and Foreign Policy.* New York, 1950.

Alperovitz, Gar. *Atomic Diplomacy: Hiroshima and Potsdam.* New York, 1965.

—— *Cold War Essays.* New York, 1970.

Ambrose, Stephen E. *Eisenhower and Berlin, 1945: The Decision to Halt at the Elbe.* Garden City, N.Y., 1967.

—— *The Supreme Commander: The War Years of General Dwight D. Eisenhower.* New York, 1970.

Armstrong, Anne. *Unconditional Surrender: The Impact of the Casablanca Policy upon World War II.* New Brunswick, N.J., 1961.

Bailey, Thomas A. *America Faces Russia: Russian-American Relations from Early Times to Our Own Day.* Ithaca, N.Y., 1950.

—— *The Man in the Street.* New York, 1948.

Barnard, Ellsworth. *Wendell Willkie: Fighter for Freedom.* Marquette, Mich., 1966.

Baruch, Bernard M. *Baruch: The Public Years.* New York, 1962.

Beal, John R. *John Foster Dulles: A Biography.* New York, 1957.

Bennett, Edward M. *Recognition of Russia: An American Foreign Policy Dilemma.* Waltham, Mass., 1970.

Berkhofer, Robert F., Jr. *A Behavioral Approach to Historical Analysis.* New York, 1969.

Bernstein, Barton J., and Allen J. Matusow, eds. *The Truman Administration: A Documentary History.* New York, 1966.

Bialer, Seweryn, comp. *Stalin and His Generals: Soviet Military Memoirs of World War II.* New York, 1969.

Bishop, Donald G. *The Roosevelt-Litvinov Agreements: The American View.* Syracuse, N.Y., 1965.

Blum, John Morton. *From the Morgenthau Diaries: Years of War, 1941–1945.* Boston, 1967.

Bohlen, Charles E. *The Transformation of American Foreign Policy.* New York, 1969.

Brock, Clifton. *Americans for Democratic Action: Its Role in National Politics.* Washington, D.C., 1962.

Browder, Robert P. *The Origins of Soviet-American Diplomacy.* Princeton, 1953.

Brown, Seyom. *The Faces of Power: Constancy and Change in United States Foreign Policy from Truman to Johnson.* New York, 1968.

Bruner, Jerome S. *Mandate from the People.* New York, 1944.

Burns, James MacGregor. *Roosevelt: The Soldier of Freedom*. New York, 1970.

Bush, Vannevar. *Pieces of the Action*. New York, 1970.

Byrnes, James F. *All in One Lifetime*. New York, 1958.

—— *Speaking Frankly*. New York, 1947.

Campbell, John C. *The United States in World Affairs, 1945–47*. New York, 1948.

Cantril, Hadley, and Mildred Strunk, eds. *Public Opinion, 1935–1946*. Princeton, 1951.

Carleton, William G. *The Revolution in American Foreign Policy: Its Global Range*. New York, 1963.

Carr, Albert Z. *Truman, Stalin, and the Peace*. Garden City, N.Y., 1950.

Chandler, Albert D., *et al*. eds. *The Papers of Dwight David Eisenhower: The War Years*. 5 vols. Baltimore, 1970.

Churchill, Winston S. *Closing the Ring*. Boston, 1951.

—— *The Grand Alliance*. Boston, 1950.

—— *The Hinge of Fate*. Boston, 1950.

—— *Triumph and Tragedy*. Boston, 1953.

Ciechanowski, Jan. *Defeat in Victory*. New York, 1947.

Clay, Lucius D. *Decision in Germany*. Garden City, N.Y., 1950.

Clemens, Diane Shaver. *Yalta*. New York, 1970.

Cline, Ray S. *Washington Command Post: The Operations Division*. United States Army in World War II: The War Department. Washington, D.C., 1951.

Coffin, Tristam. *Missouri Compromise*. Boston, 1947.

Coles, Harry, with Albert K. Weinberg. *Civil Affairs: Soldiers Become Governors*. United States Army in World War II: Special Studies. Washington, D.C., 1964.

Conant, James B. *My Several Lives: Memoirs of a Social Inventor*. New York, 1970.

Connally, Tom, with Alfred Steinberg. *My Name Is Tom Connally*. New York, 1954.

Curry, George. *James F. Byrnes*. Vol. XIV of Robert H. Ferrell and Samuel Flagg Bemis, eds., The American Secretaries of State and Their Diplomacy. New York, 1965.

Daniels, Jonathan. *Man of Independence*. Philadelphia, 1950.

Davidson, Eugene. *The Death and Life of Germany*. New York, 1959.

Davies, Joseph E. *Mission to Moscow*. New York, 1941.

Davis, Vincent. *Postwar Defense Policy and the U.S. Navy, 1943–1946*. Chapel Hill, N.C., 1966.

Dawson, Raymond H. *The Decision to Aid Russia, 1941: Foreign Policy and Domestic Politics*. Chapel Hill, N.C., 1959.

Deane, John R. *The Strange Alliance: The Story of Our Efforts at Wartime Cooperation with Russia*. New York, 1947.

Deutscher, Isaac. *Ironies of History: Essays on Contemporary Communism.* London, 1966.

Divine, Robert A. *Roosevelt and World War II.* Baltimore, 1969.

—— *Second Chance: The Triumph of Internationalism in America During World War II.* New York, 1967.

Djilas, Milovan. *Conversations with Stalin.* Translated by Michael B. Petrovich. New York, 1962.

Donnelly, Desmond. *Struggle for the World: The Cold War, 1917–1965.* New York, 1965.

Druks, Herbert. *Harry S. Truman and the Russians, 1945–1953.* New York, 1966.

Drury, Allen. *A Senate Journal, 1943–1945.* New York, 1963.

Dulles, Allen. *The Secret Surrender.* New York, 1966.

Dulles, Foster Rhea. *The Road to Teheran.* Princeton, 1944.

Dulles, John Foster. *War or Peace.* New York, 1950.

Eden, Anthony. *The Reckoning: The Memoirs of Anthony Eden, Earl of Avon.* Boston, 1965.

Ehrman, John. *Grand Strategy: October, 1944–August, 1945.* Vol. VI of J. R. M. Butler, ed., History of the Second World War, United Kingdom Military Series. London, 1956.

Eisenhower, Dwight D. *Crusade in Europe.* New York, 1948.

Farnsworth, Beatrice. *William C. Bullitt and the Soviet Union.* Bloomington, Ind., 1967.

Feis, Herbert. *The Atomic Bomb and the End of World War II.* Princeton, 1966.

—— *Between War and Peace: The Potsdam Conference.* Princeton, 1960.

—— *The China Tangle: The American Effort in China from Pearl Harbor to the Marshall Mission.* Princeton, 1953.

—— *Churchill, Roosevelt, Stalin: The War They Waged and the Peace They Sought.* Princeton, 1957.

—— *Contest over Japan.* New York, 1967.

—— *From Trust to Terror: The Onset of the Cold War, 1945–1950.* New York, 1970.

Ferrell, Robert H. *George C. Marshall.* Vol. XV of Robert H. Ferrell and Samuel Flagg Bemis, eds., The American Secretaries of State and Their Diplomacy. New York, 1966.

Fischer, David Hackett. *Historians' Fallacies: Toward a Logic of Historical Thought.* New York, 1970.

Fleming, D. F. *The Cold War and Its Origins, 1917–1960.* 2 vols. Garden City, N.Y., 1961.

Flynn, Edward J. *You're the Boss.* New York, 1947.

Freedman, Max. ed. *Roosevelt and Frankfurter: Their Correspondence, 1928–1945.* Boston, 1967.

Freidel, Frank. *Franklin D. Roosevelt: The Apprenticeship.* Boston, 1952.

—— *Franklin D. Roosevelt: The Ordeal.* Boston, 1954.

Gannon, Robert I. *The Cardinal Spellman Story.* Garden City, N.Y., 1962.

Gardner, Lloyd C. *Architects of Illusion: Men and Ideas in American Foreign Policy, 1941–1949.* Chicago, 1970.

—— *Economic Aspects of New Deal Diplomacy.* Madison, 1964.

Gardner, Lloyd C., with Arthur Schlesinger, Jr., and Hans J. Morgenthau. *Origins of the Cold War.* Waltham, Mass., 1970.

Gardner, Richard N. *Sterling-Dollar Diplomacy: Anglo-American Collaboration in the Reconstruction of Multilateral Trade.* Oxford, 1956.

Gerson, Louis L. *The Hyphenate in Recent American Politics and Diplomacy.* Lawrence, Kan., 1964.

—— *John Foster Dulles.* Vol. XVII of Robert H. Ferrell and Samuel Flagg Bemis, eds., The American Secretaries of State and Their Diplomacy. New York, 1968.

Gildersleeve, Virginia C. *Many a Good Crusade.* New York, 1954.

Gimbel, John. *The American Occupation of Germany: Politics and the Military, 1945–1949.* Stanford, 1968.

Goldman, Eric F. *The Crucial Decade and After: America, 1945–1960.* 2d ed. New York, 1961.

—— *Rendezvous with Destiny: A History of Modern American Reform.* Rev. and abr. ed. New York, 1956.

Goodman, Walter. *The Committee: The Extraordinary Career of the House Committee on Un-American Activities.* New York, 1968.

Gowing, Margaret. *Britain and Atomic Energy, 1939–1945.* New York, 1964.

Graebner, Norman A. *The New Isolationism: A Study in Politics and Foreign Policy since 1950.* New York, 1956.

Greenfield, Kent Roberts. *American Strategy in World War II: A Reconsideration.* Baltimore, 1963.

Grew, Joseph C. *Turbulent Era: A Diplomatic Record of Forty Years, 1904–1945.* 2 vols. Boston, 1952.

Groves, Leslie R. *Now It Can Be Told: The Story of the Manhattan Project.* New York, 1962.

Gunther, John. *Roosevelt in Retrospect: A Profile in History.* New York, 1950.

Halle, Louis J. *The Cold War as History.* New York, 1967.

Harriman, W. Averell. *America and Russia in a Changing World: A Half Century of Personal Observation.* Garden City, N.Y., 1971.

Harrison, Gordon A. *Cross-Channel Attack.* United States Army in World War II: The European Theater of Operations. Washington, D.C., 1951.

Hassett, William D. *Off the Record with F.D.R., 1942–1945.* New Brunswick, N.J., 1958.

Heinrichs, Waldo. *American Ambassador: Joseph C. Grew and the Development of the American Diplomatic Tradition.* Boston, 1966.

Herz, Martin F. *Beginnings of the Cold War.* Bloomington, Ind., 1966.

Hewlett, Richard G., and Oscar E. Anderson, Jr. *A History of the United States Atomic Energy Commission: The New World, 1939–1946.* University Park, Pa., 1962.

Hillman, William, ed. *Mr. President: The First Publication from the Personal Diaries, Private Letters, Papers and Revealing Interviews of Harry S. Truman, Thirty-second President of the United States of America.* New York, 1952.

Hofstadter, Richard. *The Progressive Historians: Turner, Beard, Parrington.* New York, 1968.

Holborn, Hajo. *American Military Government: Its Organization and Policies.* Washington, D.C., 1947.

Hooker, Nancy Harvison, ed. *The Moffat Papers: Selections from the Diplomatic Journals of Jay Pierrepont Moffat, 1919–1943.* Cambridge, Mass., 1956.

Horowitz, David. *The Free World Colossus: A Critique of American Foreign Policy in the Cold War.* New York, 1965.

Howe, Irving, and Lewis Coser. *The American Communist Party: A Critical History (1919–1957).* New York, 1957.

Hull, Cordell. *The Memoirs of Cordell Hull.* 2 vols. New York, 1948.

Huntington, Samuel P. *The Common Defense: Strategic Programs in National Politics.* New York, 1961.

—— *The Soldier and the State: The Theory and Politics of Civil-Military Relations.* Cambridge, Mass., 1957.

Israel, Fred L., ed. *The War Diary of Breckinridge Long: Selections from the Years 1939–1944.* Lincoln, Neb., 1966.

Johnson, Donald B. *The Republican Party and Wendell Willkie.* Urbana, Ill., 1960.

Jonas, Manfred. *Isolationism in America, 1935–1941.* Ithaca, N.Y., 1966.

Jones, Joseph M. *The Fifteen Weeks (February 21–June 5, 1947).* New York, 1955.

Jones, Robert Huhn. *The Roads to Russia: United States Lend-Lease to the Soviet Union.* Norman, Okla., 1969.

Kennan, George F. *American Diplomacy, 1900–1950.* Chicago, 1951.

—— *Memoirs: 1925–1950.* Boston, 1967.

Khrushchev, Nikita S. *Khrushchev Remembers.* Boston, 1970.

Kirkendall, Richard S., ed. *The Truman Period as a Research Field.* Columbia, Mo., 1967.

Knebel, Fletcher, and Charles W. Bailey II. *No High Ground.* New York, 1960.

Kolko, Gabriel. *The Politics of War: The World and United States Foreign Policy, 1943–1945.* New York, 1968.

Krock, Arthur. *Memoirs: Sixty Years on the Firing Line.* New York, 1968.

LaFeber, Walter. *America, Russia, and the Cold War, 1945–1967.* New York, 1967.

Langer, William L., and S. Everett Gleason. *The Challenge to Isolation: The World Crisis of 1937–1940 and American Foreign Policy.* New York, 1952.

—— *The Undeclared War, 1940–41.* New York, 1953.

Latham, Earl. *The Communist Controversy in Washington.* Cambridge, Mass., 1966.

Leahy, William D. *I Was There.* New York, 1950.

Leighton, Richard M., and Robert W. Coakley. *Global Logistics and Strategy, 1940–1943.* United States Army in World War II: The War Department. Washington, D.C., 1955.

—— *Global Logistics and Strategy, 1943–1945.* United States Army in World War II: The War Department. Washington, D.C., 1968.

Lieberman, Joseph I. *The Scorpion and the Tarantula: The Struggle to Control Atomic Weapons, 1945–1949.* Boston, 1970.

Lilienthal, David E. *The Journals of David E. Lilienthal.* Vols. I and II, 1939–50. New York, 1964.

Lingeman, Richard R. *Don't You Know There's a War On? The American Home Front, 1941–1945.* New York, 1970.

Lippmann, Walter. *The Cold War: A Study in U.S. Foreign Policy.* New York, 1947.

—— *U.S. Foreign Policy: Shield of the Republic.* Boston, 1943.

Lukacs, John. *A New History of the Cold War.* Garden City, N.Y., 1966.

MacDougall, Curtis D. *Gideon's Army.* 2 vols. New York, 1965.

Macmillan, Harold. *The Blast of War: 1939–1945.* New York, 1967.

McNeill, William H. *America, Britain, and Russia: Their Cooperation and Conflict, 1941–1946.* New York, 1953.

Matloff, Maurice. *Strategic Planning for Coalition Warfare: 1943–1944.* United States Army in World War II: The War Department. Washington, D.C., 1959.

Matloff, Maurice, and Edwin L. Snell. *Strategic Planning for Coalition Warfare: 1941–1942.* United States Army in World War II: The War Department. Washington, D.C., 1953.

Mikolajczyk, Stanislaw. *The Rape of Poland.* New York, 1948.

Millis, Walter, ed. *The Forrestal Diaries.* New York, 1951.

Moran, Lord. *Churchill: The Struggle for Survival, 1940–1965.* Boston, 1966.

Morgan, Sir Frederick. *Overture to Overlord.* Garden City, N.Y., 1950.

Morgenthau, Henry, Jr. *Germany Is Our Problem.* New York, 1945.

Morison, Elting E. *Turmoil and Tradition: A Study of the Life and Times of Henry L. Stimson.* Boston, 1960.

Morison, Samuel Eliot. *Strategy and Compromise.* Boston, 1958.

Murphy, Robert. *Diplomat among Warriors.* Garden City, N.Y., 1964.

Neumann, William L. *After Victory: Churchill, Roosevelt, Stalin and the Making of the Peace.* New York, 1965.

Notter, Harley. *Postwar Foreign Policy Preparation, 1939–1945.* Washington, D.C., 1949.

O'Ballance, Edgar. *The Greek Civil War, 1944–1949.* New York, 1966.

Paterson, Thomas G., ed. *The Origins of the Cold War.* Lexington, Mass., 1970.

Penrose, E. F. *Economic Planning for Peace.* Princeton, 1953.

Perkins, Dexter. *The Diplomacy of a New Age: Major Issues in U.S. Policy since 1945.* Bloomington, Ind., 1967.

Phillips, Cabell. *The Truman Presidency: History of a Triumphant Succession.* New York, 1966.

Pickersgill, J. W., and D. F. Forster. *The Mackenzie King Record: 1944–1946.* 2 vols. Toronto, 1968–70.

Pogue, Forrest C. *George C. Marshall: Ordeal and Hope, 1939–1942.* New York, 1966.

—— *The Supreme Command.* United States Army in World War II: The European Theater of Operations. Washington, D.C., 1954.

Pratt, Julius W. *Cordell Hull.* Vol. XII and XIII in Robert H. Ferrell and Samuel Flagg Bemis, eds., The American Secretaries of State and Their Diplomacy. New York, 1964.

Range, Willard. *Franklin D. Roosevelt's World Order.* Athens, Ga., 1959.

Rogow, Arnold A. *James Forrestal: A Study of Personality, Politics, and Policy.* New York, 1963.

Roosevelt, Elliott. *As He Saw It.* New York, 1946.

Roosevelt, Elliott, ed. *F.D.R., His Personal Letters: 1928–1945.* 2 vols. New York, 1950.

Rosenau, James N., ed. *Domestic Sources of Foreign Policy.* New York, 1967.

Rosenman, Samuel I. *Working with Roosevelt.* New York, 1952.

Rosenman, Samuel I., ed. *The Public Papers and Addresses of Franklin D. Roosevelt.* Vols. IX—XIII, 1940–45. New York, 1941–50.

Rozek, Edward J. *Allied Wartime Diplomacy: The Pattern in Poland.* New York, 1958.

Salisbury, Harrison E. *The 900 Days: The Siege of Leningrad.* New York, 1969.

Schapiro, Leonard. *The Communist Party of the Soviet Union.* New York, 1960.

Schapsmeier, Edward L., and Frederick H. Schapsmeier. *Prophet in Politics: Henry A. Wallace and the War Years, 1940–1965.* Ames, Iowa, 1970.

Schlesinger, Arthur M., Jr. *The Coming of the New Deal.* Boston, 1959.

Schoenberger, Walter Smith. *Decision of Destiny.* Athens, Ohio, 1969.

Shannon, David A. *The Decline of American Communism.* New York, 1959.

Sherwood, Robert E. *Roosevelt and Hopkins: An Intimate History.* Rev. ed. New York, 1950.

Shewmaker, Kenneth E. *Americans and Chinese Communists, 1927–1945: A Persuading Encounter.* Ithaca, N.Y., 1971.

Smith, Alice Kimball. *A Peril and a Hope: The Scientists' Movement in America, 1945–47.* Chicago, 1965.

Smith, Gaddis. *American Diplomacy During the Second World War, 1941–1945.* New York, 1965.

Smith, Perry M. *The Air Force Plans for Peace, 1943–1945.* Baltimore, 1970.

Snell, John L. *Illusion and Necessity: The Diplomacy of Global War, 1939–1945.* Boston, 1963.

—— *Wartime Origins of the East-West Dilemma over Germany.* New Orleans, 1959.

Solzhenitsyn, Alexander I. *The First Circle*. Translated by Thomas P. Whitney. New York, 1968.

Spanier, John. *American Foreign Policy since World War II*. 3d rev. ed. New York, 1968.

Standley, William H., and Arthur A. Ageton. *Admiral Ambassador to Russia*. Chicago, 1955.

Steinberg, Alfred. *The Man from Missouri: The Life and Times of Harry S. Truman*. New York, 1962.

Stettinius, Edward R., Jr. *Roosevelt and the Russians: The Yalta Conference*. Garden City, N.Y., 1949.

Stimson, Henry L., and McGeorge Bundy. *On Active Service in Peace and War*. New York, 1947.

Stuart, Graham H. *The Department of State*. New York, 1949.

Sulzberger, C. L. *A Long Row of Candles: Memoirs and Diaries, 1934–1954*. New York, 1969.

Theoharis, Athan G. *The Yalta Myths: An Issue in U.S. Politics, 1945–1955*. Columbia, Mo., 1970.

Tompkins, C. David. *Senator Arthur H. Vandenberg: The Evolution of a Modern Republican, 1884–1945*. East Lansing, 1970.

Truman, Harry S. *Memoirs: Year of Decisions*. Garden City, N.Y., 1955.

—— *Memoirs: Years of Trial and Hope, 1946–1952*. Garden City, N.Y., 1956.

—— *Mr. Citizen*. New York, 1960.

Tsou, Tang. *America's Failure in China, 1941–50*. 2 vols. Chicago, 1963.

Tugwell, Rexford G. *The Democratic Roosevelt: A Biography of Franklin D. Roosevelt*. Garden City, N.Y., 1957.

Ulam, Adam B. *Expansion and Coexistence: The History of Soviet Foreign Policy, 1917–67*. New York, 1968.

Vandenberg, Arthur H., Jr., ed. *The Private Papers of Senator Vandenberg*. Boston, 1952.

Viorst, Milton. *Hostile Allies: FDR and Charles De Gaulle*. New York, 1965.

Walker, Richard L. *E. R. Stettinius, Jr*. New York, 1965. Vol. XIV in Robert H. Ferrell and Samuel Flagg Bemis, eds., The American Secretaries of State and Their Diplomacy. New York, 1965.

Watson, Mark Skinner. *Chief of Staff: Prewar Plans and Preparations*. United States Army in World War II: The War Department. Washington, D.C., 1950.

Welles, Sumner. *Seven Decisions That Shaped History*. New York, 1950.

—— *The Time for Decision*. New York, 1944.

—— *Where Are We Heading?* New York, 1946.

Werth, Alexander. *Russia at War, 1941–45*. New York, 1964.

Westerfield, H. Bradford. *Foreign Policy and Party Politics: Pearl Harbor to Korea*. New Haven, 1955.

White, William L. *Report on the Russians*. New York, 1945.

Williams, Francis. *A Prime Minister Remembers: The War and Post-War Memoirs of the Rt. Hon. Earl Attlee.* London, 1961.

Williams, William Appleman. *American-Russian Relations, 1781–1947.* New York, 1952.

—— *The Tragedy of American Diplomacy.* Rev. ed. New York, 1962.

Willkie, Wendell. *One World.* New York, 1943.

Wilson, Theodore A. *The First Summit: Roosevelt and Churchill at Placentia Bay, 1941.* Boston, 1969.

Wittner, Lawrence S. *Rebels Against War: The American Peace Movement, 1941–1960.* New York, 1969.

Woodward, Sir Ernest Llewellyn. *British Foreign Policy in the Second World War.* London, 1962.

Wright, Gordon. *The Ordeal of Total War, 1939–1945.* New York, 1968.

Wytrwal, Joseph A. *America's Polish Heritage: A Social History of the Poles in America.* Detroit, 1961.

Xydis, Stephen G. *Greece and the Great Powers, 1944–1947.* Thessaloniki, 1963.

Young, Roland. *Congressional Politics in the Second World War.* New York, 1956.

Articles

Adler, Les K., and Thomas G. Paterson. "Red Fascism: The Merger of Nazi Germany and Soviet Russia in the American Image of Totalitarianism, 1930's–1950's," *American Historical Review,* LXXV (April, 1970), 1046–64.

Alsop, Joseph W., and Stewart Alsop. "We Have No Russian Policy," *Washington Post,* January 4, 1946.

Atkinson, Brooks. "Russia, 1946," *Life,* XXI (July 22, 1946), 85–94.

Bagguley, John. "The World War and the Cold War," in David Horowitz, ed., *Containment and Revolution,* pp. 76–124. Boston, 1967.

Barmine, Alexander. "The New Communist Conspiracy," *Reader's Digest,* XLV (October, 1944), 27–33.

"Baruch, Bernard M.," *Current Biography, 1950,* pp. 14–17.

Bateman, Herman E. "Observations on President Roosevelt's Health During World War II," *Mississippi Valley Historical Review,* XLIII (June, 1956), 82–102.

Batt, William L. "Can We Do Business with Russia?" *Sales Management,* LV (October 15, 1945), 202.

Bernstein, Barton J. "American Foreign Policy and the Origins of the Cold War," in Bernstein, ed., *Politics and Policies of the Truman Administration,* pp. 15–77. Chicago, 1970.

Bess, Demaree. "Will Europe Go Communist after the War?" *Saturday Evening Post,* CCXVI (January 22, 1944), 15 ff.

Brogan, Sir Denis. "The Illusion of American Omnipotence," *Harper's,* CCV (December, 1952), 21–28.

"Browder, Earl," *Current Biography, 1944,* pp. 69–73.

Bruenn, Howard G. "Clinical Notes on the Illness and Death of President Franklin D. Roosevelt," *Annals of Internal Medicine,* LXXII (April, 1970), 579–96.

Buhite, Russell D. "Patrick J. Hurley and the Yalta Far Eastern Agreement." *Pacific Historical Review.* XXXVII (August, 1968), 343–53.

Bullitt, William C. "How We Won the War and Lost the Peace," *Life,* XXV (August 30 and September 6, 1948), 83–97, 86–103.

—— "The World from Rome," *Life,* XVII (September 4, 1944), 94–109.

Burns, James MacGregor. "FDR: The Untold Story of His Last Year," *Saturday Review,* LIII (April 11, 1970), 12–15, 39.

Byrns, Ruth. "John Dewey on Russia," *Commonweal,* XXXVI (September 18, 1942), 511–13.

Cantril, Hadley. "Opinion Trends in World War II: Some Guides to Interpretation," *Public Opinion Quarterly,* XII (Spring, 1948), 30–44.

Chamberlain, John. "Eric Johnston," *Life,* XVI (June 19, 1944), 96–108.

Chamberlin, William H. "Can We Do Business with Stalin?" *American Mercury,* LXI (August, 1945), 194–201.

—— "Information, *Please,* about Russia," *Harper's,* CLXXXVIII (April, 1944), 405–12.

—— "Russia: An American Problem," *Atlantic Monthly,* CLXIX (February, 1942), 148–56.

—— "Russia and Europe, 1918–1944," *Russian Review,* IV (Autumn, 1944), 3–9.

—— "Russia as a Partner in War and Peace," *Saturday Evening Post,* CCXV (November 14, 1942), 124.

—— "The Russian Enigma: An Interpretation," *Harper's,* CLXXXV (August, 1942), 225–34.

—— "W. L. White and His Critics," *American Mercury,* LX (May, 1945), 625–31.

Chase, John L. "The Development of the Morgenthau Plan Through the Quebec Conference," *Journal of Politics,* XVI (May, 1954), 324–59.

—— "Unconditional Surrender Reconsidered," *Political Science Quarterly,* LXX (June, 1955), 258–318.

Clark, Dale. "Conflicts over Planning at Staff Headquarters," in Carl Friedrich and associates, *American Experiences in Military Government in World War II,* pp. 211–37. New York, 1948.

Davies, Joseph E. "How Russia Blasted Hitler's Spy Machine," *American Magazine,* CXXXII (December, 1941), 80 ff.

—— "Russia Will Hold This Summer," *Saturday Evening Post,* CCXIV (June 20, 1942), 16 ff.

—— "The Soviets and the Post-War," *Life,* XIV (March 29, 1943), 49–55.

—— "What We Didn't Know about Russia," *Reader's Digest,* XL (March, 1942), 45–50.

"Davies, Joseph E.," *Current Biography, 1942,* pp. 177–80.

"Davies, Joseph E., *Mission to Moscow,*" *Book Review Digest: 1942,* pp. 187–88.

Davis, Forrest. "Roosevelt's World Blueprint," *Saturday Evening Post,* CCXV (April 10, 1943), 20 ff.

—— "What Really Happened at Teheran," *Saturday Evening Post,* CCXVI (May 13 and 20, 1944), 12 ff., 20 ff.

Davis, Kenneth S. "Have We Been Wrong about Stalin?" *Current History,* I (September, 1941), 6–11.

Dean, Vera Micheles. "The U.S.S.R. and Post-War Europe," *Foreign Policy Reports,* XIX (August 15, 1943), 122–39.

"Death of the Comintern," *University of Chicago Round Table,* June 6, 1943, pp. 1–23.

Dorn, Walter L. "The Debate over American Occupation Policy in Germany in 1944–1945," *Political Science Quarterly,* LXXII (December, 1957), 481–501.

Drummond, Donald F. "Cordell Hull," in Norman A. Graebner, ed., *An Uncertain Tradition: American Secretaries of State in the Twentieth Century,* pp. 184–209. New York, 1961.

Dulles, John Foster. "Thoughts on Soviet Foreign Policy and What to Do about It," *Life,* XX (June 3 and 10, 1946), 113–26, 118–30.

Eastman, Max. "To Collaborate Successfully, We Must Face the Facts about Russia," *Reader's Digest,* XLIII (July, 1943), 1–14.

Emerson, William R. "F.D.R. (1941–1945)," in Ernest R. May, ed., *The Ultimate Decision: The President as Commander-in-Chief,* pp. 135–77. New York, 1960.

Ethridge, Mark, and C. E. Black. "Negotiating on the Balkans, 1945–1947," in Raymond Dennett and Joseph E. Johnson, eds., *Negotiating with the Russians,* pp. 184–203. Boston, 1951.

Eulau, Heinz H. F. "The New Soviet Nationalism," *Annals of the American Academy of Political and Social Science,* CCXXXII (March, 1944), 25–32.

Fainsod, Merle. "The Development of American Military Government Policy During World War II," in Carl Friedrich and associates, *American Experiences in Military Government in World War II,* pp. 23–51. New York, 1948.

Feis, Herbert. "Political Aspects of Foreign Loans," *Foreign Affairs,* XXIII (July, 1945), 609–19.

Franklin, William M. "Zonal Boundaries and Access to Berlin," *World Politics,* XVI (October, 1963), 1–33.

Friedman, Leon. "Election of 1944" in Arthur M. Schlesinger, Jr., ed., *History of American Presidential Elections, 1788–1968,* IV, 3009–38. New York, 1971.

Gillis, James M. "Getting Wise to Russia," *Catholic World*, CLX (October, 1944), 1–6.

Glennon, John P. " 'This Time Germany Is a Defeated Nation': The Doctrine of Unconditional Surrender and Some Unsuccessful Attempts to Alter It, 1943–1944," in Gerald N. Grob, ed., *Statesmen and Statecraft of the Modern West: Essays in Honor of Dwight E. Lee and H. Donaldson Jordan*, pp. 109–51. Barre, Mass., 1967.

Graebner, Norman A. "Cold War Origins and the Continuing Debate: A Review of Recent Literature," *Journal of Conflict Resolution*, XIII (March, 1969), 123–32.

Hamby, Alonzo L. "Henry A. Wallace, the Liberals, and Soviet-American Relations," *Review of Politics*, XXX (April, 1968), 153–69.

—— "The Liberals, Truman, and FDR as Symbol and Myth," *Journal of American History*, LVI (March, 1970), 859–67.

Hammond, Paul Y. "Directives for the Occupation of Germany: The Washington Controversy," in Harold Stein, ed., *American Civil-Military Decisions*, pp. 311–464. Birmingham, Ala., 1963.

Harriman, W. Averell. "From Stalin to Kosygin: The Myths and the Realities," *Look*, XXXI (October 3, 1967), 55–62.

—— "Our Wartime Relations with the Soviet Union," *Department of State Bulletin*, XXV (September 3, 1951), 371–79.

Herring, George C., Jr. "Lend-Lease to Russia and the Origins of the Cold War, 1944–1945," *Journal of American History*, LVI (June, 1969), 93–114.

"Is Communism a Menace?" [debate between Earl Browder and George Sokolsky], *New Masses*, April 6, 1943, pp. 11–20.

Johnston, Eric. "A Business View of Russia," *Nation's Business*, XXXII (October, 1944), 21–22.

—— "Eric Johnston Reports on What He Observed in Russia," *Export and Trade Shipper*, XLIX (July 31, 1944), 5–6.

—— "My Talk with Joseph Stalin," *Reader's Digest*, XLV (October, 1944), 1–10.

Katz, Daniel, and Hadley Cantril. "An Analysis of Attitudes Toward Fascism and Communism," *Journal of Abnormal and Social Psychology*, XXXV (1940), 356–66.

[Kennan, George F.] Mr. X. "The Sources of Soviet Conduct," *Foreign Affairs*, XXV (July, 1947), 566–82.

Kriesberg, Martin. "Cross-Pressures and Attitudes: A Study of the Influence of Conflicting Propaganda on Opinions Regarding American-Soviet Relations," *Public Opinion Quarterly*, XIII (Spring, 1949), 5–16.

—— "Dark Areas of Ignorance," in Lester Markel, ed., *Public Opinion and Foreign Policy*, pp. 49–64. New York, 1949.

Kuklick, Bruce. "The Division of Germany and American Policy on Reparations," *Western Political Quarterly*, XXIII (June, 1970), 276–93.

LaFeber, Walter. "War: Cold," *Cornell Alumni News*, October, 1968, pp. 24–29.

Langer, William L. "Political Problems of a Coalition," *Foreign Affairs,* XXVI (October, 1947), 73–89.

Lasch, Christopher. "The Cold War, Revisited and Re-Visioned," *New York Times Magazine,* January 14, 1968, pp. 26–27 ff.

Lawrence, David. "The Tragedy of Yalta," *U.S. News,* XVIII (March 2, 1945), 26–27.

Lee, R. Alton. "The Army 'Mutiny' of 1946," *Journal of American History,* LIII (December, 1966), 555–71.

Leighton, Richard M. "OVERLORD Revisited: An Interpretation of American Strategy in the European War, 1942–1944," *American Historical Review,* LXVIII (July, 1963), 919–37.

Lensen, George A. "Yalta and the Far East," in John L. Snell, ed., *The Meaning of Yalta,* pp. 127–66. Baton Rouge, 1956.

Leuchtenburg, William E. "The New Deal and the Analogue of War," in John Braeman, Robert H. Bremner, and Everett Walters, eds., *Change and Continuity in Twentieth Century America,* pp. 81–143. Columbus, Ohio, 1964.

Lindley, Ernest K. "Byrnes, the Persuasive Reporter," *Newsweek,* XXV (March 12, 1945), 42.

—— "Republican Dividing Line," *Newsweek,* XXIX (March 3, 1947), 26.

Lyons, Eugene. "Cooperating with Russia," *American Mercury,* LVI (May, 1943), 536–45.

—— "The Progress of Stalin-Worship," *American Mercury,* LVI (June, 1943), 693–97.

—— "The Purification of Stalin," *American Mercury,* LIV (January, 1942), 109–16.

McCoy, Donald R. "Republican Opposition During Wartime, 1941–1945." *Mid-American,* XLIX (July, 1967), 174–89.

Maier, Charles S. "Revisionism and the Interpretation of Cold War Origins," *Perspectives in American History,* IV (1970), 313–47.

Mandel, William M. "Russia—Our Biggest Postwar Market?" *Advertising and Selling,* XXXVII (May, 1944), 29 ff.

Matloff, Maurice. "Franklin D. Roosevelt as War Leader," in Harry Coles, ed., *Total War and Cold War,* pp. 42–65. Columbus, Ohio, 1962.

—— "The 90-Division Gamble," in Kent Roberts Greenfield, ed., *Command Decisions,* pp. 365–81. Washington, D.C., 1960.

May, Ernest R. "The Development of Political-Military Consultation in the United States," *Political Science Quarterly,* LXX (June, 1955), 161–80.

—— "The United States, the Soviet Union, and the Far Eastern War, 1941–1945," *Pacific Historical Review,* XXIV (May, 1955), 153–74.

Meyer, Leo. "The Decision to Invade North Africa," in Kent Roberts Greenfield, ed., *Command Decisions,* pp. 182–88. Washington, D.C., 1960.

Morton, Louis. "The Decision to Use the Atomic Bomb," *Foreign Affairs,* XXXV (January, 1957), 334–53.

—— "Germany First: The Basic Concept of Allied Strategy in World War II," in Kent Roberts Greenfield, ed., *Command Decisions,* pp. 11–47. Washington, D.C., 1960.

—— "Soviet Intervention in the War with Japan," *Foreign Affairs,* XL (July, 1962), 653–62.

Mosely, Philip E. "Dismemberment of Germany: The Allied Negotiations from Yalta to Potsdam," *Foreign Affairs,* XXVIII (April, 1950), 487–98.

—— "The Occupation of Germany: New Light on How the Zones Were Drawn," *Foreign Affairs,* XXVIII (July, 1950), 580–604.

—— "Some Soviet Techniques of Negotiation," in Raymond Dennett and Joseph E. Johnson, eds., *Negotiating with the Russians,* pp. 271–303. Boston, 1951.

"Mr. Hull," *Life,* XVII (December 11, 1944), 26.

Murphy, Charles J. V. "W. Averell Harriman," *Life,* XXI (December 30, 1946), 56–68.

Nelson, Donald M. "What I Saw in Russia," *Collier's,* CXIII (January 29, 1944), 11 ff.

Nicolson, Harold. "Peacemaking at Paris: Success, Failure or Farce?" *Foreign Affairs,* XXV (January, 1947), 190–203.

Niebuhr, Reinhold. "Russia and the West," *Nation,* CLVI (January 16 and 23, 1943), 82–84, 124–25.

"Not Untimely," *America,* LXVI (February 7, 1942), 490.

Pachter, Henry. "Revisionist Historians and the Cold War," in Irving Howe, ed., *Beyond the New Left,* pp. 166–91. New York, 1970.

Paterson, Thomas G. "The Abortive American Loan to Russia and the Origins of the Cold War, 1943–1946," *Journal of American History,* LVI (June, 1969), 70–92.

Pogue, Forrest C. "The Decision to Halt at the Elbe," in Kent Roberts Greenfield, ed., *Command Decisions,* pp. 479–92. Washington, D.C., 1960.

"The Prospects of Soviet-American Trade Relations," New York Institute of International Finance, *Bulletin,* No. 139, August 27, 1945, pp. 1–24.

Reynolds, Thomas F. "The U.S.A. at San Francisco," *New Republic,* CXII (June 11, 1945), 810.

Ropes, Ernest C. "The Union of Soviet Socialist Republics as a Factor in World Trade," *World Economics,* II (October-December, 1944), 69–88.

Ross, Irwin. "It's Tough to Be a Communist," *Harper's,* CXCII (June, 1946), 528–36.

Rovere, Richard H. "The Unassailable Vandenberg," *Harper's,* CXCVI (May, 1948), 394–403.

"Russia as an Ally in War and Peace," *University of Chicago Round Table,* February 21, 1943, pp. 1–18.

"Russian-American Trade: Early Developments; Peacetime Factors," *Index* [publication of the New York Trust Company], XXV (September, 1945), 62–72.

"Russia's Foreign Policy," *University of Chicago Round Table,* September 12, 1943, pp. 1–23.

Salisbury, Harrison E. "Russia Beckons Big Business," *Collier's,* CXIV (September 2, 1944), 11 ff.

Salvemini, Gaetano. "Mr. Bullitt's Romans," *New Republic,* CXI (October 2, 1944), 423–26.

Schatz, Arthur W. "The Anglo-American Trade Agreement and Cordell Hull's Search for Peace, 1936–1938," *Journal of American History,* LVII (June, 1970), 85–103.

Schlesinger, Arthur M., Jr. "Origins of the Cold War," *Foreign Affairs,* XLVI (October, 1967), 22–52.

Seabury, Paul. "Cold War Origins," *Journal of Contemporary History,* III (January, 1968), 169–82.

Sellen, Robert W. "Origins of the Cold War: An Historiographical Survey," *West Georgia College Studies in the Social Sciences,* IX (June, 1970), 57–98.

"Selling the Soviet," *Industrial Marketing,* XXX (July, 1945), 46 ff.

Smith, Daniel M. "The New Left and the Cold War," *University of Denver Quarterly,* Winter, 1970, pp. 78–88.

Smith, M. Brewster. "The Personal Setting of Public Opinions: A Study of Attitudes Toward Russia," *Public Opinion Quarterly,* XI (Winter, 1947–48), 507–23.

Snow, Edgar. "Fragments from F.D.R.," *Monthly Review,* VIII (January-March, 1957), 316–21, 395–404.

Sontag, Raymond. "Reflections on the Yalta Papers," *Foreign Affairs,* XXXIII (July, 1955), 615–23.

Starobin, Joseph R. "Origins of the Cold War: The Communist Dimension," *Foreign Affairs,* XLVII (July, 1969), 681–96.

Stimson, Henry L. "The Decision to Use the Atomic Bomb," *Harper's,* CXCIV (February, 1947), 97–107.

Stone, I. F. "Anti-Russian Undertow," *Nation,* CLX (May 12, 1945), 534–35.

—— "Farewell to F.D.R.," *Nation,* CLX (April 21, 1945), 437.

—— "This Is What We Voted For," *Nation,* CLX (February 17, 1945), 175.

Theoharis, Athan. "James F. Byrnes: Unwitting Yalta Myth Maker," *Political Science Quarterly,* LXXXI (December, 1966), 581–92.

Thomas, C. P. "Prelude to Invasion: Free European Masses from Their Fear of Bolshevism," *Catholic World,* CLVII (May, 1943), 149–54.

Ullman, Richard H. "The Davies Mission and United States-Soviet Relations, 1937–1941," *World Politics,* IX (January, 1957), 220–39.

Vernadsky, George. "A Review of Russian Policy," *Yale Review,* XXXI (March, 1942), 514–33.

Viner, Jacob. "German Reparations Once More," *Foreign Affairs,* XXI (July, 1943), 659–73.

Wallace, Henry A. "Beyond the Atlantic Charter," *New Republic,* CVII (November 23, 1942), 667–69.

Walsh, Warren B. "American Attitudes Toward Russia," *Antioch Review,* VII (June, 1947), 183–90.

—— "What the American People Think of Russia," *Public Opinion Quarterly,* VIII (Winter, 1944–45), 513–22.

Ward, Jeremy K. "Winston Churchill and the 'Iron Curtain' Speech," *The History Teacher,* I (January, 1968), 5 ff.

"What Business with Russia?" *Fortune,* XXXI (January, 1945), 153 ff.

"What Should Germany Pay?" *Fortune,* XXIX (February, 1944), 134–38, 231.

White, William L. "Report on the Critics," *Saturday Review,* XXIX (October 6, 1946), 15–17.

—— "Report on the Russians," *Reader's Digest,* XLV (December, 1944), 102–22, XLVI (January, 1945), 106–28.

"Will Russia's Abolition of the Comintern Help Win the Peace?" *Town Meeting of the Air,* May 27, 1943, pp. 3–20.

Willen, Paul. "Who 'Collaborated' with Russia?" *Antioch Review,* XIV (September, 1954), 259–83.

Willkie, Wendell. "We Must Work with Russia," *New York Times Magazine,* January 17, 1943, pp. 5 ff.

Zink, Harold. "American Civil-Military Relations in the Occupation of Germany," in Harry Coles, ed., *Total War and Cold War,* pp. 211–40. Columbus, Ohio, 1962.

INDEX